Cape Cod Railroads

including Martha's Vineyard and Nantucket

Cape Cod Railroads
Including Martha's Vineyard and Nantucket

by Robert H. Farson

Cape Cod Historical Publications
Box 281
Yarmouth Port, Massachusetts
02675

Library of Congress Catalog Card Number 90-082323

Designed by Joan Hollister Farson

Printed in the United States of America

ISBN #0-9616740-1-6 Gift

First Edition

Cape Cod Historical Publications
Box 281
Yarmouth Port, Massachusetts
02675

Dedication

For my parents whose love and devotion were a constant inspiration

Contents

Acknowledgements

Those who contributed the most: Russell Lovell, Jr., Edward C. Robinson, Philip H. Choate, William P. Quinn, Joan H. Farson.

Others I wish to thank are John Twohig, Douglas Scott, William Reidy, Walter Lenk, Rosanna Cullity, John Cullity, Barbara L. Gill, John Lobingier, Ralph Titcomb, Nancy Titcomb, H. Bentley Crouch, Gerald Otto Cash, Ben Muse, James Coogan, Stan Snow, John Perry Fish, Helen Freeman Olsen, Raymond R. Freeman, Jr., Donald Walsh, Jean Deschamps, Mr. and Mrs. George H. Stewart, Jr., Arthur Ross, Helen Angell, Ted Rose, Arnold W. Dyer, Howard Goodwin, John Braginton-Smith, George Bartholomew, William Roger Brilliant, Herbert O. McKenney, Walter H. Gifford, Elmer Landers, Robert Clifton Neal and Archelus Henry Cahoon.

The Illustrations

Edward C. Robinson did most of the dark room work and took many photos. William P. Quinn supplied a number of pictures. So did Philip Choate, John Twohig, Douglas Scott; John Nye Cullity and his mother, Rosanna Cullity, allowed me to use the photos of Samuel Dexter White's trip on the *P'town Local* and the picture of Postmistress Anna Fish hanging that mail bag in East Sandwich. Other pictures are from the collections of Archelus Cahoon, Arnold Dyer, James Coogan, Helen Angell, Art Ross, Helen Freeman Olsen, Benjamin Harrison, Fred Small, H. Bentley Crouch, Walter Lenk, Mr. and Mrs. George H. Stewart, Jr., Walter Gifford, Howard Goodwin and Russell Lovell, Jr. There are pictures, too, from the Sandwich Archives, the Sandwich Public Library and the Bourne Historical Society. Ted Rose drew five pen and ink sketches in addition to the cover painting.

Introduction

There were railroads before there were steam locomotives. The first of them had cars pulled by horses or mules. Sandwich had the first railroad on the Cape, a horse-drawn affair that ran from the Boston & Sandwich Glass Factory over the marsh to the harbor.

But the development of the steam locomotive was the most important new technology for the Railway Age for the steam locomotive made the railroads the major form of land transportation.

A group of Sandwich citizens bought shares of stock in the Cape Cod Branch Railroad that was incorporated in 1846 to run between Middleboro and Sandwich. With construction under way in 1847, Deming Jarves of the Boston & Sandwich and Clark Hoxie, a Sandwich businessman who had a contract for some of the railroad construction, bought Bourne's Neck on which to build a spur track from the Village of Cohasset Narrows down to the tidal inlet at Buttermilk Bay of the same name. Jarves had been bringing sand and coal up the coast in schooners for his glassmaking. Before the railroad, he had used large Keith wagons over the land to Sandwich. Jarves had also used the rather shallow harbor above his plant to bring in raw materials from Boston and for shipping glass.

For a short time, Deming Jarves was a director of the new railroad which reached Sandwich in 1848. After several years the line raised its freight rate on glass and Jarves responded by saying he would ship his products by water on his own boat. The railroad's general agent Sylvanus Bourne ridiculed that idea, saying, "The acorn hasn't been planted for the tree that would furnish lumber for that vessel!" Jarves would show the railroad, and one day a ship arrived, steaming into Sandwich, proudly bearing the name *Acorn*. By 1854 the railroad was finishing its extension to Hyannis, and with the lowering of freight rates on glass, the *Acorn* was tied up at the dock and Jarves was a smiling winner of that battle.

The railroad replaced the stage coaches and the sailing packets. The packets had been the prime movers of salt from the Cape where there had been a large industry using sea water and the evaporation method. The railroad was quicker. A letter from Frederick Seth Pope who ran a grocery store at Jarves and Main Streets, Sandwich, in 1861 requests Loring Crocker of Barnstable to ship him a dozen kegs of salt by train for re-sale and fish preserving.

In researching this story I found several examples of poetry created for railroad occasions. The masterpiece of the poet laureate of the Cape Cod Branch went, in part, like this:

> Hurrah for Cape Cod, for we're coming along
> To open a railroad and sing you a song.
> And though to us all very strange it may seem.
> 'Tis true we can visit the Cape now by steam.
>
> We've done altogether with packet and stage
> For railroads and engines are now all the rage.

In the late 1860s when it was decided to extend the tracks from Orleans to Wellfleet, the Reverend A. J. Church wrote:

The great Atlantic Railroad for old Cape Cod, all hail!
Bring on the locomotive; lay down the iron rail;
Across The Eastham praires, by steam we're bound to go,
The railroad cars are coming, let's all get up and crow.

By 1860 railroads were America's biggest business and our most important economic interest. Route miles were 30-thousand with 100-thousand freight and passenger cars and one-thousand locomotives. By 1880 route miles were 93-thousand, and by 1900, 193-thousand. From the 1870s until 1900, railroads provided inexpensive transportation that in one generation made possible the settling of America, a huge land area that Thomas Jefferson said would take a thousand years.

On Cape Cod in 1900 there were section crews who worked on the tracks for 48 hours a week for $9.

Automobiles had been around awhile before car dealers showed up. Once you could order one from a catalogue. You sent your money and the auto came back in a freight car. If you had a telephone, the stationmaster would call you about your big package. In Wellfleet, Dr. Clarence Bell got his first car - and the town's - that way. It was a 1907 Schacht. He read the instructions, assembling the car at the station, put some gas in the tank and drove home.

Survivors of the many shipwrecks around the Cape always left by train. The towns where the most frequent wrecks occurred had a sum of money set aside to buy their tickets. The day after the steamship *Horatio Hall* sank in Pollock Rip Shoals after a collision, in March, 1909, 67 survivors boarded the morning train at Orleans for Boston.

The railroad made possible the Annual Old Home Week that most towns held every August. Relatives came back by train, the Fall River Line, horse and buggy and later in flivvers. The event featured games, clambakes, song fests, religious activities, a grand concert and a ball.

Some stories stand out. Bill Quinn's father, Lester, was 14 and driving a horse and wagon in Orleans for a hotel, The Shattuck House. Four salesmen came in on the evening train and asked Lester to drive them to the hotel. At once they started making disparaging remarks about this small town, so Lester drove up one street and then another and finally to the hotel. He charged them several times the rate. Next morning they asked the room clerk where the station was and he pointed across the street.

Of all the materials collected for this book, one is a commutation ticket from September, 1918 issued at Yarmouth to Miss Olive Hallett for a month of rides to Hyannis where she had started her first year of Normal School. Miss Hallett, it turns out, became Mrs. Stobbart who lives just a few houses up the street.

The railroad passenger cars, referred to as the steam cars in the last century, brought hundreds of thousands of visitors to the Cape and Island and their long beaches and wind-blown dunes. The trains also carried Cape Codders from town to town on Cape and up to Boston. Of course the tracks connected with other lines and were a pathway to the rest of America. The railroad tracks near your home stretched out of sight to faraway places and unseen horizons.

At night you could lie in bed with the light out almost anywhere in this country and hear the distant sounds of the railroad: the exhaust of a locomotive, the bell ringing on its boiler, and that most universal of sounds, a chime whistle. In those days all the world seemed young.

Robert H. Farson

Above In the early days of Cape railroading the scheduling of trains was called a seasonal arrangement. The winter trains that first year, 1848, were twice a day each way in the morning and afternoon between Sandwich and Boston.

Railroads ran a great many excursions and the Cape Cod Branch was no exception. This opportunity near the middle of the nineteenth century included a round trip to Boston and admission to Brewer's Splendid Panorama! From Sandwich, just 90 cents.

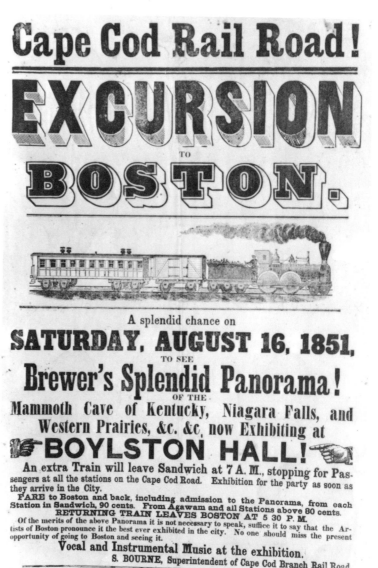

THE EARLY DAYS

The Cape Cod Branch Railroad in the first five years reached from Middleboro to Sandwich, a distance of 28 miles. It was a single-track line that was busy and profitable. It was originally capitalized at $500- thousand. Of that amount almost $422-thousand in stock was sold. The grading of the line, consisting mostly of fill, and the masonry used as abutments for the bridges together cost $106-thousand. The bridges were all constructed of wood. The major bridge was at Cohasset Narrows, but there were two others, one at Wareham Narrows and the other across the Monument River in the valley of the Isthmus of Cape Cod in the village of Monument (later Bourne). The bridges cost $28,673.

The ten way stations that were staffed and the two flag stops that were not cost $36,390, with the largest amount of that paid out for the Sandwich station, which was by far the largest, although the line never said how much.

The land totaled $57,863 and the fees for engineering the line were one of the lowest expenses at $16,710.

The four locomotives cost a total of $27,131, while the seven passenger cars and the four baggage cars totaled $16,106. The railroad owned 38 freight cars, for which they paid $34,310. Another item of rolling stock for line work rather than revenue was the gravel car; there were 60 of these by 1851 with no record of their cost. The total cost of road and equipment after five years was $633,676.

The first year of operation, 1848, with the line into Wareham in January and into Sandwich the end of May the line carried 58,802 passengers, which grew to 66,825 the following year, and in the two years following it was 69,311 and 71,539. The income from passengers in 1848 was $28,017, and in the years following up to 1851 was $35,430, $36,794 and $36,472.

The tonnage of freight carried the first year, 1848, was a modest 13,739 and the following year had a slight increase to 14,972. In 1850 and '51 the increases in freight tonnage were considerable with a growth to 20,781 in the former year and to 32,868 in the latter. The income from freight was only $7,617 in 1848, increasing each year after that from $14,972 to $18,407 and in 1851 to $18,533.

The first year that U.S. Mail was carried was 1849 and it earned just $700. That figure doubled in the two years after that. There was no express business then.

Total income the first year was $35,635, which jumped in 1849 and then stayed fairly consistent the next three years, as shown in these figures: $51,282, $56,856 and $56,736. The increase in passenger and freight business did not produce the kind of increased income one would expect, as the rates charged were reduced by the line.

The railroad had net income from 1848 to 1851 on an annual basis that looked like this: $20,679, $20,136, $17,077 and $25,738. During those years there were no stock dividends. It was a frugal operation that paid its debts, ran its trains and looked around for the next phase of growth. It didn't wait too long. Through 1853, when the next extension of the line was begun, the Cape Cod Branch Railroad had increased its total income to $68,943, while the number of passengers reached 75,170. Although freight business had dropped off slightly, the net earnings were $26,412 and the first dividend on stock was declared, totaling $20,000, which amounted to 6 and 2/3 percent. The timing of the

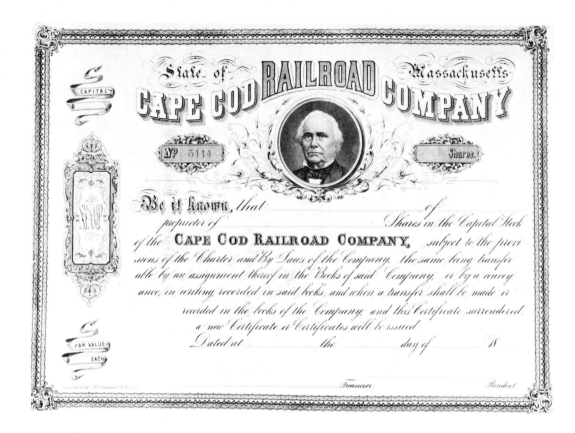

Above Unissued stock certificate printed in 1854.

CAPE COD B. RAIL ROAD
SALOON.

IN THE SANDWICH RAIL ROAD DEPOT.

REFRESHMENTS AND FRUITS
FOR THE ACCOMMODATION OF TRAVELLERS, TRANSIENT
VISITERS, AND CITIZENS OF THE TOWN.

THE SUBSCRIBER would take this method to inform his friends and the public, that he has taken this Stand, with the design to bestow unwearied pains in rendering it a place worthy of liberal patronage; and is ready AT ALL TIMES to give entertainments to such as may favor him with a call.

Passengers going to or from the Cape in the Cars, will find this a very convenient place to regale themselves, as the Coaches arrive in season to give them opportunity to breakfast before the start of the A. M. Train; and to dine before the start of the P. M. Train. Also, on return of A. M. and P. M. Trains, will find opportunity to get Refreshments, before taking the Coaches for the Cape.

Transient visiters and Parties of Pleasure will receive prompt attention; and will here find Luxuries usually afforded at similar Retreats.

On special occasions, SPECIAL efforts will be made to suit and accommodate his visiters, if previous notice be given.

☞The patronage of Gentlemen and Ladies is very respectfully solicited.

N. B. Doors open till the arr'

The saloon, or large public room, in the Sandwich station was the first on the Cape and it advertised its meals served between the time the stage coaches arrived and the train left or the train arrived and the stage coaches departed.

dividend was important, because new investment was needed to pay for the extension to Hyannis, 18 miles away from Sandwich, and the tracks had reached West Barnstable by the end of 1853. The company had legislative permission to double its capital stock to $600-thousand by issuing 5,000 new shares with a par value of $60. The dividend helped create investor interest and by the following year $230,571 worth or 3,842 shares had been purchased, $50-thousand of it by Nantucket residents and businesses, who had for many years used their influence to get the railroad to push on to Hyannis, where steamboats had a much shorter run than the New Bedford trip that they had been using. Nantucket wanted a railroad in Hyannis. In the winter of 1854 it was a matter of a few months away.

On February 22, 1854, the company got a new name: The Cape Cod Railroad, as approved by the legislature, or General Court as it had always been known.

The extension from the terminal at Sandwich to Hyannis was the first for the Cape Cod Branch Railroad. As completed in 1848 the railroad was 28 miles long from Middleboro to Sandwich. The decision to add 18 miles down the north side of Cape Cod through Barnstable to Yarmouth and then cut southeast across the Cape to Hyannis was made in 1852.

The railroad wasn't interested in keeping the end of track in Sandwich, there was too much waiting farther east, so after an application for a charter to extend the line to Hyannis was approved in 1850, civil engineers laid out three possible routes: the routes were all the same to South Sandwich or Scorton, but from there two of them stayed along the north side, one running close to the shore of Cape Cod Bay and across the head of the Great Marshes past Cobb and Smith's Wharf in Barnstable. This would have offered a fine water view. The other route on the north side was the one that was finally built and is the line today. The third route the engineers surveyed was to cut diagonally from South Sandwich cross the Cape over to Hyannis. This proposal was the shortest route, but it would have left out Barnstable Village and Yarmouth Port.

The only local man on the board of directors of the railroad was Amos Otis of Yarmouth Port. He served for several years, starting in 1849 and as cashier of the First National Bank of Yarmouth and secretary and treasurer of the Barnstable County Mutual Fire Insurance Company, he had considerable influence. His allies were the Barnstable Village group who wanted the railroad to run through their village. With Otis working from the inside and the businessmen from Yarmouth Port and Barnstable Village working public opinion from the outside, there wasn't much opposition. The end of the line would be Hyannis's Main Street with an extension to the harbor where a large wharf with tracks would be built. The wharf was what Nantucket interests cared about, for it brought the railroad to Boston just 27 miles from Nantucket by steamer.

The Nantucket Steamboat Company had been running its boats 50 miles to New Bedford where passengers boarded a train for Boston. The Nantucket Inquirer editorialized: "No person would think of going to Boston by way of New Bedford at a cost of $3.75 when he could go by way of Hyannis for about $2.50 and save four or five hours time besides."

Another newspaper, The Nantucket Mirror, put feelings about New Bedford in saltier terms: "The people of Nantucket have for the last 25 years apparently taken pains to make all their arrangements so as to add to the profit and importance of New Bedford... Yet they patronize us as a vapid city buck does his country cousin... As it is now, we have made ourselves mere bobbins to the New Bedford kite, and have to pay high for the privileges." The steamboat line had decided to close its run to New Bedford and sail between home and Hyannis once the railroad reached there.

Reaching there was a major undertaking by the railroad. In financial terms it would cost about $300-thousand just to build the line. That, of course, did not include buying locomotives and rolling stock needed for the additional trains. The company figured that more than 20,000 new passengers would be attracted by running trains to and from Hyannis. They calculated the Nantucket steamers would bring them about 7,600 new fares annually, that other ships would be worth another 6,000 and just being able to provide greatly improved transportation over stage coaches and sailing packets would sell at least 7,000 additional tickets. These were annual figures, estimates, and the railroad would have to wait a couple of years to find out just how accurate they were.

The line entered into a number of contracts for various parts of the construction: grading and masonry was the first, ties were next, followed by the rails, the chairs which were used to support the rails on the ties, next was a supply of spikes and finally crossing signs to warn about trains.

The grading contract was signed on November 23, 1852 and specified the work and what the railroad would pay. Myres, Rich and Company of Portland, Maine and Boston were to clear the land and grade, excavate and build embankments and construct all masonry for bridges, sluices, and culverts. They were to build cattle guards and grade crossings. The contractor's job was to ready the land for receiving the ballasting and the track. And for this there were four different rates of pay: for common earth excavating the company paid 14 cents a cubic yard; for hard pan (clay like material) 22 cents a cubic yard, and for solid rock $1.00 a cubic yard. Masonry construction paid $1.80 a cubic yard.

The contract specified that embankments were to be 15 feet across at the top and that all work would be similar to the line "now completed and in operation."

All the other contracts were signed in 1853 and the first was with John W. Robbins of Windham, Connecticut to provide 36,000 cross ties, which were often referred to then as sleepers. This contract specified that the ties were to be "at least seven feet long and flat on two opposite faces and of the thickness from face to face of not less than six inches and if squared on all sides have opposite faces to be no less than six inches wide and the other two opposite faces to be not less than seven inches wide each."

The ties were to be delivered between May 1 and October 1 of that year. The company would pay 40 cents each for the ties and would specify whether they be delivered by ship to the wharf at Cohasset Narrows, Wareham or Hyannis. Shipping costs were the responsibility of John W. Robbins, the supplier. The ties cost the line $14,400.

The most expensive contract was for rails and the company bought them from the Rensselaer Iron Works of Troy, New York. On June 19, 1853 the two parties signed an agreement for delivery of 100 tons of 56 pound per yard, T-rails to be delivered on board a ship at the Rensselaer dock on the Hudson River on or before July 15. The balance of the delivery of 1,600 tons in the order were to be placed on board ships at the same place between August 1 and December 1. The railroad agreed to pay $67.50 per ton for this iron rail, and they were the long tons common then, weighing 2,240 pounds. The railroad paid the shipping company to deliver the rails from Troy, a few miles up river from Albany.

The 1,700 tons delivered to the railroad were more than enough to build the main line with extra rail for sidings at each new station, an extensive yard at Hyannis with tracks into repair shops for locomotives and cars, a round house and a turntable and the branch down to and on the railroad wharf at South Hyannis. The railroad paid $114,700 for the rails.

4

The Cape Cod Branch Railroad used iron "chairs" to fasten the rails to the cross ties. Spikes were driven through the chairs to hold the rail securely and in true gauge, that is 56 and one-half inches between the inside edge of each rail in the track.

Howard Perry of Monument Village signed a contract with the line to provide "of good, tough, strong iron all such Rail Road chairs as said company may need for its Rail Road from Sandwich to Hyannis, after such patterns as may be directed by the said Company's Chief Engineer; no size to be of less weight than fourteen pounds; the same to be furnished at such times and in such quantity as said Engineer may direct." Further the contract specified that Perry shall deliver the chairs to the depot at Monument Village and load them on freight cars "if the same shall be ready when the Chairs are drawn there." The line drew a hard bargain when it could and it wrote "all said Chairs to be warranted of good quality and all such as prove in any respect bad within six months from delivery to be replaced by said Perry by others of good quality."

The price was two cents and seven mills per pound. Payment to be made on the tenth of the month for the amount delivered in the preceding month. But Howard Perry wasn't to receive all cash; for the last twenty-five tons delivered he would be given company stock at par value of $60 a share. The stock to be handed over at the completion of the contract.

Perry may have manufactured the iron chairs at the Pocasset Iron Works or its predecessor, because within a few years he was its sole owner. Ownership and partnerships seem to be in constant flux in those days with frequent change in management. However, Howard Perry had close ties to the Cape Cod Branch Railroad, having served as a director twice within the first three years of its existence.

August remained a busy month in 1853 for signing contracts with suppliers, for three days after agreeing to terms with Howard Perry on chairs, the president of the railroad, J.H.W. Page, signed with Thacher Sears & Co. of Boston "to furnish the spikes required for laying track... from Sandwich to Hyannis, 5 inches under the head (length) 9/16 inch (diameter) of best quality and warranted to be delivered... at Old Colony Depot; at four and a quarter cents per pound cash at six months from each delivery." Not a bad deal from the railroad's point of view. Sears had to wait six months for his money. Perhaps it was a slow time in his business fortunes.

Sylvanus Hinckley of Middleboro agreed to build signs for grade crossings on the extension to Hyannis. His was the last regular contract signed and it went into great detail about dimensions, paint, lettering, and erecting the signs.

Hinckley had to do a great deal of work to prepare these signs, then transport the parts to the crossings, then dig deeply to plant the supports and finally to assemble them. They had to be awkward to move and heavy to lift. The railroad was precise in its instructions.

"...the posts to be straight, not less than eight inches in diameter at the top, to be firmly set in the ground not less than five and a half feet deep and six feet where the nature of the ground will permit it to measure sixteen feet in the clear between the surface of the ground and the lower edge of the sign and more if the engineers shall direct it in any case, and to extra eighteen inches above the upper edge of the sign. The sign to be thirty feet in length across main roads and not less than twenty eight feet in the clear across other roads; to be two feet and three inches wide (high) to be made of clear thoroughly-seasoned pine planks with a cap five and a half inches thick on top and bottom from post to post. The sign to be fastened to the posts by two bolts of three quarters of an inch iron. The signs and posts painted white with three coats, and words in black Capital letters: 'RAIL ROAD CROSSING-LOOK OUT FOR THE ENGINE WHILE THE BELL RINGS,' to be well painted of at least the size of nine inches in length, painted with three coats. All the above work to be done in a substantial and workmanlike manner and to the acceptance of the engineers. The signs to be finished and placed before the trains commence running along said line."

The railroad agreed to transport Sylvanus Hinckley and the sign material to the crossings if he had a car load of materials to move, but he had to understand that he loaded and unloaded the freight car. And he only got a free ride when he was moving and erecting signs.

After Hinckley erected signs and they were accepted by the railroad, they agreed to pay him first with two shares of company stock at $60 par value each and after that the balance in cash after the work was completed. He would have needed at least one workman, probably more to move that material around and one can assume that he had to pay them with some regularity and also pay for lumber, paint and hardware. If he had enough cash on hand to meet those obligations, then he could toil on until the signs were made and planted in the ground at the new crossings from Sandwich to Hyannis, and when the company engineers approved them, he finally was paid $25 for each sign. Sylvanus Hinckley installed one sign at each of the 22 crossings and was paid $550, but the first $120 came to him in the form of two shares of company stock.

On August 27, 1853 Hinckley signed the contract along with J.H.W. Page, president of the line. Page had to be smiling; I wonder if Hinckley was by the time he finally got his money?

Two days before that on the 25th, another contract was drawn up by the railroad with Myres, Rich & Company "who declare their inability to complete the grading and masonry by the first day of September." This new contract offered a series of extensions to Myres, Rich that gave the contractors two additional months to complete their work to Hyannis Road in Barnstable and another fifteen days after that to grade the line to Yarmouth Port and finally until the first of February to complete grading all the way through Hyannis to the landing at South Hyannis where the railroad wharf would be built.

The contractors would be subject to damages if they failed to meet the new deadlines. They continued to run late, but the ballast and track gangs reached Barnstable Village the first week of May and on the eighth of that month the first passenger train came to the village.

It was a day of celebration as the train rolled in carrying railroad officials and their guests, the usual freeloaders, politicians and such. The station and nearby buildings had many flags. There were, of course, speeches which no one remembered. In Barnstable Village there was a wonderful cannon, The Patriot, a relic of the War of 1812, which was fired only on special occasions. This was one of them and its charge of gunpowder roared out its salute as part of that festive day. Church bells and other bells including those on the locomotive rang constantly and all this din was punctuated by the shrill blast of the engine whistle, a new sound in town - and all this noise on a Monday! For the Cape Cod Railroad was in Barnstable - and steam had come to the village. It would stay for more than one hundred years.

The Cape Cod Railroad reached Yarmouth Port just eleven days after that day of celebration at Barnstable. And the Cape Cod Railroad ran its first passenger train to Yarmouth Port. It was a Friday, May 19,1854. Along Old King's Highway, the main street, citizens heard that train and a few went to the station to see it. There was no organized celebration, but there would be in July when the first passenger train steamed into Hyannis.

There was an elegant new station right next to Main Street, Hyannis, a two-story affair with offices on the second floor to serve as headquarters of the line. But what was especially impressive was the Ladies Saloon on the first floor. The women of Hyannis had been asked to pay for the furnishings and decorations for this waiting room for ladies and their small children.

And pay for it they did, and in so doing created one of the wonders of Cape Cod. The newspapers of the day described it as "a spacious room, richly carpeted and as elegantly furnished as a gentleman's parlor. On one wall a mirror in which you can see yourself in full, as others see you...with chairs, rockers, sofas of luxurious lace and a table of costly style and structure, and whatnots, yes, even whatnots...Another saloon so richly and luxuriously furnished cannot be found in any depot on the Cape." There was a ladies saloon in the Sandwich depot about which similar remarks had been made in other newspapers, but this one was new and a great place to wait for the train. The term saloon in those days and for many years afterward including some of the twentieth century meant a social area like a living room, a lobby in a big hotel or the main room of a coastal steamer. The Fall River Line designated that area on their ships as the Main Saloon, a big parlor, if you will. The term so used in public areas had nothing to do with drinking alcohol, sawdust on the floor or bar stools.

It was a Saturday evening, July 8 when the first passenger train arrived to be met by a crowd estimated at 3,000. Such an important day and two months exactly from the railroad's arrival in Barnstable! Many from Hyannis drove their carriages over to get on the train at Barnstable Village so as to ride to Hyannis on the inaugural train. The few remaining seats were filled by Yarmouth Port people who had been waiting for over an hour. The train had four passenger coaches and they were filled to capacity.

As the train whistled her way into Hyannis, the crowd surged forward around the station and the tracks leading to it. The whistle frightened some of the many horses, and they neighed and tried to break free and leave. The whistle was a new, perhaps threatening sound, for until the locomotive came on the scene the horse was king of the road.

The train ground to a halt and was greeted by cheers and exploding fireworks. Several local cannons were fired, as happened in Barnstable, for this, too, was a special day. Cape Cod had railroad fever, as did so much of America. The way that first train was received - the crowds, the cheering, the noise and excitement were typical symbols of community joy!

Immediately the line started running three trains a day to and from Boston. On November 30 of that year, the railroad filed its annual report with the state senate and in it was noted total number of passengers had reached 95,000. That was 20,000 more than the year before.

The roundhouse and repair shops for building and maintaining cars were completed and hiring increased. It was not until that fall that the railroad wharf was finished out past the lighthouse in South Hyannis. The wharf was one-thousand feet long and 200 feet wide. The outside walls were made of large, granite blocks and the wharf was filled in with sand from the bluff near the light. There were several tracks and out at the end was an L-shaped wooden wharf where the steamer from Nantucket docked. The inaugural run by the *S.S. Nebraska* was September 26.

A short distance from the sidewheel steamer was a train that had backed out to wait

The round house at Sandwich was the most distinctive railroad building on the Cape. Its diameter was 100-feet and its height was 120-feet. It became a warehouse for the Boston & Sandwich Glass Company, and eight years after that company closed, this building collapsed in a storm in 1896.

for the first boatload of passengers. The *Nebraska* approached the new wharf with her walking beam pumping and paddlewheels churning the water into white foam. She saluted the train with a blast from her whistle; the locomotive returned the greeting.

In a few minutes the ship was tied up and the passengers had crossed her gangplank and entered the cars.

The Hyannis extension cost the railroad $298,747.45 for the construction. It broke down this way: for the purchase of land, settlement of land damage claims and fencing the right of way, the company spent $15,991.02. One flag stop and four way stations (staffed by a station agent) were built at a cost of $27,673.15. The clearing of the land, the grading of the right of way and the masonry for bridges, sluices and culverts was a major expense that cost $83,892.46. The small amount of bridge work in Barnstable cost $864.40. The civil engineers who handled planning the extension and inspecting the contractor's work were paid $4,344.54. The largest single expense was for superstructure and iron: placing ballast, then ties and iron chairs and spiking the rails to them and to the ties. Every station had a siding with at least one switch. The Hyannis yards were the most extensive with a number of tracks and switches and a turntable. Also tracks ran through the shops there. For this part of the work the railroad paid for material and labor $165,981.88. That amounted to $16,597.08 per mile, an extremely reasonable cost in a state where rail construction ran between $20,000 and $30,000 per mile.

The Cape Cod Railroad had done an effective job of keeping its building costs down, since the original line from Middleboro to Sandwich six years before had cost $16,974.45 per mile over 28 miles, including a rather large bridge across Cohasset Narrows and two others.

Another manner in which costs were figured was to add in the amount spent for locomotives and rolling stock. Reports to the state required this. So the cost this way of the line to Sandwich was $20,968.42 per mile.

On the other hand, the company bought additional equipment for the extra trains required for the Hyannis extension. Two new locomotives cost $15,771; six freight cars were $3,925 or $654.17 each, and for passenger trains four day coaches and two baggage cars cost a total of $11,624.65. These all came to $31,320.65, and when added to the construction costs made the total expenses for the Hyannis extension $330,068.22 or $18,597.08 per mile. Of course the railroad didn't buy nearly as much equipment for the Hyannis extension as it did when it first opened.

The railroad wharf was an important facility with its daily arrival and sailing of a Nantucket steamer, and the trains that served it. There was room for six coastal schooners

Opposite, middle The one-thousand foot long Railroad Wharf at South Hyannis was used from 1854. It was built of large granite blocks with a wooden wharf at the end for the Nantucket steamer. The wharf became a busy, maritime center. **Bottom** This schooner is unloading coal into railroad cars.

and the two tracks often had flat cars, gondolas and box cars and a locomotive moving them around and spotting them next to vessels for the unloading of lumber, cement, grain, coal, sugar, flour, fish and other freight for movement to Cape towns.

There were a number of buildings on the wharf: a lumber yard, a fish house, a grain building, a coal dealership, a ship's chandlery. There was even serious consideration given to building a hotel over the tracks on the wharf with a platform where passengers could leave the cars and walk upstairs and rent a room. It was never built.

The wharf attracted more vessels and became the center of shipping activity along that coast. Schooner size increased until four-masters were common. Sailing ships were a daily occurrence in Nantucket Sound channels, but steamers were seen more frequently and the huge coastal coal trade was slowly being taken over by large, steam tugs pulling caravans of schooner-barges.

For example in 1882 there were 1,500 ship arrivals, carrying 6,000 tons of coal, 100-thousand bushels of grain, one and a quarter million board feet of lumber and four thousand barrels of fish.

Within two years, ship arrivals had risen to 1,800 vessels, discharging one and a half million board feet of lumber, 8,000 tons of coal, 115-thousand bushels of grain, $5,000 worth of cranberries, and 1,500 bushels of oysters.

By 1893, coal delivered had reached almost 15,000 tons and the total value of all imports to the railroad wharf was $557,700. The facility was an economic bonanza to the railroad.

Shortly after the railroad wharf opened in South Hyannis the Fair Haven Branch Railroad opened from Tremont, on the Cape Cod Railroad, through Marion, Mattapoisett and to Fair Haven where passengers and freight could transfer to a ferry crossing the Acushnet River to New Bedford. The fifteen mile line, which opened October 2, 1854, was another economic plus for the Cape Cod Railroad as both lines interchanged at Tremont.

The year 1854 saw the Cape Cod Railroad have its most profitable year. On a gross income of $102,139.77 the net after all expenses was $51,658.79, an amazing profit and one that would not be surpassed until a booming Civil War year, 1863.

For the next decade the line ran pretty much as it had been for its first six years. It was primarily a passenger railroad. It ran three passenger trains a day each way and usually one freight train, but when freight traffic was light, one local freight with a passenger car on the end was scheduled, a mixed train daily. To give you an idea of what earned the money without loading you up with endless figures, let us take a few years, e.g., in 1856 passenger revenue was $94,583 and freight revenue was $23,505 (these numbers are rounded off); in 1859 passenger revenue was $83,655 and for freight $28,900; and in 1864 passenger revenue was $121,736 and freight was $33,427. In some years the ratio was almost four to one in favor of the passenger business; in other years, three to one, and the railroad accomplished that with seven locomotives, ten passenger cars and five baggage cars (every passenger train had a baggage car to carry the heavier trunks, express and the twice a day mail pick-up and delivery).

The line had declared several dividends on its stock, beginning in 1853 and continuing for three years and again in 1859, but the stock proved to be a fine investment when it declared a dividend in 1862 and every year, for eleven years, until the line was bought out by the Old Colony & Newport in 1872. The dividends were most often over six percent, but four of those years they were more than eight percent. When the line issued its first stock certificates in 1847, they were sold at par for $100. In 1851 the legislature ordered the line to reduce par value to $60. The doubling of capital stock issued from $300-thousand to $600-thousand to finance the Hyannis extension kept its value after the two dividends declared that year, 1854. The stock at times drifted as low as $18 on the market, but once those dividends became an annual event during the Civil War, the stock regained its valued and often sold for above $60.

The legislature was approached in the late 1850s for a change in the charter of the line, which restricted it to running to Hyannis. The directors were getting ambitious again and wanted to extend the tracks to Orleans, but without a charter there could be no extension. The legislature turned them down and there it sat - but not for long. It would seem that there might be a way, and there was.

A group of men, all stockholders, were asked to form a separate company and apply for a charter to build from Yarmouth Port to Orleans under the name Cape Cod Central. The charter was finally approved and the company was incorporated in March 1861.

There really was no Cape Cod Central, because the railroad would have trains run by Cape Cod Railroad workers who were operating their own equipment. The Cape Cod Central was a legal maneuver, a ploy if you will, to overcome the limitations imposed by the charter that allowed them to build as far as Hyannis. The Cape Cod Central was the Cape Cod Railroad and eventually this would all be one in name as well.

With the incorporation came the capitalization of the Central at $200-thousand with 2,000 shares of stock at $100 a share. The directors assumed that the stock would be purchased quickly and construction could begin shortly. But history stepped in and investors were concerned and cautious, for the Confederates fired on Fort Sumter, South Carolina, two weeks later and within three days Abraham Lincoln called for volunteers to defend the Union. On Cape Cod most of the young men who joined the military became navy men. The popular reference to the war was to call it "the rebellion." There was the usual talk in the early days of a short conflict. That was not to be and it ground on for a full four years.

The Civil War produced an inflation that made most things cost more, and it gave the Cape Cod Railroad steady financial success, while attempts continued to sell Cape Cod Central stock so that line could be built. The first route proposed laying track to East Harwich with a service point for Chatham. It was difficult to sell stock at that time, and it wasn't until late 1863 that a greater mood of optimism regarding the war was apparent. The change came in that summer when Robert E. Lee led his Army of Northern Virginia across the Maryland border into Pennsylvania. It was late June.

On the morning of July First just after 5 a.m. soldiers from Alabama and Tennessee sent out a skirmish line near a small bridge over a creek near the Chambersburg Pike. It was one of the routes north. Up ahead Lieutenant Marcellus E. Jones of the 8th Illinois Cavalry sighted down the barrel of his carbine until he had a man in a gray coat in his sights. Jones squeezed off one shot. It was the first fired that day. The man fell and in three days more than 40,000 would do the same. Three miles to the north where ten dusty roads came together was a place that was home for 2,400 people - a place called Gettysburg.

The Confederate defeat and withdrawal was the turning point in the war. There was a sense of ultimate victory in the north, a feeling that things would come out right. Slowly that fall and winter on Cape Cod it became a time when more people were willing to invest in a railroad.

On January 16, 1864 in the Exchange Hall in Harwich Center, President Chester Snow of the Cape Cod Central Railroad, called a public meeting to order at 10 a.m. How many shares would Harwich people buy? That was the question. Harwich responded by buying 400 shares at $100, a total of $40,000 or 20 percent of the issue. Harwich would get a railroad. Brewster pledged to buy 300 shares and the line was changed from East Harwich to pass through the Village of Pleasant Lake to Brewster to East Brewster and to Orleans as end of track - at least temporarily.

The Cape Cod Railroad shared in the general business prosperity of the country during the Civil War, and the 46-mile line carried 80,873 passengers and earned $73,336 doing it in 1861. Those figures climbed by 1863 to 135,095 passengers and earnings from them of $96,772. The last full year of war, 1864, the number of passengers carried reached 170,020 with income of $121,736. The war ended in mid April, 1865, and for that whole year the passenger lists totaled 174,100 and its income of $124,891. Freight tonnage and revenue increased too. From a mediocre 22,000 tons in 1861 it almost doubled that by '64 and '65. Freight revenues rose from $17,240 in 1861 to $33- and $34-thousand in '64 and '65. The railroad's total income went from $95,871 in 1861 to $167,030 in 1865. Times were good for the Cape Cod Railroad, and things were looking up for its prodigy, The Cape Cod Central.

In 1863 the Central's entire report to the legislature read like this: "The Cape Cod Central Railroad Corporation would respectfully report...,that the road is not yet built, but that all necessary surveys have been made, the route located, and the means secured for the building of the road."

Only the first part of that statement was true, the line had not been built. No part of it had. Final surveys had not been made, only tentative ones, so the route was not located at all, just a number of possibilities. As "the means secured for the building of the road" that is nonsense, as no stock was sold until the following year, and the bonds even later than that.

In the winter and early spring of 1864, $60,000 worth of Cape Cod Central stock, 600 shares at $100 par, were sold. Construction was to start soon and it did on July 4, 1864.

To a 46-year old Yarmouth physician, Dr. George Shove, fell the honor of digging out the first shovelful of earth. Shove had moved from Sandwich to Yarmouth Port almost 15 years before and was one of its most popular residents.

A group of workmen under the direction of Mr. Pierce, the contractor, was ready to start the grading when Dr. Shove put a new spade into the soft ground near Greenough's Pond. The doctor moved a shovelful off to one side while the on-lookers cheered. It may have been a national holiday but it was time to go to work. The doctor's ceremonial shoveling took place at 8:45 a.m. and was followed by the workmen attacking a small rise in the terrain with their shovels. The Barnstable Patriot described it this way. "In a few minutes, a considerable number of laborers were pitching into the dry sand, and a cloud of dust, through which hardly anything but the glistening of the new shovels could be seen, was enveloping the crowd. Squads of workmen have also commenced in Harwich on The Cape Cod Central Railroad."

So it began and the beginning was easy, for by August 23 three miles of right-of-way was cleared from Yarmouth east and was ready for tracks. Around Harwich work was proceeding more slowly, but there was great optimism.

The directors of the Cape Cod Railroad began talking publicly of the need to extend the tracks past the present goal, Orleans, through Eastham, Wellfleet and Truro to Provincetown, the tip of the Cape. They couldn't build it because of their charter to Hyannis only. That left it up to the Cape Cod Central. And those directors did their duty ever mindful that the country was at war. Now here was the time and a compelling argument.

In a series of weekly editorials, the Barnstable Patriot called for extending the railroad to Provincetown. The editor, Sylvanus B. Phinney, in the issue of December 13, 1864 wrote that such a development would "protect Provincetown from a future enemy...such a railroad is absolutely necessary. Private enterprise has exhausted its strength in the road from Yarmouth to Orleans. The cost for the balance must be mainly borne by the government or the fort at Provincetown will be shorn of half its strength, and that beautiful harbor will be at the mercy of foreign foes."

Editor Phinney did not identify these future foes who threatened the tranquillity of the Cape tip. He was most helpful in setting a stage for future moves, and within two months the railroad appealed to the government. On January 31, 1865, the directors of the Cape Cod Central gave their petition to the legislature, asking for permission to issue stock to finance a line from Orleans to Provincetown.

In late spring, crews completed the masonry and the bridges across the Bass River between Yarmouth and Dennis and another at the arm of West Reservoir in North Harwich, the source of the Herring River. In April the track was down for about 15 miles from Yarmouth to Brewster. The line turned north at Harwich and skirted the eastern edge of Hinckley's Pond on an embankment and crossed the sandy road, through woods to emerge on the narrow strip of land between the western end of Long Pond and Seymour Pond in the village of Pleasant Lake. From there the railroad turned in a northeasterly direction through the moraine hills of the Cape's north side and into Orleans.

Construction that summer was slow despite the urgings of the chairman of the board of directors, Captain Benjamin Freeman of Brewster. There was talk of opening the line to Orleans by October. By Halloween the line was not far from the Orleans town line, but it still had some miles to go. The stations at Harwich, North Harwich and Brewster were finished, but those at South Dennis and Orleans were still being built. The railroad was thinking about a South Yarmouth station to be a flag stop, without an agent assigned. The location under consideration was at Gray's Crossing at the eastern end of White's Path. The completion date was said to be November 25. That wasn't far off and within several weeks the company announced it would build two additional stations, both flag stops: South Yarmouth and East Brewster. November was the key and work crews labored from before dawn until after dark, completing the single track line into Orleans and the new station in early December.

The 19 mile extension began service on the morning of Wednesday, December 6, 1865 with the arrival of the train from Boston at 11:30. The Yarmouth Register, of December 8th, said "there was a large crowd on that train. The road will be equipped and run by the Cape Cod Railroad under its Superintendent Ephraim N. Winslow. The first train made its one hour run to Orleans with conductor Charles H. Nye in charge." The newspaper's story told of a promotion, saying "Leander B. Marston, a baggage master on the Cape Cod Railroad, will be the conductor on the Central." Conductors were important railroad people and well paid.

The editor and publisher of the Yarmouth Register, Charles Francis Swift, in his book, History of Old Yarmouth, paid tribute to the Orleans extension: "In the progress of the modern development of the town, we note the first train on the Cape Cod Central Railroad, which, through the energy of the citizens of this and the adjoining towns, was opened to Orleans, December 6, 1865. The villages on the south side of the town, and East

Dennis, were brought several hours nearer to Boston by this arrangement. This enterprise, prosecuted during the throes of the rebellion, shows that, notwithstanding the drains upon our resources, our people still kept up their courage and determination to develop and improve all their opportunities."

The railroad scheduled two passenger trains a day each way. From Yarmouth at 11:34 a.m. and 7:44 p.m. From Orleans trains departed at 6:30 a.m. and 1:30 p.m. The trip each way took one hour and all four daily trains carried mail. The westbound trains into Yarmouth were scheduled to meet trains from Hyannis for the run up Cape and to Middleboro where passengers could catch another train for the run into Fall River and the steamers to New York. Boston-bound passengers continued north from Middleboro into Kneeland Street Station.

Superintendent Ephraim N. Winslow appointed Frederick Nickerson to be station agent at South Dennis; Sheldon Crowell at North Harwich; Barzillia Sears at Harwich; F.H. Bangs at Brewster and Prince Rogers at Orleans.

Making way for the new whenever the railroad expanded always meant the retreat of the stage coach lines. From Yarmouth there had been four stages a day through East Dennis, Brewster, Orleans and on to Eastham and Wellfleet. The Stage service of Simeon K. Higgins and George D. Ruggles employed 50 horses on that run with four horses on each stage. The day before the first train to Orleans Higgins and Ruggles withdrew their equipment and animals to Orleans where they picked up railroad passengers for down Cape. The stage lines from Hyannis to Chatham moved their operation to Harwich, picking up passengers at Harwich depot for the trip over the sandy roads to Chatham.

Of course years earlier the Hyannis to Boston stages had their run shortened to Hyannis-Sandwich when the rails reached from Middleboro to the Cape's oldest town. Woods Hole, Falmouth, and Cataumet were still served by stage lines and would be for seven more years.

The Cape Cod Central had cost $337,647 to build. That broke down this way:(in round numbers) $14,000 for engineering; $77,000 for grading and masonry; $2,904 for bridges (most of that amount for spanning Bass River); $183-thousand for superstructure and rails; $13,750 for stations and other buildings, including a freight house, engine house and turntable at Orleans; $14,500 for land, land damages and fences; and $25,000 for commissions on bonds. Since the road was equipped with engines and rolling stock of the Cape Cod Railroad, the cost per mile was the lowest on the Cape and in the state: $17,770.94. To pay for the extension to Orleans the line sold $187-thousand worth of stock and $125-thousand worth of bonds paying 6 percent.

The 17 months of construction were longer than planned, but the contractors had difficulty keeping workers, because of the heavy demand for labor and the higher wages paid by western railroads.

The Cape Cod Central was laid with 45 pound rail to the yard, that was eleven pounds per yard lighter than the Cape Cod's rail from Middleboro to Hyannis. The Central adopted a rate of speed of 20 miles per hour, including stops for passenger and freight trains, which was seven miles faster for freight service. The only tough climb for the engines was from Pleasant Lake to Brewster, where the tracks rose 68 feet in a mile and a quarter. There were 36 grade crossings, none of them protected by a gateman, just a sign. Whether Silvanus Hinckley built and painted them as he had on the Hyannis extension is not recorded.

In its first year the Central carried 53,928 passengers and earned $8,190 from people

Above Although the Cape Cod Central was wholly-owned and operated by The Cape Cod Railroad, there were separate tickets printed to help perpetrate the legal ploy that the two lines were, indeed, separate companies.

This broadside was the first to announce service between Yarmouth and Orleans.

CAPE COD CENTRAL

RAILROAD.

WINTER ARRANGEMENT.

On and after Wednesday, Dec. 6, 1865,

Passenger Trains will leave Yarmouth for So. Yarmouth, So. Dennis, Harwich, Brewster and Orleans,

At 11.34 A.M. and 7.43 P.M.

Leave Orleans for Yarmouth and Way Stations,
At 6.20 A.M. and 1.30 P.M.

The Trains connect with the Cape Cod Railroad at Yarmouth.

☞ STAGES leave Harwich and Orleans, on the arrival of the Cars from Boston, for the Cape towns below.

E. N. WINSLOW, Sup't.

Hyannis, December 2, 1865.

people buying tickets for traveling just on its own line and no farther than Yarmouth. From tickets sold beyond Yarmouth the income was $20,202. For freight the ratio of local to off-line income was far higher: on Central tracks freight earned only $337 from within the 19 mile line. Freight that moved to and from the Cape Cod Railroad earned $2,810. The mail contract was worth $1,900 a year.

That first year the total income of the Central was given as $33,539, but that figure was based on rates proposed by Superintendent Winslow, of the Cape Cod Railroad. In its first annual report that listed income and traffic, the Cape Cod Central wrote that it did not agree with the figures and, in fact, claimed more. Such a questioning of the parent road by the stepson Cape Cod Central did not appear in later annual reports.

The Central had about the same passenger and freight business in 1867 as it had its first year. With the mail contract the same the only new service was express in baggage cars. That earned $900, and the line reported total income of $32,526.

Having extended the line to Orleans the Cape Cod Railroad decided to end the charade and bring things together under one corporate name. The Cape Cod Railroad bought the Cape Cod Central on April 21, 1868.

The Cape Cod Central records were kept up to April 1, 1868 and they indicate net earnings of a mere $5,144.76 from the opening of business in December, 1865. This may be misleading as a reflection of the earning capacity, as some loans had to be repaid quickly and the frugal management of the Cape Cod always paid bank loans rapidly, as many of them were made at 7 percent interest.

The important thing from the standpoint of management was the completion in good shape of the extension to Orleans. The legislature had approved extending the charter to build on to Provincetown and surveys were to be made laying out a right-of-way to Wellfleet, over eleven miles to the north, which would be the next terminus before the final push to the end of the Cape.

The railroad more than any single development or system of transportation brought the Cape closer to Boston, the rest of New England, New York, the south and the west. Trains brought summer people for the first time and that seasonal growth continued, producing new sources of income for Cape Codders. The railroad brought expanded mail deliveries, so that twice a day mail arrived, and of course it left as frequently. It also made possible quick trips to New Bedford, Providence and most of all Boston.

For example in the spring of 1868 the Cape Cod Railroad ran two trains a day from Orleans to Boston by having its passengers transfer at Yarmouth to a train from Hyannis that ran to Middleboro where an Old Colony & Newport engine pulled the cars to the Kneeland Street station in Boston. The train left Orleans at 6:15 a.m. and arrived in Harwich at 6:45 and in Yarmouth at 7:15. Another train left Hyannis at 7:05 a.m. for the ten-minute run to Yarmouth where the trains were combined. Passengers then reached Sandwich at 7:52 and Boston at 10:34.

From Orleans, Boston was four hours and 19 minutes away; from Yarmouth three hours and 19 minutes; from Hyannis three hours and 24 minutes; and from Sandwich two hours and 42 minutes. In the three years since the line to Orleans was completed the company had slightly modified the schedule by having the morning train leave 15 minutes earlier and the afternoon train five minutes later. That afternoon train departed Orleans at 1:35 and reached Harwich at 2:02, Yarmouth at 2:30 where passengers changed to the train that left Hyannis at 2:20. The cars were in Sandwich at 3:07 and Boston at 6 p.m.

Trains heading for the Cape left Boston at 7:50 a.m. and 4 p.m. That morning train reached Sandwich at 10:35, Yarmouth at 11:15 and Hyannis at 11:25 where it stopped at the Main Street station before proceeding down to the Railroad Wharf to connect with the steamer for Nantucket, which at that time was the beloved *Island Home*.

Meanwhile a train was waiting at Yarmouth where passengers boarded for Down Cape, reaching Harwich at 11:50 and Orleans at 12:20 p.m. All these trains had combination cars, carrying baggage, express and mail and were the first cars in the train, right behind the tender.

Freight service usually started earlier in the morning than the passenger trains. The first freight out of Orleans was scheduled to leave at 5:30 and combining with a 7:05 from Hyannis Wharf at Yarmouth. At that point the freight was in the hole and departed after the 7:15 passenger train was on its way. The freight trains were supposed to be operated on a basis of covering 13 miles per hour, including stops. That was an average for them.

That morning freight reached Middleboro sometime after 11, where it waited for the freight that left Boston at 6 a.m. and the other freight that departed Newport, Rhode Island at 7:50 a.m. All the cars then were assembled into one train that left Middleboro, or tried to, at 12:15 p.m. It usually presented no serious problem if it wasn't on schedule to leave or arrive since trains were dispatched by telegraph and there were sidings where trains could meet and pass at every station, including flag stops.

Another change was the addition of a passenger car to the 12:15 p.m. freight from Middleboro to Hyannis on Mondays, Wednesdays and Fridays.

An innovation in passenger car design appeared in 1867 when the car shops in Hyannis turned out the first day coach. It was a smoking car for men only and had long benches down each side in front of the windows, rather than two rows of double seats side by side with an aisle through the middle. One newspaper account described this first smoker "with car length seats, back to the windows, a row of cuspidors down the center, a red hot stove at the other end, and a despondent brakeman wondering how he was ever going to hoe out the vehicle when the run was finished." Before this latest addition to the company's rolling stock, one car on each trip would be designated a smoking car - for men only, of course.

Much more excitement was created when the line received in the same year its latest - and its handsomest - locomotive: *Highland Light*. Built by William Mason at his Mason Machine Works in Taunton, the *Highland Light* was a superb example of Mason's sense of style and proportion. This engine was painted brightly with reds and blues and heavily accented stripes and the tender, too. The railroad writer and historian, Lucius Beebe, is often quoted as describing it "as the handsomest steam locomotive ever built in America." Some of the artists who have painted *Highland Light* have included the road name C.C.C. or Cape Cod Central on the tender. Of course the Central owned no equipment, but it was the designated owner of the Orleans Branch when the locomotive arrived, which may account for the mistake in identifying ownership.

For the crowds attracted by the coming of a train - and there always were crowds - the *Highland Light* got the most attention and admiring glances as she rolled through Cape Cod, leaving a plume of smoke rolling back over a baggage and mail car followed by three coaches all painted a bright yellow with dark green trim.

Picture it, if you will, it is early evening and the train from Boston is due. That's the one that left Kneeland Street Station at 4 p.m. A Cape Cod locomotive couples onto the Cape Cod Railroad cars at Middleboro, leaving there at 5:20. All along the line the time of arrival is the same, no matter what season at Monument at 6:12, Sandwich at 6:35,

Barnstable at 7:05, Yarmouth at 7:12, South Dennis at 7:28, Harwich at 7:37, Brewster at 7:49 and Orleans at 8:05. It is always the same at those way stations.

At least 15 minutes before the train is due the station agent opens the ticket window. The agent walks out on the platform and moves a baggage cart to the spot where the first car will stop. If he has any express or mail that will be moved through an open door to the car. He will assist the agent in the car in unloading mail and express. The crowd gathered around the platform and along the sides of the track look for arriving passengers whom they have come to meet. Others are there to see if they have any mail, for that will be taken to the post office by the station agent after he has brought the express in and locked it in his office if there isn't anyone there to claim it. Any telegrams that have come in the few minutes before the train arrived are sealed in envelopes and delivered if the person is there. The person may well be there, for watching the evening train arrive is a most popular social activity. Any earlier telegrams have been sent out in the care of a local boy with a bicycle. The ritual of the train's departure never changed. The brass bell on the engine would start to ring, the conductor would check his watch and never give the signal to leave early. Then he would glance along the train both ways if he was next to a middle car and shout "BOARD!" Two short blasts on the whistle, and as the conductor climbed the steps to an open platform day coach, the engine was working steam and the tempo of machinery quickened and the sounds came from farther and farther away.

As the train moved away so did the people, alone or in groups. It always took longer for a crowd to gather than it did for them to vanish. After they had gone, the station agent locked the outside door and headed for the post office. Then he went home. That is unless he lived upstairs in the apartment that some stations had.

Up ahead at the next stop it was the same. A train was approaching, a baggage cart was spotted on the platform near the tracks and a waiting crowd. The station was the center of activity. If you went any distance at all, you went by train. Anything that you used that wasn't local in origin came to you by round wheels turning on rails, for the railroad was the most important single factor in the development of modern America.

In 1868 the line was surveyed to Wellfleet and some land was acquired for the right-of-way. Passenger traffic increased while freight tonnage was down but not seriously. What continued to be the role of the line was its earnings from its business strictly on the 64 miles of main line as compared with its interchange business. On passenger revenue the ratio was four to one in favor of interchange with the Fairhaven Branch at Tremont and with the Old Colony & Newport and the Middleboro & Taunton at Middleboro. Freight was earning about the same or a little less than four to one. Income from carrying mail was up to $7,833.28. For 1868, total income rose by more than $21,500 to a new high: $219,516.83. The net earned was $50,659.80, that despite the largest damage fees the railroad had to pay in its 20-year history. A spark or ember from a locomotive passing through Sandwich Woods had set a fire that destroyed not only woodlands but houses and out buildings, including barns. The fire occurred in 1866, but the line finally agreed to damages of $27,349.16 in 1868 and the checks were mailed then.

The *Highland Light* had to be paid for a year after delivery and a check for $6,500 was sent to William Mason at Taunton, who was always generous with his terms of purchase, especially with his New England neighbors. The *Highland Light* increased the locomotive roster to eight. For rolling stock the line had 15 passenger cars, 6 baggage and mail cars, 67 freight cars and 52 gravel cars, which were used for ballast and right-of-way maintenance. That year there were 140 employees. For the first time the railroad analyzed its ticket sales and announced that the average distance traveled was 21.71 miles.

There was something more on the minds of the company directors than the extension to Wellfleet and past that to Provincetown, and that was the move by the Vineyard Sound Railroad Company that had since 1861 a charter to build a line from Cohasset Narrows or from Monument Station, one mile east, down through Cataumet to Falmouth and Woods Hole. On April 13, 1868 the Vineyard Sound Railroad Company changed its name to the Plymouth & Vineyard Sound Railroad Company, and this renewed an old threat, i.e., to build a railroad to the Cape from Plymouth. The stockholders were happy with the Cape Cod Railroad, because despite that large settlement of claims from the Sandwich Woods fire, the line declared a 6-2/3 percent dividend, distributing $42,666.

The following year was even better for the line with total income reaching $250,517.32, producing a net of $64,879.16. The railroad declared its eighth straight dividend, and its largest at 8-1/2 percent. That dividend amounted to $56,665.

In 1870 construction began on the line from Orleans to Wellfleet, an 11.61 mile extension. The railroad to Wellfleet took most of 1870 to build and involved a great deal of fill across marsh areas above the Orleans Station for much of the nearly three miles to the Eastham Station. The line was laid out to avoid the many Cape ponds, but Eastham had marshes extending far inland from Cape Cod Bay on the west and from Town Cove and Salt Pond Bay from Nauset Harbor on the east. The engineers designed a straight right-of-way on as much dry land as could be found from just below the Eastham station to just above the South Wellfleet station, a distance of six miles.

The problem of stable fill in marshes began around Orleans and three tidal creeks - Little Namskaket, Book Creek and Boatmeadow Creek - run from Cape Cod Bay on the west into a wide area. To the east much of the area was spongy from Town Cove north to Salt Pond Bay and little tidal streams like fingers ran through the area both sides of the track below Eastham station. Horses and wagons and some tip carts were used for the extensive fill needed there.

The Eastham station was built just to the south of Depot Pond where the line ran between there and the smaller Jemina Pond. A water tank was constructed there with a line to Jemina Pond. Later when the water level was low, another tank was built a few hundred feet away with a pipe to Depot Pond.

From a short distance below the Eastham station to just above the one at South Wellfleet there was an absolutely straight stretch of track - six miles long. From North Eastham to South Wellfleet a four mile run was an invitation for engineers to open it up for there on the Plains of Eastham and South Wellfleet was flat track with no grades. At Wellfleet the railroad built a trestle across the inner section of Duck Creek on the southern end and a long fill from the trestle to Wellfleet station above it. Construction moved along well and the stations within the new line - Eastham, North Eastham and South Wellfleet - each had a passenger and freight depot and a siding. Wellfleet, as the new terminus, had in addition an engine house, a car shed, a turntable, a water tank, a wood station and a coal shed. The railroad had started burning coal in one locomotive in 1859, but its conversion from wood went slowly and it continued using both fuels, although by then coal was predominant.

With all the fill required the Wellfleet extension was by far the least expensive the Cape Cod Railroad built. The land cost the railroad $4,614.76; the station's wood and coal facilities and water tanks cost $13,613.10; the engine house, car shed and turntable at Wellfleet cost $1,037.13, and the biggest expense was $107,745.87 for the grading, masonry and tracks. The total was $127,010.86. The per mile cost was the lowest in Massachusetts history - $10,939.78 per mile. That was about a third of what most railroads cost to build those days in the Commonwealth.

Service began December 29, 1870 and again steam came to another Cape Cod town. The stage coaches now made their runs to Truro and Provincetown from the Wellfleet station, moving there from Orleans.

By the late spring of 1871 the morning train for Boston left Wellfleet at 6:10, Orleans at 6:40, Brewster at 6:53, Harwich at 7:05, South Yarmouth at 7:19 and Yarmouth at 7:30 where the passengers got on the cars from Hyannis, which had left there at 7:20. The train would be turned around at Yarmouth and wait to pick up passengers that left Boston at 8 a.m. for Down Cape on the train that would then go on to Hyannis and to the Railroad Wharf for the steamer to Nantucket. After the arrival of the 8 a.m. from Boston at Yarmouth the train that had come from Wellfleet would start back at 11:27 a.m., reaching South Dennis at 11:41, Harwich at 11:50, Brewster at 12:03, Orleans at 12:15, Eastham at 12:22 and Wellfleet at 12:40 p.m. So Wellfleet was a four hour and 40 minute train ride from Kneeland Street Station, Boston.

The locomotive and cars - usually one head car for baggage, mail and express - followed by two day coaches and a smoker would be turned at Wellfleet and spotted at the station there to leave at 1:17 p.m. for Yarmouth. The thirty-seven minute layover at Wellfleet was not a lot of time for the passenger brakeman to assist in cutting the locomotive from the train and helping turn her on the table and then recoupling the engine after running past the cars on the siding. When that chore was done the brakeman had to clean the cars and, if it was winter, shake down the fires and add fresh coal in the car stoves. The appearance of the passenger cars was his responsibility under the supervision of the conductor, which meant the brakeman did the work.

The afternoon train from Wellfleet covered the 31 miles to Yarmouth in an hour and a quarter. Once there the passengers changed trains and headed up Cape on the cars from Hyannis. When that train left Yarmouth the Wellfleet train would be turned to wait for the afternoon train from Boston. Leaving Yarmouth at 7:00 p.m. the run to Wellfleet reached there at 8:15. One locomotive and four cars handled the passenger, mail, express and baggage business between Yarmouth and Wellfleet. One set of equipment and one crew ran the four passenger trains a day - a day that began about 6:00 a.m. and ended when the train was turned, heading south after 8:15 p.m. and ready for the next morning's run. It was more than a 14 hour day, counting the two layovers at Yarmouth. Still, it was a long time to be on duty.

In the early days of Cape travel by rail when the end of track was in Sandwich a ticket to Boston cost $1.50, which meant that for the 62 mile trip the per mile cost was $.0242. The line frequently ran special excursions - usually to Boston - to exhibitions or a theatrical performance and the ticket rate was much lower, sometimes as low as $.90. The fares stayed much as they had been set originally for passenger tickets, but during the Civil War with its inflation, ticket prices rose as did freight rates, which earlier had been reduced in several attempts to create more business.

In that period of 1868 to 1870 the per mile cost of a ticket, including season or monthly commuting tickets, was $.0372, which made one way to Boston $2.31. But the average rate of local fares was higher; it was $.0474 per mile. From Orleans to Middleborough - the longest run on the railroad: 60 miles - cost $2.10. If you just wanted to go from Orleans to the next station, East Brewster, it cost $.10. From Brewster to Harwich, just under five miles, was $.20. From South Dennis to South Yarmouth, with a view of the Bass River from the railroad bridge, was a dime, as was East Sandwich to Sandwich, a little more than two and a half miles. It also cost a dime to ride from West Sandwich to Sandwich and from West Sandwich to North Sandwich. Even though it was a mile and a quarter longer from Monument to North Sandwich, a ticket between those stations was also $.10. At $.0369 per mile that was one of the lowest rates except for Hyannis to South Yarmouth for a quarter, a per mile rate of $.0331. Finally, the rate per mile was high but the fare was the lowest on the line from Wareham to Parker Mills - just a nickel, but the stations were only three-quarters of a mile apart.

Early in 1870 the Board of Railroad Commissioners issued its First Annual Report and in it the longest section dealt with a hearing on a petition from 55 citizens around Rock Village in Middleborough, complaining of their treatment by the Cape Cod Railroad.

The station, first called Rock Meeting House, was the first one below Middleborough and located five miles south on the way to the Cape. It seems that when the line was contemplated there was general agreement that a station would be built there and regular service maintained. The railroad designated it a flag stop and for a period of eleven years followed the usual procedure of stopping when anyone flagged down a train there.

About 1860 the company discontinued the station and ignored anyone signaling them. In 1865, the legislature enacted a statute providing that no railroad should "abandon any passenger station or depot which is on its road in this Commonwealth, except by the consent of the legislature." The law was not retroactive and so did not apply to Rock. Two years after that the petitioners brought the matter to the legislature in hopes of getting the provisions of the statute extended to cover their case.

While the hearing before the Committee on Railways was being held, and before any action was taken, an agreement was reached between the attorneys representing the line and the petitioners. The railroad agreed to stop its trains at Rock on three alternate days of the week. Unfortunately, no record of the agreement was made and the petitioners later denied that it was made with their knowledge, so they felt that they were not bound by it. "About 800 people looked to Rock for service," said the report, "and receipts from the station amount to $900 in fares and $3,027 in freight, and of that total of over $4,000 the Cape Cod Railroad keeps almost half. A box factory near the station has increased the freight business there."

The Railroad Commission was set up as a board of referees on questions of accommodation arising between localities and the railroad corporations. The Commission had no final power in these matters, but if after a hearing either side wished, they could appeal to the legislature.

What the railroad wanted to do was close the two stations at Rock and South Middleborough, two and a half miles below it, and then build a new station at some intermediate point between the two. But that was out of the question, because "it violently disturbs the customs, business relations and arrangements which have grown up during twenty years, and must be dismissed as impracticable," said the Commissioner's report.

The report recognized the desire on the railroad's part to speed up its train service, especially for through passengers. The line ran only two passenger trains a day each way and could not very well run some express and some all local. The Old Colony did this with some of its through trains and in fact steamed through most of the stations between Boston and Middleborough without stopping. "In other words," to quote the report, "the inhabitants of Rock, as a rule, travel but a short distance over the road, and must travel over it, no matter how far they have to go to reach it; the road therefore is sure of their patronage; - the more distant and valuable travel, if inconvenienced, may seek other lines, and must, therefore, be accommodated at the expense of the local travel."

Still, the Railroad Commission felt that what "is reasonable to the public is the daily stopping of a morning and evening train each way, when any passenger wishes to get out, or the train is signaled that passengers wish to get in." Thus the Commission "find the prayer of the petitioners to be reasonable in its character and do accordingly recommend the Cape Cod Railroad Corporation to hereafter cause one daily morning and a daily evening train each way to stop at Rock station when any passenger wishes to leave such trains at that place, or whenever signal is made that any passenger wishes to take such trains at that place."

So Rock was a twice daily flag stop once each way. The line took the suggestion of the Commission; it seemed to be a good move. After all some of the original owners of land who had sold it for a right-of-way were among the petitioners. All along those people had said they had been promised fair service years before when the railroad first came to town and asked to buy some of their land.

With the extension to Wellfleet bringing total length of the main line to 72 miles, the railroad was serving a greater area through its 29 stations. By 1871 the number of employees had risen from 140 to 200 in three years. The employment picture had remained quite stable through the Civil War and just afterward, but the addition of stations from Orleans to Wellfleet and steady increases in passenger and freight business and construction of rolling stock in the Hyannis car shops required more personnel.

For the additional traffic the Cape Cod Railroad ordered two locomotives. The one from New England was a Boston Locomotive Works product of Hinkley & Williams, the successors to Hinkley & Drury since 1866. The other engine was built by the Rogers Locomotive Works in Paterson, New Jersey. The Boston locomotive was named *Right Arm*; the Rogers machine was the *Bounty*. Each engine cost the same - $8,000. They were in service from May of 1871.

The railroad that year listed the various categories of freight it carried and the tonnage. Leading all categories was iron and other ores at 12,807 tons; associated with that were castings and other iron at 7,961 tons; less than carload merchandise was next with 10,989 tons; grain with 4,010 tons lead agricultural shipments, followed by 1,481 tons of other agricultural products and 554 tons of flour. Coal arrived entirely by sea, landing at Cohasset Narrows for glass manufacturing at Sandwich and some of it at Wareham docks and the Railroad Wharf in South Hyannis. Bituminous totaled 3,721 tons and anthracite 809. The Cape was importing more of everything, including building materials with lumber at 1,653 tons leading stone and brick at 245 tons and lime, cement and sand at 169 tons. That year the road built four cattle cars to carry the 654 tons of live stock that was moved. The final category was "other articles" that didn't fit any of the above and all of that "other" weighed 5,989 tons. The iron ore and castings were major items and reflected the iron business around Wareham with its foundries and mills. However, there were several iron businesses on the Cape at Sandwich and Monument.

A total of 59,298 tons of freight was handled by the line in the ten months ending September 30, 1871, the new reporting date set by the legislature to coincide with a new and popular fiscal year. For this growing part of its business the railroad had 41 eight-wheel box cars; 13 four-wheel box cars; 25 eight-wheel flat cars and seven four-wheel flat cars, plus the cattle cars.

The average rate charged for freight was $.0339 per ton per mile on company tracks and $.0391 per ton per mile on freight interchanged with other roads. The line earned $25,116.36 carrying freight from town to town on its own tracks and $40,407.13 from freight to and from other lines with which it connected. In addition the Cape Cod Railroad earned $4,990.53 from freight over other roads as tolls or for the use of its cars by other roads. Total freight income was $85,804.79.

Passenger traffic was divided to earn $42,313.04 on tickets between company stations and $133,238.93 on interchange with other roads. Receipts from passengers over other roads as tolls and for use of Cape Cod Railroad passenger cars by other roads earned $20,149.10. Total passenger revenue was $195,701.07. Mail contracts reached $13,712.45 and express $9,040.88. For 1871 total income was a new high: $308,928.93. After all expenses and bond interest was paid, the net income was $63,857.50, and all of that went to stockholders as an 8 and 1/3 percent dividend.

The stockholders had two more reasons to be happy investors with plans to build a line from Cohasset Narrows to Woods Hole announced on September 9, 1871. It was on that day the Plymouth & Vineyard Sound Railroad was transferred to the Cape Cod Railroad. Three days later ground was broken for the 18-mile long Woods Hole Branch. The other good news was the announcement of plans to push tracks from Wellfleet to Provincetown. The fort would be saved yet from future enemies and Major Phinney could at last relax. For stockholders, a great deal to look forward to - more expansion of the line, increased earnings and dividends every year!

Of the $900-thousand dollars of stock issued, almost $818-thousand had been sold to 1,230 stockholders. All but 45 of whom were Massachusetts residents. The directors were some of the principal stockholders and year after year the board was composed of the same names with the same addresses: Richard Borden, president, of Fall River; Ephraim N. Winslow, treasurer and superintendent, of Hyannis, where the company had its offices; George Marston, clerk, New Bedford; Jefferson Borden, of Fall River; Prince S. Crowell, of East Dennis; Nathaniel S. Simpkins, of Yarmouth Port; Matthew Starbuck, of Nantucket; and Minor S. Lincoln, of Wareham.

Since the arrival of the tracks on Cape Cod a number of residents discovered commuting, which allowed them to live in one community and work in another. Before the railroad this was only possible if one had a fast horse to cover a short distance. Stage coaches were not for commuting - railroads were. So the company started selling three month season tickets, which entitled the buyer to two trips a day, one each way, five days a week. By 1870 the cost per mile with a season ticket was only four mills, four-tenths of a cent, a real transportation bargain. In 1871 Cape Codders bought 27,436 of them. The following year the number reached 38,555. The commuters were beginning to crowd the cars which for so long had seen only occasional travelers. Not only was the railroad carrying more people to and from work, but it opened up Cape Cod as a summer resort, attracting more tourists to New England's great asset - the sea. Passenger trains to the Cape from June through early September carried six and seven cars, instead of the usual four. The popularity of the area grew as a summer playground as it became easier to get there by train, and the Cape and Islands have never been the same.

Falmouth had had an interest for years in getting a railroad line extended there, and finally a group of businessmen from the town formed The Vineyard Sound Railroad Company and later petitioned the legislature to grant a charter for its construction. On April 11, 1861 the Vineyard Sound Railroad was incorporated by an act of the legislature to build from Cohasset Narrows to Woods Hole. The timing could not have been worse. The next day Confederates in South Carolina fired on the Federal fort at Charleston called Sumter. President Lincoln called for troops three days later, and on the nineteenth he proclaimed a blockade of the South. It was not a time to raise money to build an extension of the Cape Cod Railroad up Cape.

After the war ended in 1865 the possibility of a Woods Hole branch was revived. The success of the Cape Cod Central to Orleans provided an example and an inspiration to the group from Falmouth, and the following year subscriptions to stock were offered. Engineering surveys were ordered for two routes and in the spring of 1867 they were complete. The first was a more direct route that turned to the west sharply around Little Sippewissett Lake and then down the shore of Buzzards Bay and across the entrance to Quissett Harbor and into Woods Hole from the west. The other route followed the same line southward from Cohasset Narrows and along the west fringe of the Buzzards Bay glacial moraine, but at Little Sippewissett Lake it turned southeasterly to cross the belt of hills diagonally into Falmouth Village at its eastern base and then through the southern end of the moraine along the edge of Vineyard Sound and then directly west inside Nobska Point along the edge of Little Harbor, Woods Hole, and to a terminus on the waterfront at Great Harbor. This second, or Falmouth Village route, was longer by a mile and a third and more expensive by $30,000. With so much support from Falmouth business people, there was never any doubt as to the final plan. The railroad would go through Falmouth Village. Period! With the Cape Cod's extension to Wellfleet almost complete the annual town meeting in Falmouth on November 11, 1870 had an item on its agenda that called for the town to purchase $60-thousand worth of stock in what had become known as the Plymouth & Vineyard Sound Railroad, incorporating the Vineyard Sound Railroad. The citizens of Falmouth overwhelmingly approved the purchase, 259 to 14. The stock issue totaled $260-thousand, but the sale of the rest of the shares was left up to the Cape Cod Railroad, the owner of its subsidiary, The Plymouth & Vineyard Sound.

The year 1872 was to be the time of greatest change for the Cape Cod Railroad. There were two extensions of the line: to Woods Hole and Provincetown. The former was already under way and the latter would soon begin. These moves were to prove important for the railroad and the Cape and Islands, but the greatest change of all followed rumors that had been circulating for some time: the line would be part of a merger with another railroad.

Officials of the two companies had been meeting in Boston secretly and they reached agreement on terms, but the legislature and the stockholders had to agree. The legislature gave its blessing on March 27, 1872, authorizing The Old Colony & Newport and the Cape Cod to unite under one corporation. The legislature put it this way. "If the companies should vote at a meeting to form one corporation, then upon the passage of votes the Cape Cod Railroad Company is authorized, according to terms agreed upon, to assign and convey to the Old Colony & Newport Railroad Company its franchise and property. This (new) company is also permitted to issue new stock in lieu of the stock of the Cape Cod, but the whole is not to exceed the capital of both corporations. If the union is approved the company may change its name to the Old Colony Railroad Company."

The votes were taken and the merger approved. By May it was over and the coming marriage was announced to the world. On September 30, the Cape Cod was deeded in escrow to the Old Colony and the conditions of fulfillment met, because the next day the two lines were consolidated as the Old Colony Railroad. The final, legal merger took place on January 17, 1873 until death do they part. The Cape Cod was quite a bride. She was born in 1846 and construction started the following year. She was about to reach as far as she could, and at the age of 26 she was a prize. The stockholders received 17 shares of Old Colony stock for 23 of the Cape Cod. The formula was based on the market price of each. No one seemed disappointed.

The two bridges on the Woods Hole Branch were finished in July, 1872. The longest was the wooden trestle over the Monument River at Cohasset Narrows - 320 feet with stone abutments at each extreme. The other was at Back River in Monument where a shorter, 40-foot span was erected with stone abutments for support. The line was finished and the first train rolled down the branch to Woods Hole July 18. There was no ceremony, no speeches and no cannons fired. The railroad had a contractor build a dock with tracks right up close to the edge where the steamers tied up. The first day the *Island Home* met the train, having transferred from the Nantucket to Hyannis run. After that, Woods Hole was the shortest way to reach Martha's Vineyard and Nantucket.

The branch was 17.54 miles long from the station at Cohasset Narrows. At first there were only four stations: North Falmouth, West Falmouth, Falmouth and Woods Hole. The trip took 49 minutes, making an average speed of 21.7 miles an hour, including stops.

In the final annual report issued by the Cape Cod before it became the Cape Cod Division of the Old Colony, the railroad had a new total length of 94.06 miles with a length of sidings of 7.80 miles, making an aggregate length of 101.86 miles. The telegraph ran on poles along the entire 94 miles of line. The telegraph was owned by a separate company, but operated jointly with the railroad. There was a telegraph office in 14 stations. The two bridges just built on the Woods Hole Branch brought the total number of bridges to 22. There were 120 grade crossings, but only one with gates and a flagman on duty: Main Street, Hyannis, just east of the station. With the completion of the Woods Hole Branch, the company had hired 25 more workers, bringing total number of employees to 225. The Cape Cod had issued $260-thousand in stock to build to Woods Hole from Cohasset Narrows. It wasn't enough and bonds were sold and loans were made. The branch cost $340,163.96, or $19,393.61 per mile.

Passenger income, including two and a half months of service on the Woods Hole Branch, was $220,745.74. All freight receipts totaled $79,244.61; express income was $9,146.64 and from U.S. Mails, $12,056.50. Total income was $321,798.38. After all expenses and bond interest were paid the Cape Cod Railroad earned a net income of $65,873. The officers declared a dividend of 8.07 percent. The Old Colony Railroad paid $33,180.50 of that dividend. For new equipment the Cape Cod, in its last year, bought eight passenger cars, three baggage, express and R.P.O. cars, two cabooses and six flat cars.

As it was about to become part of the Old Colony, the Cape Cod had used only 500 cords of wood in its locomotives, while burning nearly 3,000 tons of coal in that last year. Finally there was a great banquet in Hyannis in the Masonic Hall in celebration of the railroad merger. The new president of the Old Colony, who was also the Governor of New Hampshire, Onslow Stearns, was there. The toastmaster was Major Phinney and part of the evening's business was presenting a gold-lined silver service to Ephraim N. Winslow, who was retiring after 20 years as superintendent. His replacement, Charles H. Nye, who was born in Falmouth in the 1820s, had worked for years as a conductor on the Cape Cod Railroad. Nye was the new Cape Cod Division Superintendent and his office would be the same one that Winslow had used on the second floor of the Hyannis station.

EARLY LOCOMOTIVES

The Cape Cod Branch Railroad was already under construction from Middleboro to Wareham when the company took delivery of its first two locomotives in the fall of 1847. The Boston firm of Hinkley & Drury manufactured the pair, the *Wareham* and the *Sandwich*, delivering the former on October 8 and the latter December 4. The names were a smart move as both towns the railroad was soon to serve were honored by having a locomotive named for it. Each engine was a standard 4-4-0 or American type eight wheeler with five foot diameter driving wheels. For the Cape Cod Branch Railroad these engines were ideal, for they were general service machines that could be used for passenger or freight trains and for yard switching of cars. Naming locomotives rather than numbering them was common here and in Great Britain in those early days and the Cape Cod Branch Railroad followed that practice.

The fifteen mile track to Wareham was opened for public use on January 26, 1848 and its passenger and freight trains were hauled by those two engines now running between there and Middleborough for its connection with the Fall River Railroad to Fall River and its famous steamboats to New York and north on the Fall River Railroad to South Braintree where it joined the Old Colony tracks to Boston.

Most of the early business and income was passenger service, but the company had another goal and that was to reach Sandwich, thirteen miles to the east where, in addition to more passengers, was the potential of moving freight to and from the Boston & Sandwich Glass Company, a thriving industry. Additional passenger and freight cars were on order for what the company saw as a busy future, beginning in late spring.

The third locomotive, the *Cape Cod*, steamed into Middleborough on April 27 from Hinkley & Drury in Boston, and after a trial run it began service for the company that was completing its right of way to Sandwich, having bridged the water at Cohasset Narrows and the Manomet River, a much smaller stream, in the valley of the isthmus of Cape Cod where a canal was spoken of long and frequently, but was yet to be built.

On May 13, a train with the railroad's directors aboard arrived at end of track at Scusset for an early inspection. They were pleased, noting that from there to Sandwich was a mere two miles and that the pace of construction was strong, although behind their announced schedule.

The track to Sandwich was completed several days earlier than the grand opening of Friday, May 26, 1848 when trains arrived with extra locomotives on each as a thousand people from out of town walked from the cars into the main room at the new depot, an expanse 80 feet by 120 feet and sat at row after row of tables to be served food, drink and speeches. Sandwich had its railroad and it loved it!

At this terminus of the Cape Cod Branch Railroad the most prominent structure had to be a stone roundhouse with a cupola on top and a turntable within for reversing engines and their tenders for the trip west. The roundhouse rose 120 feet on a 100 foot diameter base; it was unique and impressive.

Close by was the station with several tracks and beginning Monday, May 29, 1848, trains left Sandwich for Boston at 5:45 a.m. and 3 p.m., while two trains left Boston for Sandwich at 7:45 a.m. and 4:15 p.m. The fare was $1.50 one way and for that sum for the first time Boston was a three hour, 62-mile train ride away.

Later the company's annual report to the legislature blamed the six month delay in completing the line to Sandwich on "the disappointment in receipt of iron," a reference to the rails that were being rolled at a Wareham iron mill. A shortage of local labor due to a building boom in Sandwich may also have held up construction, but the railroad company just blamed slow delivery of rails.

With completion of the thirteen miles of track from Wareham to Sandwich, the Cape Cod Branch Railroad was now a 28-mile long, single track main line from Middleboro with a mile and a half spur to the docks at Wareham under construction.

That November a fourth locomotive from Hinkley & Drury, the *Barnstable*, joined the others, and that was enough motive power to haul passenger trains to and from Middleborough and a daily freight each way except Sunday when nothing moved on the rails.

So two years before the middle of the nineteenth century Cape Cod had its railroad with all the excitement of the wonder of that age: the iron horse, the one part of railroading that was its greatest attraction. The steam locomotive had size and motion, along with fire, smoke and steam and their sounds - whistles, bells and exhaust. And for boys of all ages two glamorous new figures - an engineer and a fireman.

As people thrilled to the sight of the steam locomotive in Sandwich when it arrived and elsewhere on the Cape and across America years later, it would change, the locomotive would, in an evolutionary way, but remain throughout the years that it was the prime mover of people and goods, the most fascinating machine ever devised. Through a huge catalogue of inventions over centuries nothing comes close to the popularity and affection with which the steam locomotive is held. Nothing. Its numerous survivors today, whether in museums or on tourist railroads, prove its durability in our memories.

For six years the end of track was at the Sandwich station and the nearby Boston & Sandwich Glass Company. In the railway age growth was inevitable and pressure, mainly from Nantucket interests, caused the Cape Cod Branch Railroad to extend their rails to Hyannis via West Barnstable, Barnstable Village and Yarmouth. By making the new terninus Hyannis, Nantucket businessmen had a much shorter steamboat trip there rather than the much longer one to New Bedford where they caught the train for Boston.

Work began in 1853 down the north side, reaching Barnstable Village where the first passenger train arrived on May 11, 1854 and to Hyannis two months later on July 8. During construction the directors of the line had their application to change the name to Cape Cod Railroad approved, dropping the name Branch.

Two new locomotives were on order in 1854 for the additional traffic and distances to run trains. Four stations were added in the 17 miles from Sandwich to Hyannis and work was nearing completion on a new railroad, the Fair Haven Branch, from Tremont on the Cape Cod Railroad through Marion and Mattapoisett to the edge of the Acushnet River where a ferry would complete the journey to New Bedford and vice versa. This new line which opened in October would feed additional traffic to the Cape Cod Railroad, so new engines were necessary as business had increased annually and the company had added passenger and freight cars to accommodate it.

Since management was satisfied with the four engines it had from Hinkley & Drury it turned to them once again. And in late April another inside-connected locomotive, the

This locomotive, the *Nantucket*, was a typical inside-connected machine built by Hinkley & Drury's Boston Locomotive Works. She was the fifth engine the Cape Cod Railroad bought from Hinkley. The column rising from the boiler in front of the cab is an early pressure gauge of modest reliability. The spark arrestor on the stack looks like an inverted milk pail.

The *Cape Cod* was the third locomotive on the Cape Cod Branch Railroad. She was built and delivered in the spring of 1848 before the tracks reached Sandwich. She cost $7,800. When new she was an inside-connected engine. Years later she was converted to outside valve gear and appears that way in this photo at West Barnstable.

This big wood-burner, the *Burgess*, was one of many locomotives assembled as a mass-produced experiment by the Massachusetts firm, Lawrence Locomotive Works. The Cape Cod Railroad bought it in 1854 to help with the extra trains on the Hyannis extension.

The *Highland Light* was one of the finest locomotives built by William Mason of Taunton, Massachusetts. This engine was delivered in 1867 and worked all over the Cape Cod Railroad and later on the Old Colony and the New Haven.

Nantucket, was delivered at Middleboro.

The regional design favored by Hinkley & Drury and others in New England, the inside-connected locomotive, had no outside driving rods from cylinders over the leading or front wheels. The cylinders were inside the wheels and the only connecting rods were between the driving wheels on the axles.

Then for the first time management turned to another supplier for a locomotive. It was the Lawrence Locomotive Works in the city of that name about 25 miles north of Boston. The engine, the *Burgess,* was a handsome, outside-connected American type, 4-4-0, decorated with strips of brass and lots of red paint.

How the Cape Cod Railroad came to buy it is a story that tells much about locomotive manufacturing in New England. The Lawrence company was a small machine shop working with iron products that, like so many other similar operations, turned to steam locomotives in the late 1840s because of heavy demand from new and expanding railroads. Lawrence, turning out good machines, had an aggressive sales force that created large numbers of orders and subsequent profits. The combination of good engines and good salesmanship worked and profits increased to a point where management decided to build standard engines for a stock of them from which deliveries could be made at once, something that was new and different in the industry. This was only a good idea as long as demand remained high. Parts were ordered and machined for 42 locomotives, a large inventory for 1854. Then the market collapsed with about half of them completed and Lawrence had great difficulty in selling them. They approached the expanding Cape Cod Railroad, which needed another engine and offered a good buy which the Cape Cod accepted. It would be 17 years before the Cape Cod Railroad bought another Hinkley locomotive. The *Burgess* was an outside-cylindered engine and this type, unlike the Hinkley machines, was what railroads everywhere were turning to.

The bank panic of 1857 hurt business so badly that at least half of the 20 locomotive manufacturers went out of business. Lawrence had made some bad decisions within a few years by accepting land from western lines in payment for engines. In 1862, the second year of the Civil War with the U.S. Government buying large numbers of locomotives, this was a great opportunity for business, but it was too late, for Lawrence had its assets sold off including that western land to satisfy creditors.

Lawrence was one of many New England shops that switched at least part of their manufacturing to railway locomotives. Some of the other better known plants were Locks and Canals Machine Shop of Lowell, the Portland Company in Maine, Taunton Locomotive Works, John Souther who had left Hinkley, Manchester Locomotive Works in New Hampshire, Matfield Manufacturing in that Massachusetts town, and Mason Machine Works of Taunton.

Although most companies involved in locomotive building were first manufacturers of several other lines, at least ten such concerns existed in this country about 1840. Within ten years the number had doubled and the panic of 1857 cut that number in half. By the early 1860s the more successful firms were capturing greater shares of the market because of their growth, professionalism and specialization. Although all railroads created mechanical departments to maintain their engines, most of them never built them. A few New England lines did.

The six locomotives of the Cape Cod Railroad were typical of their day - light, flexible, simple and inexpensive. The Hinkley shop of Boston that had built five of them favored the inside-connected locomotive, which became a regional design. New England builders almost exclusively assembled inside-connected engines through 1855.

Most of these regional builders utilized a local system of construction called "job hands." The foremen of various departments were hired for a set fee to machine the parts and assemble or sometimes just assemble a part of the locomotive. This could be the underframe, the cylinders and rods, the tender, or the trucks, boiler or steam fittings. The foreman would get a crew together and agree to pay so much to each man. Each sub-assembly was priced according to the amount of work and time involved. The foremen had to be familiar with these and he would pay each man according to his skills and usually by the day. Workdays were from 7 a.m. to noon and from one to 6 p.m. - ten hours, six days a week. It was sub-contracting and it made uniform the labor cost of most locomotives, because of fixed prices. The "job hands" system may not have been the whole reason for generally poor workmanship, but the reputation of the New England builders as a group was not high. There were some exceptions, but not enough to remove the stigma.

The Cape Cod Railroad had no other type of engine besides the 4-4-0, the basic steam locomotive of the nineteenth century. The builder of these first five engines, Holmes Hinkley, was born in Hallowell, Maine in 1793. He worked as a carpenter, and later in the Boston area at the age of 30 he began to learn the machinist trade. In 1831 in partnership with Gardner P. Drury and Daniel F. Child the three opened a machine shop. Nine years later, in order to help satisfy a growing demand for locomotives, they produced their first, a small 4-2-0 designed by John Souther, a pattern maker who later started his own firm in South Boston where he produced steam excavators, machinery for sugar mills and railroad locomotives.

The little 4-2-0 that Hinkley made as his first was a general service engine that proved to be too light. The next, the American type or 4-4-0, was to be quickly adopted everywhere as the most popular wheel arrangement. The 4-4-0 came from the imagination of Henry R. Campbell of Philadelphia, an associate of Matthias Baldwin, who would become the most famous locomotive builder of them all. Campbell received his patent in 1836 and completed his first 4-4-0 the following year.

Hinkley stayed with the 4-4-0 for many years as did other machine shops and small foundries that made a variety of iron products and hoisting and other stationary engines and boilers while still others, in addition to those, manufactured textile machinery, farm equipment and pumps. Locomotives were just one of their product lines.

The Middle-Atlantic states and New England dominated locomotive building. Philadelphia had the Baldwin Locomotive Works and the Norris Locomotive Works, the latter by mid-century was America's largest. Paterson, New Jersey was the other major center and its biggest concern was the Rogers Locomotive Works.

New England had a number of small firms but its grandest was Hinkley & Drury of Boston, which dominated the region for many years. In 1845 they had 45 of their engines in service; in 1850 it was 291; in 1855, 581. By the end of the Civil War there were 750. Hinkley died a year after the war, but his company lasted until 1885 by which time its production exceeded 1,600.

It was three years after the Hyannis extension of 1854 when the Cape Cod Railroad bought another locomotive and this time management turned to a small firm, the Matfield Manufacturing Company located on the line about a mile north of Bridgewater in Matfield. It was May 1857 when the *Daniel Webster* was delivered at Middleboro. She, like the others, was an American type with 66-inch diameter drivers, matching those in size on the *Nantucket.*

31

The metal industry through this period underwent some changes. The greatest amount of material in locomotives was wrought iron, which could stand the stresses of motion, because it is strong and malleable. By 1856 steel was being made with the Bessemer process, but it was more expensive than wrought iron and contained too much carbon, making it too hard and often brittle, a dangerous material for boilers. Within 15 years, alloys produced a safe steel for higher pressures in boilers. Wood was used sparingly and usually in cabs, tender frames and pilot beams. Cast iron was used in smokebox fronts, cylinders, journal boxes, cab decks and bell stands. Boiler tubes and firebox walls were of copper, and in the 1850's a 20-ton locomotive had up to two tons of it. Steel replaced copper in firebox sheets and iron in driving wheel tires by 1870.

The Cape Cod Railroad's mechanical department, which was in the engine house at Hyannis recorded low maintenance costs for its 4-4-0 locomotives because that type, as the national engine, was a simple machine, having few parts, low in cost, easy to repair and quite powerful. It could operate on uneven tracks and the Cape Cod Railroad had many of those, like other American roads of its day.

The Railway Age began in Great Britain as a phase of the Industrial Revolution. British railroads were models of engineering skill and construction. They had gentle turns and bends, frequent tunnels and bridges and were running for the most part on flat roadbeds with crossties and rock ballast. Their early cost was over $175-thousand a mile, partly due to high land prices.

American railroads in those early days were built quickly along the natural contours of the countryside. Most American railroads cost between $20-thousand and $30-thousand per mile, including the land, the grading, bridges, tracks, engines and cars. The Cape Cod Railroad between Middleboro and Hyannis cost just under $21-thousand dollars per mile, using the above formula.

After the standard 4-4-0 locomotive, the ten-wheeler, or 4-6-0, was the next most popular wheel arrangement of those years. It was built in Philadelphia for the Reading Railroad, a coal-hauling line. Another type with New England origins and great longevity in the region was the Mogul, or 2-6-0. The year after the Civil War, 1866, the Taunton Locomotive Works built an engine of that wheel arrangement for the Central Railroad of New Jersey, which assigned the name Mogul to it. Locomotive historian John H. White, Jr. believes that may be the origin of the name for that class of engine. The New Haven had a bunch of k-1 class Moguls, running around branch lines, including Cape Cod, until the end of steam in the 1950s. The Mogul was ideal for high speed freight service, but when it was first introduced the Cape Cod Railroad showed no interest, staying with the American type.

A larger freight locomotive, the 2-8-0 or Consolidation type, was used for heavy trains after 1875. The bigger railroads, with expanding freight business, turned to Consolidations by 1880 and that moved, at least there, the 4-4-0s to passenger traffic only.

Slow speeds were favored by the railroads, since operating costs escalated with faster trains. One western railroad, the Rock Island, reported it had reduced running costs per mile from 30 cents to 21 cents by cutting speeds. This was done between 1857 and '59. A train could be run for half the cost by reducing speed from 30 to 20 miles per hour. Trains operated at high speeds made for more wear and tear on bridges, rolling stock and the track. Speed increased fuel costs, too, and in order to run continuously that way it would require extensive rebuilding with heavier rail and bridges and improved roadbeds. The Cape Cod Railroad from the 1850s through the 1860s reported running its passenger trains at 21 or 22 miles per hour, including stops, while its freight trains, including stops, were given as 14 miles per hour, occasionally 13. The passenger trains stopped at every one of the way stations, 13 of them, and there were two flag stops. Every one of the stations had a siding for freight cars and a freight house. The Cape Cod Railroad was a bit above the U.S. Bureau of Statistics, which reported in the 1870s that maximum profit from freight trains is achieved at ten miles per hour. Before that time most railroads ran light, short trains at low speeds with high mileage for engines and rolling stock.

In the 1850s and on there were three factors involved in the expense of railroading - fuel, wages and locomotive repairs, in that order.

Fuel prices, the largest single expense, varied by season and available supply, but in those early years it was wood mostly. In 1857 the average cost of wood for engine fuel on Massachusetts railroads was 20-cents a mile. From the early 1850s through 1858 wood for fuel on the Cape Cod Railroad averaged 16-cents a mile. All of the Cape Cod engines burned wood until management converted one of them to coal in the winter of 1859 "and is successfully running. It is contemplated to make the same change in others when they are taken into the shop for repairs, and we confidently anticipate a very material reduction in the expense of fuel," stated a company report of June 22, 1859 to the stockholders. Some 90 percent of American railroads were burning wood as fuel in 1860. However, coal was the future and within a decade wood and coal split the market evenly. By 1870 the Cape Cod Railroad was spending almost four times for coal what they did for wood, but they were still burning some wood.

From 1848, Cape Cod management had purchased wood locally from farmers or others with wood lots who brought it by horse and wagon to platforms spaced adjacent to the major stations at Sandwich, West Barnstable, Yarmouth and both ends of the line where engines spent the night: Hyannis and Middleboro. These platforms were a little higher than an open wagon so that tossing wood from there to a locomotive tender wasn't such a long throw. The railroad contracted with individual suppliers who cut the wood - hard wood and pitch pine usually - to firebox length, about two feet.

Prices varied through the 1860s from $4.75 per cord to $8.00, with the highest paid during Civil War inflation. Those Cape Cod locomotives carried about one cord of wood in the tender and about one-thousand gallons of water. In hauling a typical passenger train of four cars or a freight of eight or ten cars, those engines burned a cord of wood every 25 miles and used about 925 gallons of water. Able-bodied passengers would often climb down from the cars and help "wood up," throwing pieces to the engine crew on the tender. Water tanks were situated along the track, often next to wood platforms, so as to eliminate additional stops.

Before 1880 the usual railroad average was 140 cords of wood per mile every year. New England had huge amounts of wood for fuel and some of the far northern lines were still burning it in the 1890s. The Cape Cod Railroad turned to coal almost entirely by the 1870s because Cape forests and woodlands were decimated for building materials, fuel and fences. It seems that most property on the Cape used long, wide boards for fences to keep animals out, especially in town.

Coal came in as the best fuel because it had greater heating properties. But it had to be the right kind of coal. The first American coal was anthracite, hard coal, a nice thing to burn on a grate in a fireplace or slowly in a pot-bellied heating stove or in a kitchen stove. In the small fireboxes of the 1850s it did not have the quick combustion qualities needed in a steam locomotive. When bituminous coal was discovered and made available in Western Maryland, the move to coal was on. But the distances from the coalfields kept prices high for New England customers who received most of it by water, schooners first, then long tows of schooner-barges by coastal tugs, finally steam colliers. The abundance of coal finally brought prices down in an industry that had no production agreements because there were so many coal operators, so many mines.

Larger fire boxes and careful attention to firing by engine crews solved the problems of coal as fuel. Most of the coal burned by the Cape Cod Railroad came into Hyannis by schooners from Philadelphia and Baltimore and was unloaded at the Railroad Wharf that was completed in 1854 in South Hyannis. Coal cars were spotted on the sidings on the wharf next to the ships. A coal dock was built in the yards just west of the Hyannis station. Coal was also landed at Wareham docks for that end of the line and Middleboro.

In 1865 the railroad opened the line from Yarmouth to Orleans and passenger and freight service began December 6, 1865. This 19-mile long extension ran through South Yarmouth, across the Bass River to South Dennis, then to Harwich and up through Pleasant Lake to Brewster, East Brewster and Orleans. This new line was called Cape Cod Central, a wholly owned appendage of the Cape Cod Railroad, which created it, but made a separate corporation as a legal device to circumvent the restrictions of its own charter that limited the Cape Cod Railroad to building just to Hyannis.

Construction had started during the war, and after several delays, was finally completed. The Cape Cod Central had no rolling stock and no locomotives, although two years later in 1867 on November 14, the *Highland Light,* Cape Cod Railroad's most famous steam locomotive, was delivered from the Mason Machine Works in Taunton. The best-known photo of this American type, 4-4-0, shows its builder William Mason sitting in the tender wearing a stovepipe hat and looking uncannily like Abraham Lincoln. Railroad historian, Lucius Beebe, called the *Highland Light* America's most beautiful locomotive. It certainly was one of them, which is not surprising since Mason had a fine sense of grace and proportion. He turned out beautiful locomotives that were fine examples of precision machinery. The bad reputation that many New England engine builders had developed with shoddy workmanship and engineering earlier hurt Mason, but no railroad ever denigrated his excellent locomotives. They were first class examples of their kind. The *Highland Light* was no exception.

The difficulty of marketing quality locomotives in the late 1800s was pointed out by even as skilled a manufacturer as William Mason of Taunton. "My principal business has been making cotton machinery. My locomotive business is now the meanest part of it and always was. I took an interest in it and told my friends that I got up locomotives for fun, but that it was the most expensive fun I ever had. I make just enough money from my cotton machinery to make up the losses on locomotives," he said.

When he said that, Mason was one of the few New England locomotive builders still around, since many others had closed and most of the business was going to the Middle Atlantic states where Baldwin in Philadelphia had long since grown into the biggest producer of them all.

In the first few years of the Railway Age it became apparent that safety devices would be needed. One of the first to be considered was some form of a locomotive headlight. At first trains were restricted to daylight running, because there was no way to illuminate the rails as a way for train crews to see properly and further to warn people away from the track to avoid injury to themselves from an approaching train.

The South Carolina Railroad in 1832 placed two flat cars in front of the engine. The head car had sand over the flooring on which were piled pine knots set afire. It made a bright glow and it was reflected forward by a piece of sheet iron mounted on the second car. This was the headlight, possibly the first, and it introduced the two factors necessary: a light and a reflector.

Headlights were adopted on railroads after 1850 for night running, but the Cape Cod Railroad had headlights from its beginning in 1848. The first scheduled trains, leaving Sandwich in wintertime ran before sunup and the afternoon train from Boston arrived after dark.

Those early headlights advanced past open fires on flat cars to a large sheet metal box with a glass front and a cast metal reflector. A lamp inside the box case burned whale oil at first, then petroleum. If the lamp chimney broke - and they often did - the early cast reflector melted easily. The search for a better reflector came up with spun copper, silver plated. They were stronger and did not dissolve in back of broken lamp chimneys. The reflectors, of course, were parabolic.

Oil lamps gave a yellowish glow, provided some illumination of the rails directly ahead of the locomotive and served to warn approaching trains from the opposite direction over single-track railroads, that is most railroads, and certainly the Cape Cod Railroad, whose main line was all single-track. The reflectors in those early box case headlights had diameters of 18 to 23 inches and cost about $100. The light was attached on a metal mounting frame slightly above the front of the smoke box. The most popular fuel for the lamps was oil, but many others were tried. Calcium was one; gas was another. Lime lamps burned with too great an intensity and were dropped as an alternative. In Russia in 1874 battery-powered electricity was an early experiment five years before Thomas Edison's incandescent bulb. In France in 1883, a generator powered by steam was tried. Before the turn of the century that idea was given another try, and this time it was in the United States - and successful. A federal law made the railroads put it on every locomotive by 1915. Still, oil-burning headlights had a long run from the 1840s.

Another safety feature was the locomotive bell and an early Massachusetts law forced railroads to adopt it. What the state was looking for was some reliable device to use at grade crossings to give warnings about approaching trains. The state passed the law requiring the bells in 1835, an early indication in rail history of the seriousness of crossing accidents; in fact, the problem is still with us.

The early "A" frame to hold bells on locomotives was a Hinkley & Drury device, but it was never used on engines made for Cape Cod. By 1860 some engines had huge brass bells weighing over 200 pounds that could be heard for a quarter mile. The bells of the nineteenth century were all rung by hand using a cord that ran back into the cab. Bells served well on engines engaged in yard work: moving cars, leaving engine houses, or making up trains. They indicated a moving engine or one about to move. But clearly something louder was needed. It was called a whistle, and it was louder. In fact at first it was piercing, ear shattering and because of its high tone - a shriek! The shrill sound of a whistle could be heard for a mile or more. The unprotected grade crossing was the greatest hazard and they were everywhere. Crossing tenders and gates were almost unheard of. Most rights-of-way were not fenced and people and animals strolled along and across the tracks at will.

Locomotive historian John H. White, Jr. gives credit to the British for the origin of the steam whistle, referring to "a full account of its invention in 1832-33 and first used on a British locomotive in 1835." The Locks and Canals Machine Shop in Lowell, Massachusetts "probably was the first company to apply the whistle in the United States to several locomotives it built in 1836," according to White.

Some years later, manufacturers produced chime whistles with three or more chambers, each with a different tone and the blending of those simultaneous sounds made a more pleasant noise and one that became associated with railroads. The chime whistle was in the key of G, most pleasant to the ear, and sounded a bit like Woooooo-ooooo!

Cape Cod ear drums in the years the Cape Cod Railroad ran, 1848 to 1873, never heard chime whistles, as those earlier locomotives all had one-tone shriekers.

Another problem that management had to deal with was the frequency that cattle strolled along the tracks, wandering from fields where they were grazing, oblivious of trains, time, the change of seasons, literary trends or state politics.

They were big, slow, dumb and apparently deaf. A cow or bull, weighing over half a ton could derail a locomotive weighing up to 20 tons. Actually it was quite common and expensive. One of the answers was a device on the front of the locomotive to clear such obstructions from the track. In the 1830s a leading set of pilot wheels was added to the front of locomotives to guide the machine over rough track. To this was applied a cowcatcher that looked like a plow. Its purpose was to throw the animal or anything else such as a stalled wagon at a grade crossing off to the side and not allow it to get under the locomotive wheels.

At first cowcatchers were made of wood, and a solid one could toss a one-ton animal up to 30 feet. The poorly made ones would buckle, allowing the animal to pass under the locomotive, derailing it.

The attractive wooden cowcatchers, or pilots as they were called by railroad men, were replaced by iron and later steel. From the photographs of the early Cape Cod engines, those cowcatchers appear to have been made of iron.

The boilers on the first American-made engines were thin, wrought iron capable of holding pressures up to 50 pounds per square inch, but within a few years - the late 1830s - their capacity had increased to 90 pounds. By 1850 most engines had working pressures of 100 pounds, which reached 110 by 1860 with some as high as 140, which was standard by the end of the Civil War. By the late 1880s 150 pounds was standard with some as high as 175. American railroads always ran boilers with higher pressures than those considered safe in Europe. Of course we had more boiler explosions too.

In order to warn engine crews of dangerous pressure, a safety valve with a spring mechanism was the most common type of gauge before 1850. After that a mercury gauge that was attached to the top of the boiler indicated pressure. These were high, thin columns and were an additional measure to the safety valve, which sometimes would stick.

An invention in 1849 became standard equipment in less than ten years. A French inventor, Eugene Bourdon, discovered that a bent metal tube would react to steam pressure and indicate that pressure on the face of a dial. It was above all accurate and compact and could be attached to the back-head of the boiler within the engine cab. It performed well and was quite inexpensive - no small consideration - at $30 each. It helped relieve anxiety among engine crews and by 1857 every engine had one - the universal device.

Steel alloys in the 1880s made better and safer boiler material than wrought iron, which had an upper pressure limit of 150 pounds. Steel fireboxes were in use before that time. The Taunton Locomotive Works built a steel firebox for the Erie Railroad in 1860. They soon became common, since with soft water they could last 15 years or about 300-thousand miles. Iron fireboxes lasted about three years. The railroad industry turned to using steel just about everywhere iron had been in that post Civil War era of the greatest rail development.

One of the worst problems the railroads had was never solved completely, only partially. It had to do with the nature of firing locomotives and their exhaust. In the early wood-burning days live embers and sparks flew out of the smokestacks of locomotives, setting fires in dry grass and weeds, burning barns, houses and the railroads' own rolling stock. This fire damage was expensive and Cape Cod had its share of railroad fires, including some in the 1950s at the end of the age of steam locomotives. The high flying sparks looked like fireworks at night and were described by Charles Dickens "which showered about us like a storm of fiery snow." He saw that one night from the window of a passenger car on the Boston & Lowell.

The amount of money paid out for damages was huge and this nuisance was a difficult one for the roads. All sorts of inventions were patented - over one thousand were issued - for spark arrestors. What was needed was a screen or similar device to trap the embers without obstructing the draft that pulled the fire through the boiler tubes and made steam. The more effective the screen to trap embers and sparks the worse the draft. The diamond-shaped stack you see on the *Cape Cod* and the *Highland Light* were typical of a design that had wire netting inside as a spark arrestor as well as a cone that deflected the sparks. The New Haven Railroad tried making longer smokeboxes on the front of the boiler. Eventually steel screens and deflectors inside smokestacks were replaced by smokebox designs, but again, nothing worked completely.

Attached to each locomotive and directly behind it was a tender that often weighed as much as the locomotive, that is about 20 tons in the 1850s for the typical eight-wheel tender. Some Hinkley & Drury tenders in the late 1840s had six wheels, a single axle toward the front and a pair of two wheels on a truck toward the rear. This didn't help their rolling ability because tenders were the worst tracking rolling stock the railroads had. They were hard riding and they damaged the rails.

On the average tenders had the capacity to carry one cord of wood and one-thousand gallons of water - enough for 25 miles of steaming. That didn't pose much of a problem as trains stopped often anyway. Their water tanks were made from sheets of heavy gauge iron, which had to be replaced at least every ten years, sometimes earlier, as they were subject to heavy rusting. Rubber hoses carried the water to the locomotive. The trucks were wood beam type and sometimes had heavy leaf springs mounted outside above the wheels. The tender frames were heavy wood beams.

From the beginning, locomotives had to use quantities of grease and oil as lubrication for moving parts. Some of both fell to the rails and caused slippage when driving wheels ran across it, especially when starting up. You've heard the sudden burst of exhaust when that happens. The solution was one of the simplest in the annals of a business that had few easy ones. By applying a small amount of dry sand on the tracks before the driving wheels the problem was solved and the trains went on their way. A sand box was mounted on top of the boiler behind the smoke stack with tubes running down both sides of the boiler jacket to the track. The flow of sand was operated from the cab on either wet or oily rails. It worked! Cape Cod sand was known to be ideal for such work and the Old Colony and the New Haven Railroads used to ship it off Cape, usually at night, to other parts of the line for use in company sand boxes on the top of locomotives. The train that left Provincetown on the New Haven had a nickname - The *Sahara*.

The earlier locomotives were strictly for work and had a spartan look to them, perhaps with the exception of some decoration on their big steam domes. Through the 1830s and 40s locomotives were plain, simple machines and unadorned with decorations. But at about the middle of the century that changed.

From 1850 to 1865 or so the times were characterized by great optimism and the spirit of growth and expansion. The railroad locomotive was a fascinating machine, a symbol of the pride which Americans felt about this new industrial age. So engine manufacturers and the railroads themselves decided to glamorize the iron horse. They did it in three ways - with paint, brass and ornamental designs of headlights, bell stands, wood boiler lagging, steam domes, piping and cabs. The brass was bright and so was the paint, a lot of red and some green. Red wheels, green trim and black stacks and smokeboxes on the front of the boiler. This was a widely used color scheme. William Mason's engine, *Phantom*, was painted mostly blue as was John Souther's *Washington*. The *Highland Light* of the Cape Cod Railroad was not only its most celebrated engine but its most colorful. Blue from the cowcatcher - I mean pilot - through all the wheels, the headlight, most of the stack, the boiler, the cylinders, bell frame and the piston rods. The trim was red, yellow and brown with some white striping on the wheels and rods. The cab was red as were the sand dome and the steam dome. Strips of bright, polished brass were vertical on the boiler every three feet or so. The name *Highland Light* was painted in white under the cab windows. There was scrollwork on the tender both sides of the railroad name.

William Mason of Taunton, one of the great locomotive stylists, built the *Highland Light* and his shop featured painting every part of the locomotive and tender and all those surfaces were striped or scrolled with bold lettering, shaded and then outlined with thin stripes.

The paint shops seemed to feel they were in competition with those of other manufacturers. Even though the Civil War was such a tragic period for the nation, it did not have the effect of reducing the richly ornamental or garish color schemes that had become such a part of railroading.

After several starts the Cape Cod Railroad extended its tracks another 19 miles, reaching from Yarmouth to Orleans with service beginning on December 6th, 1865. Two passenger trains a day were scheduled each way with those leaving Yarmouth for Orleans at 11:34 a.m. and 7:44 p.m. The westbound trains left Orleans at 6:30 a.m. and 1:30 p.m. The railroad's official name was Cape Cod Central by its charter from the legislature. The Cape Cod Central had no engines or rolling stock, so all of those were supplied by the Cape Cod Railroad which had created the Cape Cod Central. It would all have the same name in a few years.

The Cape Cod Railroad ran trains to and from Orleans without adding new locomotives from 1865 to 1871, when two new engines were delivered to the road by that September. The first was named *Right Arm* and it was built by Hinkley & Williams, the successor in name to Hinkley & Drury of Boston. The second locomotive, named *Bounty*, came from the famous Paterson, New Jersey plant of The Rogers Locomotive Works. The *Bounty* was the only locomotive the Cape Cod Railroad purchased that came from either of the great locomotive production centers of Paterson or Philadelphia. They were both standard 4-4-0 types, but the *Right Arm* had smaller driving wheels of 54 inches diameter, making her better for freight service.

The company was extending its tracks in two directions at opposite ends of the Cape. The eleven and one-half mile addition from Orleans to Wellfleet was nearing completion and would open the end of December of that year, 1870. The branch from the

Village of Buzzards Bay to Woods Hole had been started that year and would open in July, 1872. Plans to push tracks through Truro to Provincetown were well under way, but reaching the tip of the Cape was a year away from completion of the line to Woods Hole.

With its ten locomotives, the Cape Cod Railroad was running passenger and freight trains over its 71 miles of main line.

The standard locomotive of the 19th century is this 4-4-0, American type. This engine was designed by the Old Colony, which built several, but sent its plans to the Manchester Locomotive Works in New Hampshire where most of the 25 engines acquired between 1891-93 of this type were built. They were identical, weighing 49.5 tons with 18" x 24" cylinders and 69" drivers. This engine, #256, became New Haven #1660 and was still running in 1919.

PROVINCETOWN EXTENSION

The year the Cape Cod Railroad merged with the Old Colony, 1872, the branch to Woods Hole was completed that summer and the steamer service to Nantucket moved from Hyannis to end of track at Woods Hole. From there the first stop on the trip to the islands was Martha's Vineyard, which previously had been served by steamer from New Bedford three days a week. A boat trip then to the Vineyard usually meant taking a Cape Cod train to Tremont and transferring to one of the Fairhaven Branch for a 15 mile run to the end of that line at Fairhaven and there taking the ferry across the Acushnet River to New Bedford. The new steamer run from Woods Hole was shorter, faster and daily.

The final extension - and the long-awaited one - of the Cape Cod Railroad was started and completed by the Old Colony. That was the 14 miles of track between Wellfleet and Provincetown, once considered a necessary federal project for the rapid land protection of the fort and harbor at Provincetown. The rail line's completion there would enable troops to be brought in quickly, if needed, or so the theory went. This military justification for the railroad extension had long been a special issue of Major Sylvanus Phinney in his newspaper, The Barnstable Patriot. The year that Phinney sold the Patriot, 1869, to the owners of the new Provincetown Advocate there appeared a new rationale for building a railroad to the tip of the Cape. The editor of the Advocate, Dr. John M. Crocker, wrote, "Thoreau declared that it was the destiny of Cape Cod to become one of the greatest 'watering places' in New England. It only remains to make these towns of easy access by rail to turn the outside world toward them for a summer resort." Crocker used the contemporary great event of tying the nation together with the joining of the Central Pacific and the Union Pacific and its golden spike ceremony north of Salt Lake City to remind his readers that the extension from Orleans to Wellfleet was moving ahead, but that nothing was being done about the railroad's coming to Truro and Provincetown. That idea became almost a weekly part of Crocker's editorial agenda. His persistence paid off.

With the end of track just across from Duck Creek in Wellfleet from December 1870, the final distance seemed tantalizingly close. The Cape Cod Railroad said it had to sell $200-thousand worth of construction bonds to finance the end of the line. A special town meeting was called in October, 1871 at which citizens would consider the recommendation by the Provincetown Railroad Committee that $98,300 in company bonds - the limit allowed by state law - be purchased by the town. Crocker had suggested members for the committee. He also proposed - then promoted - the special town meeting. After the full report was read by the committee, comment was called for and most of it was heavily in favor. When the vote was taken, the citizens - by an almost unanimous vote - approved the town's buying the bonds. The headlines the next day in the Advocate were pure Crocker; he could barely contain himself: "SET THE FLAG! FIRE THE BIG GUN! We Are Going to Have A Railroad!" Of course there remained the matter of selling the rest of the construction bonds, more than $101-thousand worth. Major Phinney, now a Barnstable banker, said he would guarantee sales of $25-thousand, and Truro was expected to buy an additional $25-thousand. But there was still $51,615 unsold and that amount was left up to Provincetown citizens to buy on their own.

They finally did and 13 months after that special town meeting, railroad construction began in Provincetown, Truro and Wellfleet. It was November, 1872 and workmen began a deep cut through a hill across Commercial Street from the Wellfleet Station. A bridge was put over the cut for Holbrook Avenue and the area beneath it became known as "The Tunnel." While the heavy digging was underway at "The Tunnel," the material removed was taken by horse and wagon northward as fill across the extensive marsh areas. This was a tedious and long process to raise a filled area wide enough - in some places one hundred feet - to support the road bed and tracks across the marshes in a northwesterly direction toward South Truro, three miles away.

The line was surveyed to avoid hills and it did, but because so much of the route was fill, progress was slow. Nearby hills were attacked by workmen with shovels - much of it was hand labor - and the sand and other material was thrown into wagons with extra wide wheels to cart out of the way of the line or deposit somewhere as fill. The wide wheels helped the wagons negotiate the sandy trails. From Wellfleet to South Truro much of the three mile stretch was across Bound Brook and the streams from Duck Harbor and the Herring River north. A great deal of that area was marsh and much fill was needed just to establish a base for the fill on which the roadbed would lie. There were also marshes around the area of the South Truro station, from which the railway line ran in a true north direction parallel to Cape Cod Bay for another two miles to the Truro station on the south bank of the Pamet River. For a half mile below the Pamet and a thousand feet above it wide fill was used to support the tracks through more marshland. The Old Colony built a pile trestle over the mouth of the Pamet River and a fill across the western edge of the marsh on the north side and than a long curve to skirt the lowlands at Corn Hill toward the Bay and then away from it and them back again along the shore to Pond Village where the company planned a station, North Truro. At Pond Village, the railroad fill closed off a tidal inlet. After the line was completed it used to take a passenger train six minutes to cover the three miles, sometimes they made it in five. From there to Provincetown station the line ran close to Cape Cod Bay for much of the way, especially along Pilgrim Beach. The distance was slightly more than six miles.

The work was slow and difficult that winter of 1873, because of cold weather and frequent snow. Conditions were harsh for the men and were made worse when a subcontractor named E. J. Farrell suddenly left town, taking the payroll cash. Police caught up with Farrell and arrested him on a train from Wellfleet to Boston. Not all of the money was recovered.

The workmen had to be satisfied with $.80 on the dollar due them. Many of them were employed in the fishing industry that had been plagued by slim catches and low prices the previous summer. The railroad construction had offered them a chance to recover financially from those dismal days on the water. The shortness in pay didn't help, but at least the work continued through that spring and into summer. At Provincetown Harbor a pile driver pounded away on wooden supports for the new railroad wharf, while schooners arrived carrying cross ties, rails, spikes and chairs. By the second week in June tracks were being built toward Truro from Provincetown and from Wellfleet. From the south all the track equipment arrived in Wellfleet by freight train.

Masons had finished the footings and the foundation and carpenters were working 12 hour days to complete the Provincetown station. Around July 20 somewhere in that 14 miles of new railroad the last rails were joined and there was a final spike driven into a cross tie. The record doesn't tell us where, but we know it wasn't gold.

On July 23, 1873, at 6:25 a.m. a train left Kneeland Street Station, Boston, pulled by locomotive # 25, named *Extension*. In the cab was engineer Zachariah P. Buchardt, accompanied by his fireman Charles Sawyer. At first there were four of the bright, yellow Old Colony day coaches. By the time the train reached Harwich it had 13 cars and every seat occupied. From Harwich to Wellfleet passengers on station platforms had to watch the long train pass and wait for the next one. It was an hour away.

A number of prominent people were on that second train, including three governors, one candidate for governor, the mayor of Boston, many Cape political and business figures and railroad officials. When that train arrived old cannons boomed out salutes, church bells were rung and a brass band helped the crowd march up to the Pavilion on High Pole Hill. Provincetown had never seen so many flags displayed on its buildings. The Advocate listed the menu on the banquet tables: "hot turkey, chicken, lobster salad, cold meats, cakes and pastries, fruits of the season, tea, ices, lemonade and coffee."

The speeches followed the meal and the tone of success of the rail line was set by the Honorable James Gifford who spoke first and concluded, saying, "the ocean has been flanked and we forever allied to the continent by bands of steel." The candidate for governor, General Benjamin F. Butler, later bought a house on the highest hill in town from which he went forth by train to cross the Commonwealth in search of votes. He persisted and finally was elected to serve a two-year term in 1883.

Fishermen loved the railroad as it gave them a chance to ship quickly their catch to Boston and New York. The packet owners detested the railroad, for soon the line was carrying everything they had been. The railroad eventually killed off the packets.

And there was another mode involved. In each town as the tracks arrived, the stage coaches retreated - always losing ground. After the rails reached Wellfleet, Samuel Knowles withdrew his stages and his horses from Orleans and ran shorter trips from Wellfleet to Provincetown. He was retreating. That was in 1870.

In July 1873 his stage routes were covered by trains. So several weeks after the steam cars arrived, Samuel Knowles gave his stage coaches fresh coats of paint and began meeting trains at the Provincetown station where he would take passengers and their baggage to the various hotels. Shortly after the steam cars started running to the tip of the Cape, editor Crocker wrote: "The story that the station at North Truro is indicated by a milk can isn't so. They have a pile of ties there with a man sitting on it, and are soon to possess a nice little station." And they did, too.

For years the dream and the goal of the Cape Cod Railroad was to run trains to Provincetown. The line was finished from Wellfleet by the Old Colony in July, 1873 and this locomotive, named *Extension*, brought the first passenger train to the tip of the Cape. This picture was taken moments after her arrival.

As the railroad advanced the stage coaches retreated, and finally vanished.

OLD COLONY RAIL ROAD,

PARTICULAR NOTICE.

On and after Wednesday next, 17th inst., there will be a change in running the Engines and Trains between South Braintree and Boston, from the right to the left hand track; of which all persons interested will please take notice.

F. B. CROWNINSHIELD,
PRESIDENT.

BOSTON, MAY 13, 1854.

The 1854 change to running on the left track from South Braintree to Kneeland Street was so incoming passengers might land on the South Street side, as the opposite side was a freight area and there was no street. For outgoing trains it meant avoiding crossing the inbound track. Running on the left in that area made sense for these reasons to the Old Colony management, so they changed over to it. This printed announcement was for company personnel.

OLD COLONY RAILROAD

The Old Colony Railroad eventually became the dominant system in Southeastern Massachusetts, following a rocky and somewhat aimless beginning. The legislature granted its charter in 1844 and it opened in November, 1845, 37 miles from Boston to Plymouth, running two passenger trains a day each way. The route passed most of the larger shoe manufacturing towns and the iron works in that area directly south of Boston. Once the line was in operation it began building branches and leasing other roads in a search for more traffic. The Old Colony was not strong financially and quickly had a debt of $640,000. In desperation it started selling $100 a share par value stock for $75 and short term bonds for a discount price of ninety cents on the dollar.

The line hired some of the big stars of New England railroading, but that didn't help the sorry financial picture they had painted. In exasperation the stockholders brought in outside analysts who, among other things, thought that irregularities by the officers were responsible for the bleak outlook. They found none.

In 1847 two powerful families in Fall River, the Bordens and the Durfees, built the Fall River Branch Railroad as an adjunct to their textile and iron enterprises. They first tried to forge a connection to the Boston & Providence. Failing that, they looked at a line of their own into Boston. The goal was better transportation to the capital of Massachusetts for their industries.

Finally the Fall River Branch and the Old Colony agreed to meet at South Braintree from where the Old Colony would double-track its line to Boston. With such an agreement in hand the Bordens could now run their steamboats between New York and Fall River and move the passengers and freight from that overnight service into Boston. That move began the world's most famous night boats, the Fall River Line, and its railroad connection from Boston to the wharf on the waterfront of Fall River, making that city the gateway to New England. The steamers and their boat train were to last ninety years.

The two railroads signed a ten year contract in which they divided traffic income on a mileage basis: The Old Colony paid the Fall River Branch one half cent per mile for each ton of freight and each passenger on the Old Colony that had come from the Fall River. In addition neither line was to divert any business from the other or charter any new lines that would harm the other. This was to begin a new chapter for the Old Colony and a new direction - to the south and west with improved company finances.

Much of the ten year agreement between the two saw periodic fighting in which each claimed to be a victim. The charges were made in public and each line thought its future lay in an extension. The Old Colony went so far as to survey a line to Newport where, it announced, it would start its steamboat service to New York. The Fall River looked at extending its rails into Boston from South Braintree, bypassing the Old Colony.

In 1854, the two got together and formed one corporation - the Old Colony and Fall River Railroad. That union also included a number of smaller roads that had merged with both. The addition of the Newport & Fall River Railroad helped create a new corporate name: the Old Colony & Newport in 1862. Newport became the terminus of the new

One of the earliest locomotives the Old Colony had was the *Governor Bradford* built by Hinkley & Drury. This engine was used as a switcher in Boston. This is early, simple motive power - just the basics.

steamers that had moved 16 miles south of Fall River. It remained so until 1869 when the ships returned to Fall River but included a stop at Newport on the way. The next big move of the Old Colony was to merge with the Cape Cod Railroad in 1872. In the view of Cape Cod stockholders it was about time, since they had expected - and many of them had been told - that upon completion of the original line from Middleborough to Sandwich in 1848 the line would be bought out by the Fall River Railroad, whose owners were the biggest investors in the Cape Cod. Instead the Cape Cod stayed independent for the next 24 years.

With the merger of the Old Colony & Newport and the Cape Cod, the new corporation reverted to its original name - Old Colony. That name was Southeastern Massachusetts terminology for the part of the land occupied by the first settlers at Plymouth. It seemed fitting and appropriate, since the railroad built first to Plymouth from Boston in 1845.

When the Old Colony bought the Cape Cod Railroad in 1873 the 85.7 miles of Cape Cod main line and 22.4 miles of its two branches - Woods Hole and Hyannis - brought the total trackage of the Old Colony to 294 miles, all but 16 of which were in Massachusetts. This total did not include the distance covered by the steamers the company operated between New England and New York - the Old Colony Steamboat Company's Fall River Line.

That year the Old Colony was authorized by charter to issue $7,950,000 in capital stock with a par value of $100 a share. The actual number of shares sold was 65,610 and the average price paid was $100 for each share. The stock paid an annual dividend of 7 percent and by investment standards of its time was a good buy and one to hold on to. Its bonds totaled $3,255,000. The railroad had cost $9,080,000 to build. That figure represented the actual cost of its own building programs and those of the numerous lines it had purchased, leased, merged with, consolidated, controlled financially and operated jointly.

The Old Colony had 59 steam locomotives, 153 passenger, mail and baggage cars, 1,168 freight and other cars and ten snow plows.

This motive power and rolling stock was valued at $1,134,000. The locomotives weighed an average 26 tons and their tenders (full of fuel and water) averaged 20 tons. Each locomotive and tender was valued at $7,313 for a motive power total of $431,500.

The 129 passenger cars, day coaches, cost on average $2,792 each for a total value of $361-thousand. They were wooden construction as were all cars in those years. They weighed on average 17.67 tons each. Most of them were built at the company shops in South Boston and at the car shops in Hyannis that once were part of the Cape Cod Railroad.

The 24 mail and baggage cars were also company-made for an average $1,500 and weighed 15 tons each.

The line had 281 eight-wheel box cars valued at $450 each for a total of $126,400. The largest number of freight cars were the 444 gondolas for coal and gravel. They cost the company $300 each.

Locomotives were getting heavier but the company stayed with iron rails of 56 pounds to the yard in 1873, but gradually heavier rails would be used.

For New England winters the Old Colony built ten wooden snow plows in its shops. Each one weighed three-quarters of a ton and was valued at $220.

The smallest rolling stock on the roster were the dozen four-wheel flat cars that weighed close to three tons and cost $75 each; the eleven four-wheel box cars at $100 each, weighing 3.3 tons; and the six-wheel flat cars at $350 each, weighing five tons. The Old Colony had 72 of the latter.

The rate of speed of express passenger trains, including stops, was 33 miles an hour. For local passenger trains it was 23 miles an hour. Fast freight trains with limited stops averaged 16 miles an hour, while slower freights, including stops, averaged ten miles an hour.

Passenger trains, including baggage cars, were averaging 4.5 cars in make up. Freights had an average 22 cars of the eight-wheel variety.

Tickets in day coaches on company-operated trains averaged 2.7 cents per mile. The lowest rate of fare per mile was 2.5 cents. Through passengers to and from connecting railroads paid two cents per mile on Old Colony trains. Passengers who commuted to work on the line paid the least. The monthly ticket based on 12 rides a week - twice a day for six days - was nine mills per mile. In the year ending September 30, 1873 the number of commuters to and from Boston was 378,963 each making one round trip a day. All over the system there were 449,448 commuting passengers. The railroad called them season-ticket holders. Total passengers that year were 4,256,840, paying $1,431,708. Of that figure $1,110,000 was from local passengers on company trains.

Express business was $74,781 total that year; mail contracts were worth $28,459. These two were added to ticket sales, since express and mail were always moved in passenger trains, making total receipts from the passenger department $1,534,948.

At Cohasset Narrows the Cape Cod Branch Railroad built the longest bridge on its line from Middleboro to Sandwich. This bridge is a later one than that and probably dates from the 1880s during the Old Colony tenure. Two main spans are through trusses, while that iron isosceles triangle on this end opens for boat traffic between this arm of Buzzards Bay and through the rail bridge to Buttermilk Bay. In 1869 the first bridge was washed out by a hurricane and its tidal surge.

This train is about to leave for Woods Hole from Buzzards Bay. This might be an excursion or otherwise something special, since most scheduled trains had two passenger cars. The locomotive, #127, was built in 1885 at the Old Colony shops in South Boston. The headlamp is an oil burner with a large reflector. The locomotive looks new and well maintained. That is a large train crew with eight men from the engine back to the lead steps on the first day coach and a conductor or trainman on the ground. The man next to the gang way with that track bar is a section hand. All ten of these men have beards and mustaches. In the middle of each passenger car was a carved, wooden oval design with the number or the name of the car.

A four-car passenger train leaves the yard at Buzzards Bay, heading south for Woods Hole. Two tracks in foreground merged at switch by second coach into single track across the Monument River trestle. Large coaling dock in left foreground was a busy facility at this junction. Bridge at left was for road traffic: horse-drawn vehicles, horseback riders, cyclists and pedestrians. The public was warned by signs on both sides not to walk on the railroad's trestle, but many people did anyway.

At Cohasset Narrows this 320-foot wooden trestle was finished in July 1872 for the Woods Hole Branch. This is the Monument River and that is Buzzards Bay in the distance at the upper left. Across the water back of the bridge is Bourne's Neck, later known as Taylor Point. Yards at the junction of the main line and Woods Hole Branch are off camera to the right. From here to Woods Hole, left, was 17 and one half miles. With four stops along the way passenger trains covered the distance in 50 to 55 minutes. It was short of breakneck speed, but compared to the stage coaches it replaced, which had often taken most of a day, it was heaven on earth.

OLD COLONY R.R.
MAIN LINE DIVISION.

NOTICE TO PASSENGERS
☞ Important Changes in Time Table

Commencing SUNDAY, Sept. 25, 1887, the Sunday Passenger Train heretofore leaving BOSTON at 7.30 A.M. for NANTUCKET, COTTAGE CITY, WOODS HOLL, FALMOUTH, HYANNIS, SANDWICH, BUZZARDS BAY, MIDDLEBORO, BRIDGEWATER, and BROCKTON, and the RETURN Sunday Train from those places will be run only between BOSTON and MIDDLEBORO.

On and after MONDAY, Sept. 26, 1887, the week-day Passenger Trains leaving Boston at 1.00 and 4.05 P.M. for BROCKTON, MIDDLEBORO, and points on CAPE COD, WILL BE DISCONTINUED; and the Passenger Train leaving Boston at 11.40 A.M. will make connection for HYANNIS, WOODS HOLL, COTTAGE CITY, and NANTUCKET.

The Fall River and New York Express Passenger Train leaving Boston at 7.00 P.M., on week-days, WILL BE DISCONTINUED ON AND AFTER MONDAY, Sept. 26, 1887.

SEE OTHER IMPORTANT CHANGES.

J. H. FRENCH, Division Supt.
J. R. KENDRICK, General Manager.

BOSTON. Sept. 23, 1887.

GEO H ELLIS PRINTER 141 FRANKLIN STREET BOSTON.

The Old Colony had a great many broadside produced to tell the public of schedule chang and, in other cases, to promote ticket sales.

The carpenter shop of the Old Colony Railroad Car Works in Hyannis had been a going concern for the Cape Cod Railroad long before the Old Colony bought it out. The nineteenth century saw the rise of the wooden car, because it was easier to build and inexpensive. Many wooden cars lasted until the middle 1930s on the New Haven. Three of these workers can be identified. The second man from the left over by that door was William Cannon. On the right side of the picture, the man in the middle, Henry Hallett, was the brother of Asa Hallett, who is standing to Henry's left and facing the other direction. This building burned in 1898.

This is a rare photo taken inside an Old Colony round house in Boston in the 1880s.

Freight trains earned $774,752 and represented about one half the revenue derived from carrying people. Total revenue was $2,309,701, including rents and leasing of some of its cars to other roads. From the net earnings of $504,796 the company paid a 7 percent stock dividend, including a dividend on Cape Cod Railroad stock that was exchanged prior to the dividend.

The line had 282 grade crossings, but only 21 with gates and flagmen. All the company's 117 bridges were wooden. More than half the depots had a telegraph - 62 out of 110. The Old Colony operated the telegraph itself in 45 of those depots and in the other 17 it was a joint operation with the telegraph company. With the telegraph in so many stations, train dispatching was safe, quick and easy. When the Old Colony bought out the Cape Cod, there was already in place an extensive telegraph system.

The early growth of manufacturing in New England is reflected in Old Colony freight business in 1873. The largest single category in tonnage was the 342,623 tons of general merchandise. Coal was the second largest item of freight with the line carrying 105,520 tons of anthracite and 12,000 tons of bituminous within Massachusetts, a reflection of the huge volume of coal that came up the coast on schooners and landed at the Port of Boston. East Boston and Everett had major coal docks with hoisting equipment and tracks running right out on the piers. With all the track capacity entering New England, the bridge lines brought very little coal. Most of it came in by water to three major ports: Providence, Boston and Portland, Maine. Of those three Boston was the largest, although most of the small ports had coal pockets, too. The coal business was a maritime affair. The railroads became involved delivering it to customers inland once it arrived on the docks.

Building materials were the next largest cargo on Old Colony tracks with 46,859 tons of lumber, 33,778 tons of stone and brick and 5,912 tons of lime, cement and sand. Cities and suburbs in Massachusetts were in a boom period of growth in construction.

That boom had been fueled by the financial growth created by the heavy government spending of the Civil War. After that conflict the prosperity had continued and it helped expand a growing middle class. The railroads had become the nation's first billion dollar industry and they underwent steady and huge growth.

The fourth largest category of freight carried on the Old Colony in 1873 was grain and flour. Its total weight was 48,863 tons.

More and more meat was being raised at a distance and shipped to customers by rail. The Old Colony carried 6,354 tons of livestock that year.

Of all the technical changes the railroads adopted, many were to make train travel safer. None was more important than brake systems, and of those the air brake devised by George Westinghouse was the best and in time became almost universal in the business. Westinghouse applied for his patent in 1869. The Old Colony by the fall of 1873 had equipped 16 of its locomotives with the Westinghouse train brake and installed it on 70 of its passenger cars. Hand brakes were still in use on all freight trains and the company's 59 other passenger cars, but the Old Colony was one of the first lines to use the Westinghouse air brake and within a few years it was in use on all its trains.

More people rode in railroad cars from the 1850s until 1920 than any other conveyance. At first these coaches had a row of small windows, open platforms and a roof that was slightly arched. In the 1860s their appearance changed. They became longer, had larger windows and featured a raised roof down the middle about a foot and half high where small windows were placed for additional light and ventilation. Architects had used such a device for years, calling it a clerestory. When these roof additions were added to

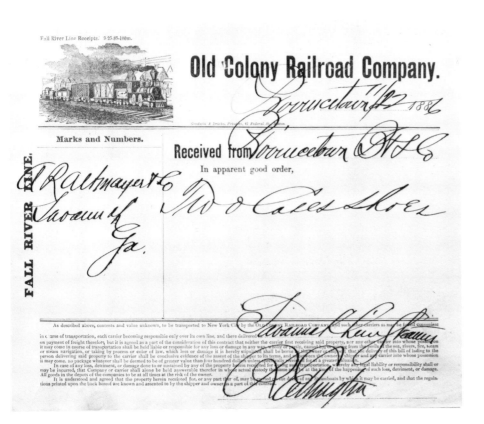

The Provincetown Boot & Shoe Company was a steady shipper on the Old Colony. This order to Savannah went to Fall River by train and New York by steamer-as far as the Old Colony went.

passenger cars new names were applied, such as raised, lantern, deck, monitor and steamboat. The windows could be opened for ventilation, but one of the chief benefits was the additional light admitted. These clerestory roofs gave more headroom and space for lighting fixtures for oil and later gas. The price of the clerestory was an additional $600 per car and it produced a much nicer appearance than the earlier, almost flat styles of roofs.

One failure of the clerestory in its first applications to the wooden coaches of the day was its structural weakness. It had no lateral strength, and gave little support to the sides of the car because the clerestory was the weakest part of the entire car. But it looked good, so the railroads liked them and put one on each piece of new passenger equipment, including combination and baggage cars. In fact the clerestory roof lasted on new cars until just before World War II.

From the 1860s until close to the turn of the century the size of passenger cars remained about the same. They were 50 to 60 feet long and weighed from 18 to 25 tons and seated a total 50 to 60 passengers on double seats each side of the aisle.

On the side panels the wood was batten-board and in the center there were oval picture frame moldings called name panels. Within them was the car's name or its number.

Inside the first class cars the interiors were finished in cherry, black walnut and mahogany - the rare cabinet woods. Ordinary day coaches had wood interiors of less expensive pine; it was easy to work. The excursion cars of some railroads were the only ones that were painted. When the Old Colony took over the Cape Cod Railroad in 1873, the car works at Hyannis continued to build coaches and baggage cars. Their parlor cars were made by Pullman.

The Old Colony had scenes painted on the outside of its passenger cars and these were done by company painters and artists. On one of its cars there was the scene of a buffalo hunt, on another a woman on a horse accompanied by a dog and still another car featured an African scene with a lion springing from a tree on to a gazelle drinking at a brook.

After the Civil War the painted scenes began to disappear and to be replaced by striping and lettering and scrollwork at the corners and around the doors. The name Old Colony on the space above the windows and the car numbers were double-shaded and every nut and grabiron was highlighted by stripes. The cars were painted a bright yellow with striping either black or dark green. They could be seen at a considerable distance and there was no denying their exciting visual qualities.

The yellow color of passenger cars also had a practical effect of hiding or at least blending of the sandy dust that swirled around moving trains. A yellow car covered by yellow dust still looked pretty good. Once a year all this equipment was taken back to the shops and given a cleaning and another coat of varnish. Every eight or ten years the finish was burned off and the application of five coats of paint was started again. There was a great deal of labor involved and time in applying primer and filler coats followed by varnish and two coats of finishing varnish. The drying time was two months but the results were a glistening car with a waterproof finish.

The bright yellow cars gave way to darker colors in the late 1880s. There were dark greens, chocolate browns and even plum-colored cars. The dark colors required only three coats of paint and were longer lasting than the light. Car lettering and decorations such as striping still took a great deal of time with layers of gold leafing on the dark surfaces. Six men might work 50 to 60 hours each to complete that work on one car.

The wooden cars were attractive, but in a serious wreck at high speed they could be death traps for passengers. The adoption of the Westinghouse air brake was a major advance in safety, but a derailment or collision between trains still could cause the telescoping of one wooden car into the next one with hideous results.

One horrible example was on the Eastern Railroad, running north out of Boston. Train travel was heavy that day, August 26, 1871, with train after train running late out of the Causeway Street station that Saturday. Employees lost track of time and how close trains were running to each other. At the Revere station that evening a local was stopped when the *Portland Express* came out of the twilight and crashed into the rear car which surged forward through the next which in turn slid into the one ahead of it. The cars were illuminated by oil lamps which broke open dousing the interiors of the cars and the passengers with the flaming liquid. Twenty-nine were killed and 57 injured in the Revere wreck. The Eastern Railroad hadn't adopted telegraph dispatching and the express wasn't equipped with air brakes. Some of the wrecked cars on that local were turned into furnaces.

There was still another problem and that was the platforms, which allowed the rear car to climb up on the platform of the car ahead and then by sheer momentum to break through the car end and telescope into the passenger section. This happened with great frequency in collisions. But a solution was on the way.

Since many cars had different heights above the rail, in a crash the sill of one would slide above or below the next one, or it could. After the Civil War an engineer, Ezra Miller, devised his Miller platform with three elements. Each car platform was heavily braced by long sills and all were on one level; the contact between each platform was a buffer working against a compressed spring; when the cars were brought together in making up a train, the couplers attached to springs in tension slid by each other and snapped into a

The Woods Hole Branch is new, 1872, and this Old Colony locomotive is at the water column before backing up for a train. The end of a train for down Cape is to the left of the water tank. Buzzards Bay had long, wooden platforms and a large engine house across the tracks in the center of the picture. This was an important junction for the Old Colony.

This is the second Old Colony locomotive named *Pilgrim*. She was built in 1883 at the South Boston shops of the Old Colony by J.K. Taylor, the railroad's master mechanic. She was the largest locomotive in New England.

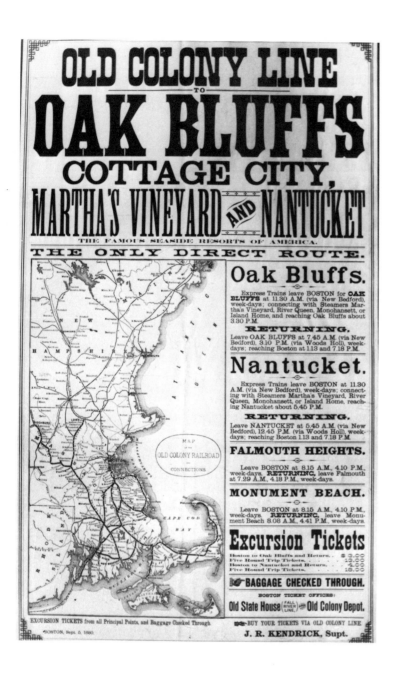

Below Some of these Old Colony wooden, open platform day coaches were built at the car shops in Hyannis. They had a capacity of 72 people in their 36 double seats, 18 on each side of the aisle. The clerestory roof helped to ventilate the interior, but it was a weakness in construction and added no strength which could protect passengers in case of an accident.

union. The pressures between cars tightened the train into a single unit. The Miller platform was a decided safety measure and along with Miller's automatic couplers were installed on many railroads. That installation did not take place quickly or on all roads, but the Old Colony by the late 1870s was advertising Miller platforms and Westinghouse air brakes on its Fall River boat trains and other expresses.

There were hundreds of coupler inventions in those years and the ultimate winner of that financial sweepstakes was the Janney. The Old Colony installed them, too.

The Janney was named after its inventor, Eli H. Janney of Alexandria, Virginia, who apparently was interested in helping to eliminate the number of hideous injuries to railroad workers from the link and pin coupling systems then in use. An iron pin dropped through a chain link coupled the cars together. It was a simple technology, but dangerous to switchmen, yard men and brakemen who had to step over the rail and lift or drop the pin in the middle of the sill at the car end. When he was in between the cars coupling or uncoupling, he could not be seen from the locomotive. If the engineer moved the train, the result could be a crushed hand or arm, amputated fingers or even death. Such accidents were commonplace, for example in 1885 four Old Colony employees were killed and 15 injured; in 1886 nine were killed and 14 injured; and in 1887 six were killed and seven injured. For many years the casualties were even higher, and coupling accidents - although not the only cause - were among the most common.

In 1873 Janney received a patent for his open jaw type of coupler that looks similar to those in use today, which resemble a closed fist for a hook and a hinged jaw for the fingers. Janney's passenger coupler had a spring catch and his invention was clearly a major step for safety and convenience. Its adoption, like other innovations, was uneven, but its clear superiority to the old link and pin and other couplers assured its eventual universal adoption. Within five years the Old Colony was installing Janney couplers to its Miller platforms on passenger cars that early in the 1870s were among some of the earliest to have had Westinghouse train brakes.

The adoption of safety devices and the use of the telegraph for dispatching were not enough in some cases to avert disaster because of employee error. The worst cases of this on the Old Colony took place in Quincy a dozen years apart.

On October 8, 1878 shortly after 7 p.m. an excursion train derailed at high speed near Wollaston Heights south of Boston. The switches were not set for the main line and signal lamps on the end of an outward local freight for Newport were not displayed as required in such movements.

The collision and derailing of the passenger train killed 17 passengers and two railroad employees and further injured 166 passengers and four employees. So the death toll was 19 and the injured, many of them seriously hurt, numbered 170. The total cost to the Old Colony was $348,453 of which $324,651 were for death and personal injuries. The remaining $23,801 was the damage to a locomotive and passenger cars, six of which were destroyed by the impact.

Employee negligence was again responsible for a carnage in Wollaston on August 19, 1890. On that occasion the train was bound from Cape Cod to Boston. It was one of those trains that combined cars from Woods Hole with a train that originated in Hyannis. The three cars from Woods Hole were carrying mostly passengers who had come in from Nantucket and the Vineyard by steamer with some picked up at stops from Falmouth north to Buzzards Bay where the trains were joined and became an express for Boston with only a stop at Middleboro.

The nine car train had slowed to 40 miles an hour through an area of track work that Tuesday morning when it derailed. A crew had been reballasting the main line and apparently had worked almost up to train time, running back to safety just as the locomotive appeared. In their haste they left a heavy jack used to lift rails and ties and the engine ploughed into the jack and left the tracks, continuing forward for some 280 feet. The train, of course, followed with the first passenger car climbing up the tender and crashing onto the locomotive. That impact burst pipes and flooded the car with live steam, scalding the passengers. The carnage was 23 dead and 170 injured.

The wreck in Yarmouth on the Hyannis Branch in November, 1890 was also caused by employee error. The shuttle train to Yarmouth was supposed to wait for a work train following to clear. Instead it backed down the line where the work train crashed into the single car and telescoped inside the combine, killing one passenger and injuring ten others. It was less than three months after the second Wollaston wreck.

The cheapest and simplest way to heat railroad cars in the nineteenth century was an iron stove. Several seats were removed on one side of the aisle in the middle of the car as space for the heater. About 1870 many lines dropped that method, replacing it with one stove at each end of the car. Neither system worked well, since the cars had thin walls and were not insulated; the windows rattled loosely and admitted plenty of outside air and the doors were frequently opened as trainmen passed between the cars and passengers got off and on at each stop. On a cold night - or a cold day for that matter - the grimmest experience was when a train was underway and suddenly the doors at the opposite ends of the car were opened simultaneously. The through blast of Arctic temperatures which also stirred up dust and dirt from the floor was a fearsome thing.

So car heating was a problem and all kinds of solutions were tried. Some attention was gained by the cone disc stove invented by Gardner Chilson of Mansfield, Massachusetts. A common cast iron stove of the 1870s except for a large diameter disc that deflected the heat, preventing the immediate rise of hot air to the clerestory and circulating some heat to the floor where it was most needed. As a safety feature in the event of a wreck, long bolts secured the stove to the floor, and the fire doors could be locked as another precaution against the scattering of live coals. The worst defect of most car stoves was the intense heat close to the stove. Experienced travelers made a dash for those seats not too far or too close to the heater. The atmosphere was dry and very hot near the stove's simmering walls. The brakeman was responsible for keeping the stove going and he most often kept it going like hell on wheels - too hot and this by overstocking. These stoves inside the cars produced dust, ashes and, sometimes, smoke. When trains lurched or made sudden stops some passengers were burned or bruised on contact with the stove. Hot air stoves were tried by putting wind scoops outside on the tops of the coaches and brought the outside air to the base of the stove then warming it and sending it through registers along the floor. Of course the greatest threat to life was in a wreck with wooden passenger cars thrown off the track on their sides, rolling over and telescoping into adjacent cars and the stoves spewing hot coals over the passengers and the wooden interiors, setting fires and burning to death trapped and injured people. There were enough of such accidents to concern railroad management about the danger from free-standing stoves inside the cars.

The Old Colony experimented with a form of under-the-floor furnace as early as 1846. It was not successful, but management showed that early in its corporate history the line's willingness to improve matters.

It was left to William C. Baker from Dexter, Maine to design a hot water heater for

This illustration from a contemporary magazine was drawn from photographs made of rescue efforts at Braintree. In the early evening of October 8, 1878 an Old Colony excursion train crashed into a freight, killing 17 passengers and two railroad employees. There were 170 people injured. The accident cost the company nearly $350-thousand, most of it for death and personal injury claims.

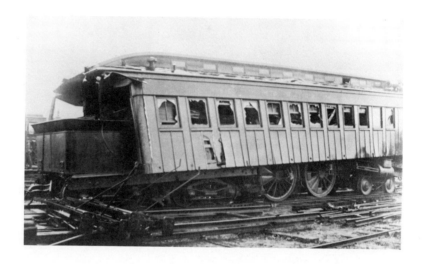

On the morning of November 11, 1890, a one car shuttle train from Hyannis to Yarmouth Port was involved in a collision that killed one passenger and injured ten others. The early passenger train from Provincetown to Boston was met first at Harwich by a shuttle train from Chatham with passengers and then met at Yarmouth Junction by a shuttle train with passengers from Hyannis. On that November morning early, around 7 a.m., an Old Colony steam locomotive pulled one combination baggage-passenger car from the Hyannis depot to Yarmouth. The shuttle train was under orders to wait at Yarmouth for a work train from Hyannis, which would leave Yarmouth after the Boston train. After picking up passengers for Hyannis from the Provincetown train, the shuttle backed out of Yarmouth toward Hyannis, ignoring its orders to wait. Meanwhile the work train was heading north on the single track toward Yarmouth. In railroad slang these were called "cornfield meets." At Deep Cut Curve at the north end of the Yarmouth Camp Grounds the work train locomotive plowed all the way through the passenger-baggage car, telescoping it. The wooden car was a shambles and the locomotive not much better with the smoke box destroyed and side rods torn loose. The wreck was taken back to the Hyannis yards with the day coach still riding the engine. **Above** The first photo is how it looked back at Hyannis. **Left above** The second is the locomotive after the shell of the car was removed.

railroad cars similar to systems used to heat homes and other buildings by circulating hot water. Baker's system became the best known with its small, coal-burning stove in one end of the car surrounded by sheet metal. Inside the stove was a coil of pipe that was laid out on the car floor along the baseboard with a loop under each seat, forming an iron radiator that pulsed with hot water throughout its length and returned the circulating water to the reservoir and back to the stove. The brakeman could charge the fire with coal and then bank it where it would run the system for many hours without attention from him. Baker's system warmed the complete car with even heat, doing the job of two regular stoves and took up less space. In 1865 he tested his patents by installing it in the New Haven Railroad president's private car. It proved to be impressive and later tests were conducted on New Haven's day coaches. The greatest drawback of Baker's hot-water heater was the $500 cost per car. Most railroads felt inexpensive coal stoves - not more than $10 each - would suffice. But by 1890 about 7,000 cars were equipped with hot water systems. That was about one out of four passenger cars and most of these had the Baker system. The Old Colony stayed with two free-standing stoves in each coach and only gradually - in the 1880s - installed Baker's more elaborate system in coaches except for their earlier use in parlor cars and all the rolling stock on the boat trains to and from the steamers at Fall River.

Many Old Colony trains, especially on the longer runs - Boston to Provincetown or Newport - had young men called news butchers. They wore a uniform, a blue suit and cap with a brass nameplate, identifying the company that had the concession. They were at first, at least in the 1850s, called train boys, then newsboys or news agents. It is not clear when they became known as news butchers. They sold newspapers and magazines, candy and tobacco products. They even sold ice water before the railroads put water tanks in the coaches with a spigot and a glass tube dispenser with Dixie cups.

The news butchers ranged in age from 12 to 18. Most often they were on commission, usually 20 percent of their sales. They were aggressive young salesmen, entering the coaches and immediately shouting out their wares. They were brash and cocky and acted in a masculine way far older than their years, waving from the trains at farm girls in barn yards, other girls near grade crossings and winking at female passengers of all ages.

One ability they developed soon on the job was to make change quickly - in fact so quickly that customers often did not know whether it was the right change. Often it was not. The most famous news butcher in American history was Thomas Alva Edison, who, in 1859, at the age of 12 became a news agent on the Grand Trunk Railroad's 7 a.m. local from his home town of Port Huron, Michigan to Detroit.

Edison worked the train with his stock of goods until its arrival at 10 a.m. Then he went to the Detroit Free Library where he read magazines and books on chemistry until six that evening when he left for the station where he worked a local back to Port Huron.

Edison invested some of his profits in chemical equipment, setting up a laboratory for experiments in a corner of the baggage car. After hawking his merchandise through the cars following each station stop, he would go to his laboratory and continue his experiments and writing the results in a notebook. He hired boys to help him on other trains. A year after he started as a news butcher, he further expanded his enterprises by buying a handpress and some type to become a publisher. He asked telegraphers along the line to save news items that came over the wire. He would edit these into a newspaper, the Weekly Herald, which soon reached a circulation of 800, earning the 13-year old editor/publisher a monthly profit of $45 from that effort alone. Unfortunately, trouble was coming.

A derailment ahead of his train caused the baggage car to slew to one side, tossing his chemicals onto the floor where they burst into flames. The conductor, shouting at the youngster, first extinguished the fire after which he boxed Edison's ears, causing the beginning of deafness. The conductor's fury caused him to throw Edison, his laboratory and printing press off the train. The youngster continued as a news butcher, but Edison decided to change careers and become a telegrapher, which he did before turning to a long life of invention.

In 1889, 15-year old Harry Thomas of Taunton was hired as a news butcher on the Old Colony, working a train from there to New Bedford. Thomas described the open platform day coaches as "rolling palaces" even though they were the standard accommodation trains with wooden combination cars and day coaches, featuring kerosene lamps, stiff-backed seats and a round coal stove for heat.

Years later he recalled how important he felt, sitting in the back of a car "announcing the station names just before we stopped. As soon as we got in motion again I would go to the baggage section of the first car where I stored my merchandise, pick up my tray and slowly promenade through those coaches, calling out my wares."

His big day was June 1, 1889 when he sold out of his newspapers, after shouting, "Boston morning papers - all about the great flood in Johnstown, Pennsylvania."

Harry Thomas sold magazines, tobacco, cigars and candy besides newspapers on trains between Taunton and New Bedford and return, but peddling drinking water was a money maker for him and others who worked trains in those days. "Most of my sales were of drinking water, which I peddled up and down the train. I carried a carrier resembling a teakettle. On each side of the spout was a holder," he said. "In each holder was a glass, and the passengers drank from these two glasses. Sure, the glasses were washed once in a while, when I wasn't too busy selling merchandise."

About that time the railroads were beginning to install ice water tanks, so that passengers could get water for themselves, but Thomas recalls that his train had no such modern convenience.

As Edison graduated from selling in the cars to a telegrapher's job on the railroad, others moved from candy butchering to other rail positions. The same year that Harry Thomas started working Old Colony trains out of Taunton, 1889, the June 29th issue of the Yarmouth Register told its readers that a local man, A. Howard Crocker, "who sold fruit and confectionery on the Cape Cod trains is now employed as brakeman on the accommodation train between Hyannis and Boston."

One of the horrors of railroad travel in the nineteenth century was the collapse of bridges. The Old Colony inspected its bridges and the entire line on a regular basis and this as a precaution seemed to work. Also the company built its own bridges rather than have outside firms do them under contract. Some firms were notorious for cutting corners on construction materials and for sloppy workmanship.

One New England bridge disaster pointed up what could happen if management didn't routinely check bridges, especially those built by outside firms.

It happened on the morning of March 14, 1887 at the Bussy Bridge in Roslindale on the Dedham Branch of the Boston & Providence. A passenger train was crossing the structure that carried the tracks over a street, when the iron bridge suddenly failed and the cars fell to the road below. There were school children among the commuters and the death toll was 24. The following year the Old Colony leased the Boston & Providence and one of the first things it did was the thorough inspection of the road, concentrating on bridges.

In August of that year the Bussy Bridge collapsed, 1887, employee negligence was blamed for a mid-western horror when a small wooden trestle over a culvert burned and collapsed when a passenger train crossed it. A section crew had been burning weeds along the tracks of the Toledo, Peoria & Western near Chatsworth, Illinois and that evening as a precaution the trestle should have been checked. It wasn't. After midnight a nine car excursion train headed for Niagara Falls was making up lost time when the engineer spotted fire ahead. Seeing that it was a small trestle burning, he whistled for brakes and put the engine in reverse. The first engine passed over the bridge, but it collapsed under the weight of the second and the wooden cars started telescoping, turning over and breaking up. The violent effects of the crash and the fire that followed killed 82 passengers - wooden cars with oil lamps and in a violent accident there was always a fire.

The illumination of railroad cars had begun with candles and graduated to sperm oil lamps and kerosene until the late 1880s when a petroleum gas called Pintsch was beginning to be installed. Pintsch lamps came to be the principal method in car lighting until World War I, when electrical systems replaced them. The earlier oil lamps were the most dangerous in a train wreck, for they spread the contents of the oil reservoir over the wooden wreckage and burst into flame. The Revere wreck on the Eastern was the infamous Massachusetts example of a high speed rear-end collision of wooden cars and oil lamps, creating death by impact and then fire. The Pintsch lamps gave the brightest light and were safer than their oil predecessors. Far safer.

In the winter, severe train wrecks always resulted in fire in the broken cars from the free-standing stoves used for heat. The Baker heaters were safer than the inexpensive iron stoves, but they still depended on a coal fire. The obvious source of heat was steam from the locomotive and applied to the cars through a system of pipes and hoses. American railroads lagged behind their European counterparts in steam heating by 20 years, but it finally was introduced in America in 1889. One of its greatest features was its safety and freedom from stove fires in wooden cars, besides its even quality of comfort, improving on the Baker system. The Old Colony installed its first steam heat radiators in the 1890s.

The pace of change varied on each railroad, but generally the Old Colony adopted new safety devices and progressed as a leader among New England railroads. Increased earnings from passengers and freight contributed to a management attitude welcoming change and a willingness to pay its price.

One of the most important parts of modernization was the replacing of iron rails with steel that had at least 20 percent more strength than the older metal, with which the railroads had been built. It was the first year after the Cape Cod had been purchased by the Old Colony that the parent company began its program of putting in steel rails. In 1874 a total of 12 miles of new steel rail were on the main line running south of Boston. The following spring 16 additional miles of steel rails were laid. And so it went as locomotives and rolling stock increased in size and weight, so did the miles of steel rail and its weight per yard. The Old Colony and most of the Cape Cod Railroad had put down 56 pounds per yard rail. By the late 1870s the Old Colony was laying mostly 67 pound rail and in the 1880s that increased to 70 and 77 pound. The 80s were the years of change in the roadbed as the opening year of that decade saw 33 miles of new steel track put down, two years later 53.7 miles of steel track were added. Cape Cod began to get an allocation of new steel and by the fall of 1886 only the line from Orleans to Provincetown had the older, 56 pound iron. That final 26 miles received the heavier steel rail by the end of summer 1887.

Along with the new rails came a replacement of the smaller wooden ties as part of

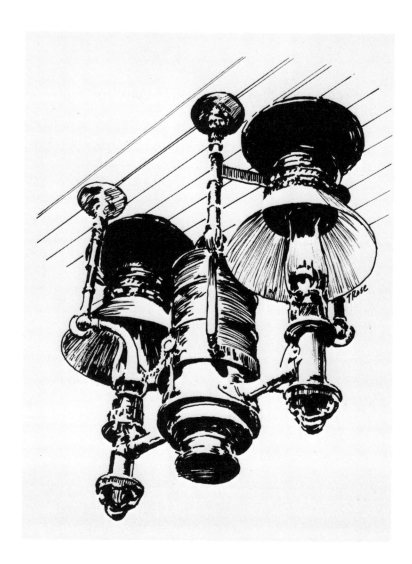

Ted Rose drew these oil lamps.

These trackmen worked out of one town and had more or less permanent assignments for a stretch of track, usually not more than 20 miles. No location came with this picture, but it is probably the 1880s when the Old Colony on Cape Cod used untreated ties and sand for ballast, and everybody - that is everybody - wore a hat. This handcar carried them to the work site.

the rebuilding program. In 1879 there were 193,000 new oak ties put down. Within three years new ties totaling 232,000 were placed from spring to that fall. And every year there were large orders for new rail and ties. By 1885 more than 458 miles of track were of the heavier steel. The Old Colony and the Cape Cod Railroad that it had bought had a total of 117 bridges and all were built of wood. The heavier trains required a change to iron and steel for these bridges, and so the modernization of the line included replacement of them, too. In late September, 1888 after the last train of the evening, a large gang of workmen began on a Saturday night to replace the Bass River bridge. First they tore out the wooden structure and put heavier stone in the abutments. By late Sunday morning they had iron beams in and by that night the main line had been put back on the new bridge. The schedule suffered no interruptions, since after the summer season there were no Sunday trains. On Monday morning the early train from Provincetown rolled slowly over the bridge before 7 o'clock as inspectors watched carefully. The first passage was uneventful and the bridge crew moved on to their next job.

The pay of skilled railroad men didn't change a great deal during most of the Old Colony's days given the number of years involved. Locomotive engineers were paid $1.97 a day in 1850; $2.03 in 1860; $3.35 in 1870; $3.30 in 1880 and $3.67 in 1890. For locomotive firemen their pay was $1.15 a day in 1850; $1.16 a day in 1860 and in 1870, 1880 and 1890 it was the same, $2.00 a day.

Passenger conductors were in charge of the train and their pay was the highest. In 1850, it was $2.30 a day; in 1860, $3.20 a day; by 1870 it reached $3.50 a day; ten years later it had risen only by two cents a day, and in 1890, because of business conditions it was reduced to $3.43 a day.

Passenger conductors were paid better than freight conductors for two reasons: their job was dealing with the public and the passenger side of the business was by far the most profitable. Freight conductors made only $1.68 a day in 1850; by 1860 their daily rate had dropped four cents to $1.64; by 1870 it had risen to $2.61; ten years later in 1880 it had dropped to $2.58 and by 1890 it had only risen two cents a day to $2.60.

Brakemen had the worst jobs on the railroad. Whether they worked passenger or freight they were paid the same daily rate. They were easily the hardest working crew members on passenger trains, and on freights they were riding the tops of box cars in all weather, turning brakewheels, and jumping on and off moving trains. For all those joyful experiences their pay was the lowest of anyone in train crews. In 1850 their daily pay was $1.11; ten years later it had risen to $1.22; by 1870 because of Civil War inflation it reached its peak in the nineteenth century, $2.00 a day; in 1880 it dropped to $1.90 and ten years later in 1890 it had dropped even further to $1.83. It seems unusual that brakemen who suffered more injuries and deaths on the job were paid the worst. Coupling cars was a constant hazard as we have seen. Racing along the tops of swaying freight cars at night had to be the most dangerous exercise in railroading. And the brakeman had to do it in response to the engineer's whistling for "down brakes." Another hazard while riding the tops of cars was posed by low bridges and other overhead obstacles. The railroads used to hang a series of a dozen or so ropes over the tracks up high on a horizontal line to warn men on top of cars they should duck down. These were called tell-tales and busy preoccupied brakemen either ignored or didn't feel their slap while passing. A steady number of accidents involved overhead obstacles sweeping brakemen off cars to either fall to the tracks and be run over or off to the side where they were sure to suffer some injury.

Brakemen regularly climbed on and off moving trains in the course of their work.

The accident reports the Old Colony Railroad filed annually with the State Senate listed the many injuries and deaths suffered by workers.

Among the many deaths and injuries reported there were some on the Cape. On December 21, 1881 George Burgess, a railroad employee, was injured at Wareham by coming in contact with an overhead bridge. On May 27, 1887, Sylvanus Freeman, a peddler, attempted to get off a train before it reached Bourne station had his right arm crushed. And the same year at Tremont on November 3, H.G. Baxter, a freight brakeman, fell from a car and was fatally injured. In 1878 within one week there were two serious accidents on the Cape. On December 14, a Mrs. Lutz stepped from a moving train at Sandwich station and had one foot crushed. On the 21st, a boy named George G. Copeland was run over by a train that crushed both his legs at Hyannis "when he was attempting to jump from a moving freight car upon which he had got a ride." He died as a result of those injuries. On February 2, 1882, a passenger on a moving Cape Cod train was killed at Quincy. William Jackson jumped from the platform of a car and struck his head against a stone wall, fracturing the base of his skull, which caused his death.

A startled horse bolted as a locomotive blew its whistle at a Harwich crossing. The horse headed across the tracks, but it was a tie. The engine struck the wagon, killing the driver and his horse.

The last year the Old Colony operated before it was leased to the New Haven was 1893. In its final accident report the Old Colony listed 25 of its train workers killed and 70 injured, many of them seriously. Railroading was dangerous work, and the job with the greatest danger was that of brakemen. And they were paid the least.

Among the public there were deaths and injuries, but most of them were caused by a complete disregard of common sense. Many railroad travelers, despite written warnings in the cars, routinely jumped on and off moving trains. In the days of open platforms on passenger trains people would walk between the cars while the train was moving. This was forbidden by the companies, but it was done anyway. Steel gates were put over the steps to keep passengers from leaving the cars early or late, but some travelers would unfasten them for a quicker exit or entrance. It earned some ticket holders a quick entrance to a cemetery. Others were injured in a fall.

Some members of the public treated the right of way as property to explore and enjoy. It may seem improbable, but people did just about everything you could imagine on railroad tracks: walking, running, sleeping, reading, relieving themselves. One could sometimes understand, as dangerous as it was, trying to beat a train to a grade crossing while on foot, a bicycle or on a horse. But too many accidents on the tracks were caused by just plain mindlessness, and in a few cases by suicidal impulses. As dangerous as railroads could be for company employees, they were even more dangerous for the public. In 1893 a total of 34 people died on Old Colony rights of way by leaping on and off moving trains or walking or otherwise being on tracks and hit by trains. Another 21 were injured from the same behavior.

The Old Colony had to pay for injuries as well as death benefits if the railroad was at fault. Shippers had to be reimbursed for damaged in-transit merchandise. Steam locomotives set fires in meadows and woodlands on a regular basis during dry seasons. Sometimes buildings burned up and the railroad had to pay.

On December 1, 1875 the superintendent of the Cape Cod Division, Charles H. Nye, approved a payment of $10 for injuring a cow belonging to Elisha Rich in South Truro. On October 7 of that year the cow was struck by a locomotive. The cow died from

When the Cape Cod Central built to Orleans in the last year of the Civil War, the crossing of the Bass River required a major fill from both banks out to stone abutments which support the deck truss bridge. The original bridge was wood. This steel bridge replaced it. The train is heading east toward South Dennis and Harwich.

injuries and Rich was reimbursed.

The Old Colony's roster of motive power was heavy with New England products. Besides its own shops that turned out locomotives in South Boston, the two builders in Taunton - Mason Machine Works and Taunton Locomotive Works - supplied many engines. Most of the Boston companies sold to the Old Colony, such as Hinkley, John Souther and Jabez Coney. Other suppliers were Lawrence Machine Works, Manchester Locomotive Works and the Rhode Island Locomotive Works in Providence. The best known company in America, Baldwin Locomotive Works of Philadelphia, only built four engines for the Old Colony.

Most of the machines were American type, 4-4-0s, the standard of the nineteenth century, which the Old Colony used for all kinds of work - passenger, freight and switching. For fast freight use the Old Colony built a few 2-6-0, Mogul types, in the early 1890s, but that was hardly a daring experiment since the Mogul was introduced in the 1860s.

The rugged looking standard engines of the Old Colony were the work of James N. Lauder, superintendent of motive power who designed them. It was he who got rid of the long-time custom of naming locomotives and assigning them to a particular engineer and his fireman. No doubt that old way had created a feeling of tender loving care by the cab crew for their machine, and interest by the public, but Lauder changed the system to simply putting numbers on locomotives and assigning crew to trains that had engines coupled on the front by what was available. The names vanished and the numbers appeared in 1884.

There had to have been some broken hearts from the days of "driving my engine." That move to numbers was a corporate one and away from the personal touch of the past. And with it something was lost.

In 1874 there were 64 steam locomotives on the roster. By 1876 there were 69 and within four years there were 109, and by 1886 the list had grown to 133 to include 74 passenger, 41 freight and 18 switchers. The growth included those under lease when the Old Colony leased another line and added its equipment to the parent company. For example the 212 locomotives listed in 1888 represented the 146 machines owned and 66 under lease.

The new engines on order were larger as the weight for road locomotives grew from 40 tons to 48 tons. Costs, too, increased as prices climbed from $7,300 each in 1872 to $8,400 in 1890.

Older and smaller rolling stock was annually replaced by new and heavier equipment with larger capacity. The 162 passenger, baggage and express cars of 1874 had increased to 268 by 1880. Within six years that passenger equipment list totaled 309 with its 255 passenger cars, 12 parlor cars and 42 baggage, express and mail cars.

Trains were longer, too, as the four and five car passenger units of the past grew to average seven cars each, which included a baggage and express car behind the locomotive, five day coaches and a parlor car. Some trains added a baggage and express car which had a section for mail sorting along the way, as the railroads became the principal means of handling intercity mail with their R.P.O. cars. So seven car passenger trains were the average, but ten car trains were seen, especially for excursions and times of traditionally heavy travel around holidays.

Heavy travel to Martha's Vineyard and Nantucket on Fridays in the summer often required as many as 15 coaches pulled by two locomotives to Woods Hole. Yarmouth Camp Meetings attracted thousands in the summer where doubleheading was necessary to pull up to 16 coaches.

Freight trains were also longer. The 21 car freights of the early 1870s had reached on average 30 cars in 1880 and 33 cars in 1883, which was more or less the maximum into the early 1890s.

The roster of freight equipment also grew in size as the success of the Old Colony continued through the decades of the 1870s and 80s. The line listed 1,224 freight cars, mostly boxes and flats, in 1874. By 1882 the number reached 2,159 and in 1888 the total was 3,184.

One number that remained almost constant was the dividend. Most years it was 7 percent on the par value of $100 a share. A few years in the early 80s it was 6 percent, but then it had a nine year run of 7 percent that dropped to 6.4 in 1892 and rose to 9.58 in 1893, the last year of Old Colony's independent existence before the road was leased by the New York New Haven & Hartford.

When the Old Colony bought the Cape Cod Railroad it took over a line that ran two passenger trains a day from Boston to Provincetown. These trains did not change times. The morning train left Kneeland Street at 8 and split at Cohasset Narrows for Woods Hole. It was met at Yarmouth by a shuttle train for Hyannis and continued on to Provincetown where it arrived at 1:40 that afternoon. That was train #1 as all trains leaving Boston were given odd numbers. So #1 took five hours and 40 minutes to cover the 120 miles. The next train was #3, leaving Boston at 11:30 a.m. for Cohasset Narrows at 1:35 p.m. Passengers could change for a Woods Hole local from Cohasset Narrows that reached "The Hole," as railroad men called it, at 2:10 p.m. The next train from Boston was #5, leaving Kneeland Street at 4 p.m. where again it dropped off the rear cars, or split, at Cohasset Narrows for Woods Hole. The #5 continued to Yarmouth where passengers for Hyannis changed to a shuttle train, usually a locomotive and one car, sometimes two. The main line train continued out to Provincetown, leaving off the evening mail and newspapers plus express shipments at every station where there was a depot master. This was the evening train that was met by so many Cape Codders who walked down to the station in town after town to watch it come in and then hike over to the post office to see if there was anything in the lock box. With all the stops #5 took four hours and 55 minutes to reach Provincetown, which was less by 45 minutes than #1 took in the morning. The last train from Boston, #7, left at 6 p.m. and again left the rear cars at Cohasset Narrows where they became a Woods Hole local, reaching there by 9:23, a few minutes before the last steamer left for the Vineyard and Nantucket. She arrived at Hyannis at 9:40.

From Provincetown the first of the two daily trains for Boston left the Cape tip at 5:10 a.m. as #4, even-numbered trains were always inbound, and took five hours and a quarter to reach Kneeland Street at 10:25. The other train left Provincetown at 12:20 p.m. as #8 and arrived at Kneeland Street at 6 p.m. Hyannis had service three times a day from Boston, two of which were shuttle trains from Yarmouth. Woods Hole and the other stations on that branch had the best service with four trains a day each way, except in the morning when there was an additional train to Cohasset Narrows.

Through the 1870s and 80s the schedule changed slightly on the twice a day service through to Provincetown. The morning train left Boston 15 minutes later than before; it became the 8:15. The afternoon train from Boston left ten minutes later at 4:10. On the Hyannis Branch there were four passenger trains a day, but only two made connections at Yarmouth for Boston.

The Old Colony heavily promoted its passenger services and on all timetables, billboards and newspaper advertisements the Cape and Islands were prominently mentioned. Its summer business that stressed traveling to New England on the Fall River Line was included in annual booklets that listed every Cape and Island town and village where there were summer hotels and guest houses. The price of the railroad tickets was listed along with the daily rates at the hotels and guest houses, plus the distance from the station and the public conveyances available to reach them.

Older maps and railroad timetables had two spellings for Woods Hole, sometimes making it Woods Holl. The story goes that the change in name to Holl was brought about by the first summer resident, one Joseph S. Fay, who first came there in 1850. Fay was interested in the name hole and guessed it to be a local term that came from the Icelandic word holl. which means a small hill. Fay thought the word was evidence of explorations by Vikings who are reputed to have visited the New England Coast long before anyone else. Fay made his feelings into a cause and in 1877 convinced the United States Post Office to change the name to Woods Holl. It remained that way until changed back to Woods Hole nineteen years later. In 1896 the time tables, the maps and the name boards on the station at the end of the branch all read the same - Woods Hole.

The last year of independent corporate existence for the Old Colony before it was leased by the New York New Haven & Hartford, saw this highly successful Massachusetts business at its height. It long ago had reached a degree of success that enabled it to grow and modernize constantly. Everything about the Old Colony - its size, its equipment, its traffic, its finances, its steamboat company, its number of employees - increased.

This American type locomotive is a good study of the archetypal steam power of the nineteenth century...solid, powerful, a tool for work. When built in 1887 she was named *Stoughton* by the Old Colony, which was before locomotive names were dropped and numbers were added. She was built by the Hinkley Locomotive Works in Boston as one of the last engines they produced. Of course, Hinkley was to New England railroad operations as Gillette was to New England beards - well known.

In 1893 the total length of track owned was 858 miles, which included 369 miles of main line: Boston to Plymouth, Provincetown, New Bedford and Newport and from Taunton to Fitchburg and Framingham to Lowell.

The company-owned branches such as Woods Hole with its 17.54 miles of single track, Hyannis with five miles of single track and Fairhaven with 15 miles of single track were part of the 126 miles not considered part of the main line.

The Old Colony also operated branches under lease or contract. On Cape Cod that meant the seven miles of single track from Harwich to Chatham that was a contract with the Chatham Railroad Company and the 12 miles of the Fall River Railroad; the seven miles of the Nantasket Beach; the 63 miles of the Boston & Providence; the 15 miles of the Plymouth & Middleborough; the 14 miles of the Providence, Warren & Bristol and the four miles of the Attleboro Branch. The rent for the Chatham Branch was $2,839.79 for the year ending June 30, 1893.

The company's gross was $9,401,885 that final year and its net profit of $1,428,837 made for a 7.58 percent dividend. The total permanent investment was $26,790,093. Its bonded debt was $12,576,200. Its roster of employees reached a new high of 7,231.

Its motive power and rolling stock had increased to 250 steam locomotives with 158 passenger engines, 54 freight engines and 38 switch engines. Passenger and freight engines averaged 56 tons each in weight and all but seven freight locomotives were equipped with Westinghouse air brakes. There were 544 cars in passenger service, including coaches, combination cars and baggage, mail and express cars. All of this rolling stock had air brakes and the safer Miller platforms and patent couplers. The Old Colony's modernization program was converting its freight cars to air brakes too. Out of 3,097 cars, 560 had Westinghouse air brakes with orders for equipping half those with hand brakes to be converted within a year.

The heavier engines and rolling stock required better road beds and, of course, heavier rail. The main line contained all steel rails as did most of the branches, owned and leased. The newer rail was 70 and 78 pounds to the yard and was laid on larger oak ties for stability and longer life.

The greatest income was accomplished with lower ticket prices. Rail travelers were paying on average two cents a mile on regular coach tickets and .733 mills per mile on commutation tickets. On interchange tickets to and from other railroads, the per mile average was 1.985 cents.

The railroad's highly successful Old Colony Steamboat Company had received its new giant of Long Island Sound, the *Puritan* in 1889. She was 420 feet long and had the first steel hull on the Sound. She was the first with feathering paddlewheels and powered by the largest beam engine ever built. As the first four-deck steamer of the Fall River Line, she had 321 staterooms.

The Fall River Line was so heavily traveled that the Old Colony ordered another vessel that was completed a year after *Puritan*. The *Plymouth* was designed for winter service and was built at the same yard as *Puritan*: Delaware River Iron Shipbuilding & Engine Works at Chester, Pennsylvania. *Plymouth* entered the overnight service at New York on November 6, 1890. In its last year of operating the Fall River Line, the Old Colony ordered the steamboat that was to become the most famous vessel in Long Island Sound history - *Priscilla*. Her friends and admirers numbered in the millions and her fame was literally world wide.

To the 1893 World's Fair at Chicago the Old Colony sent this equipment: the largest engine is #252, built the year before by the Manchester Locomotive Works in New Hampshire, next is the inside-connected *Daniel Mason* from the railroad's earliest days. The stagecoach on wheels at the far right of the picture is the historic passenger coach of the Boston & Providence Railroad and used first in 1833 and typical of the day coaches of her time. The Old Colony had taken over the B & P a few years before this picture was taken, and in fact shortly afterward the New Haven leased the Old Colony.

One of the last locomotives the Old Colony built in 1893 at its South Boston shops was #89, completed the same year the New Haven leased the Old Colony. A heavy engine at 57 tons, she ran on the New Haven until 1922.

Above These boys are Cape Verdeans selling flowers to departing passengers from the Harwich station. This was a Sunday afternoon ritual during the summer so many years ago.

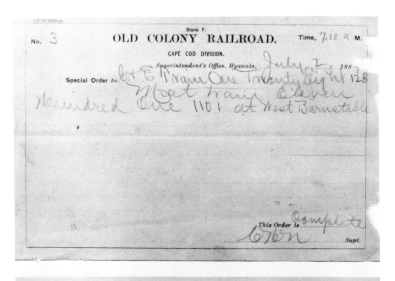

Right The telegraph had a key and a sounder in so many stations that it was the natural means of sending train orders. These two examples from the late 1880s are from Hyannis (top) and from Boston (below). Clear instructions were vital on single track lines such as the Cape had. When a conductor received a train order he read it to the engineer who read it to the firemen and each of them in turn read it back aloud.

OLD COLONY RAILROAD.

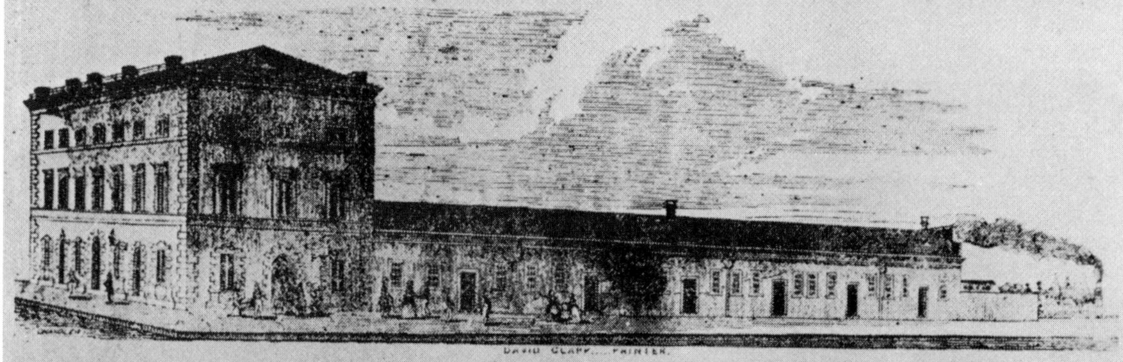

DEPOT CORNER OF SOUTH AND KNEELAND STREETS.

ON AND AFTER FRIDAY, APRIL 6, 1849,

Trains will leave Daily (Sundays excepted) as follows.

Boston for Plymouth and Bridgewater, 7¾ A.M., 5.20 P.M.

Boston for Quincy and Braintree, 7¾, 8¾ A.M., 1½, 2½, 4¼, 5.20, 6¼, 9¼ P.M.

Boston for Weymouth, Hingham and Cohasset, 8¾ A.M., 2½, 6¼, 9¼ P.M.

Boston for Dorchester and Milton, 7⅓, 9¾ A.M., 1¼, 2¾, 5½, 7 P.M.

Boston for Fall River and Cape Cod Railroads, 7¾ A.M., 4¾ P.M.

Boston for New York (Steamboat Train), 5 P.M.

Plymouth for Boston and Bridgewater, 6½ A.M., 4¼ P.M.

Bridgewater for Boston, 6.52 A.M., 4.35 P.M.

Bridgewater for Plymouth, 8½ A.M., 6 P.M.

Cohasset for Boston, 6¼, 7¼, 11 A.M., 4 P.M.

Dorchester and Milton for Boston, 6¾, 8.10, 10½ A.M., 2, 4½, 6¼ P.M.

JOS. H. MOORE, ***Sup't.***

Boston, April 6, 1849.

A woodcut of the Kneeland Street Station was used for many years on Old Colony timetables. The two daily trains in 1849 for the Cape Cod connection at Middleboro are listed on the fifth line down.

KNEELAND STREET STATION

The Kneeland Street Station was the terminus of the Old Colony in Boston and its corporate headquarters from 1847. The railroad had built a smaller station that it quickly outgrew after a year's use. That area of the city was filled land as was so much of Boston. The mud flats were filled in 1842 in the space bound by Kneeland, South and Cove Streets.

The building, constructed for $39,000, was three stories high with the ground floor for passengers and the two above for offices. The structure was of brick, fronting on Kneeland Street and was 544 feet long by 113 feet wide. This front area was called the head-house; to the back was the car-house "for the shelter and occupation of trains arriving and departing, and of passengers when they enter and leave the cars," said the company in an annual report to stockholders.

Twenty years after its construction it was extensively rebuilt in 1867 to serve a successful and expanding business. In the front of the head-house on Kneeland Street, according to that report, "are two doorways communicating with a hall of one hundred and twenty-five feet in length by twenty-nine feet wide, and twenty-two feet high." On the west side of the building on South Street was a gentlemen's room, a newspaper stand, a hackmen's room, a baggage room, and a water fountain. Above all of this on the west side was a half story containing a kitchen with a pantry attached and a dining room. On the east side was an area almost exclusively for women passengers: a ladies' waiting room, a ladies' retiring room, a ladies' package depository, a public restaurant with a ladies' restaurant attached, an "inward" baggage room, a telegraph office and a ticket office. The restaurant opened upon the main hall from Kneeland Street and had a vestibule for passengers waiting to take horse cars or other vehicles. At the south end of the main hall was a clock with two faces for those looking from either direction.

The half story of the east wing contained a station agent's room, a conductor's room, and apartments for ticket agents. The head-house fronting on Kneeland Street held the offices of the Old Colony president, treasurer, superintendent, auditor, clerks and secretaries. Those were on the second floor, while the third floor had a committee room, a hall for stockholder's meetings and a storage room for company documents. The entire head-house was heated by steam and lighted by city gas.

The car-house for the trains was divided into three areas in width by two rows of columns which had a clerestory with upright walls with windows for its entire length. The roof over this was circular and had a ventilator the whole length of the car-house to allow the smoke from locomotives to escape. Across the head of the tracks was a platform on the north end of 112 by 25 feet. That platform was separated from the rest of the car-house by an open fence with gates to allow passengers to and from the trains to pass. There were four platforms of 20 foot width each parallel to the four tracks, two for entering trains and the other for departing. Each track entered the car-house through a large, arched opening. The center corridor, with a domed ceiling, ran from Kneeland Street more than 600 feet to the rear of the car-house.

The exterior clock tower was placed to be seen from Summer Street through South

Street. The clock face was illuminated by gas, as the company put it, "to give notice of the hour to approaching passengers and others in the night-time." The Old Colony Railroad, in a mood of almost constant self-congratulation, wrote to its stockholders "the original head-house, which has been so successfully re-used as a part of the new building, has always been considered a well-proportioned structure, of more than ordinary merit in architectural taste." A large brass bell warned passengers of imminent departures - two rings meant two minutes and one ring at leaving time. Along various walls were posted maps and timetables of the different lines. The entire Old Colony Railroad was in heavy black and connecting railroads were thinner. On weekday afternoons between four and six there was a steady, unbroken line of people moving through the station to their trains. The north end of this Boston landmark faced Kneeland Street with its intersections from South to Cove Streets. To go to Boston on an Old Colony train was a trip to Kneeland Street Station.

OLD COLONY RAILROAD
CAPE COD DIVISION.

Summer Arrangement

On and after MONDAY, June 22, 1874,

Passenger Trains will run as follows:

DOWN TRAINS.

LEAVE	No. 1 A.M.	No. 3 A.M.	No. 5 P.M.	No. 7 P.M.
Boston,	8.00	11.30	4.00	°6.00
Middleboro,	9.39	12.55	5.18	7.36
Rock,	9.52			7.46
So. Middleboro,	9.59			7.53
Tremont,	10.09	1.16	5.40	8.00
So. Wareham,	10.14			8.05
Wareham,	10.23	1.25	5.49	8.12
Agawam,	10.29		5.54	8.19
Cohasset Narrows,	10.40	1.35	6.04	8.28
Monument,	10.45			8.32
No. Sandwich,	10.52			8.41
West Sandwich,	10.57			8.47
Sandwich,	11.07		6.25	8.55
West Barnstable,	11.25		6.41	9.15
Barnstable,	11.34		6.51	9.24
Yarmouth,	11.44		7.00	9.30
Hyannis, (arrive)	11.54		7.10	9.40
So. Yarmouth,	11.55		7.11	
So. Dennis,	11.59		7.15	
	P.M.			
No. Harwich,	12.04		7.20	
Harwich,	12.09		7.25	
Brewster,	12.19		7.35	
East Brewster,	12.24		7.40	
Orleans,	12.30		7.47	
Eastham,	12.38		7.55	
No. Eastham,	12.44		8.01	
So. Wellfleet,	12.52		8.08	
Wellfleet,	1.00		8.17	
So. Truro,	1.09		8.25	
Truro,	1.16		8.31	
No. Truro,	1.25		8.40	
Provincetown (arr.)	1.40		8.55	

UP TRAINS.

LEAVE	No. 2 A.M.	No. 4 A.M.	No. 6 P.M.	No. 8 P.M.
Provincetown,		5.10		12.20
No. Truro,		5.24		12.34
Truro,		5.32		12.42
So. Truro,		5.37		12.48
Wellfleet,		5.46		1.00
So. Wellfleet,		5.53		1.06
No. Eastham,		6.00		1.13
Eastham,		6.08		1.21
Orleans,		6.16		1.29
East Brewster,		6.21		1.34
Brewster,		6.29		1.42
Harwich,		6.40		1.53
No. Harwich,		6.45		1.58
So. Dennis,		6.50		2.03
So. Yarmouth,		6.54		2.07
Hyannis,	‡5.15	6.55		2.07
Yarmouth,	5.24	7.10		2.22
Barnstable,	5.31	7.17		2.29
West Barnstable,	5.41	7.27		2.39
Sandwich,	6.00	7.43		2.58
West Sandwich,	6.07			3.05
No. Sandwich,	6.12			3.10
Monument,	6.19			3.17
Cohasset Narrows,	6.24	8.07	12.05	3.26
Agawam,	6.32	8.14		3.33
Wareham,	6.37	8.20	12.16	3.40
So. Wareham,	6.44			3.46
Tremont,	6.49	8.35	12.27	3.55
So. Middleboro,	6.58			4.03
Rock,	7.05			4.10
Middleboro,	7.20	9.05	12.55	4.25
Boston, (arrive)	8.57	10.25	2.22	6.02

*(vertical notes: †Mondays only; between Hyannis and Sandwich. / *Saturdays only; between Sandwich and Hyannis.)*

WOODS HOLE BRANCH.

DOWN TRAINS.

LEAVE	No. 1 A.M.	No. 3 A.M.	No. 5 P.M.	No. 7
Boston,	8.00	11.30	4.00	
Cohasset Narrows,	10.41	1.36	6.05	
Pocasset,	10.50		6.13	
North Falmouth,	10.56		6.19	
West Falmouth,	11.04		6.27	
Falmouth,	11.12	2.02	6.36	
Woods Hole, (arr.)	11.20	2.10	6.45	

UP TRAINS.

LEAVE	No. 2	No. 4 A.M.	No. 6 P.M.	No. 8 P.M.
Woods Hole,		7.20	11.30	2.35
Falmouth,		7.29	11.38	2.44
West Falmouth,		7.38		2.53
North Falmouth,		7.46		3.02
Pocasset,		7.52		3.10
Cohasset Narrows,		8.07	12.05	3.26
Boston, (arrive)		10.25	2.22	6.02

The summer schedule from 1874 was typical of timetables posted in and around railroad stations. Buzzards Bay is still listed as Cohasset Narrows, but was changed shortly afterwards. These schedules measured 24" by 13".

DUDE TRAIN

Cape Cod had a private subscription train for 32 years that was used by Boston businessmen to take them and their families to and from their summer homes on Buzzards Bay. These wealthy men approached the management of the Old Colony Railroad in the winter of 1884 about chartering a passenger train for them and their friends to be run during the summer months - roughly June 1 to October 1.

For these men the regular trains just took too long, stopping too often. Regularly scheduled trains took just under three hours from Woods Hole to Boston, that is, ten minutes under three hours. The trip covered 72 miles.

A price was worked out by the Old Colony based on cost of crew, usual return on equipment and rules on tariffs set by the Massachusetts Railroad Commission. The special, private train would start that spring, and it did although later than planned; its first run was June 23. The train consisted of three cars, the first was a combination baggage and smoker, followed by two drawing room cars. The first locomotive on the train was the *Foxboro*, # 100, a 14-year old machine, a typical American type from the Rhode Island Locomotive Works with 66 inch drivers. The cars were plush and fit for wealthy patrons, while the engine was quite ordinary and without distinction. The three car consist was the minimum.

The train quickly became known as the *Dude*, a name applied, apparently, by the first conductor, Harry Meyers, who had started railroading with the New Bedford and Taunton in 1871 and with the Old Colony in 1875 following one of the frequent mergers that created the system. The term dude usually referred to city-bred men who were concerned about their clothes, appearance and manners. That certainly fit the wealthy men who owned companies or were bankers and investment people or perhaps scions of moneyed families or who just married well. It had always been true that one can acquire wealth by patrimony or matrimony. However they got their money, they had it and used some to buy land and build estates along the shores of Buzzards Bay from just across the Monument River at Cohasset Narrows to various places all the way south to Woods Hole and to the Islands.

Such people were referred to as Boston Bluebloods and their names read like this: Beebe, Forbes, Fay, Parkinson, Weld, Minot, Eustis, Wilson, Paine, Ditmar, Bartol and Baxendale. Some of them built their palatial summer homes around Marion and Mattapoisett on the north shore of Buzzards Bay, an area that could be reached by the Fairhaven Branch Railroad, but not by the *Dude*, at least not at first.

The *Dude* was chartered to its riders who formed a group known as the Train Club or Club for short. This club had a small executive committee who negotiated annually with the Old Colony and, after 1893, with the New Haven. The committee signed a contract with the line, guaranteeing a minimum income from the train of $22,185 for each season. Club members paid $100 for each family member and bought tickets based on the regular fares charged for their trip. The members could bring family packages, including suitcases or trunks up to 60 pounds for no extra charge. Larger baggage was charged at regular rates as were pets, including horses and sometimes their carriages brought to the western end of the Cape for the summer. Later the annual fee was increased and each member and his family bought season tickets at the lower, commutation rate.

One of the earliest and one of the many locomotives that hauled the *Dude Train* was #1 of the Old Colony. This photo dates from the 1880s.

The *Flying Dude* always stopped at Cataumet where wealthy Bostonians had summer homes overlooking Buzzards Bay. This is the original depot with its gingerbread and church windows. All depots in those days had platforms made from wide, wooden planks. The train is heading for Boston in this photo.

Here is Augustus S. Messer, the *Dude's* conductor for 14 years, the man most closely associated with the train. The car behind him is one of those plush drawing room cars that were the only passenger cars the *Dude* ever used to bring wealthy home owners for easy summer days from Wareham to Woods Hole, where some of them took a steamer for the islands. Messer wore that uniform of his office for 32 years and all of it on the Boston to Woods Hole Branch.

The *Dude* was an express train that stopped only when a passenger told the conductor. The train never stopped before Tempest Knob, which was just below Wareham, where there were many summer homes of train club members. House guests were frequent riders, and they had to present an invitation card signed by a subscriber and show a ticket, too. The *Dude* was a private train that ran roughly from June 1 to October 1 on weekdays only. Its schedule varied but at first it left Boston at 3:10 p.m. and reached Woods Hole at 4:50, a one hour and forty minute trip. The best time on the run was between Brockton and Middleboro with so much straight track that 60 miles an hour was the standard. It was that part of the run that enabled the train to do so well overall. In the morning the run to Boston took five minutes longer. Out of Woods Hole at 7:40 a.m., the train reached Kneeland Street at 9:25.

The public couldn't ride the train and that exclusivity plus its speed created an aura. Today we'd call it mystique. The speed of its trip soon had given it an adjective *Flying* before *Dude*. The crew took special pride in their assignment by keeping the cars and the engine polished, even gleaming. Nothing in the records indicates they were paid extra, besides the boost to their egos of working a private express train - the only one on the line.

The stops after Tempest Knob were Buzzards Bay (formerly Cohasset Narrows), Monument Beach, Cataumet, West Falmouth, Falmouth and Woods Hole. After the railroad built a station at Gray Gables for President Grover Cleveland, that stop was added. The sign that was hung next to the track at Kneeland Street station in Boston indicating the *Dude*, is now at the Gray Gables station moved to the site of the Aptuxcet Trading Post in Bourne.

In 1892 after eight seasons the *Dude* added a second section, another train that followed and turned at Tremont off the main line and stopped at Marion, Mattapoisett and Fairhaven. Four years later the two trains were joined with the Fairhaven Branch cars dropped off at Tremont and picked up by another locomotive that for those 15 miles, at least, became another *Dude*.

Elmer Landers of Cataumet worked around the station there as a youth, delivering telegrams, polishing lenses on switch stands, taking the mail to the post office and to the trains. He recalls the *Dude*. "Those passengers had the privilege of bringing down all kinds of edibles with them," he said. "They'd be piled up on the platform next to the baggage door on the first car. One day there was a leg of lamb on top of the pile, and a dog took a liking to it and he took off with it, and the station agent right after him; he never did catch the dog."

Like a lot of other people, Landers dreamed about a ride on the *Dude*, probably because it was so difficult. "I had to wait a long time to get a ride on the *Dude*," he said, "because the conductor had such an eagle eye. There was a time when I climbed on the back car and rode to Buzzards Bay and nobody knew about it. I was out on the back platform all the way to Buzzards Bay. Wow! Were we moving! Trains always stopped there, because it was a junction. I hopped off and walked away, so don't say anything about it." Elmer Watson Landers told the author that story in February, 1978. He died the following year in August at 83. It was unusual to get such a ride on the *Dude*, and I haven't said anything about it, Elmer, until now.

In the season of 1890, the seventh for the *Dude*, a new conductor joined the crew. He was Augustus S. Messer and no stranger to the Woods Hole Branch, having been in charge of the first train on the line in July, 1872. That was his first assignment as a conductor and he served on that branch with trains to and from Boston until his appointment to the *Dude* 18 years later. Messer was a huge man with walrus mustache, a vast stomach and all supported by big feet. The vest of his official, railroad uniform had the usual brass buttons and gold watch chain. The outer blue coat - regulation as prescribed by the general manager - was not wide enough to cover his ponderous girth, so he buttoned the top button which was less than a foot beneath his chin and allowed the rest to separate over his stomach in an inverted V. He mixed easily with the passengers - bankers, manufacturers, importers, insurance executives, shipping magnates and others of wealth - and their families. In a business suit he would have looked like one of them; with some gold braid and a different hat he could have passed as a steamboat captain on the Fall River Line. By company rules the conductor had general charge of the train, and according to the written regulations, "he must be polite and obliging..see that order and decorum are preserved in the cars." Augustus S. Messer looked like order and decorum. There was one time, according to Elmer Landers, when Messer was less than his dignified self. "Yes, that was the time the *Dude* took off for Falmouth and Woods Hole without him. He was left standing on the Cataumet platform, waving at the train. The engineer had to back up almost a mile. Messer climbed back on, an embarrassed and distressed conductor," said Landers.

The *Dude* Train's equipment during the other eight months of the year ran between Boston and Taunton by way of Quincy and Braintree. In 1904 the New Haven Railroad ordered five cars from the Pullman Company to use on the *Dude*. Three of them were parlor cars and each cost $16,800. The other two were combination baggage and parlor - smoking cars for the head end. The New Haven paid $13,700 for each. To Pullman the whole order was worth $77,800. The five cars arrived in South Boston on May 11 and were made up as the *Dude* Train that began the new season Friday afternoon, May 20, 1904.

A new train, a new season, and the fourteenth year for its venerable conductor, Augustus S. Messer, and the twentieth year for the *Dude* Train. An exciting day for everyone involved, perhaps too exciting for Messer who suffered a stroke. It was fatal. He had served as a conductor from Boston to Woods Hole for the 32 years the branch had existed. Those years made him the oldest conductor in point of service on the New Haven Railroad. He lived at a time that set great store by continuity of office. For 14 years he was the *Dude* Train to his passengers and to those who watched it. He was a good old gentlemen who made the run his own. Augustus Messer was a railroad man who took pride in his work, as he wore for those 32 years his dark blue coat of office with a fresh pink daily in its buttonhole. He died in harness and his memory is still green in New England.

The private express train rolled on - a money-maker for the New Haven - until the railroad ran its last *Dude* Train on October 2, 1916. It was the end of the thirty-second season. World War I had raged since the summer of 1914 with no certainty that America could continue to stay out of the conflict. In such an atmosphere the New Haven announced that the *Dude* would not run again until the emergency was over. The following year America entered the war until its conclusion in November 1918.

In the first months of 1919 the old committee from the Train Club met several times with New Haven officials in Boston. The railroad proposed continuing the *Dude* as a subscription express train, but its cost would be twice the previous guarantee with higher ticket prices. The committee took the proposal to previous members, but there was not enough interest. It never ran again. The *Dude* Train was different. It ran for 32 years from Boston to the Cape and back on weekdays in the warm weather. It was fast, elitist and had an undemocratic social aloofness to it.

THE FALL RIVER LINE TO CAPE COD

At the very end of the nineteenth century the New York, New Haven & Hartford Railroad had put together a monopoly of all the steamship lines and railroads that ran between New York and Boston. The railroad was controlled by J. P. Morgan who had the financial influence to remove any and all competition.

Before the Civil War, the railroads of southern New England were primarily lines that fed passengers and freight to the steamers. Those small railroads ran from inland manufacturing towns down the river valleys to Long Island Sound or to Narragansett Bay. But the affluence created by the war and its aftermath was a boon to the railroads, which enjoyed unprecedented growth and attracted great amounts of new capital, making the railroad industry one of this country's most prosperous. By the end of the war the steamboat lines were extensions of the railroads.

This was what the system had turned into in a relatively few years. For it had started in 1822 when Robert Fulton of Hudson River fame had started sending his steamers through Long Island Sound and up Narragansett Bay to Providence where passengers caught a stage coach to Boston. For that 45 mile trip behind horses, it took six hours. Steamers plied that route to Providence for the next 120 years. Before Fulton's boats, New York and Boston were linked by several stage lines that consumed four long days on the road and three short nights of sleep at inns en route. The travelers arrived late on the fourth day, feeling more dead than alive from such an endurance test.

Fulton began to provide the badly needed improvement in transportation that New York and New England needed. In 1835, with the Railway Age barely under way the completion of the Boston & Providence Railroad provided a two hour train trip to and from the steamers, while reducing the land journey to one third of what it had been. The stages had to go elsewhere for business. By this time, 1835, the steamers were making the run between New York and Providence in 12 hours. This route was the way to go, but it didn't last in popularity because just two years later another railroad was completed between Stonington, Connecticut and Providence. This new line used the amazingly ambitious title of New York, Providence & Boston. Steamboats were put on the run from Manhattan to Stonington, making for an eight hour trip, passengers leaving New York at 6 p.m. and arriving at Stonington at 2 a.m. and traveling to Providence by train for two hours. The station of the New York, Providence & Boston was in the west side of Providence and a ferry trip across the Providence River was necessary to reach the Boston & Providence station where one got on a train for the final leg of the trip, arriving in Boston at 6:30 a.m. That time was an earlier arrival by several hours over the steamer trip directly to Providence, but that saving was enough to make the Stonington trip more popular, even with those middle-of-the-night moves.

A few years later another steamship line opened between New York and Norwich, Connecticut, but the railroad connection was north to Worcester and the area served was above Boston and to the west and never became a factor in the growing Boston-New York competition.

The primacy of the Stonington route to New England was to last ten years, and what ended that dominance was to create a new gateway to New England. It was a railroad and a steamship line.

Colonel Richard Borden and other Fall River, Massachusetts businessmen had created the Fall River Branch Railroad which was quickly consolidated with several other small roads that together gave the Fall River Railroad a line to the Old Colony and over those tracks a route into Boston. In 1847, the owners of the Fall River Railroad placed a brand new steamboat, *Bay State,* on the route from Fall River to New York. The *Bay State* was the largest inland water ship in America. The Fall River Line was born and for almost 91 years it not only dominated the Long Island Sound steamship business, but it became world famous as the standard by which overnight boats were compared.

In 1854 the Fall River and Old Colony Railroads combined, and the new company owned a line from Boston to Fall River and connected with the Cape Cod Railroad at Middleboro. The Cape Cod connected at Tremont with the brand new Fair Haven Branch which connected to New Bedford by ferry at Fair Haven. From Fair Haven there was a three day a week steamer to Martha's Vineyard. The Cape Cod had recently completed its expansion from Sandwich to Hyannis where a steamer offered daily service to Nantucket. From Boston a daily train ran right out on the pier at Fall River. A few steps from the train to the gangplank and one was on a Fall River steamer. The train was the longest scheduled passenger train in American history - over 90 years.

The train was called the *Fall River Line Express* and sometimes in company timetables The *Fall River Line Special,* but most people called it The Boat Train with the boats always being Fall River steamers. During the 90 years the train and boats ran there were three stations used in Boston: the first was the Kneeland Street Station from 1847 to 1890; next came the Park Square Station from 1890 to 1899, and finally the huge South Station from 1899 to 1937. The Old Colony Railroad put some of its best equipment on the run, since for many years the railroad seemed to exist to take passengers and freight to and from the steamboats. The boat train at first left Boston at 5 p.m. In 1856 the departure was changed to 5:30 p.m. and in 1875 it was set back a half hour to 6 p.m., where it remained for 62 years - right up to the end.

Perhaps its most unusual cars were two British-type passenger cars, the ultimate in American travel, but not for the train crews who had to go outside the cars to move from one to another as they did not have platforms on the ends like American day coaches. They were on the line for several years and considered a novelty by travelers. They were given the distinction of numbers 1 and 2. The latter was destroyed in 1878 in the Wollaston wreck; #1 was sold to a Canadian railroad.

Parlor cars were regularly part of each boat train and the Old Colony owned a number of them. Two of the better known were *Pilgrim* and *Puritan* after the Fall River steamers of the same names. In the 1890s the Pullman Company provided the parlor cars *Violet* and *Pansy* to the train. The conductor who was on that run for more than 30 years was Asa Porter who had the knack of remembering names and recognizing travelers who used the boats. He rode the train from Boston accompanied by a key man, carrying a large board containing stateroom keys which were distributed to passengers on the train, a convenience that eliminated waiting at the purser's window in the entrance hall of the steamer. Some writers say Porter made the Fall River Line. Maybe. Up to his death in 1896 his charm and courtesy certainly helped build friendship and good will for the line.

The Old Colony used a number of locomotives on the boat train, among them the

Above One of the first locomotives to pull the boat train was the *Randolph*. The train left Kneeland Street Station in Boston over the tracks of the Old Colony. The first run was on May 19, 1847, and the train left at 5 p.m., arriving at the Fall River Wharf at 6:50: the first steamer, *Bay State*, left at 7.

Left The *Fall River Line Express* pulled by the former *Highland Light* of the Cape Cod Railroad in a circa 1875 photo. Switch stand in foreground had wide boards painted for easy daylight visibility in addition to the lamps.

The waterfront at Boston is an appropriate background for a locomotive named *Plymouth Rock* on a railroad called Old Colony, for Plymouth was the Old Colony. In 1878 the company shops built her and added the #9. She pulled the boat train for many years and later was Old Colony's 609 and was renumbered 1816 by the New Haven, serving until 1918 - a 40-year career.

The *Old Colony* was built in 1869 in Providence by the Rhode Island Locomotive Works, a company owned by well-known Civil War General Ambrose Burnside. Around the time when this engine was built her 66" driving wheels were the largest used on the line. Her diamond stack was shaped to enclose a spark arrestor. Her number was 37.

The *Fall River Line Express* leaves the wharf on a summer morning in 1906. The twin stacks of the *Puritan* tower over the second car in the train. The express of that time was usually six cars: one combination baggage and passenger car on the head end, four day coaches, and a parlor car - in that order.

The Fall River Line wharf and station on the Taunton River where the trains and steamboats met side by side. The station is behind the crossing gate and those automobiles: the company had offices upstairs. Tracks ran both sides of that platform canopy out onto the wharf. You stepped off the train and were a few feet from the gangplank, or if you were coming from New York it was the other way around. Porters from the ship carried your luggage. The crossing gates protected traffic along Water Street. Tracks led away from here to the right of this picture and several blocks away turned north for the way to Middleboro, Cape Cod and Boston. Oh, yes, the steamer behind the station is *Commonwealth*.

The Old Colony shops turned out this 55-ton engine, #232, for the *Fall River Line Express* in 1891. This was one of the first compound locomotives in New England, using steam twice as ships often did, but she wasn't fast enough for express service and wound up pulling freight cars.

The *Falmouth* was built in the Old Colony locomotive shops in South Boston, in 1876. Designed for passenger service with 66" driving wheels, she weighed 35 tons and was lighter than some engines of her time. The company numbered her 68.

Boston, Randolph, Hudson, Old Colony, King Philip, Neponset, Plymouth Rock, Falmouth and *Middleboro.*

It was the New Haven that finally marked the boat train cars "Fall River Line" in the spring of 1922 when on June 10th the six-car train left South Station for Fall River. It was made up of a combination baggage and smoker, four steel day coaches and the Pullman parlor car *Dighton.*

From Cape Cod there was a *Fall River Line Special* and so named in timetables, but during the summer only. It carried a parlor car and from the early 1920s until the end of service the additional cost for a reserved seat was $.75 from Hyannis and Yarmouth to the Fall River dock. That train ran most years from early June to mid-September, leaving Hyannis at 5:20 p.m. Tickets were also sold at Yarmouth, Barnstable, West Barnstable and at Buzzards Bay for those traveling on the Woods Hole Branch train which had no parlor car. Both trains reached Fall River Wharf within a few minutes of each other: the train from Boston was due at 7:20 and from Hyannis 7:25 p.m. with the ship's departure scheduled for 7:30 p.m.

When going the other way in the summer the 6:55 a.m. train from Fall River Wharf had a parlor car for Hyannis but not one for Woods Hole, Chatham or Provincetown.

From the beginning the Fall River Line made sense for many reasons. New England had for so long an economy based on using the water for moving people and goods: the sea was a part of New England, an old addiction. Railroads were not as comfortable a way to travel as the steamers, nor as economical. Water transport is usually a less expensive way to move heavy freight than by rail.

Through the Civil War and afterwards, cities in New England experienced great population growth that accompanied the expansion of industry throughout the region.

New England became the heart of American textile manufacturing. The raw cotton that was turned into cloth came north on steamboats as did coal from Pennsylvania and Virginia and leather and other products from the south and west. New York, with all those railroads coming in there, became the distribution center of the country.

The valuable products of New England: fish and other seafood, boots, shoes and different leather goods, cranberries, strawberries, asparagus and other expensive agricultural exports moved south the easiest way to reach New York by overnight steamers that docked in early morning in downtown Manhattan.

New York City never had large railroad yards and because Manhattan is an island there was a great deal of lighterage. Freight at Boston could take as long as four or five days to reach New York in a box car, but get the shipment to a Fall River steamer and after leaving Newport at 9 p.m. it was non-stop to the North River by 8 a.m. next morning.

It was difficult to bring bulk freight through New York by rail, so a far easier way to reach plants in New England was to ship it on steamers through Long Island Sound. Along with the freight, companies were sending salesmen and other management representatives between New England and New York by steamer. A good example, but only one, was a busy concern like Provincetown Boot & Shoe. When a salesman went on the road to New York, he would leave on the afternoon train and change at Middleborough for Fall River and the overnight boat. Arriving around 8 a.m. at the start of the next business day, the salesman could call on customers and make the late afternoon steamer back, leaving at 5 or 5:30. That way the ship is transportation and a hotel, a moving one. It was inexpensive, fast, efficient and a safe voyage through protected waters.

Vacation travelers became a whole class of business for the Sound lines. From the

1870s on summer holidays became extremely popular for the new urban middle class. New England was the great magnet, drawing families to the beaches of Cape Cod, Martha's Vineyard and Nantucket, the mountains of New Hampshire and the coast of Maine, and for the wealthy there was Newport.

The prosperity of New England during the last 20 years of the 19th century increased travel and made that period from 1880 through 1917 the great days of the night boat. During those years, starting in 1890 the Fall River Line, then operated by the Old Colony Railroad, built the steamer *Plymouth*. Four years later and just one year after the New Haven Railroad bought the Old Colony and its Fall River Line, the *Priscilla*, the most famous of all the Sound steamers, joined the fleet. Two older boats, *Pilgrim* and *Puritan*, were still running when the last steamers were built: the *Providence* in 1905 and the huge *Commonwealth* in 1908.

In those days before the Cape Cod Canal made for a safer and shorter trip by 70 miles between New York and Boston, the coastal steamers ran between New York and Portland, Maine. At first they stopped on the Vineyard at Oak Bluffs, but in the late 1890s they added two new boats which were faster and after that stop was eliminated they could make the one way voyage in under 24 hours via Nantucket Sound and Pollock Rip Slew below Monomoy Island. The Maine Steamship Company operated these boats successfully for years and on that same route even after the canal opened to deeper draught vessels in 1916.

The major freight traffic moving northeast was raw cotton to Fall River where even in the 1920s there were more than 120 cotton mills, or one quarter of the spindles in the country. Finished cotton products and other quality merchandise moved toward the water and onto steamers for New York, the west and the south, as New York was a major distribution center.

When J. P. Morgan was putting together his combination of steamship lines, railroads and trolley lines in New England, it seemed as if nobody could stand in his way. He had that kind of economic clout. He was challenged domestically only occasionally and then not for long.

One man who tried was Charles W. Morse of Maine, a man who had made money in the ice business and had turned to shipping and banking. Morse acquired Eastern Steamship Company with its lines from Boston to Maine ports and St. John, New Brunswick. Also in the early years of this century he acquired the Hudson Navigation Company with ships running between New York and Albany; the Clyde Line, serving from Boston to Jacksonville and the West Indies; the Metropolitan Line, running between New York and Boston, mostly freighters; the New York and Cuba Mail Steamship Company; the Mallory Line from New England to Galveston and the New York and Puerto Rico Line.

Where Morse came into directly challenging J. P. Morgan and his shipping and railroad interests was on the Metropolitan Line between Boston and New York. In 1905 Morse announced he was going to build two luxurious, turbine passenger ships to run around Cape Cod and through Nantucket Sound between Boston and New York. This had never been done with passenger ships with any amount of success.

Morse had his academic twins, the *Yale* and *Harvard*, built at Chester, Pennsylvania with the avowed goal of outdoing the Fall River Line's service by boat and train. The *Yale* and *Harvard* were finished in the late spring of 1906. With them it was all-the-way-by-water with no changing. They were 407 feet long, fast and comfortable - and immediately

Below Built at Chester, Pennsylvania in 1883, *Pilgrim* was a noteworthy steamer. The first with an iron hull on the line and the first American ship with a double hull; the first with an electric thermostatic system of fire alarms, and the first to be lighted exclusively by electricity. It was said the Fall River Line had electricity before the White House. "The Iron Monarch of Long Island Sound" served until 1913.

In 1889, the Old Colony Railroad took delivery of the *Puritan* from W & A Fletcher Company of New York who had installed the world's largest beam engine as her power plant. Travelers loved her comfort and space: this first four deck steamer was 420 feet long and had 321 staterooms. After *Commonwealth* joined the Fall River Line in 1908, *Puritan* became a spare boat.

The gallery deck of the Fall River steamer *Old Colony* was pure Victorian. This steamer built at Greenpoint, New York in 1865 had part of the engine from the *Bay State*, the first boat of the Fall River Line. Throughout *Old Colony* her lighting fixtures were operated by city gas stored in tanks on the upper deck. She was retired in 1894, the year *Priscilla* started her career.

Above The Fall River steamer viewed with the most affection was *Priscilla*. She is shown here at Newport, the first stop from Fall River and New York. **Left** The Peacock Lounge, or main saloon, of *Priscilla* was the largest room afloat when she was built in 1894. Up those stairs is the Gallery Deck. **Right** The *Providence*, launched in 1905 at Quincy, Massachusetts, was the only Fall River passenger boat built in New England. She was designed for winter service. **Below right** In 1908 *Commonwealth* was the largest inland water steamer in the world. Many summer nights she carried two-thousand passengers and many of them dined 50 feet above the water next to the boat deck at the stern.

This area represented one thing: power; the engine room of the *Commonwealth* was a brightly lighted space dominated by huge crankshafts and piston rods painted a bright red. The fascination here was watching those huge cranks rising out of the pit, turning and then falling out of sight only to rise again. This 12-thousand horsepower engine turned a set of 100-ton paddlewheels, moving the ship at 22 knots.

popular. They were sold out every night. *Yale* had that university's colors: blue and white for decor. Of course the *Harvard* had crimson and white. Their speed reduced the trip over that route by three hours.

The New Haven's owners had to respond and they did. They ordered four steamers. The largest was the *Commonwealth,* which at 456 feet was the biggest inland water steamer in the country with a passenger capacity of 2,000. The other three ships were designed as express freighters, but with the capacity to be changed to passenger service if necessary. Those three were the *Old Colony, Massachusetts* and *Bunker Hill.*

The *Commonwealth* was to be the new queen of Long Island Sound on the Fall River Line as a summer boat running with *Priscilla* while *Puritan* would become a stand-by vessel or reserve.

The three fast freighters were to begin a new service between New York and Boston on the same route *Harvard* and *Yale* traveled around the Cape and over Nantucket Shoals. They were called the Boston Merchants Line.

So in 1907 Morse's plans were made for his two new passenger ships and the counter moves by the New Haven Railroad to meet the challenge. Morse decided on a new strategy and he offered to buy New England Navigation Company for $20-million. The stock in the wholly-owned subsidiary of the New Haven had a par value of $5-million. Charles S. Mellen, the president of the New Haven since 1904, considered the offer "very attractive" and would have sold all those steamboats, if the choice had been his. It wasn't and when told of the offer owner J. P. Morgan shouted: "No deals with Morse!"

The three freighters were launched in 1907, and the last of them, *Bunker Hill,* was christened by Rose Fitzgerald, daughter of the mayor of Boston, "Honey Fitz," and later to be the matriarch of the Kennedy clan of Hyannisport.

In the fall *Harvard* and *Yale* began sailing between Boston and New York. In January, 1908 the Boston Merchants Line started regular freight service and with rates reduced by a fourth under the competition, was doing nicely. The *Harvard* and *Yale* were back on the water in May for another summer with a heavy advertising campaign stressing "All the Way By Water." The Fall River Line trip by water and rail covered 233 miles with 180 miles by boat. The Morse ships by water around the Cape had a total voyage of 330 miles. Of course one could go by train, and thousands did, over the 229 miles. The fast limiteds - *Merchants, Bay State* and *Knickerbocker* - covered the distance in five hours. By Fall River Line and the boat train took just about 13 hours and the Metropolitan Line around the Cape 15 hours.

A word about New York-Boston rail service in 1908. The New Haven scheduled nineteen through passenger trains every day and that's each way. Eight trains along the Shore Line Route; three by way of Hartford - Willimantic, and eight via Springfield-Boston & Albany Railroad. In addition there were two express trains daily from Washington to Boston with a ferry trip to the Harlem River and no stop in Manhattan.

The Fall River Line then not only offered a fine sea voyage, but it cost the traveler less. A one way ticket, including train fare from Fall River to Boston, was $3.65 and for that amount you had a guaranteed bed in a dormitory. An excellent dinner for $1.00 was available. Staterooms were $1.00, and if you chose one, your whole tab was $5.65. By train the New Haven charged two cents per mile with a total coach fare of $4.58. If you wished to go in five hours on one of the limiteds the price was $6.65 in a parlor car. If your trip was around noon or evening meal time, add $1.00 for the dining car meal. So, an elegant train ride was by far the fastest way and at $7.65 the most expensive.

The most famous pair of Eastern Steamship's vessels to make the New York to Boston run was the *New York* and her sister, the *Boston*. Launched in 1924, they soon became symbols of the Cape Cod Canal; they drained off thousands of passengers each year from the Fall River Line. Eastern Steamship's "All-the-way-by-Water" campaign was so successful that the Cape Cod Canal and Eastern's ships were usually blamed for helping to kill the Fall River Line.

The *S. S. Yale* and her twin sister, the *Harvard*, were the first serious challenge to the dominance of the New Haven Railroad's Fall River Line New York-Boston service. The pair started sailing on Metropolitan Line between the two cities in 1907 and made the 330 mile trip around Cape Cod and through Nantucket Sound in 15 hours, a record by at least three hours. They were on that run for two years when the New Haven bought and then banished them to the west coast through a series of dummy corporations.

In 1916 after the Cape Cod Canal was deepened to charter depth of 25 feet the Eastern Steamship Corporation began using the canal on daily New York-Boston trips from April to October. The *S.S. Massachusetts* and her sisters, *Old Colony* and *Bunker Hill*, were on that run until purchased by the U. S. Government for use in World War I. Eastern substituted steamers from its Down East fleet after the three were taken for war service. The three were those built by the New Haven Railroad for Boston Merchants Line as competition to *Harvard* and *Yale*.

Eastern bought steamships in pairs to better serve overnight routes with vessels running in opposite directions. After the federal government bought the Cape Cod Canal in 1928 and eliminated tolls, Eastern began year round service between Boston and New York further reducing patronage on the Fall River Line. The *Evangeline* and *Yarmouth* at first sailed from New York and Boston to Yarmouth, Nova Scotia in the summer and Boston-New York through the canal in the winter during the 1930s.

The challenge of Charles W. Morse to the New Haven was short lived and much of it caused by the financial panic of 1907. In March of 1908 Morse was indicted on charges of falsifying records and misapplying funds of the National Bank of North America, of which he was the vice president. After his conviction, Morse was sentenced to fifteen years in a federal penitentiary. Before going off to jail from which he would be pardoned by President Taft in 1912, Morse agreed to receivership for his steamship company. The New Haven agreed to close the Boston Merchants Line and got a half interest in the Metropolitan Line and through a maze of dummy corporations sold and then banished the *Harvard* and *Yale* to the west coast where for many years they sailed between San Diego, Los Angeles and San Francisco. The three express freighters were transferred to Eastern Steamship and converted to passenger service.

So around 1910 the New Haven Railroad had control of 90 percent of New England water transportation. It would not remain that way, for in 1914 the Panama Canal Act prohibited ownership by railroads of competing steamship lines except by permission of the Interstate Commerce Commission.

So the New Haven's New England Navigation Company had to sell its stock in Merchants and Miners Line, which it did at a loss and also its shares in Eastern Steamship, Morse's old company.

The Fall River Line remained the old lady of Long Island Sound with its big, white side-wheel steamers.

The high point, the peak year for the Fall River Line was 1906 with almost half a million passengers. From then into the middle 1920s some 400-thousand passengers traveled those ships yearly. When the Cape Cod Canal opened in July, 1914, it was not finished to charter depth of 25 feet in the channel. Two years later in the spring it was, and Eastern started in April sending through steamers from New York to Boston daily until mid-October. At first the former express freighters now converted to passenger use were on that line. Of course Eastern advertised "All-The-Way-By-Water" as Morse had done with *Harvard* and *Yale.* The canal company charged tolls based on size and weight of vessels and passenger ships and yachts paid the most. But the canal trip saved about 70 miles and hours of time, so that Eastern ships leaving either city at 5 in the afternoon reached the other end of the trip by 8 in the morning.

The Cape Cod Canal seriously began to drain off Fall River Line passengers when Eastern put its two new steamers, *Boston* and *New York,* in daily service in June 1924. They were comfortable ships of 402-feet length, turbine powered, oil-fired, double steel hulled with room for 900 passengers. They had dance orchestras and a ballroom on the top deck and their nightly passage through the canal from about 8 to 9 p.m. was a major social enterprise along the shore of the narrow, sandy waterway with crowds along both banks and on the cantilever bridges to watch "The New York Boat."

The Boston-bound steamer especially took business from the Fall River ships because of the early arrival time in Newport and Fall River as compared to being able to sleep later and step off the ship at India Wharf, Boston at 8 a.m. The trip by Eastern was a little easier on your constitution. The Cape Cod Canal offered a protected voyage through safe waters with the only encounter with rough water being that part of the Long Island Sound trip from the entrance of Narragansett Bay for about an hour west of Point Judith, and the Fall River boats had to navigate that, too. Many travelers came east through the canal and returned by way of the Fall River Line. Two years after Eastern's new ships, *New York* and *Boston,* arrived in 1924, the Fall River Line began operating in the red, but the company kept its ships running along with the other marine properties of New England Steamship, which since 1912 had been the title of the reorganized branch of the New Haven.

By the early 1930s the number of passengers carried annually had dropped to about a quarter of a million. In 1935 the New Haven Railroad declared bankruptcy and entered its first reorganization. A year later the ICC told eastern railroads they had to reduce coach fares to two cents a mile, which was what some lines in New England charged in 1848 and the New Haven did in 1908. This new fare also took passengers from the steamers. In 1936 Fall River Line passenger lists sank to 128-thousand. Early the following year the New Bedford Line and Providence Line were closed down and the management thought some of that business might move to the Fall River Line. The New Haven intended to keep the ships running, but a labor dispute between A. F. L. and C. I. O. called a sit-down strike.

It was July and a few days later a federal court in New Haven, looking at $5-million in losses from 1932-36 for the line, ordered the New Haven to shut down the most famous overnight steamers in the world and sell the vessels. The New Haven put the four steamers - *Priscilla, Commonwealth, Plymouth* and *Providence* - up for sale with the provision that they could not be operated on Long Island Sound. A Baltimore company paid $88-thousand for the ships and towed them down the coast for scrapping late in the year and early in 1938. That spring they were broken up. So the Fall River Line died before it was dead. For the better part of a century the big, white steamers sailed between New York and Fall River, the gateway to New England. Their safety, comfort and luxury made them a unique American institution. They were viewed with such affection that books, songs and poems were written about them. And it seems that everybody - or just about everybody - rode them.

On the last timetable issued by the company it says "Fall River Line to Boston, Cape Cod, Martha's Vineyard and Nantucket." And for all those days and years there was a ride to and from the Fall River Line Wharf on a boat train. A trip that came from Boston, Provincetown, Chatham, Hyannis, Yarmouth or Woods Hole and all the stations in between.

The last trip of *Commonwealth* was on this tow line in January 1938 as she is slowly pulled away from the Fall River wharf out of camera range to the right. The crowd on the adjacent pier looks like a wake. It was one of Fall River's saddest days.

SUSPENSION

FALL RIVER LINE

Including

RAIL AND MOTOR COACH CONNECTIONS

EFFECTIVE JULY 20, 1937

(All Times Shown Eastern Standard)

Account of labor trouble Fall River Line Steamer Service between New York and Newport, R. I. and Fall River, Mass. is temporarily suspended.

Fall River Line Cape Special leaving Taunton at 6:42 A. M. daily for Middleboro and Hyannis and leaving Hyannis at 4:00 P. M. daily for Middleboro and Taunton is annulled between Taunton and Hyannis.

Fall River Line Special (Boston) leaving Fall River Wharf at 6:10 A. M. daily and leaving Boston at 5:00 P. M. daily is annulled between Fall River and Fall River Wharf.

Train leaving Fall River Wharf at 5:10 A. M. Saturdays only for New Bedford Wharf and train leaving New Bedford Wharf at 6:00 P. M. daily for Fall River Wharf are annulled.

N. E. T. Co. bus leaving Fall River Wharf at 5:20 A. M. except Saturdays for New Bedford Wharf and bus leaving Fall River Wharf at 7:00 A. M. daily for New Bedford Wharf are annulled.

N. E. T. Co. busses leaving Fall River Wharf at 5:55 A. M. and 6:55 A. M. for Providence, and leaving Providence at 6:23 P. M. and 6:55 P. M. for Fall River Wharf, will continue between Providence Terminal and Fall River Terminal as regular operations of the New England Transportation Company.

N. E. T. Co. bus leaving Hyannis at 8:05 A. M. and Yarmouth at 8:20 A. M. for Provincetown will leave Hyannis at 6:30 A. M. and Yarmouth at 6:42 A. M. on Tuesdays, Thursdays, and Saturdays connecting with NIGHT CAPE CODDER from New York previous night.

N. E. T. Co. bus leaving Provincetown at 2:20 P. M. daily for Yarmouth and Hyannis will leave at 7:05 P. M. and run on Tuesdays and Thursdays only connecting with NIGHT CAPE CODDER. On Sundays connection for NIGHT CAPE CODDER from Provincetown will be by train leaving at 6:40 P. M. as at present.

See New Haven R. R. timetables for through rail service between New York and Cape Cod Points with steamer connections to and from islands of Martha's Vineyard and Nantucket.

The NEW HAVEN R. R.
The NEW ENGLAND STEAMSHIP COMPANY

TO BE POSTED UNTIL AUGUST 20, 1937

This poster published in newspapers and put up in railroad stations tells of a temporary suspension of service. A federal court in New Haven later decided on abandonment.

End of track on the Chatham Branch with station on the left as it was built in 1887 and appears today. This drawing by Ted Rose is based on a photo from about 1910.

THE CHATHAM RAILROAD

Chatham had a long wait for its railroad station and regular service. A wait of close to 25 years, almost a quarter century of waiting. When the railroad finally reached Chatham it was late in the year 1887. That was 14 years after trains were serving Provincetown, 15 years after Woods Hole, 17 years after Wellfleet, 22 years after Orleans, 33 years after Yarmouth and Hyannis and 39 years after Sandwich got rail service. The 25 years began in 1863, during the Civil War, when the Cape Cod Central had been created to run from Yarmouth to Orleans. In February Chatham residents voted to petition the legislature for the town to be able to issue bonds to assist the Central in building eastward from Yarmouth, providing the line went where it was indicated in the subscription book for stock. What Chatham wanted was a railroad that would be closer. What Chatham got was the Cape Cod Central building from Harwich north instead of east. Brewster pledged to buy enough stock to insure the rails through there and so the Central built through Pleasant Lake to Brewster and East Brewster and on to Orleans by 1865.

What Chatham also got were committees, lots of them that were supposed to bring the tracks to the town. What the committees brought were meetings and discussions and proposals and votes and dissolving of committees. Later, more committees would be formed, and later still they would vanish.

And Chatham residents were willing to put up money, too, as other towns had to bring the railroad. For some years during the 1870s the Old Colony put the cost of the seven-mile long line at $200-thousand. That was more than $28-thousand per mile for a fairly easy route with small stations in-between and a terminal yard, engine house, passenger and freight station and turntable at Chatham. In fact, it was high, since no additional motive power or rolling stock was called for to be purchased, even though one locomotive would have to be assigned to the branch along with a combination car and two day coaches.

Even when it appeared that there was no interest on the railroad's part or the town's, the subject never went away; it was a constant source of conversation by many and of planning, sometimes by only a few. The Cape Cod Railroad suggested to the town that it should look over the land and decide where the line should be; that was in 1871. An informal group did ride and walk over the ground from Chatham to the Harwich station. The route suggested was southerly and close to the water of Nantucket Sound. That was because the fishing interests were to be given first consideration. Wherever the railroad had gone, the fishermen had used express cars for fast delivery of their catches to Boston and other major markets. The fishermen and the railroads were allies who got along fine. Fishing interests had pledged support in buying railroad stocks and bonds and they were sure to be among the biggest shippers.

After South Harwich heading toward Chatham the line should go south of the main road, as the grading would be easier there. The line, once in Chatham, should be as close to the fish companies as possible and should touch Oyster Pond with its outlet through Stage Harbor to Nantucket Sound and the sea. Things seemed to be looking up with this latest planning, but with the Chatham Railroad things always seemed to be looking up, that is, until they crashed.

At the annual Chatham town meeting on February 4, 1872 the voters were asked to consider an article to buy 550 shares of Cape Cod Railroad stock at $100 par and to create another committee to negotiate with the company. The voters chose to pledge five percent of the next evaluation of the town's property for railroad stock purchase and they created another committee to represent them. One member of that committee, Josiah Hardy, informed the town meeting that there was a distinct possibility of a merger between the Cape Cod Railroad and the Old Colony & Newport. Hardy suggested that Chatham "keep quiet." After that remark, most of the voters got up and left. Chatham kept quiet. Nothing happened. One wonders if at that time the committee had shown greater desire to reach an agreement with the railroad, perhaps something substantial might have happened. Perhaps not with the consolidation and completing the Woods Hole Branch and starting the extension to Provincetown. Still, it might have been a moment for starting a strong effort to build a line to Chatham.

One year later - and no closer to having a railroad than before - a new idea was brought in - to build a narrow gauge railroad. There was no strong support for such a line, but some favored a narrow gauge if that was all that could be had. The question of land values kept coming up with many taxpayers thinking if the railroad didn't come close to their property, their land would be worth very little. This was cause for a great strain in relationships between people and sections of town. There followed more meetings, one in South Chatham that was especially boisterous, committees started marching around the countryside and up Great Hill where they could see more. Marching seemed to be the one activity that followed every meeting or suggestion about a route. In the winter of 1874 Chatham voted to issue bonds on five percent of its evaluation with interest of seven percent with annual coupons for ten years. A committee was formed to represent the town's interest, naturally, and the line built from Harwich to Chatham would become part of the Old Colony Railroad. The town was to receive stock at par of the railroad in the amount of its bond investment, except it would receive no dividends on that stock for five years. The Old Colony was to build the line and run it. The running was to start by no later than July 1, 1875. The Old Colony president, Onslow Stearns, replied that the line would cost $110-thousand and his company would furnish the track and its materials - ties, chairs, spikes - or $40-thousand as a loan with the line furnishing cars. The Old Colony to keep one-third of the passenger income and $.25 a ton on freight. The other company suggestion was to provide engines and rolling stock for which it would be reimbursed by the average cost of running its trains. A committee of 15 was appointed and they added the Barnstable banker and former publisher, Sylvanus B. Phinney, as a liaison between Chatham and others. The 15 fell to arguing among themselves and there was no agreement reached and soon there was no committee, although some of the members submitted expenses to the town. The largest bill was from banker Phinney who asked for $1.35.

The periods of intense interest in the railroad were followed by no discernible activity and from 1874 to 1878 was one of those. In November 1878 a special town meeting was held to consider a proposal from one, Chester Snow, who wished to buy an eight and one-half mile long two-foot narrow gauge, The Billerica & Bedford Railroad, northwest of Boston. The builder of that Lilliput line was George E. Mansfield, who had traveled to Wales where he saw some of those small gauge lines and returned to Massachusetts filled with enthusiasm for what he saw as the ease of construction and economy of purchasing equipment and operating it. The citizens of those two towns were mesmerized by Mansfield's vision of this small gauge line and what he promised it would do. They bought the idea and paid for it. Mansfield had Hinkley Locomotive Works in Boston build two locomotives, *Ariel* and *Puck,* and had others manufacture rolling stock, including freight cars, flat cars, combination cars and day coaches - even an excursion car, based on the open air trolleys that were to become a city fixture later.

The line cost more than Mansfield said it would and the traffic, passenger and freight, never lived up to his predictions. The Billerica & Bedford ran for six months and went broke. George Mansfield wanted to pick up and plant it somewhere else. Why not from Harwich to Chatham? Chester Snow and his town friends thought it might be the solution to Chatham's railroad woes. The line would cost, according to Mansfield, $22-thousand. Snow asked the small crowd in attendance that night to approve Chatham's purchase of half that in bonds of ten years duration at 5 percent per year. It was further asked that Chatham pay for any land needed, erect fences to keep cattle off the track and further to assist the new enterprise, not to charge it with property taxes. Following a remark that the town's occasional high winds might push the Lilliputian cars off the tracks, there was an attempt to get Chatham to buy the bonds. It didn't pass and soon after that there was adjournment.

The narrow gauge talk had wakened some of the dormant feeling about a railroad, and another meeting was called at which it was made known that some 400 passengers were getting off trains at Harwich and traveling to Chatham by stage coaches every month and 150 tons of freight were moving on the same route. This was made in an effort to get some action toward purchasing the Billerica & Bedford.

Nothing was approved and some time later it was learned the locomotives had been sold to a New Hampshire man, a Mr. Brown, and the tracks could not be moved without permission of the towns, which would certainly involve difficult legal problems. George Mansfield took his vision north to Maine, where a number of small towns were willing to consider a small-gauge railroad on the order of 24 inches between the rails. Mansfield solved the legal problems of moving the 25 pound rail and had the Sandy River Railroad buy the *Ariel* and the *Puck* from Mr. Brown. The miniature locomotives lost their names and acquired numbers one and two.

In the winter of 1886 at a town meeting it was suggested that a new method of building railroads be tested between Harwich and Chatham. The method was the invention of Mr. H. L. Stillman, of Rhode Island. His method did away with cross ties, which railroads placed 2,640 per mile and spiked the rails to them. Stillman wanted to place hard pine stringers on short cedar posts and place the rails along the stringers. Stillman brought a model of his invention and spoke of its great savings in the cost of construction. The meeting seemed to be impressed and a new committee was formed. This one with 32 members.

After many meetings about surveys, finances and Stillman's method they did little that was new, much that had been done before, but they thought Stillman's idea "too venturesome." The committee did feel that the Old Colony Railroad was willing to run the branch if Chatham - or anybody under the sun - would only build it. That still left it up to finding a way to build a little more than seven miles of railroad. The committee made an agreement with a concern in Boston that went out on its own and eventually had to be paid off early in 1887, a venture that cost the taxpayers of Chatham $2,443.

Without looking further to outside sources, Chatham called a series of meetings and stock subscriptions were taken. In a short time that winter and spring $70-thousand dollars worth of stock was sold in The Chatham Railroad Company with a par value of $100 a share. All 700 shares were subscribed. A management team was formed with Marcellus Eldredge as president and Charles Bassett as clerk and treasurer. For a board of directors, Eldredge - who was one of the largest stockholders - was chosen along with Osborn Nickerson and the three selectmen, because the town of Chatham had purchased 310 shares for $31-thousand.

A crowd estimated by the Chatham Monitor as 100 people, or more, was gathered shortly before 9 a.m. on May 24, 1887 for the ceremonial first shovelful. The digging began with Marcellus Eldredge saying: "I accordingly proceed to the business in hand." He then took a new shovel and plunged it into the ground and lifted and threw the soil a distance to one side on a small hill near the eastern end of White Pond. Several other directors took turns with the shovel, followed by a number of Chatham citizens until the youngest, two year old Eddie Howard, got his chance.

It was a Tuesday and nearby, waiting for the ceremony to end, were about 75 men with horses, tip carts and shovels. This group would dig its way through hills and fill cuts for more than seven miles and on their work the Old Colony would place sand as ballast, then ties and finally spike rails down. The line had been surveyed, but still there were those pleading for a different route, including tracks over Watch Hill and along by the Chatham Lighthouses and down to the wharves at Stage Harbor. This route would better serve the fishing fleet and give a fine view of the Atlantic from the bluff near the lights. A more southerly route along Oyster Pond had been urged for most of the quarter century that a railroad had been sought; this idea was repeated to no one's surprise, but it didn't happen.

The work crews kept long hours that summer and fall and with the ground prepared the oak ties started to arrive by schooner from Maine down to the Railroad Wharf in Provincetown where they were transferred to flat cars and pulled to Harwich and moved forward, even by crews working during the night for others to spike down the rails in the daylight hours.

There was an urgency to the construction effort made no doubt by the officers and directors who had lived so long with one dead-end idea after another for all those years. Finally the track gangs reached close to the end of the line in Chatham. This was a great day! The sand ballast was down and the ties were placed and sections of track were carried forward and joined to the one next to it and then spiked to the ties. Slowly moving forward were flat cars with rails, spikes, chairs, and fish plates - all pushed slowly by an Old Colony steam locomotive. A crowd was on hand - and growing larger by the minute. The steam whistle on the engine blasting - no, screaming its signal. And there were bells - all kinds of bells - school bells, church bells, the engine bell, and even dinner bells. This was too much for the schools and they let the children out to join the crowd.

Opening day was set for Tuesday, November 22, 1887 and almost six months to the day that Marcellus Eldredge "did proceed to the business in hand" and picked up that shovel. Travel was free that day on the one train that had a locomotive and six coaches. The trip started at Harwich at noon and took 20 minutes. All six cars were filled with passengers for the return trip. The Chatham Railroad Company had built a station, a car house,an engine house with a turntable in front of it, a windmill to pump water for the engines and a small building for track tools and hand cars. The station with its Oriental-type tower was unique in Cape railroading. There was no other like it. That opening day crowds watched with fascination as the locomotive was uncoupled from the train and changed direction on the turn table for the trip to Harwich. Again all seats were filled as some people just rode the train back and forth.

There were two other new stations on the 7.4 mile long branch: South Chatham and South Harwich. Two years later a station was built at West Chatham for a new hotel, the Hotel Chatham. A one way ticket from Harwich to Chatham cost $.35 or $.048 per mile. Freight charges were $.05 per 500 pounds. Sales of tickets averaged about 50 per day. The line was a success and the Old Colony took over its operation immediately.

Four years after it started the Chatham Branch of the Old Colony carried more than 23-thousand passengers annually. Boston was 91 and one half miles from Chatham and the trip took about two and a half hours. Chatham had been slowly growing as a summer resort. The coming of the railroad increased the tempo of that growth. The line to Chatham was the last one to be built on Cape Cod. It was to last a half century, just twice what it had taken in years to bring it there.

ove This share of stock in the Chatham
ailroad was bought for $100 about one month
fore the line opened that fall of 1887.

n the Chatham Branch the first depot east of
larwich was this building at Harwich Center,
ine-tenths of a mile away. The New Haven
ook three minutes to cover that.

Two miles farther and five minutes later the train stopped here, at South Harwich.

The South Chatham depot was next, one mile away and for some reason six minutes on the time table. The next station was a flag stop, West Chatham, and sometimes called Hotel Chatham after a local hostelry. The depot sign was on an Ocean Spray cranberry plant once.

The end of track was Chatham with this unique depot, its tower and candle snuffer roof..."a fine balance...and adds a bit of drama that is very welcome. The color is soft yellow with soft red trim," according to Clair Baisly, author of Cape Cod Architecture. This picture was taken in 1887, the first year the branch operated. The engine house is a little misty and shows between the engine and the depot. A turn table was in front of the engine house facing to the right of the picture.

Almost everyone is looking eastward and there wasn't much track that way. Crowds on Sunday afternoon were often the largest of the week during the summer days of so long ago. All the depots on the branch were built the year it opened, 1887. The one remaining is this Chatham station now used as a railroad museum. The others, like the railroad, are gone. The Chatham depot was 7.1 miles from Harwich and 92 miles from Boston, a three hour journey in 1926.

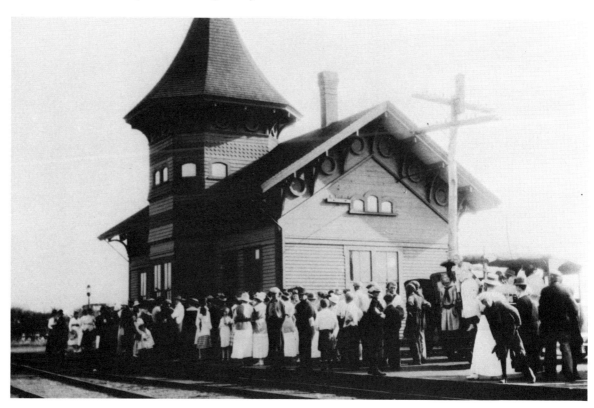

A daytime wreck involving a passenger train killed the locomotive crew on Wednesday, August 31, 1921. It was the worst accident on the Chatham Branch and a good example of why railroads preferred to run locomotives forward rather than in reverse. The locomotive and three cars had run forward from Chatham to Harwich, but later on the return trip the engine and tender ran past the train and coupled onto the day coach at the rear and ran backwards to Chatham. Just north of Queen Anne Road crossing between West Chatham and Chatham when either the rails spread or the wheels of the end truck on the tender jumped the track the tender wrenched itself and flipped over and turned upside down to one side, separating itself from the locomotive which was off the rails and settling on its side across the track from the tender. The day coach, a standard wooden car with closed vestibules, angled to one side and lost its wheels but did not overturn and no passengers or conductor George Snow were hurt. The engineer, William Drew, and the fireman, William McKenna were both killed in the wreck. Drew wound up under the boiler where he was crushed, and McKenna was pinned and scalded to death by escaping steam. The throttle was off and the air brake lever turned for "brakes on" in the crushed cab of locomotive # 1597, a 4-4-0 American type built at the New Haven's Roxbury Shops in 1899. The passengers, the mail, express and baggage were moved to Chatham in automobiles. A wreck train cleaned up the accident and the track crew rebuilt the torn up right of way next day. William Drew was a popular resident of Chatham who once lived in his own home on Main Street, Hyannis. He was born in Tioga County, New York and moved to Wellfleet at age 15 where he started a railroad career as a section hand. His uncle, Joseph Drew, was a roadmaster on the New Haven and had built the Chatham Branch in 1887, and it was through him that young William was promoted to locomotive fireman, and after four years to engineer working on the night freight from Provincetown to Hyannis. His best promotion came as engineer on passenger trains from Provincetown to Boston and then later from Hyannis to Boston. In his last years he was engineer on Chatham Branch passenger trains. It was a nice life since he lived in Chatham where he and his wife raised their four children, and he sat on the right hand side of a New Haven steam locomotive rolling over a seven-mile branch line to Harwich. He had two brothers, both of whom were railroad men: Fred Drew of Boston, also an engineer, and Myron Drew, formerly the roadmaster at Hyannis. If Drew were living, he would call himself a Born Again Christian for his beliefs, and he practiced those beliefs and gave the land, the building and the organ to the Zion Mission Church on North Street, Hyannis, as a religious center for black people. He was a man ahead of his times. These wreck photos were taken the day of the accident and the following day. The couple on the bench are William Drew and his wife, Bessie, whom he had married when he was 19 and a newly-promoted fireman. She was from Hyannis and their marriage lasted 36 years. When he died in that Chatham wreck, he was 54.

The man in the center of the picture with the oil can is Matthias P. Slavin, who was the engineer on the Chatham Branch from the opening of the line in 1887 until his retirement in 1910. He was succeeded by his fireman William Drew who is the second from the right. This picture was taken at the Chatham station.

On a Sunday morning in August, 1911, a passenger train on the Chatham Branch was approaching the wye just east of Harwich station at full speed just after eleven o'clock when the locomotive jumped the track and ran along the ties and the ground for more than one hundred feet and finally stopped in front of the engine house by plowing up sand to its headlight. The fireman, William S. Stinson, from Boston was standing in the gangway between the edge of the cab and the front of the tender. Stinson was leaning out the side and watching for signals when the engine left the rails. The accident happened so suddenly that Stinson was trapped and crushed in that space. When they removed him, the space where he had been trapped measured just under two inches. He was taken quickly to a train to carry him to Boston for medical care, but he died in the train near Buzzards Bay.

MARTHA'S VINEYARD RAILROAD

Martha's Vineyard is the closest of the two major islands off the south coast of Cape Cod. At its closest point it is four miles from the Cape across Vineyard Sound to Nobska Point in the town of Falmouth. The Vineyard is 23 miles long by seven miles wide and covers about 100 square miles. Today its attractions are yachting, fishing, beaches and a rather mild climate. After a visit by the explorer Bartholomew Gosnold in 1602 he named the island after his daughter Martha and the grapevines he found there. The growth of railroads and coastal steamboat lines helped introduce New England's great asset, the sea, to ever larger numbers of summer visitors. The general prosperity in the north after the Civil War allowed more and more of middle class Americans to travel for summer vacations.

The extension of track to Woods Hole opened up that whole area from the Village of Buzzards Bay south along the coast, which caused the Hyannis steamer to be moved to Woods Hole and from there to stop first at the Vineyard before reaching Nantucket. In fact no area of the Cape itself prospered as quickly as did that served by the Woods Hole Branch from the summer of 1872 on. Steamers from Woods Hole stopped at the three ports on the north side of the Island: Vineyard Haven, Oak Bluffs and Edgartown. Once on the island people moved about drawn by horses and even a trolley.

In the age of steam with great construction projects everywhere in the country building railroads, there were powerful interests on Martha's Vineyard who saw a railroad there as a necessity. In the summer of 1873 there was completed a horse railroad that ran from Highland Wharf to a loop around a camp area. The line had open, four-wheel cars pulled by two horses. It was a strictly summer-only local line built for a modest $8-thousand.

As was the case on Cape Cod and elsewhere the incessant prodding by local publishers and editors helped bring about rail lines or expansion of existing lines. On the Vineyard there was the Vineyard Gazette whose editor Edgar Marchant said, "The snort of the iron horse will arouse men from their lethargy and infuse new life into their veins." The occasion was a call to duty, a town meeting at which good citizens will vote to approve a railroad from Oak Bluffs to Edgartown and on to Katama near the South Beach on the Atlantic.

It all came about quickly, unlike most similar proposals. Quickly, that is, considering the push that began that winter of 1874 to build by that coming summer. The proposal was to build a cross-island narrow gauge, three feet between the rails. It was to be nine miles in length. Recent developments on the island, including large hotels for the growing vacation trade, were the impetus for the kind of transportation that then only a railroad line could provide.

There were many social activities around the Vineyard, but one had to reach them. The railroad - its supporters said - was the answer. One of the railroad's biggest supporters was Captain Nathaniel M. Jernegan who rose and made his case that March evening. "The horse railroad...sold 40-thousand tickets last year (its first year). Our summer population,"

111

he continued, "is a community of idlers, and they grasp at everything that offers which is calculated to vary the monotony of existence. Fifty-thousand people will ride down to our South Beach every summer, and at fifty cents apiece, or even half of that, will afford a handsome profit." Captain Jernegan, who was the agent and a director of the Katama Land Company, a major developer, pushed his case on the easy economics of building the railroad. "It can be run for $30 a day, which is one half the cost of running a steamboat. The road will cost $80-thousand and money can be had for 7 percent." He returned to traffic predictions to support his case. He said, "About 50-thousand people come to Oak Bluffs and vicinity during the summer, who would average one ride apiece. Everyone who has noticed the success of enterprises similar to this will have to agree with me as to the probable success of this one."

As in the case of towns on the Cape and almost everywhere in the nation the public was asked to commit tax money to build this line. One of the chief opponents was the inspector of customs for the district. He was Ichabod Luce - tall and bearded. He was against putting town money to work this way. "Towns which mix themselves up in private enterprise commit a fatal blunder," he said. "Take care of your poor, your schools, your roads - these are the legitimate functions of a town government. The Katama Land Company is abundantly able to develop their property, and if they want a railroad let them build one. Katama has money enough and ability enough, but lacks confidence in its own scheme," said Ichabod Luce.

There were others who questioned such a use of tax dollars; they said steam locomotives would frighten the horses, endanger the children, set fire to the fields and woods, bring undesirable elements from the mainland and generally disturb the peace of this off-shore paradise.

A leading figure in the whaling industry was Samuel Osborn, Jr. who favored limited town participation in building the line. Osborn, who had been sheriff, state representative and a member of the Governor's Council during part of the Civil War, suggested that $25-thousand be raised independently before the town pledged $15-thousand and with that total sale in stock the company could bond the remaining $35-thousand from its property. The statutes allowed a railroad to bond its property for an amount equal to the capital subscribed. Osborn was certain that the Old Colony Railroad, if necessary, would buy the $40-thousand in bonds. Osborn thought the line could be built for $75-thousand. He found that to be surprisingly low. Later Osborn spoke to the question of whether such a railroad would pay. "To run over a few figures, a train can complete a round trip in an hour," he answered. "For the first six weeks of the season, with only one trip a day, there would probably be an average of 200 passengers a trip, or 7,200 for six weeks, which at fifty cents a ticket would amount to $3,600. The following six weeks would be, say five trips a day with an average of 100 passengers a trip, making 18-thousand passengers who would pay $9-thousand. The total would be $12,600, and the cost of operation $2,500, leaving a net of $10,100." With that he concluded, "I expect a net of 10 percent."

Samuel Osborn, Jr. was used to the kind of cash return one could get from successful whaling voyages. While some vessels in fleets of east coast fore and aft wooden schooners earned as much as 25 percent of their cost in one year. That of course was a return from a good year of commerce - and they were not all good years. Still, Osborn was an optimistic businessman from Edgartown who had read Cape Cod Railroad and Old Colony Railroad annual reports to stockholders with their yearly dividends and been impressed. This was the Railway Age, after all, and Samuel Osborn, Jr. wanted a railroad for his island.

Time passed at the meeting with those in favor and those opposed to public investment challenging and answering each other's arguments. One of the main objections to investing in the railroad was concern over a growing town debt. The other was not mixing the public's money into private enterprise. One opponent put it this way: "If the investment was as good as they say it is, every dollar would have been taken before the town could get together."

It was finally the turn of editor Edgar Marchant of the Vineyard Gazette, who, with no little drama to his delivery, made the final case for the railroad plan. "We want a railroad," he said, "and we are going to have it. As for manufactures, they will come with some of the men this road will cause to come here." He went on, his voice rising. "Build this road and manufactures will come along, Katama will grow, and we shall become a very vineyard indeed. Refuse to encourage and lend our aid to this enterprise, and this town will disappear into the darkness of oblivion. All spirit of improvement will depart from our borders, men of brains will go where they can use them, and for aught I can see to the contrary, the town will become a waste, a howling wilderness; rats and mud turtles will crawl over our streets, and owls and bats sit in our high places."

It had all been said by both sides. Now it was time to vote. As voters names were called, they marched past the ballot box and placed a slip of paper through the slot. Each slip said "yes" or "no." Finally the town moderator gave the tally. A two-thirds vote was required to pass. Those in favor of the town investing in the railroad numbered 149; against 72. The railroad passed - barely by two votes. But it passed.

There was another order of business at the meeting and that was where to locate the track on the way south from Oak Bluffs, its northern terminus. The voters felt the track should not go down Nantucket Sound along the Edgartown Bathing Beach parallel to Edgartown-Oak Bluffs Road. They favored a route inland and west of Sengekontacket Pond. The main reason for avoiding the beach route was the proximity to that road with all the horses that traveled it. The train would frighten them!

The promoters made a different case for the beach route. It offered a magnificent view, they argued, was shorter and thus less expensive to build, not much of a grade, offered no need for paying land damages or erecting fences, required little trestle work and would save two weeks in construction time, since the line was to be in operation that coming summer. Railroad men who looked at both routes liked the route along the sandy beach.

Since the main objection to the beach route was the fear of the locomotive frightening island horses, the solution was to buy a dummy locomotive, a type used on the New York City elevateds. With wary citizens convinced their concerns were being addressed by the railroad, the next step was to buy track supplies and hire workmen.

A Neponset company, Dacey Brothers, was hired to build the line. Dacey agreed to be bonded for completing the roadbed and track by July 20! In late May about 40 men arrived on the site with another 50 expected. The Martha's Vineyard Railroad offered the workmen $1.75 a day. They asked for another $.25 and went on strike when they didn't get it. Then they got it.

The sand started to fly and some of the fastest railroad building in Massachusetts was under way. A group of company management men took the steamer to Woods Hole and the train to Boston and to Worcester. They had a budget of $9-thousand and in Worcester they signed a contract with Jerome Wheelock, who would build a dummy locomotive that looked like a passenger car far less threatening to horses and their peace of mind. It would have a monitor roof, guarantee 25 miles an hour, accommodate 24 people, pull a train carrying 150 people total and consume about 500 pounds of coal while covering 80 miles of track. It seemed almost too good to be true.

There were some minor problems with a bridge, but they were solved and on August 3, which wasn't far off the target date, the railroad was ready for use. It had taken 66 days to build the nine mile Martha's Vineyard Railroad. The dummy engine and the rolling stock - a passenger car, an excursion car and a box car - were waiting. The two passenger cars were identical in size - 35 feet long by 8 feet wide. The passenger car had seats for 47 people, sitting four across. The seats were red plush. The excursion car could carry 56 people seated on long benches, one on each side lengthwise under the windows. The box car, when not used for freight, could be a smoker with seats for 22, portable seats.

The trial trip of the dummy engine was August 5. The president of the new line, E.P. Carpenter - first president of the Mansfield & Framingham - was on hand with his directors. Many residents showed up, too; they wanted to see their new railroad in action. The dummy engine left Oak Bluffs and headed south. All went well until it reached the first curve. The engine stopped as it was unable to take the curve. The power to the wheels from the upright engine and boiler was a direct sprocket drive and the design would not allow the truck and its wheels to turn but slightly. The track turned more than slightly and the dummy stopped.

The problem was apparent - the Martha's Vineyard Railroad didn't have an engine that worked. Not on that track! However, the worst fears of horse lovers were realized when the dummy approached a road and there were horses nearby. Some of them bolted and ran and others tried to. The dummy was backed up to Oak Bluffs and shunted aside. The company lawyers were told to sue the builder, Jerome Wheelock.

A telegram to the H. K. Porter Company of Pittsburgh ordered a regular narrow gauge steam locomotive with a diamond stack, a huge headlight, sand dome, bell, whistle, cylinders and nothing dummy or camouflaged about it. As luck would have it, H. K. Porter had an 0-6-0 which they had just completed and it was three foot gauge and so would fit the Vineyard's tracks. Porter named it *Active* and shortly afterward it was chained down to a flat car and shipped to Woods Hole where it arrived on August 17 in the afternoon. It was moved next to the end of the wharf to await the steamer *Martha's Vineyard* and a trip to Oak Bluffs. Several freight cars were moved to the same track but farther up in the yard. Their brakes failed and on they came, striking the flat car which carried the *Active*. The car surged ahead and stopped only when it struck the caplog of the wharf. The *Active* broke its chains and went over the end of the wharf and sank in the water of Woods Hole Harbor. The *Active* may have been the first engine in America to join the Flying Locomotive Corps. The engineer who had come from Pittsburgh to teach the Vineyard railroaders how to run it was on the wharf and escaped the sudden flight.

Since it was the Old Colony's responsibility, they hired a diver and moved a crane to position and two days later brought up the *Active*. She was placed on a flat car and taken to the Old Colony's locomotive shops in South Boston for repair to her broken pilot. The shop men cleaned her up and removed seaweed from her cylinders. The Porter engineer pronounced her in good shape and off she went to Woods Hole on a flat car.

This time there was no swimming and *Active* was loaded on the forward deck of the steamer *Island Home* which brought her around Martha's Vineyard to the south shore and the Katama Wharf. A brass band saluted the new engine and she was run off the ship to

The first trolley line on the islands was a horse-drawn affair that ran from this boardwalk by the Highland House to a Methodist camp ground and back. This line was built in 1873. Cars bought later had greater passenger capacity. This horse line became part of an electric street railway system.

All the rolling stock of the Martha's Vineyard Railroad is behind the *Active* on the steamboat wharf at Oak Bluffs in this picture from long ago. The steamer *River Queen* was built in 1864 and used by General Ulysses S. Grant as a dispatch boat in the Civil War.

Another train load of passengers and their baggage leave the wharf at Oak Bluffs behind the locomotive *Active* on the Martha's Vineyard Railroad. This picture dates from the middle 1870s. The *Active* will run down the beach to the right and on to Katama where the train will turn on a wye track like the one on this wharf. Island steamer in the background is the *Martha's Vineyard*, a fast side wheeler which joined that popular fleet in 1871.

All the elements are here on a summer day long ago on Martha's Vineyard. The locomotive *Active*, followed by baggage car #5 and the three coaches with a trainload of tourists in front of Mattakesett Lodge, which was built in 1873 at the Katama section of Edgartown along South Beach. The railroad was built the next year. Train has backed up on the wye track in order to return to Oak Bluffs.

The wharf with train loading on a busy summer day at Oak Bluffs. The camera is high on the tower balcony of the Seaview Hotel. That building alongside the train was used as a baggage room by the Old Colony Railroad for passengers traveling between the Vineyard and Woods Hole and by the New Bedford, Vineyard & Nantucket Steamboat Company for connections, including boats to New York, via New Bedford. Track running off to the left was a wye used to turn the locomotive.

Typical summer train on the Martha's Vineyard Railroad on the wharf at Oak Bluffs with Seaview Hotel in background, the largest building in the area. The *Active* is about to leave on its eight-mile trip to Edgartown and South Beach. The track to the left ran along the shore for over half that distance. The cars were in reverse order here because the wye track for turning was just long enough to handle the locomotive alone. On the back of the baggage car a Vineyard Tom Sawyer and his mysterious friend are ready for a free ride to Katama and South Beach, hanging on that short platform looks dangerous. The rails were light at only 30 pounds per yard.

This train shows the locomotive *Active* and all the rolling stock of the Martha's Vineyard. When the locomotive arrived from its builder at Pittsburgh it already had the name *Active*. The railroad changed the name to *Edgartown* and later to *South Beach*. But to most people she was the *Active* for her 22-year career on the Vineyard - and even today. The third car was the nicest, joining the line in 1877 and named *Oak Bluffs*.

the land. With steam up she moved slowly at first, pulling the two passenger cars. The train stopped at the Edgartown station and was greeted by a large crowd. She whistled off and ran along the beach tracks and on to the Sea View Hotel at Oak Bluffs on Nantucket Sound. For most of the nine miles one of the line's directors, Henry Stumcke, rode in the tender and kept setting off firecrackers. The large verandas at the Sea View were crowded with vacationers that sunny afternoon, August 22, 1874.

The season was almost over, but the Martha's Vineyard was running, which was quite remarkable considering workmen had started construction the last week of May. For the first full week of operation the company announced it had earned $375 a day. By the end of the season receipts totaled $5-thousand from hauling 2,900 passengers a total of 12,554 miles. The road and its equipment had cost $90,757.

The railroad sued the dummy's builder, Jerome Wheelock, asking for $6,300. That seemed fair compensation for lost revenue for the 21 days the Martha's Vineyard was without a locomotive at a daily rate of $300. Wheelock filed a counter suit, which he lost. Two years later he paid the company $2-thousand.

The Martha's Vineyard Railroad was heavily in debt, and since it ran only for a few weeks that summer after all the grand promises, many stockholders and some taxpayers who had pledged public money to support it wanted to sell out and forget it. The locomotive was placed in the engine house next to the turntable in Edgartown for winter storage. It was never intended to run the line except in the tourist season. In November the sheriff attached the rolling stock to pay some debts of the line. Some of the directors put up enough money to recover the cars, while other directors favored a sale of the assets. The board met and voted that idea down. They would stay in the railroad business.

That first winter began the problems that lasted as long as the Martha's Vineyard Railroad. Winter storms and wind undermined the track along the beach and covered other parts with drifting sand - some quite deep. The route along the beach favored by management because it was shorter and less expensive to build, turned out to be a heavy annual expense and filling in washouts and locating buried track every spring was a heavy burden for the island narrow gauge.

In 1875 the line was extended from Katama to South Beach on the Atlantic Ocean. There was a wye at Oak Bluffs and another one at Katama with a turntable at Edgartown. At Oak Bluffs the tracks ran out on the trestle wharf for the steamers and that wharf had a wye for turning around and backing trains out next to the steamers for loading.

In 1877 the railroad bought another passenger car from Jackson & Sharp's Delaware Car Works in Wilmington, the same outfit that built the first three. That June at an Edgartown town meeting the taxpayers, disappointed in the sorry financial state of the line, voted to sell the town's share for a mere $315. The rest of the stockholders and creditors, which included a very patient Old Colony Railroad Company, paid off the loans.

By the end of that season the railroad showed a modest profit. One reason was the number of people attracted to social events at the Mattakeeset Lodge at Katama where they had dances, picnics and clam bakes that drew hundreds on weekdays and as many as three thousand on a weekend. Most of those people took the Martha's Vineyard Railroad which sold tickets for $1.00 round trip from Oak Bluffs to Katama and included a meal.

On one occasion an Old Colony passenger train, a special from Boston to Woods Hole, had three engines pulling 30 day coaches. The boat line had to put on extra steamers and then at Oak Bluffs they had to await their turn at the wharf. The *Active* - which had her name changed to *Edgartown* and later to *South Beach* - clipped along at 30 miles an hour with all four cars filled with passengers. On the way back trains were run late at night to bring the crowds back to the Bluffs.

The island did everything it could to promote itself as a resort, since its once great whaling days had faded years before. It even changed Oak Bluffs to Cottage City, which sounded more like a summer place. It helped for awhile. But the railroad limped along, always hurt by a short season of earning power and the annual rebuilding of roadbed and removal of drifting sand.

The Martha's Vineyard never killed anyone, but it had an accident once at the end of the wye outside the Mattakeeset Lodge at Katama. The train failed to stop and went through the wall of the hotel and crashed into the dining room. The depression of the early 1890s hurt resort business and tourism fell off. A fire in September, 1892 destroyed the Sea View House, the Casino nearby and the wharf with the railroad's wye at Cottage City. None of these were rebuilt; business had declined too far. The following summer trains ran north head first and returned backward. That fall the Highland House, a medium-sized hotel near Cottage City, burned.

The following season, 1894, the area around Katama was a ghost of what it had been, so the railroad ran only as far south as Edgartown, ignoring Katama and South Beach. The Martha's Vineyard Railroad ran for two more seasons and following a dismal 1896 summer, the line shut down that fall.

Everything was for sale, and a Boston contractor purchased the *South Beach*, ex-*Edgartown*, ex-*Active*, that charming little narrow gauge steam locomotive. She was loaded on the deck of a schooner, which later ran into some heavy Cape Cod fog in Nantucket Sound. An approaching coastal steamer almost collided with the schooner, but someone on the schooner frantically rang the locomotive's bell, warning the larger vessel to change course - in time to avert an accident. It was a nice touch to the story of a stout engine that ran for 22 years on Martha's Vineyard as she ushered in the age of steam to that beautiful island, and ushered it out, too.

The island steamers to the Vineyard and Nantucket came under New Haven ownership in 1911 when the railroad bought controlling interest in the New Bedford, Martha's Vineyard and Nantucket Steamboat Company. The steamers became part of New England Navigation Company, which later renamed its marine division New England Steamship Company that owned in 1930 a total of 129 vessels. When the New Haven sold the island steamer line on December 31, 1945, there were but two ships left: *Martha's Vineyard* and *Nantucket*. The New Haven got $750,000 from the Massachusetts Steamship Line. Service under the new private company deteriorated, so the state created an authority in 1949 and bought out the line. The steamer *Island Home* was the first vessel to carry passengers and freight from Woods Hole to the islands.

Right The last sidewheel steamer bought for the company was the *Uncatena* in 1902; she ran until 1930.

Below The *Gay Head* at 203 feet was larger by some 19 feet when she was delivered new in 1891 from Philadelphia, and she ran until 1924.

In 1925 *Nobska* was delivered to the company by her builder, Bath Iron Works. She was a steam, propeller vessel that was sold 50 years later, in 1975, to a Baltimore man who wanted to convert her to a floating restaurant in his home town. She is back in New England waters where steamship buffs plan to run her.

On the Woods Hole dock there were always trains and other passengers waiting. In the middle to late 1950s Diesel locomotives moved trains to within a few hundred feet of the newer and larger island boats. Local service to Boston by train ended in June, 1959, but summer trains from New York continued to this dock until 1963.

In the older post card view of a steamer coming toward the landing next to the tracks at Woods Hole you see people sitting in their automobiles on the forward deck of a paddle steamer. It was a nice way to take a short sea trip cooled by ocean breezes and much more comfortable than sitting on hard wooden benches up on the boat deck. The steamers carried lots of automobiles once they were permitted on the islands.

The double-ended *Islander II* joined the fleet in 1946 when she started running from Woods Hole to the Vineyard where at both places special debarkation ramps were constructed. She was built in 1906 for the Pennsylvania Railroad and used in lower Hudson River service between Manhattan and Jersey City. She began life named *Hackensack* and though that name had been changed once she was at Cape Cod, the steamship people most often referred to her as *Hack*! She ran to the Vineyard, four trips a day, through 1949. She is approaching Woods Hole where to the left in the photo is the Oceanographic Institution.

NANTUCKET RAILROAD

The other major island off the south coast of Cape Cod is Nantucket. It is 18 miles from the Cape and 15 miles east of Edgartown, Martha's Vineyard. Like the Vineyard it is a summer resort and like the Vineyard it was, starting in the 1700s, a whaling port - in the case of Nantucket at one time the most famous whaling port in the world with as many as 125 whaling vessels calling it home port. Its name is Indian from the word Nantucket, meaning The Far Away Land. Nantucket is 15 miles long by 4 to 10 miles wide. The Railway Age came there seven years after the Vineyard got its road. It was privately owned and so there were not the pro-and anti-camps and town meeting bitterness that existed on the island to the west. There were a number of similarities, however.

Both lines were narrow gauge with three feet between the rails. They were built to carry summer tourists and then shut down for the winter. They were single track and built close to the ocean; they suffered serious damage from that. The Martha's Vineyard Railroad ran from 1874 to 1896, a 22-year life. On Nantucket that railroad ran from 1881 to 1917 or 36 years, but one year, 1906, it did not run at all. The Nantucket Railroad became Nantucket Central for awhile and then went back to being Nantucket Railroad once more. On Nantucket there were more locomotives and other equipment, including some gasoline-powered machines. The Vineyard road was 8.8 miles in length; the Nantucket was 11.6.

A former Nantucket resident, Philip H. Folger, was the major figure in bringing the railroad to Nantucket. When he first brought a civil engineering team to the island in 1879 to survey a route, he was living in Boston. The second newspaper on the island, a recent publishing enterprise, The Nantucket Journal, was all for Folger's railroad, saying: "...it will be a speculation by capitalists from abroad (meaning Boston and New York). A steam railroad is a thing to be most devoutly desired by all having the prosperity of the island at heart."

There were voices in opposition. One suggesting that a toll road to Siasconset from Nantucket Town would bring about the better transportation the former needs in order to grow. A town meeting that fall to allow comment on the proposed railroad, especially objections, produced none. It would seem the selectmen were very much in favor of the line, as they scheduled a meeting "on location and building of the Nantucket Railroad" for the afternoon of the day before Christmas. Only a few people showed up and after "gazing at each other for 15 or 20 minutes, 'according to a report,' the meeting adjourned."

In April, 1880 the legislature granted a charter for the company to build a narrow-gauge railroad from the Town of Nantucket to the Village of Siasconset. A Boston contractor was hired and he brought about 25 men in by the evening steamer on May 3. The following day they started shoveling and soon had a raised roadbed within the town limits of Nantucket. Within a week another 75 men were in the work force with some 40 or 50 teams of horses and wagons. Their efforts were monitored daily by curious islanders who gathered by the hundreds to watch. Many Nantucket people had never been off the island and thus had never seen a railroad. Their innocence in that regard would not be changed that summer, for the ties arrived in June, but the rails never did that year and the work stopped for 1880, although some 60 percent of the roadbed had been built by fall.

Management of the line moved quickly in 1881 to raise money to finish construction by issuing $60-thousand in 20-year bonds paying 7 percent and $30-thousand in stock with $100 par value shares. The bonds were sold at discount - $500 for $425. The company said it would have the road in operation that spring.

In early May the rails and two passenger cars were bought and then management looked for a used narrow gauge locomotive, which it found in Illinois. On the 30th the schooner carrying the rails was spotted by the town crier, William Clark, from his high cupola and he shouted the news around Nantucket Town. The next day at flood tide the schooner reached Commercial Wharf where a temporary track was laid with Clark doing the honors driving the first spike.

All during June work gangs moved fill, relaid ties and spiked down light rail. A locomotive engineer had been hired and he came by steamer from Woods Hole on June 30. Clarence M. Stansbury arrived the day before the locomotive and two passenger cars did on the deck of a lighter from New York. The first locomotive was an American type, 4-4-0, that was built by the famous Baldwin Locomotive Works of Philadelphia that year for the Danville, Olney & Ohio River Railroad, an eight-mile line in Illinois that shortly afterward was standard gauged. The engine was hardly broken in by its midwest owners.

Its name was, however, a surprise. When it was unloaded there was the tender with "Dionis" printed in large gold letters. That name belonged to the wife of Tristram Coffin, the leader of the group which settled Nantucket Island. Later that summer there was to be a huge Coffin family reunion and the naming of the first steam locomotive after Dionis seemed an act of genius, creating even more interest in the new road, if that was possible.

While Dionis was being checked over by Stansbury the two passenger cars were painted yellow. They had come from the Long Island Railroad where they had been used as summer excursion cars in which the seats were reached from the outside running boards rather than a middle aisle. They were truly open cars with glass partitions at either end for protection against engine exhaust and cinders, even though a new type spark arrestor had been installed in Dionis's diamond stack to avoid setting grass and woods fires. At least that was the hope. With somebody's new spark arrestor there was always hope it would work all the time. They never did.

Three miles south of Nantucket Town was Surfside, the terminus for the first year on the South Beach. The Surfside Land Company had talked of great plans to build a resort village there to the east of a life-saving station. The railroad had been influenced by such talk and was anticipating running back and forth to a resort until they could extend the line eastward to the Village of Siasconset. It was left to the Nantucket Railroad to build something that people would go to. That turned out to be a station - Surfside.

At least it was a station at first. More was planned for later, but for the opening run, Monday, July 4, there was a barn-like structure at the end of the tracks on the Atlantic Ocean side. There was a wooden platform for passengers and set back about 50 feet was the station of about 100 foot length and 25 foot width. A porch with a low-pitched hip roof ran along the entire side facing the railroad. There was a ticket booth at the center, bigger than a bay window. There was more planned, including a dining room for Surfside. But for now that was all.

The inaugural run left Nantucket shortly after 2 o'clock and reached Surfside without incident. The passengers were invited guests and the train backed up on the return run for more passengers. Each of the open cars could carry between 75 and 90 people. The second train was filled and within a few minutes of its Nantucket departure it arrived back at Surfside. If there was anything to fault, one woman said, it was that the trip was too short.

Since it was the nation's birthday there were festivities planned to take place after the large shore dinner that was served on long tables set up at the station. Glee Club selections started it off, followed by poetry readings and finally political speeches about patriotism with a reference to "the industrial and mechanical developments of the age." After which there were kind remarks made about the Nantucket Railroad. There followed several other long-winded talks which rambled about a number of subjects, but often concluded with praise for the line that was "keeping the island abreast of the rest of the world in technical achievements."

There were four, way stops for picking up and discharging passengers along the line. Two were in town at Washington Street and at Orange Street, both crossings, another was at Hooper's Farm and the last at Miacomet Pond where people went to fish. It was that kind of line where a man who lost his hat on the trip to Surfside could retrieve it after the conductor stopped the train on the way back. There were a few excellent spots for picking blueberries along the three mile track. The train let passengers off for picking, even though it wasn't one of the four way stops. Just tell the conductor.

When the station was finished later in July at Surfside there were dances with an orchestra and roller skating. In August for three days was the major summer social event, the Clan Coffin Celebration. Much of it took place at Surfside where 500 gathered for dinner, speeches, poetry readings, singing and conversation. The railroad had to make five trips to bring everyone out, including the New Bedford Brass Band. The second day of the Coffin reunion had its activities in town, but the final day was again at Surfside and six trains were necessary to carry the large crowd.

There seemed to be one person at least who was not happy with the line and twice tried to wreck a train later in August by placing a tie on the track near the Brass Foundry in town and again with a large rock near a switch at Commercial Wharf. In each case the

The first locomotive of the Nantucket Railroad was *Dionis,* which came from an Illinois short line. *Dionis*, the most popular of the locomotives, ran until 1901. The island narrow gauge had a total of four steam locomotives and two gasoline contraptions.

obstruction was discovered and taken away.

The first season's final run was on a Saturday, September 24, carrying the teachers and pupils from the Sunday School of the Summer Street Baptist Church out to Surfside for a clambake. That evening upon its return the train was covered by a temporary shelter at South Beach. It stayed there until spring of 1882. The company estimated that its trains ran as many as six-thousand miles, carrying more than 30-thousand passengers. Management seemed satisfied.

In May, 1882 it was time to get ready for the line's second season, and Clarence Stansbury was the man for the job. Stansbury had been hired as engineer for the *Dionis*. First, he checked his locomotive and then used it to pull the two cars to Surfside for a coat of paint. After that he took charge of workmen who repaired winter damage to the three mile railroad and added a siding with switches to move the engine at Surfside around the train, so the cars could be pulled back to Nantucket rather than shoved.

The middle of June the summer train schedule was announced as seven trains a day each way, leaving Nantucket, starting at 10 o'clock. The return from Surfside was a half hour later. A round trip ticket cost $.35. Most people who used the train frequently saved a nickel by buying three tickets for a dollar. Groups paid even less.

Again the Fourth of July was the big summer event with seashore dinners, brass band concerts, literary readings, patriotic speeches, hot air balloon ascensions and at night - fireworks. All of this was at Surfside at the depot where bath houses had been built, adding to the dances and roller skating parties. Surfside was the center of summer fun on Nantucket Island, because of the railroad and its large depot, which had become more a social hall than a railroad station.

The Surfside Land Company had divided up lots, averaging 50 by 100 feet and by November had sold 300 of them. A hotel had been bought in Providence by the railroad which planned to dismantle and move the parts to Surfside and rebuilt it there. The location for the Surfside Hotel was about one mile east of the depot and so the track was extended to the excavation. New flat cars were used to move the parts to Nobadeer. The hotel assembly started in February and finished in June as a four-storied wooden building with verandas. The social events formerly held at the depot were moved to the hotel for that season of 1883.

The number of tourists to the island was 10-thousand or about one-thousand fewer than 1882. In October at the stockholders' meeting, management said the railroad would be built to Siasconset in 1884.

Work on the extension from Nobadeer to Siasconset - another seven miles - began in March and finished July 1. During the final weeks of the construction a work train pulled apart when a coupling pin broke, throwing Thomas Hall, a laborer, under the wheels of a flat car. His was the first death on the tracks of the Nantucket Railroad.

On July 8 Siasconset's biggest crowd gathered to watch William Clark, the town crier, pound in what was referred to as a golden spike, an eastern re-enactment of the joining of the Central and Union Pacific lines in May, 1869 in Utah. The Mechanic's Band played Yankee Doodle and it was done. The Nantucket Railroad had been chartered to go to Siasconset on the eastern end of the island. And now it was there.

That first summer there were six trains a day from Nantucket town to 'Sconset - as the islanders call it - beginning at 5 a.m. One train a day ran only to Surfside and back. On Sundays that summer there were four trains to 'Sconset and eight to Surfside. A round trip to 'Sconset cost an adult $.80, children's tickets were $.40. Five adults riding on a group ticket paid $3.50 or $.70 round trip. A round trip was 22 miles. Tickets to Surfside - six miles round trip - were still $.35 for adults and $.15 for children.

Early in September daily trains were cut back to three round trips to 'Sconset, and after the 21st ticket prices were cut too, becoming $.50 for adults and $.25 for children. Despite the cost of the seven mile extension from Nobadeer to 'Sconset, management said its profits rose three percent: perhaps the summer mail contract to 'Sconset, the first for the line, helped.

In 1885 a shipwreck at Surfside produced some unexpected freight revenue. It was two days before Christmas when a schooner loaded with cotton bound for Boston ran aground. The crew was rescued and the owners waited for the surf to subside before lightering off the bales after Christmas. The ship's owner made a contract with the railroad to bring the cargo from Surfside to Steamboat Wharf in Nantucket for the steamer *Island Home* to carry to Woods Hole for the Old Colony to deliver to Boston. The flat cars used to move the hotel parts to Nobadeer were pulled down to Surfside by *Dionis* and she made a dozen trips with 60 bales per trip, salvaging more than 700 of the 1,000 bales on the schooner *Warren Sawyer*. The whole affair lasted two weeks.

That next season, 1885, saw the railroad increase its motive power and rolling stock by one each. The goal was to have two trains running that summer. The new locomotive was named *'Sconset* and was purchased from the Boston, Revere Beach & Lynn, a nine-mile narrow gauge that ran from Lynn south to East Boston where it operated a ferry across Boston Harbor to the business district. It was a short commuting railroad built in 1875. Local people called it "The Gauge." The new locomotive was ten years old and built for a Georgia line by The Mason Machine Works of Taunton. "The Gauge" bought it from its Georgia owners. Actually the Nantucket Railroad leased the engine, an 0-4-4-T or tank locomotive, on one frame with the tender on the back of the frame. The new passenger car actually was new and contained 32 double seats with an aisle between for a capacity of 64 people. This closed car was built by the Brill Company of Philadelphia.

In October the engineer Clarence Stansbury chartered the equipment for a few weeks and ran one train to 'Sconset at 10 in the morning and returned at 4:45 p.m. Stansbury charged a modest $.40 round trip. This may have been one way for the company to add some compensation to the engineer for his many contributions. Management never said.

Early in 1886 heavy storms undermined the bank near Surfside and caused washouts in other locations along the line. The track had to be relaid farther inland and the season went by without further incident, except the railroad's business fell off that year. Its income of $7,431 was dwarfed by $10,797 in expenses, including interest on bonds for a net loss of $3,366. The little line was in trouble and needed to raise $36-thousand to settle debt and repair storm damage, including moving the track back from the shore. So new owners took over and there would be more of them in the future.

One part of the island picture was not bleak - the steamboat lines that sailed between the Massachusetts mainland and Nantucket and the Vineyard. There was a merger between the New Bedford, Vineyard and Nantucket Steamboat Company and the Nantucket and Cape Cod Steamboat Company in 1886. The new company called itself The New Bedford, Martha's Vineyard and Nantucket Steamboat Company. The *Martha's Vineyard* joined the *Island Home* plying those waters and the line ordered a new boat, the *Nantucket*. In July she joined the fleet following her construction in the Pusey & Jones yard at Camden, New Jersey. The *Nantucket* sailed between Woods Hole and her namesake from that summer until 1915. She is the beautiful, white side-wheeler approaching the wharf at Woods Hole in the cover painting of this book by watercolorist Ted Rose. The painting was commissioned for this book.

In 1887 the Surfside Land Company was in financial trouble and about 900 acres of its land was sold at auction for $2.80 per acre! The cottage building that had been expected there took place on a much smaller scale, and the land company bailed out for pennies on the dollar.

The next year the Surfside Hotel got a refurbishing and the usual track repairs from winter's storms preceded the summer business. The topic of interest on the island switched to trolley lines in 1889 when there were two petitions to build them. One was a horse car street railway in Nantucket Town and that was approved and actually run until 1894. The other was an electric line that wanted to reach Siasconset. Voters turned it down as there was a great deal of suspicion regarding electricity.

The railroad line seemed to be deteriorating with *Dionis* turning over and later three derailments in one month in the summer of 1891. Every spring the winter storm damage that had wracked the eleven mile long Nantucket Railroad had to be repaired. At that time of the year after the sand was removed and twisted tracks and ties were righted, the line looked like two forlorn streaks of rust. So far the railroad always ran again in late spring and through the summer.

In 1894 management decided that it should run a more direct line to 'Sconset and also sell the railroad. Of the two ideas the latter was uppermost in their planning. The tracks along the south shore from Surfside east were again badly damaged and so the trains ran just to Surfside - the original three miles. That summer the tracks along the shore to 'Sconset were either twisted like pretzels or covered with as much as three feet of sand. That October at a mortgagee's sale in Boston the Nantucket Railroad was sold to a trustee for $10,800. The little narrow gauge was 15 years old and in poor shape.

The new owner set up a management team and petitioned the legislature to change the company name to Nantucket Central, making it a new corporation and a new route to 'Sconset, an inland route that would not suffer the severe damage from south shore storms that the old line had. Work began on the short cut that was two miles under the old line in length. The legislature approved the new name. In mid August, 1895 the new line was finished and service resumed but with fewer trains. The last years of the century saw the line limp along while Surfside turned to a ghost area once the railroad moved inland from it. Part of the depot was moved to 'Sconset and the hotel was abandoned and by 1899 had collapsed part by part.

By the spring of 1901 *Dionis* was in such poor shape that a replacement was needed. The Nantucket Central went back to the Boston, Revere Beach & Lynn, "The Gauge," for a locomotive. The engine available was a 22-year old, 4-4-0 American type built by Hinkley of Boston for a New Hampshire line, Profile and Franconia Notch. It was owned by the Concord & Montreal, which was part of the Boston & Maine, which standard-gauged that line, selling the engine to the Boston, Revere Beach & Lynn. Of course the *'Sconset* came from the same line.

The next four years were not unusual for the Nantucket Central, but in 1906 there was talk of selling the railroad by a bank that was the bondholder for the company. The sale did not come about and for the first time since it started running in 1881 the railroad lay idle for the entire year. Several old horse-drawn barges, four-wheeled wagons with hard seats, were the way to reach 'Sconset and return to Nantucket Town for the summer season

On a cold day the stove in combination car makes more smoke than the locomotive, at least at the moment this picture was taken at Easy Street in Nantucket with Old North Wharf Basin in background.

The Hinkley-built #1 takes a train to Surfside for the annual Fourth of July celebration.

At the foot of Main and Easy Streets locomotive #1 is turned on crude turntable in Nantucket Town. This engine came from the Boston, Revere Beach & Lynn and earlier had seen service on several other New England lines. The headlamp burned oil.

In this scene #2 is off to 'Sconset with passengers, their baggage and the mail. The two black stacks at the left belong to steamer *Sankaty* which was owned by the New Haven Railroad's marine subsidiary, New England Steamship Company, and used on the islands service from 1911 to 1924 when she was burned out by a fire while docked at New Bedford. This picture was taken in the summer of 1915 when most of the fishing fleet was in Nantucket Harbor along with a few dories and cat boats.

Number 2 was the only steam engine the railroad bought new. These two cars were new, too. This whole train showed up on barges in 1910. The locomotive seems out of scale pulling these attractive open platform cars.

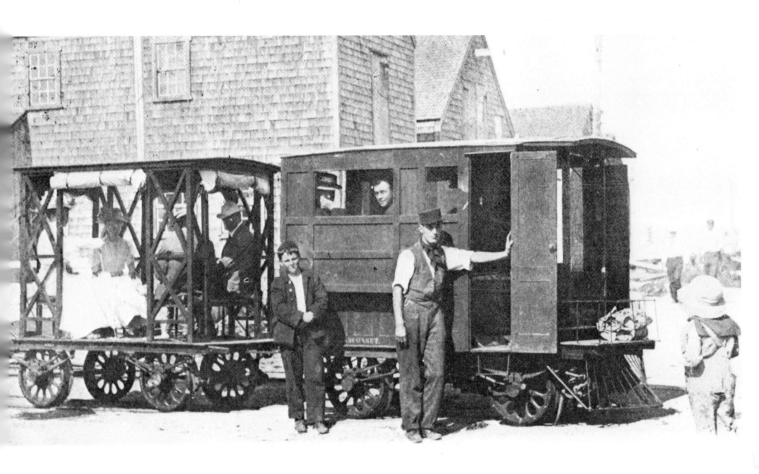

This 12 horsepower gasoline unit became known as *"The Bug."* The little see-through open car in the back is a passenger and baggage unit called the *"Bird Cage."* The *Bug* ran from 1907 until 1913. Her formal name was *Siasconset* and that is where she ended her career, crashing into a steam locomotive after her brakes failed.

Now this looks like a Nantucket scene on the waterfront. This picture from about 1900 is of locomotive #1 and a car with the railroad station under that long roof to the right.

This is locomotive #1 on the Washington Street siding in Nantucket after an accident in which she turned over, suffering internal damages that were mortal. She was righted and moved here, then boarded up in case repairs could be made; they could not and the railroad bought #2 as a replacement. This scene is close to the junction of Fayette and Washington Streets where later this engine was buried under sand.

Under the bank at Siasconset was the end of the line. Trains ran this way from Nantucket with the locomotive forward pulling the cars. This train returning to Nantucket and *Dionis* has moved around the cars on a passing track and coupled onto the end and will run in reverse. For most of the railroad's 36 years they ran that way.

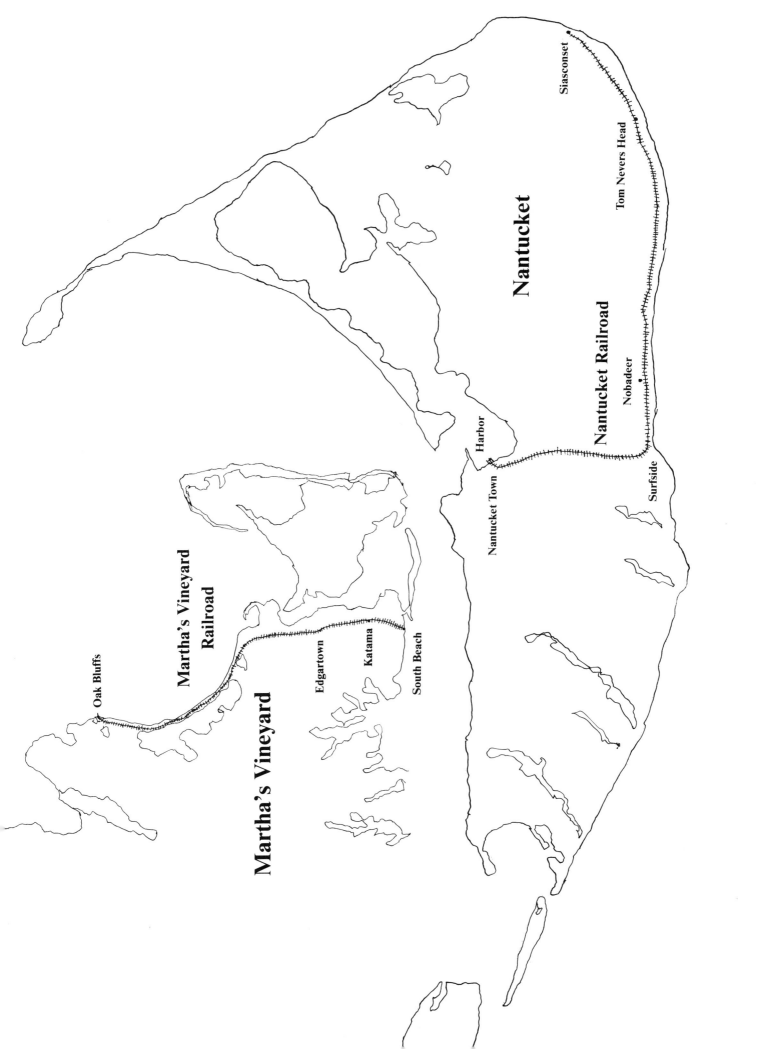

of 1906. It was an awful way to travel over those rutted, sandy roads. There was no train.

After a year of idleness the Nantucket Central Railroad was being looked over as a possible purchase. An old Nantucket hand, Thomas G. Macy, headed the successful group that bought the line for $12-thousand dollars in 1907. Macy, who had been clerk of the horse car line in town - The Beach Street Railway Company - became general manager of the Central. His brother, Cromwell G. Macy, Jr., was treasurer. They thought that $5-thousand if wisely spent could restore the island railroad to running condition. The state Board of Railroad Commissioners was petitioned to allow the line to issue $17-thousand in ten-year bonds at 6 percent. The line opened in July for the first time in two years.

In the fall when the summer-only railroad usually was put into hibernation, the new management announced that service would continue through the winter and it would be provided by a small gasoline motor car. The new vehicle was quite small, about nine feet long and seven feet high and resembled a box with four wheels and a windshield. It had a canvas top with roll-down curtains and three seats with a capacity of ten people, one of whom was the driver. The two rear seats faced each other and were leather. The wheels had discs rather than spokes. The machine looked similar to those motor cars used for either track inspection on standard gauge lines or for section hands to reach work areas. The Fairbanks-Morse Company of Michigan manufactured the motor car, which was powered by a two-cylinder, 12 horsepower gasoline engine. The motor car reached Nantucket late in November and was given its trial run with passengers the next day with a factory engineer in charge. On the way to 'Sconset and two miles east of Nantucket Town the motor conked out. It was late afternoon. The engineer tried to restart the engine, but it would not respond. Finally the six of them pushed the machine back to Nantucket where they arrived after dark.

Two days later the engineer found the trouble in the carburetor and the machine ran well and twice a day to 'Sconset, which was also the motor car's name, or rather the more formal *Siasconset.* The trip usually took about a half hour each way for the more than nine miles. The new machine ran through the winter and the Nantucket Central even got a government contract to carry mail on an annual basis rather than for summer only as before. A ticket cost $.40 one way, and you could sit on that nice leather upholstery. The success of the little motor car convinced management that the future lay with gasoline engines. They decided to order a bigger vehicle and they did.

The famous Mack Truck Company of Allentown, Pennsylvania designed and built the 25-foot long car for the Nantucket Central. The machine looked like a four-wheel trolley and had a capacity of 24 people. The engine was 60-horsepower and moved the car on level track at 38 miles per hour. It also had enough power to pull a passenger car. To management it was the answer. A small turntable was built in town to reverse the new machine. There was great anticipation among the railroad people and the islanders who had been told of the coming of this wonderful new machine. She finally arrived on the deck of a schooner from Woods Hole July 28, 1908. All dressed up with new paint and varnish the *Nantucket,* as she was called, was lifted off the deck and placed on the rails. Now here was a handsome and noble railroad car - new and gleaming. Her designer and a mechanic from Mack Brothers came along to show the Nantucket Central people how to operate her. Two days later was the trial run to 'Sconset and the return with 15 passengers. In the middle of August she ran the route, towing a passenger car and carrying a payload of more than 50 passengers. Things looked good, but then they turned sour.

At first little problems kept nagging at its success. Overheated journal boxes were followed by several derailments. Then transmission gears failed as did the drive shaft. Parts were ordered from the factory, but the problems through September were almost constant, and the Mack Company asked that the Nantucket be returned to the plant in Allentown. It did not return to the island.

While so many hopes had been riding with the *Nantucket,* the little motor car, *Siasconset,* had been running along well, and, in fact, had another car to run with it. A small trailer had been purchased and fitted out with seats at front and back facing each other. There was lattice work at each corner, roll-down rain awnings on all sides and a roof. It had been built to carry baggage, which it often did, but those seats could hold six or eight passengers. The motor car now had wooden panels and some windows. There was a small metal pilot down in front. It looked as if it belonged on tracks. It seems that nobody called it the *Siasconset,* its given name. It was in its early island days known as "the Benzine Buggy," but that didn't last. Soon it was called "the *Bug.*" The trailer acquired an alliterative name, too; it became "the *Bird Cage,*" and so they were the *Bug* and the *Bird.*

In the spring of 1909 it was no secret that the Macy group wanted to sell. The railroad had defaulted on its interest payments on the bonds and it had other unpaid obligations, and so a federal circuit court in Boston appointed a receiver who in turn handled the sale of the railroad to a group from New York and New Jersey. The new management decided to drop Central from the name after a 13 year tenure. So the line went back to being the Nantucket Railroad.

The new owners decided the plant needed rebuilding, and so they ordered new ties and rails, which arrived by barge in June. With 140 laborers putting in long days the old track and ties were removed and the new put down in their place. The trains ran smoothly, but the financial picture didn't and the line was sold at a receiver's sale in Boston in November. It was only three months after it had been entirely rebuilt.

It was late May, 1910 when a new locomotive and two cars ordered by the management arrived on a lighter from Woods Hole. It was all new equipment, including a combination baggage and passenger car and a passenger car. They were painted a bright red and had been manufactured in Wilmington, Delaware by Jackson & Sharp. The steam locomotive was a new 4-4-0 tank type from the Richmond Works of American Locomotive Company. The engine was coupled to the combination car with the passenger car trailing.

Something seemed wrong, either the engine had been ordered without considering the size of the cars or the other way around. The cars were good looking, first class. The locomotive looked too small in comparison, as if it didn't fit or really belong. The engine was # 2. Its steam whistle had a good, solid shout to it, but the bell sounded anemic. What could be done about it, since the railroad and its equipment were of great public interest?

For the time being nothing could be done. The new equipment started the season on June 7 with three trains a day each way, beginning at 5:45 a.m. from 'Sconset in order for passengers to catch the early steamer. The last train left Nantucket Town at 7:15 p.m. after the late steamer and stayed in 'Sconset overnight. The railroad had a successful year and when the season ended October 1 there was no talk of its being for sale.

The railroad started the next June with an old but different sound. The bell of the *Dionis* had been found in an antique shop on Pearl Street, Nantucket and was installed by the local blacksmith, John C. Jones, on # 2 as a replacement for the factory bell that had proven so unsatisfactory. The *Dionis* had the first railroad bell on Nantucket, and a substantial brass instrument it was. A good, loud, clear peal and not that tinny sound they had to listen to last year. Now # 2 had a bell to match her whistle. People were pleased, including newspaper editors; everybody said so. In the spring of 1912 # 2 needed new side rods and while she waited for them to come from the factory, the *Bug* and the *Bird Cage* ran the line for three weeks and then went back to reserve after the locomotive was steamed up for the summer.

The *Bug* was starting its eighth year in 1913 when after several weeks of work on her engine it was time for a test run. The man who did the work on her was Jeremiah W. Diamond who claimed to know "all that was necessary about gasoline engines." It was an afternoon in early June and Diamond wanted to give the *Bug* a test of record-breaking proportions. He was to get more than he bargained for. With the three friends that he had invited along, Diamond ran the *Bug* out of Nantucket Town from the wharf and headed for 'Sconset. The *Bug* was clipping along and her engine chugging beautifully with everything right that warm Tuesday. The engine had to work a little harder on the grade up to the station at Tom Nevers Head on the southeastern end of the island. Once at the top of the hill she started down the other side, approaching Low Beach and then end of track at Siasconset. Jeremiah Diamond decided it was time to shift gears from power forward to neutral and apply the brakes. The first part was easy, but then the brakes didn't work. The *Bug* was gaining speed and up ahead was the end of track. Staying on the *Bug* was not a reasonable choice. One by one the three friends jumped clear and into the sand at Low Beach. Up ahead was the # 2 steam locomotive on the end of the same track. Diamond jumped last and seconds later the *Bug* crashed into the locomotive. The #2 did not move; the *Bug* crumpled into instant junk. Diamond and his three friends suffered some abrasions in hitting the ground at speed, but they were not seriously hurt. For the *Bug* the crash was fatal. Two days later what was left of the *Bug* was loaded onto a flat car and taken toward Nantucket and buried near the car barn. The railroad's conductor, William Sandsbury, wrote an ode for the funeral that ended this way:

> For Your chugging days are o'er-
> Yes, your song's forever hushed
> Now that your're so badly squashed
> By gum! Ne'er again you'll make me tug-
> You pesky, cranky, gol-durn bug!

Twice that August the locomotive tossed sparks from its stack that set large brush fires on the moors. This had been only a small problem before, but islanders worried about fire, and one blaze back in 1846 had burned out the entire business district and nearby homes.

In 1914 the line offered passengers a major saving on tickets for the whole line. A block of 20 for a $5 bill meant that one way was a quarter and round trip just $.50. Each of those single tickets was a dime more.

In 1915 about 2,000 acres of land which covered about two miles along the south shore were sold to a group who started to develop the area for cottages on small lots. The railroad had built a station at Tom Nevers Head to serve that whole area and its expected development. A lodge was built on the tip of the hill there, and once again, as at Surfside years before, there was great optimism expressed at the lot auctions. With five trains daily each way there was always a long stop at Tom Nevers Head.

In 1916 the railroad finally after 35 years of running built small turntables for the locomotive at both ends of the line. There had been a turntable in town installed for the

Mack gasoline car years before, but it had washed away during high water one year. 'Sconset hadn't one before, but now engines could be turned both ways on the flat tables. Up to then, locomotives ran forward pulling the cars behind them running east and then at 'Sconset uncoupling and using the passing track to run around the train and coupling to the last car and reversing itself back to Nantucket. Now the engines could be turned at both ends of the railroad for forward operation. It was easier - and safer.

In 1916 World War I was getting closer to Nantucket when German submarines were sinking allied vessels with deck guns after allowing the crews and passengers to row away in lifeboats where they were taken aboard the Nantucket Shoals lightship. The unrestricted submarine warfare of the German navy was turning American public opinion against Germany.

In 1917 the sinking of neutral ships by the German navy caused the United States to declare war on Germany and the other Central Powers. After America's entry into the war in April, there was a huge mobilization and by June some American troops had landed in France. The first Liberty Bond Drive that month sold $411-thousand worth to Island residents.

On June 20 an accident at lower Orange Street crossing killed the driver of a team who disregarded a signal to stop by the watchman at the crossing. The train was approaching Nantucket and the driver of the team, William Dodge, tried to beat the train to the crossing. The locomotive hit the rear of the wagon and threw it around, tossing Dodge forward where his head struck the hoof of a bolting horse. He died of a fractured skull, and his passenger who was heading for a steamer was thrown and bruised but not badly injured.

The railroad ran on through the summer and into the fall. President and Mrs. Woodrow Wilson visited in September from their yacht *Mayflower* and took a carriage to Siasconset to visit relatives. They returned by carriage. No train trip for them. And soon no train trips on Nantucket for anyone.

The stockholders met January 3, 1918 in the station on Steamboat Wharf. They were told that the directors of the line had authorized the sale of "all the property of the Company, except land, buildings, right of way, and franchise." The physical railroad property - tracks, cars and the locomotive, # 2 - could be sold for more than they cost, because of the war. The previous year the line had run $1,500 in the red and had an unpaid fuel bill of $3-thousand.

Within two months the tracks were taken up with engine # 2 pushing flat cars of rails to the wharf for shipment to Woods Hole. The rails were loaded onto barges as were the cars and finally # 2, the last Nantucket locomotive. The Nantucket Historical Association bought the bell that had come originally from *Dionis*.

The rails, cars and # 2 were sent to Bordeaux, France to be run by the Allied Expeditionary Forces. The war lasted five more months. The bell from *Dionis* is today in a Nantucket Museum along with the headlight from locomotive # 1 and other memorabilia. They are all that is left of 36 years of railroading - narrow gauge style - on Nantucket.

THE STATIONS

This is the second station built at Middleboro. This was always considered the beginning of the Cape Cod Branch Railroad, but the station and other facilities there were built by the Fall River Railroad in 1846. The Old Colony built this station in 1887.

On the Cape Cod Branch Railroad Rock Meeting House was the first stop below Middleboro, in fact five miles below Middleboro. There were a number of businesses around there, generating freight revenue as well as passenger. Later the station was called Rock, for Rock Village, part of Middleboro. In February 1888 the snow from a blizzard was so heavy that a passenger train, running from Hyannis to Boston, was stuck in drifts for two days here. People from nearby heard about it and used horse-drawn sleighs to bring blankets and food for the passengers and train crew.

More than two and a half miles below Rock was this station, South Middleboro. This picture was taken in the 1880s and you are looking south toward Tremont. On this platform is Charles Hatch, the flagman at Spruce Crossing. On the other side is the station agent, Frank Wallen. This was in the Old Colony days. Just before World War II the New Haven eliminated service here, and the trains rolled through without stopping.

Tremont was important as the junction for the Cape Cod Railroad and the Fairhaven Branch. From here to Fairhaven was 15 miles. There were turntables here and at Fairhaven. The *Flying Dude* used to carry extra cars for Marion and Mattapoisett and they would be dropped here and picked up by a locomotive to take them down the Fairhaven Branch, while the *Dude* went on to Woods Hole. The name came from the Tremont Iron Works.

This is the original depot at Marion, on the Fairhaven Branch, that was built in 1854. It was moved across the street in 1904 for use as a combination express office and trolley station. This building is still there and is a home.

One of those original stations that was not replaced during its long life, was Mattapoisett on the Fairhaven Branch with a large apartment upstairs for the station agent and his family. Those wooden cutouts under the eaves of the upper roof are more of the early railroad Gothic than later gingerbread. The station at Tremont had them, too. The New Haven stopped running passenger trains on the branch in 1935 and this old building was torn down after World War II. This structure looks solid, doesn't it?

This station on the waterfront at Fairhaven was a brick building and the third depot to be built here in the 1850s. The first two were destroyed by fire between 1858 and '59. This building lasted from 1859 until taken down in 1929, though passenger service continued, in the summer only, until 1935. Passengers took the ferry on the other side of this depot across the Acushnet River to New Bedford. This station was 15 miles from Tremont, and the Old Colony passenger trains in the 1880s took about 27 minutes from either end, including stops at Marion and Mattapoisett. The Fairhaven Branch was unusual in that the four stations were about five miles apart. Leases, purchases and merges were a big part of small railroad economics in the earlier days. It had to happen, as there were so many small lines. The Fairhaven Branch Railroad was incorporated in 1849 and built in 1853 and '54. The ferry to New Bedford had been operating since 1832, and it became part of the Fairhaven Branch. In order to protect itself from another line taking away its traffic, the New Bedford & Taunton bought the Fairhaven Branch in 1861 for $300-thousand, which was its capitalization and, in 1861, the total of its debts. The Fairhaven Branch was completed the same year the Cape Cod extension reached Hyannis. Years later the Fairhaven became part of the Old Colony and then part of the New Haven.

This station called Tempest Knob was in Wareham; one of the smallest depots in America it was the first stop of the *Flying Dude*. Many of the *Dude's* patrons had summer homes nearby. This depot was later made into a shelter for a crossing guard.

This station was South Wareham, the next stop below Tremont on the line to Cape Cod. When the Cape Cod Branch Railroad was built through here in late 1847, this stop was called Burbank. In 1871, the Cape Cod Railroad changed the name to South Wareham. The foundation of wealth around Wareham was the iron industry, which depended on local deposits of bog iron. There was a foundry near here that made horseshoes, and the existence of that plant was a big reason for this station and a siding into it. This photo is from 1926. This station was torn down later.

Another depot in Wareham was this one, Parker Mills, named for a New Bedford industrialist, John A. Parker, whose interests included banking, textiles and whaling. Tremont Nail Company is in the original Parker Mills. In 1925 the New Haven shut this depot.

This station was East Wareham, but it also had a lot of other names. When the Cape Cod Branch Railroad came through Wareham in January 1848, this station was Agawam, then East Wareham, Onset Bay, Onset Beach, Onset Junction and Onset. That litany of names covered more than a century. Dummy trains ran once over a bridge south to a religious camp ground, and around 1901 the New Bedford & Onset Street Railway after the station was moved made a connection with it. Actually this station was moved twice.

The depot at Wareham was built by the New Haven in 1900, as the second one there. It was torn down in 1965. Twenty years later the town built a shelter and restrooms. Amtrak trains and those of the Cape Cod & Hyannis Railroad stopped here.

This small station was built in 1892 where President Grover Cleveland could catch or leave a train a short distance from his summer home, Gray Gables. This depot, also called Gray Gables, had a direct telegraph line to Washington and the President's home nearby, the Cape's first summer White House. After careers as a summer cottage and real estate office, this station was bought and moved by the Bourne Historical Society to the Aptuxcet Trading Post where it is today.

This station at Monument Beach was the third at the location and it is still there. The first depot was built three years after the Woods Hole Branch opened, and was a small structure operated just during the summer months. The second depot burned down in a huge fire that destroyed half the village in May 1906. Its replacement is this present station, shown in this photo from 1915. An apartment has been added on the second floor.

A single track, a sandy road, a country depot, a touring car and a local train pulled by a 4-4-0 steam engine with high-hat cylinders, boiler-mounted marker lights, a big steam dome and a tall, straight stack - that's how it appeared on a summer morning in 1915 at Pocasset. They called it waiting for the morning train.

This is the Pocasset depot on August 4, 1929 with a train from Woods Hole slowing to a stop. All the stations on the Woods Hole Branch, except the one at Falmouth, were close to the waters of Buzzards Bay. This station was on Barlows Landing Road, below the Pocasset River. Pocasset is one of the villages of Bourne, and in the 1870s and '80s there was another depot in Pocasset, but it was phased out because a stop was built at Cataumet, just to the south.

Eighteen years after the line opened to Woods Hole Cataumet got its first depot. It was 1890 and during the summer months the *Dude* train always stopped here.The second floor was the agent's apartment. This is looking north. A fire destroyed the building in 1925. The next year the brick building to replace it was erected, and it is still there owned by a civic association.

A mile and a quarter below the Cataumet depot was this stop called North Falmouth. This is the second station there and was built in 1905. The picture is from around that time with the train heading toward Buzzards Bay. In the later picture, a Mack railbus from Buzzards Bay has replaced larger trains in this 1937 scene of a unit heading for Woods Hole. This station burned in 1969.

The station at West Falmouth was close to West Falmouth Harbor and running north from Woods Hole the trip from Falmouth to this stop was the longest run between depots on the Woods Hole Branch - three and three-quarter miles. Old Colony passenger trains covered that in eight minutes. It is a sunny afternoon in July of 1915.

This is the New Haven yard at Woods Hole and this station was built of brick in 1899 and lasted for 70 years or one more year than the tracks did. After this line was completed and opened in the summer of 1872 there was a wooden station on the end of the wharf where the island steamers met the trains and where the ferries still land. This spot became the busiest rail-boat transfer dock on Cape Cod with the others being South Hyannis and Provincetown. The cover of this book is entitled the *Woods Hole Connection* by noted railroad artist, Ted Rose.

Opposite bottom This is the first station in Falmouth and it dates from the beginning of operation of the Woods Hole Branch, 1872. Two years after this was built, a well-furnished saloon, or waiting room, was added to the interior. A platform canopy was extended on this side and finally in 1912 this building was sold to the Swift family who moved it across the tracks and the New Haven Railroad built a replacement of brick. **Below** In 1989 a $1-million renovation took place here just 21 years after the tracks to Woods Hole were taken up and a bicycle path put in its place.

About a mile east of Cohasset Narrows was the station known as Monument. This station was there until the railroad built one. The family name was Swift and they operated a grocery store, which included the post office, express office, freight office and railroad ticket office. Since all these services were in the same building, it made a trip to town easier and less complicated. In 1884 when the legislature passed a bill separating those villages from being part of Sandwich and created the Town of Bourne, the name board on the station was changed from Monument to Bourne. There were many cousins Swift in the area and the family name achieved immortality when Gustavus Franklin Swift from West Sandwich moved his meat-packing business from the Cape to Boston and later Chicago.

This depot started its life at the other side of the Monument River and it appears there on the opposite page in the lower photo. Before the dredges of the Boston, Cape Cod and New York Canal Company started to chew their way through that area and down the valley, the railroad moved the building to the south side and placed it here and surrounded it on three sides by a new wooden platform.

Opposite This is the station the Old Colony built at Bourne, formerly Monument, with the tracks running down the valley of the isthmus in the distance toward Sandwich. Those reflections directly in the middle of the picture are in the Monument River. The single track on the right was the main line and it crossed the river on a trestle. The crossing here was old Bridge Road, later Bridge Street, running from Swift's Corner to Bourne Four Corners and was the main road to Bourne Center in those days. Look closely. The pole with the white stripe in the middle has a steel rod holding the wire for the trolley line to Monument Beach, which is off to the right and across the marshes.

When the Cape Cod Branch Railroad built through here in 1848, this place was known as North Sandwich. It was also called Herring River after the herring run on the other side of the valley. The station was Bournedale, but the New Haven designated its telegraph name as Sampson.

The New Haven built this station at Sagamore in 1909 similar to those at Buzzards Bay and West Barnstable. The Keith plant is gone and the canal is widened in this scene from June, 1937. A year later this depot was closed.

Many local residents lived on the opposite shore. The canal company provided four ways to cross: two highway bridges, a railroad bridge and this ferry here at Bournedale below the bank and near the station. This craft had a small gasoline engine that could do little against a strong current that often had frustrated passengers shouting to trains that left without them.

The largest station on the Cape Cod Branch Railroad was at Sandwich, for its time it was a big depot when Sandwich was the end of track for six years. That station was replaced in 1878 by a brick affair shown in these photos. The track off to the left went to the roundhouse and on to the Boston & Sandwich Glass Company, although when this picture was taken in 1912 the B & S was long gone.

On a summer day in the late 1890s at the right on the wooden platform is Postmistress Anna Fish. To the right is West Barnstable. In his black cap and black uniform is Albert Hall, the station agent, at the East Sandwich depot. The woman holding the baby on the left accompanied by an older daughter who is sitting on the bench is probably waiting for the next train. The photo may have been taken by her husband who crossed the track and told everyone to smile, including Hall and Fish. This was the second station at East Sandwich and was built in 1889. The first depot was moved some 300 feet to the west, toward Sandwich, where it became the freight house on the right in the crossing picture of what was then Main Street, now 6A, and the area was known as Spring Hill for the numerous fresh water springs in and around there. The springs are still there and they supply much of Sandwich's water. In this century there was a telegraph here and the New Haven identified this station as Royal. After the station was closed a former New Haven Railroad employee bought it and moved it across the tracks beyond the Route 6A crossing and added some ells, but that eight-pane upper window can still be seen. In October barrels of cranberries were shipped from here harvested from bogs that still exist.

s depot at West Barnstable was almost five miles from
East Sandwich station, and was one of the longest runs
ween stations on the Cape. The building was erected in
2 and its architecture is similar to the depots at Buzzards
and Sagamore from the same year. Many passengers,
uding the family of Joseph P. Kennedy, used to get on
off trains here and drive south on Meetinghouse Way
continue on Barnstable Road to Osterville, Centerville
Hyannisport. The siding here had a capacity of 18
ight cars. The New Haven's telegraph name was
ment. The platform canopy is gone, but the depot is still
re with a concrete raised platform for passengers on the
stern end of the station.

At Barnstable Village the Old Colony Railroad built this depot in 1889; it was the
second at that location. The crossing in the foreground is rather narrow, but it was
wide enough to carry Railroad Avenue down the hill to Main Street, left. The
Barnstable Patriot was published near here in a two-story building just out of the
picture to the left. The editor's wife would climb to an upper floor window around
train time and, using binoculars, see who was arriving and leaving the cars. The editor
would work this information into the next edition, usually. Pity the man who greeted
an attractive woman, or an unattractive one, on the platform when his wife was away.
The courthouse is also down Railroad Avenue. Passenger service began here in May,
1854 with a noisy celebration.

The first station at Yarmouth was in Yarmouth Port and when the Cape Cod Railroad built its extension from Sandwich to Hyannis in 1854 it was a sure thing the line would go through here, because there was great influence on the railroad company from stockholders in Yarmouth and a prominent ex-publisher on the board of directors. The first station burned in a spectacular night fire on November 17, 1878. **Opposite upper left** This depot replaced it and lasted until it burned in 1941. The Cape Cod Central built from here to Orleans in 1864-65 and this station then became a junction with the Hyannis Branch turning south and the main line running east toward Harwich. In this photo from around the First World War you see the north side with the main line to the east to the left. On the other side of the station the platform served trains to and from Hyannis. **Left** The water tank serviced locomotives that had long layovers here, such as morning passenger trains from Provincetown that would stay until late in the afternoon and pick up people for down Cape from trains from Boston. There was a gasoline-powered pump that Gerald Cash used to fill the tank when he was a baggageman. **Lower left** In the other photo from a family album it looks cold enough for a Smith Brothers cough drop or syrup when this couple waited for a train. The hand writing looks feminine; she wrote, "Yarmouth railroad station. All set to leave for Miami & Cuba. 1939." This small brick depot replaced the burned out one. In this picture taken in 1946 you are looking west down the main line. Willow Street, which was built because the railroad came through here, is behind you and the track to Hyannis runs behind those buildings to the left of the picture. **Above**

Looking west from Depot Square the photographer stood close to the middle of Main Street in the days of sandy roads. **Above** From the opposite side of the tracks looking east from the belfry of the Hyannis Federated Church a train is shown in the station, heading for Yarmouth. **Below** The sign over Main Street to the right is a crossing warning. The picture is from the late 1870s. The Main Street crossing in the early 1890s looked this way with the crossing tender's shanty behind the fence and Murphy's Bakery across the tracks that ran to the right down to the Railroad Wharf, South Hyannis. **Opposite top** Crossing gates were hand cranked by the tender, and the crank is visible several feet above round weights. All the gates were controlled from this position. The building next to Murphy's was an ice cream parlor. Baggage carts on the station platform contain barrels of fish for express delivery. **Bottom** In this 1923 photo an ice wagon is at the right next to an early version of what Detroit later called a station wagon. It's close to train time.

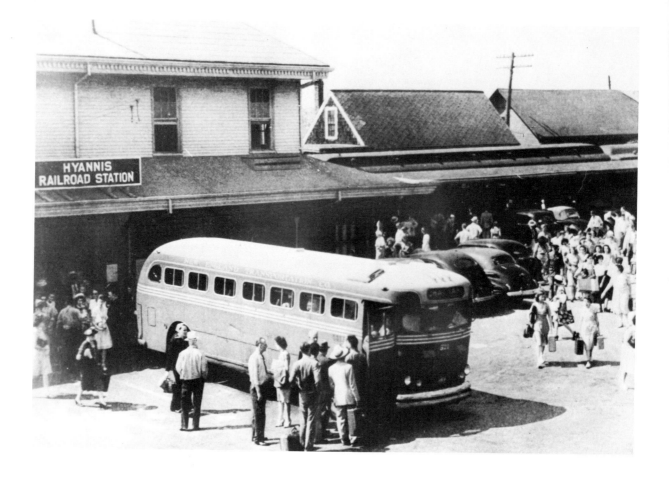

Above After the Chatham Branch was pulled up and passenger trains stopped running east past Yarmouth in the late 1930s, the New Haven ran its own buses from the Hyannis station to Chatham and from the Yarmouth station along the north shore to Provincetown. This picture was taken in the summer of 1946, and World War II had been over one year.**Below** This Pacific type locomotive on the Hyannis turntable was the most popular engine the New Haven used on Cape Cod passenger service. The roundhouse had eight stalls. Behind the water tank to the right the hopper car is on the coal trestle which supplied steam locomotives for years. This picture dates from 1947, and it is getting close to the end of steam power. Tracks reached here in July, 1854 when the train brought the world to Main Street.

This is the Bass River depot, just to the east of Station Avenue in South Yarmouth. A depot was built a mile east of here in 1865 and was first called North Yarmouth, then East Yarmouth and finally Yarmouth Farms. With the town developing more around Station Avenue, especially to the south of it, the New Haven decided to move Yarmouth Farms depot from Great Western Road. On a Sunday in August 1901 the partially dismantled two story building was placed on flat cars and moved here where it was renamed South Yarmouth. When the New Haven became concerned about confusion in train orders and decided to drop all West, South, North and East names of stations they almost called this depot Mozart. They came to their senses and named it Bass River. In 1906 John Frank Crosby became station agent, a job he held until the railroad closed the depot in 1936. He stayed on a year as caretaker in order to qualify for a full pension. The building was taken down in 1937, after Crosby became eligible for that pension.

The depot at South Dennis was a typical one-story affair of which the Cape had many. The Old Colony built this station in the latter years of the 1880s. The train racing to a stop is an early action photo. Those on the platform were leaning quite a bit, maybe too close to tracks, but they got back in time. This location is now the end of track. It used to be equidistant between Bass River and North Harwich - a mile and a half each way. Either way took four minutes when the Old Colony ran the trains.

There were four stations in Harwich and running east this was the first - North Harwich. There was once a large Ocean Spray cranberry plant here. The New Haven designated this station as Norman in railroad communications.

There are nine people waiting for the train at North Harwich in this picture from about 1912, but it doesn't seem possible that they all came in that automobile.

Harwich itself had the largest railroad plant in the area, with a passenger and freight station, a windmill, a water tank, a turntable, a wye to reverse whole trains, lots of side tracks and a junction where the Chatham Branch started and the main line to the tip of the Cape turned northward. Harwich was a wonderful spot for railfans. The overpass to the east of the platform is still here, but the tracks are gone. So's the station gone. When construction began on the Cape Cod Central, there were two gangs of laborers - one here and the other in Yarmouth Port. The first trains came through in December 1865 with the first freight to Harwich consigned to William H. Underwood.

The largest agricultural product on Cape Cod is cranberries and has been since before the Civil War. These wagons have brought barrels of cranberries to the Harwich depot, circa 1890, from the autumn harvest. The town also had a large cooperage, most of whose product was used by the cranberry industry.

This fill carried the single track main line into the Village of Pleasant Lake where the station had always been in a general store across Pleasant Lake Avenue. Hinckley's Pond is to the left. The track ran through those woods behind the buildings, including the general store in the center of the picture and wound around the western end of Long Pond with Seymour Pond to the left. It was a most attractive ride through here.

The Brewster depot was at the corner of Route 137 and Underpass Road. It was torn down before World War II.

This depot at East Brewster was sold and moved around the Nickerson State Park where it is used as a cottage. This picture is one of the few station scenes on Cape Cod where there is not a bicycle leaning against the building.

In December 1865, the Cape Cod Central completes its track from Yarmouth to Orleans where the first train is shown after arriving. As was often the fashion of those times, the railroad built a covered station, shown at the right. Such depots may have been popular, but they had problems with excessive smoke gathering under the roof and billowing around the passengers who were supposed to be protected from the weather by the overhead structure. At the left is the turntable before the door of the one-stall engine house.

This is the Orleans station in the center with a taxi and its driver, Ralph Rogers of South Orleans. The freight house is to the left. The line of buildings behind the station and off to the right is along Main Street. H.H. Snow's is a few hundred feet down the tracks and back of the box car. Snow's was a major railroad customer. This scene is from 1916.

This station served Eastham from the 1880s until 1940 when it was closed and then dismantled. The two water tanks were built years apart, as each had pipes running to a different pond nearby. The plains of Eastham are flat through here, and it was a place for engineers to make up time.

One of the smallest depots was at North Eastham. This station had the telegraph name Hastings. It was closed in 1935 and sold.

For much of its existence this depot at South Wellfleet was a flag stop. When these people were waiting for a train in the year 1912, this station had a full-time agent. In the 1920s he was gone and the building was locked with railroad business handled through Wellfleet. This depot was three and a half miles from North Eastham and two and two-thirds miles from Wellfleet. This building was demolished in May 1939.

The Wellfleet station from across the tracks, and a large number of people on the platform, is a Sunday afternoon photo. This could be the end of summer with visitors heading home. Behind the station was a warehouse and office for the hay and grain business of A. C. Freeman. There always seemed to be freight cars unloading there as well as hopper cars with coal for A. L. Wiley's general store and coal company.

Wellfleet was the terminus of the Cape Cod Railroad from 1870 to the summer of 1873 when the Old Colony completed the line to Provincetown. This station was about three miles from South Truro and 14 miles from Provincetown and 106 miles from Boston. The last train brought the evening mail and the motion pictures for the theater. They used to say "the movies start 15 minutes after the evening train gets in."

There was a large amount of paper work for the agent and telegraph operator, Howard Albert Dickey, at Wellfleet where he worked for many of the forty years of service he put in on the Old Colony Division of the New Haven. When he retired in 1956 he was the agent at West Barnstable. Behind him is the lever to operate a semaphore on the roof to signal trains. Company reports and way bills were a daily part of the job. Other necessary items in view are a scissors phone, a telegraph key and sounder, stamps and ink pads, books of ticket prices and freight rates, an alarm clock with a bell on top and a kerosene lamp in case the electricity failed. It was a self-contained world and the business came to him. Everybody in town knew the station agent. They also knew the time of trains, too.

Wellfleet oysters were an extraordinary epicurean delight, a rare product of local waters that could not be duplicated elsewhere. There were many years after 1900 when annually 200-thousand bushels were shipped by rail either by express from the depot or by freight from the platforms of these oyster houses along the railroad dike on Duck Creek. There were four companies there: Wellfleet Oyster Company, R. R. Higgins, D. Atwood Company, and Williams & Kemp. Oysters were packed in barrels and left on the loading docks for the night freight from Provincetown. Those shipments were for Boston and New York and customers who were not that far away. Express shipments were brought to the depot - a few hundred feet down the dike - by 2:30 in the afternoon, so the express agent, Vess Howland, could finish the waybills for the afternoon train. Wellfleet oysters were a feature in the dining rooms of the Palmer House in Chicago and other expensive eating places in that city and others in the Middle West. Once at South Station, Boston, the barrels were quickly moved to express cars on the Boston & Albany tracks for overnight trains to Chicago via the New York Central.

Heading north from Wellfleet you reached this depot at South Truro, the first of three in the town. There was a sameness, a uniformity, a consistency in these small Cape Cod railroad stations: one or two windows on each end, a wooden platform for well into this century, the wooden train signal facing the tracks, several doors on both sides, metal downspouts draining the gutters. This summer picture from long ago has a company conductor at the right who looks somewhat like the skipper on the Toonerville Trolley. Remember him? Much of the line from Wellfleet to South Truro was built on a filled embankment across the many marshes.

The depot at Truro was just below the Pamet River entrance which the Old Colony Railroad had bridged with a wooden pile trestle. Across from the station and closer to the water was a freight siding. This station was built by the Old Colony in the late spring of 1873; the approach to it was called Depot Road. The Portland Storm did extensive damage all through this area.

Truro station in 1912.

The New Haven provided this large settee at the Corn Hill station because the depot was a flag stop and was closed and locked most of the time. An unfinished road with two ruts, a sandy knoll with beach grass and bayberry bushes and a sense of Pilgrim history were at Corn Hill. Now this is country railroading! This station was only a half mile from the one at Truro.

There was more industry at North Truro, or Pond Village as it was called, than elsewhere in the town. The place had a fish freezer near the tracks, a fish canning plant and a bayberry candle factory. From the village you climbed a steep grade to the depot where you could see the fish freezing plant between the railroad and Cape Cod Bay. This is a summer afternoon scene, and it's close to train time.

This is the Provincetown station where the Old Colony completed the main line on the Cape in the summer of 1873. All the end of track facilities were here and a railroad wharf besides. Passenger service by train ended to Provincetown in the late 1930s. This station was 120 miles from Boston by rail.

ALONG THE RAILROAD

Cape Water Views

The location of tracks on Cape Cod gave tantalizing water views to passengers. First there was the bridge at Cohasset Narrows. If you were heading toward the Cape the right hand side was better at that bridge and if from the junction you were heading south for Woods Hole, the right hand side was still the seat for you. At the end of the yard at Cohasset Narrows (in the 1870s renamed Buzzards Bay) there was a pile trestle over the mouth of the Monument River. When crossing that bridge there was a nice expanse of water between Bourne Neck and Grey Gables where the Cape Cod Canal would be completed in 1914. South of the bridge the tracks ran quite close to the water, within a couple of hundred feet in places, following the western fringe of the glacial moraine, a belt of hills one to two miles wide from Woods Hole to the Monument River. From the train, passengers could see the islands, beaches and spits of the shore along Buzzards Bay. At Red Brook Harbor, Cataumet, and at West Falmouth Harbor there were water views. The tracks turned inland after that and the next water was south of Falmouth station on the left hand side where the line was within fifty feet of Vineyard Sound for over a half mile. The tracks turned west away from the Sound and offered a waterview next at Little Harbor and moments later from the railroad yard at Woods Hole.

Taking the main line east from Buzzards Bay one had to sit on the left side and get a quick view of sand dunes and Cape Cod Bay around Sandwich, East Sandwich and West Barnstable. You saw a little more in the late fall and winter, because the foliage was gone, but water views were quite fleeting through there, as some of the hills of the Sandwich Moraine shut out the Bay, still here and there could be seen marshes, tidal streams and dune beaches. The only water on the Hyannis Branch was around the Railroad Wharf at South Hyannis.

Down toward South Wellfleet on the left hand side passengers could see the tidal streams at Fresh Brook and Blackfish Creek. Crossing the railroad dike over Duck Creek there was Wellfleet Harbor and the Bay to the west. But from Wellfleet north there were the longest views of Cape Cod Bay. From the Truro station at Pamet River the tracks were on the fill and one could see over the Harbor Bar west of the Pamet River trestle. Once past Corn Hill the view to the west was constant and much of the line from there past Pilgrim Lake was so close to the water that the view approximated the one from Henry Flagler's Florida East Coast Railway to Key West.

From Boston to Provincetown by train was 120 miles and in the 1870s took between five hours and a quarter to five hours and 40 minutes. From Boston to Woods Hole was 72 miles and took three hours and 20 minutes. The Woods Hole Branch was 17 and a half miles long from Buzzards Bay and took 40 minutes. The Old Colony designated the tracks of the Cape Cod Railroad, i.e., from Middleboro south, to be the Cape Cod Division. Middleboro was 34 miles south of Boston. The Fairhaven Branch was 15 miles long and ran from Tremont through Marion to Mattapoisett to Fairhaven. That run took a half hour. The Hyannis station on Main Street was three and one-third miles from Yarmouth and passenger trains covered the distance in eight minutes. From Hyannis station to the Railroad Wharf was a mile and a half and after the Nantucket steamer was moved to Woods Hole in July, 1872, passenger trains stopped running to Hyannis Harbor. Freights continued to, of course, for it was a growing source of traffic for the Old Colony.

Keith Car

In the Village of Sagamore the largest family business on Cape Cod was named for the family Keith. It had its origins when Isaac Keith, a 22-year old blacksmith and wheelright, formed a partnership with Ezekiel Ryder to make carriages in 1829. The partnership dissolved when Keith bought out Ryder and named the little company Isaac Keith & Sons. Keith made tools, carts, carriages, wagons, wheel barrows and sleighs. He furnished Conestoga wagons that carried five tons of freight and were pulled by as many as six horses along the American trails that led westward. Keith's prairie schooners were smaller and used by families to carry household goods and the family along those long trails. His products were a response to land transportation needs and when those needs changed, so did his products.

Isaac Keith welcomed the Railway Age, following his building of two cars for the Boston & Sandwich Glass Company to move their products to Cohasset Narrows where ships were loaded for the coastal trip to New York. The Cape Cod Branch Railroad ran right past Keith's plant, located in what then was West Sandwich, later Sagamore. Keith had a spur built into his property and through the main building. By 1870 most of what came out of the Keith plant ran on railroad tracks, although the company still produced wagons and carts, in fact in January, 1879 one cart and nine wagons arrived in New Bedford on flat cars for a sea voyage to California.

The Keith family stayed with the business as Isaac's sons, Hiram T. Keith and Isaac Newton Keith, joined their father in the 1860s. The boys bought the business from their father in 1869, a year before his death.

The production of wooden box cars increased and the plant was enlarged as the Railway Age expanded. In the early 1880s Isaac Newton Keith bought out his older brother's share after Hiram was disabled in an accident. Isaac Newton Keith followed his father's interests, filling the postmastership and position of station agent for the Cape Cod Railroad, later Old Colony, at West Sandwich. In the case of the railroad the position was more honorary than anything, since another man performed the many duties of the job.

In 1884 when Bourne was split off from Sandwich that area became the Village of Sagamore. The Old Colony built a new station, a tall structure in which Isaac Newton Keith had his company offices upstairs.

Isaac's son, Eben Sturgis Smith Keith, worked as a machinist for four years in his father's plant following graduation from Bourne High School. After that Isaac promoted his 22-year old son to a management position. Isaac served three terms as a Republican senator in the legislature and on the executive committee of the town.

Isaac Keith died in 1900 and Eben inherited the firm, changing its name to Keith Manufacturing Company. Seven years later Eben Keith was elected state senator. That was in 1907 the same year the firm became part of Standard Steel Car of Pittsburgh and got a new name: Keith Car & Manufacturing. The plant expansion that had begun with Isaac Keith in 1830 continued through his grandson Eben who acquired additional land and erected more buildings until the property extended for more than a mile running roughly east to west alongside a mill pond through which in a few years the Cape Cod Canal would be built parallel to the Keith plant.

In the early years of this century the average pay for a common laborer was ten cents an hour. For the typical work week of 58 hours that meant a pay envelope of $5.80. Skilled machinists, blacksmiths and foremen were paid $3.00 a day. Men came from all over the Cape to work at Keith's. They commuted by train, getting off the cars at the depot which was right next to the Sagamore plant. Keith brought in foreign labor for many years, especially Italians and Finns. For the young Italians he built a number of tenements in Sagamore and later when their families joined them they moved into the same apartments. Those tenements are still there along Route 6A across from the baseball field and just east of the Sagamore Bridge. Eben Keith liked their work ethic and he hired more and more of them.

The plant remained busy and reached its peak during World War I when Standard Steel Car won the contract from the French Government to build 40-thousand, four wheel "40 and eight" cars for their railroads. The "40 and eight" designation was a reference to the car's capacity, 40 men or eight horses. The cars were about half the size of a standard American freight car. The last year of that war there were more than 1,200 men on the Keith payroll, turning out 20 of the small cars each day with 27 being the record.

During the 1920s Keith Car was turned into a repair facility by Standard Steel Car, its parent company. New Haven steam locomotives would haul damaged and sometimes aging box cars to the Sagamore plant where parts were fixed or replaced and the cars otherwise made new again. Keith Car repaired thousands of New Haven freight cars, but the contracts were occasional ones and the size of the work force declined steadily through that uncertain decade.

In 1928 the Pullman Company of Chicago bought Standard Steel Car and phased out some of its numerous plants, including Keith Car. The machinery from Sagamore, at least a large part of it, was loaded on cars in the plant and moved to the Worcester facility of Pullman. Then the Keith Car & Manufacturing Company shut down forever. It was 99 years old.

Within a few years the United States Government bought the property and demolished the buildings to make way for a much wider Cape Cod Canal.

Eben Sturgis Smith Keith lived on in the big white house just south of where his plant had been in Sagamore. He died there in 1935.

This photo from about 1905 is taken from the north side looking toward the Keith plant just across that mill pond, which was a source of water for manufacturing and fire fighting, when necessary. To the left of the stack and water tower is a yard where finished cars were parked before leaving the Cape on the New Haven tracks just back of the power house.

This strange looking structure was the second in this location. It was built in 1887 with Isaac Newton Keith very much in mind; his company office occupied the second floor. He was called the station agent, as was his son, Eben, after him.

This New Haven passenger train is stopped at the old Isaac Keith passenger station in Sagamore just short of the road that ran through the plant to the right. By stopping at the end of the wooden platform, horses, wagons, pedestrians and cyclists could cross the tracks while the train was at the station. The locomotive is an older American type of a class that was rebuilt between 1898 and 1903. This train is headed east on the main line for Hyannis or Provincetown.

The main line of the New Haven Railroad's Cape Cod Division runs straight ahead between the old Sagamore station on the right and the Keith Car plant at the left. Track next to Keith's is the siding from which spurs ran into the plant. Large building in left background is the paint shop with clerestory running along its entire length.

In the winter of 1918 Keith Car was manufacturing 20 of these "40 and eight" freight cars for the French Railway System every day. The man on the right was Charles Streicher, the plant's general manager. A few feet behind the telegraph pole is the Cape Cod Canal.

Keith Car built 6,550 of these hopper-bottom gondolas for coal hauling between 1906 and 1911. Also steel underframed, wooden box cars made from Cape Cod pine were a steady production from 1902 to 1912. There were 25,000 of those built at Sagamore for the New Haven. For three years beginning in 1926 the Keith shops overhauled steel underframes and built new wooden bodies on 12,576 New Haven freight cars.

The new Cape Cod Canal in July, 1914 before its official opening looked like this with signs of expansion at Keith Car including piles of sand this side of the buildings. Dredges are working in the channel beyond the draw of the Sagamore bridge; the waterway will be dedicated the end of the month, and smoke from the power house and a large number of box cars in the Keith yards indicates a lot of company activity.

The gateway to Cape Cod ran past Keith's plant, which in this 1935 photo is closed. Bridge in foreground is the present Sagamore Bridge, a fixed span 135 feet above high water. The old Sagamore draw bridge is to the left in about the middle of the plant, which had closed six years before. That June of 1935 the new bridge was dedicated and the old bridge dismantled.

This aerial was taken in the summer of 1935 on the western end of the land cut of the Cape Cod Canal. There are four bridges here. In the foreground is the new Bourne Bridge that opened that June. Next, in the middleground is the old Bourne Bridge which was built around 1912. One of its cantilevers has been removed; the other is in the up, or open, position. In the back those tall steel towers are under construction and will raise the span of the new railroad bridge. The rolling lift bridge carrying the tracks of the New Haven Railroad is just back of the construction of its replacement.

1935 Canal Bridge

The long negotiations for the purchase of the Cape Cod Canal by the United States Government resulted in the sale of the waterway in 1928 with the Army Corps of Engineers taking over the operations on March 31, 1928.

The New Haven Railroad had long had an interest in and been affected by the plans to build and finally the construction of the sandy ditch through the Isthmus of the Cape connecting the waters of Buzzards Bay and Cape Cod Bay to the east.

The construction work and rail relocation plus the double track bridge at Buzzards Bay are all dealt with in this book.

The canal was not heavily used by merchant ships and as a toll waterway it lost money for its investors and operators. The canal was narrow, too narrow, with only 200 feet surface width and a 100-foot wide channel of 25 foot depth. The government consulted coastal shipping interests and they suggested a wider waterway, a reduction in the current and removing the three draw bridges, including the bascule bridge carrying tracks of the New Haven. The open draw between fenders on all three bridges was 140 feet.

In September, 1933 the Public Works Administration granted a $5.783-million appropriation to widen the canal channel and build a railroad and two highway bridges to replace the three draw bridges. The highway bridges were to be fixed structures. The rail bridge was to be a single track, vertical lift bridge with a movable span 544 feet long. The Corps wanted a 500-foot wide clearance between piers and the fenders in front of them.

The new bridge which was built between 1933 and 1935 was actually done in two stages. The substructure or foundation work with deep piers cost $325-thousand and entailed cofferdams, hundreds of oak piles, concrete on top of that with concrete and granite channel piers above that. It was difficult construction with as much of it done by hand labor as possible to provide jobs for the unemployed during modern history's greatest financial depression.

With the foundations in by January 4, 1935, the steel men started to erect the two towers to carry the huge movable span. The Phoenix Bridge Company of Pennsylvania had that $987-thousand contract for the superstructure. For five days in September of that year the canal was closed to shipping while the middle panels were completed and the span could be raised giving a 136 foot clearance above mean high water.

Four days after Christmas, 1935 the first train crossed the new bridge in the morning. It was a passenger train from Boston to Hyannis.

The span weighs 2,050 tons and is balanced on either end by a one-thousand ton concrete counterweight covered by steel. More than 4,000 tons of steel were used in the bridge's construction.

The span is raised and lowered by four, 150-horsepower electric motors. There is an emergency generating plant on the north side in case of trouble with normal power from the utility company.

It takes usually two and a half minutes to lower the span and to seat it properly.

The Bay Colony Railroad employees operate the span, but are paid by the Corps of Engineers. The Buzzards Bay tower operators are Bay Colony employees and half of their pay comes from the federal government.

It works this way. When a train needs to cross the bridge, the tower operator calls the bridge operator in his control room on the north side. The bridge operator then calls the marine traffic controller in the canal administration building several hundred feet west of the bridge. For the traffic controller to give permission to lower the span there must be a wide clearance of big vessels, including tugs and barges, in and approaching the canal. If those conditions prevail a patrol craft is dispatched to about a half mile up current from the bridge to warn smaller craft that the span is being lowered which, when it is down for rail traffic, has only seven feet of clearance above the water.

Once the span is seated properly in the down position, the bridge operator calls the tower and tells him that the train can be moved through the bridge.

The speed limit for trains is 30 miles per hour.

For 23 years the Cape Cod Canal's railroad lift bridge at Buzzards Bay was the longest of its type in the world. In 1959 a similar bridge was finished at Staten Island, New York with 14 more feet in its length, so the Cape bridge was demoted to second place in the vertical bridge sweepstakes.

During World War II long convoys of merchant ships were assembled in Buzzards Bay behind anti-submarine nets and extensive mine fields as precautions because of Nazi U-boats. Once convoys started moving through the canal with ships at least a thousand feet apart, train movements were on hold both sides of the waterway. The presence of so much shipping moving through on the way to North Africa, England and Russia created frequent bottlenecks on the New Haven Railroad at Buzzards Bay. Troop movements to Camp Edwards and to Camp Wellfleet and from there often had to wait at either side of the bridge for an opportunity to cross.

The extensive track changes in the Buzzards Bay yards when the canal was first constructed were not necessary when the lift bridge was built in the 1930s to replace the original bascule bridge of 1912, because the new bridge was constructed some 60 feet east of the older one. On the south bank a new switch was necessary to move trains from the single track of the bridge to either the Woods Hole Branch or the main line parallel to the canal.

The twin towers and the 540 foot span are completed at Buzzards Bay. The old bridge is still used in this photo taken in late November, 1935. The tug and dredge in the center are part of a fleet of vessels that were enlarging the Cape Cod Canal, a project that was completed by 1940 in time for the convoys of World War II.

Camp Station

About one mile south of the Yarmouth station on the Hyannis Branch there was a Methodist camp ground from 1863, where summer religious gatherings were held, until 1939. Camp meetings had started in the United States in Kentucky in 1799 and moved eastward where the first New England camps were in Connecticut three years later and in Norton, Massachusetts in 1805.

On Cape Cod in South Wellfleet the first camp meeting was held in 1819 in August. The camp location was moved to Wellfleet and in 1836 to Eastham in an area called Millennium Grove. There was seating there for 1,000 people and on a Sunday as many as 4,000 attended, arriving on horseback, by stage coach, wagon and packets. Some began the journey by train first to Plymouth, then, later to Sandwich and to Yarmouth, making a trip combining railroads, ships and stage coaches. Eastham was difficult to get to and so there was unhappiness with that location, and after the 1862 meeting, it was decided to move the camp.

A search committee had shown interest in Yarmouth Port on the south side of Dennis Pond. About ten acres were purchased, running eastward from the Barnstable-Yarmouth town line. The Cape Cod Railroad built a station there in the spring of 1863, calling it Camp station. The building was 15 feet by 37 feet and was surrounded by a six foot wide wooden platform. Inside was a small waiting room, ticket window, a room for the station master, telegraph operator and baggage master. There was a large room for baggage. The building was staffed by the Cape Cod Railroad several weeks before the services started in August until a week or two afterward. The railroad paid for the building. It was located right at mile post 76, that meant it was exactly 76 rail miles from Kneeland Street Station. That first meeting was five weeks after the Battle of Gettysburg and there was a great deal of discussion about how to enlist the camp's draft quota, as half the eligible men were at sea either in the U. S. Navy or merchant marine. There was obvious satisfaction in Lee's defeat and his retreat, but talk persisted of the need to fortify Provincetown, which was considered vulnerable.

By 1870 the Methodists had bought a total of 43 acres of that spot that was a working woodland, mostly oak with some pine. The cost was about $56 an acre. The camp ground grew to 60 acres eventually. The largest crowds topped 7,000 in one day, and the smallest 3,000. Often the railroad brought in 2,000 people daily. To accommodate such numbers the railroad extended the wooden platform 240 feet along the track in 1866 and four years later put in a siding, because of the great quantities of baggage and freight, much of it food, handled there from the station to beyond Oak Avenue, the entrance that is still there.

When the station was open in the summer, guests and owners of cottages could use the telegraph, and starting in 1882, the telephone, one of the few on Cape Cod. Letters could be mailed there and picked up by the trains and stamped "Boston & Cape Cod Railroad Post Office." Incoming mail was dropped off at the Camp station. When not in operation, the station was a flag stop. At first the railroad built a crossing at the north end of the station, but it was not successful as traffic would back up from the long delays in unloading passengers, baggage and freight that blocked it. That crossing and later the one at Oak Avenue were off Willow Street, which was built in 1854 because of the railroad line to Hyannis.

To cross the Cape before Willow Street and the railroad were built, one used Old

Yarmouth Road, which then passed Dennis Pond on the east and joined Summer Street to Old King's Highway (now 6A) by Olde Yarmouth Inn.

At the southeast corner of that intersection, starting in 1855 the first telegraph office was located in Yarmouth Port in the Yarmouth Register's building. Much of the traffic on that wire was news dispatches.

Methodist camp meetings were so popular in the 1800s that excursion trains were scheduled from Woods Hole, Providence, Boston, New Bedford and Provincetown and after 1887 from Chatham. As many as eight excursion trains would arrive daily, carrying more than 2,000 passengers. At least that meant 40 day coaches, and some of those trains were so long they needed two locomotives. A number of excursion trains ran every day for a week before camp meetings began; these trains brought those who had cottages or would stay in tents for the five days or more that the camp services lasted. Some excursions were for just one day. Those trains arrived about 9 a.m. and left the camp grounds around 6 p.m.

The railroad ran shuttle trains between Hyannis and Yarmouth Port to meet trains from Chatham and Provincetown. Steamers from New Bedford stopped at Woods Hole, Martha's Vineyard, Nantucket and then sailed to the Railroad Wharf at South Hyannis where a shuttle train ran to the camp grounds and then on to Yarmouth to pick up additional passengers from Boston and up Cape stations. The shuttle between Hyannis and Yarmouth stopped at the Camp station as many as 12 times each day. A ticket from Hyannis to Camp was $.20, from Yarmouth to Camp was $.15. Later both cost one dime. The railroads gave rebates to the camp from the sale of excursion tickets but not on shuttle fares.

In 1890 attendance during the summer was still rising and the camp built a large wooden tabernacle that was circular, 103 feet in diameter and 58 feet high with a capacity of 1,800 people. As many as 750 would take part in communion, a regular function, and even baptisms were held at intervals. Hurricanes in 1938 and '44 weakened the tabernacle and it was dismantled in 1945.

Attendance at camp meetings started to drop off after 1900 and the station was a flag stop all year round after 1910. The New Haven sold the Camp station to a Harwich man in 1925 who took it away to use as a bungalow. Captain Lorenzo Dow Baker of Wellfleet, the banana grower and importer, was a devout Methodist who built a cottage at the Camp in 1891. Around 1900 Baker enlarged his cottage and then bought six identical ones nearby. He had the six moved by flat cars to Wellfleet and planted them just north of the present Town Pier, where they became known as the "Lemon Pie" cottages for their 60-degree roofs and their ownership by Baker and his work with tropical fruits.

The last Methodist camp meetings were held in 1939. There are still many cottages that are occupied year round on those grounds. On May 24, 1944 two residents of the camp ground were killed at Oak Avenue Crossing when their car was struck by a New Haven passenger train. Mrs. Fannie Ruoff and her friend Mrs. Minnie Reade had been shopping in Hyannis when they drove in front of an afternoon train from Boston.

Railroad Avenues

Often when the railroad came to a town in America in the 1800s, a road had to be built to the station. That road was named after the railroad, the station or the depot, an older term now mostly out of favor.

Cape Cod was no different from this small town practice. And these roads still have

Camp Station at the Yarmouth Camp Ground was open a few weeks each summer.
At one time there was a long, wooden platform along the side of the station.

The two Cape Cod Railroad Company tickets were sold at a reduced fare and were
limited to use during that August of 1866 and "good one day after close of meeting
only." The Old Colony ticket was unrestricted and could be used any time up to 30
days after purchase.

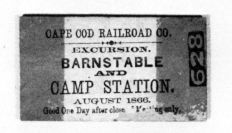

the old designation that indicated to the uninformed or the lost just where the trains were. Where the tracks have been taken up and removed the street signs tell you what was there. The streets never got new names after the tracks and the trains left and there were no more whistles in the night.

There is a Railroad Avenue in Barnstable and it runs to the tracks back of the court house. Hyannis has an Engine House Road where the locomotives used to be serviced. Bourne has a Depot Road, as does Brewster and Chatham. Dennis has two streets named Depot, but Harwich can beat that with four - one Depot Street and three Depot Roads, one of which was actually near the railroad when it ran through Harwich.

Eastham has one of each, a Depot Road and a Railroad Avenue. Wareham has a Depot Street and a Railroad Avenue. Truro has a Depot Road that winds down to the Pamet River where the station used to be close to a trestle that carried the single track across the mouth of the Pamet. Provincetown has a Railroad Avenue, while Wellfleet has the same and an Iron Horse Drive besides. Yarmouth has a Station Avenue and two Railroad Avenues, one by the wye where the track turns for Hyannis and the other near the Yarmouth Camp Meeting Grounds off Willow Street.

The Town of Falmouth has four railroad-associated streets: Depot Avenue off Palmer Avenue in Falmouth, Depot Road in North Falmouth, Railroad Avenue in Woods Hole and Depot Street in Woods Hole.

In Cataumet the single track to Falmouth crosses this deck truss bridge over Scraggy Neck Road, which intersects Depot Road. The paintings on the sides of the bridge of the 1872 Cataumet station were for America's Bicentennial in 1976 by local artist, Priscilla Levesque, who lives just down Depot Road from here. She repainted them in 1984. In 1977 a man driving a truck load of marijuana from Florida to a local destination drove the truck under this bridge and it became stuck there from the low clearance. The Cataumet depot is the other side of the bridge.

Jenny Lind Tower

On a bluff in North Truro about 200 feet above the shore of the Atlantic Ocean is a granite tower. It is by itself and appears to be completely out of place in that location. Its construction is of blocks of granite with a brick lining. The famous Cape Cod Lighthouse, or Highland Light, as it is sometimes known, is nearby. The granite tower is over 50 feet high and looks as if it might be a corner to an old castle from the Middle Ages. It is called the Jenny Lind Tower, and it has a story.

The tower was one of four at the corners of a railroad station in Boston, actually not the whole corner, but the top 55 feet of a 90 foot high tower. The station was built by the Fitchburg Railroad, a line that opened in 1843 to Waltham and reached across the Charles River to Boston five years later. The station took nine months to build and received its first train in August, 1848. The station with its towers was 306 feet long and 96 feet wide. It had two floors with the ground floor for trains and platforms and ticket offices. The second floor, where the important part of our story took place, had company offices on both sides of the building with an auditorium or concert hall in the center with 1,500 seats and an area for 300 people to stand. The station was on Causeway Street.

The Swedish Nightingale, Johanna Maria Lind, better known as Jenny Lind, came to America in 1850 under contract to Phineas T. Barnum of circus fame. Barnum guaranteed Jenny $175-thousand for a series of concerts. After half a dozen concerts in New York City in early September, she came to Boston where she was scheduled to sing four concerts at a hall called Tremont Temple. After two concerts and a one day trip for a single concert at Brown University in Providence, it was decided that because of poor acoustics and lack of space at Tremont Temple, the final two performances would be held in that big hall on the second floor of the Boston station of the Fitchburg Railroad.

The concerts were set for October 11 and 12 with seats priced at $15 and standing room $1. The first concert was a promoter's dream - a magnificent voice, a sold out house and an enthusiastic audience. The next night was different when ticket agents had sold more than one-thousand tickets over the hall's capacity. That was the worst problem but the heat was another. It was a warm evening and in the hall it was stifling. Those who had reserve seats were allowed in first and they were followed by the others who surged into the entrances and up the stairs. There were large crowds outside on Causeway Street and many of them were holding tickets. They were not happy.

The concert began but the noise in the hall continued with brawling and the smashing of the inside glass partitions that separated the hall from company offices. Some women passed out and others, men and women, were trampled by the crowds inside the hall.

There are several versions of what happened next, including Jenny singing and eventually calming the crowd while the orchestra fled by way of stairs to the train floor. Another story has it that after singing and soothing the crowd in the hall, Jenny, with great dignity, walked to the tower, the same one that is in Truro now, and sang without orchestra or piano and so enchanted the crowds on Causeway Street and on nearby roofs that they gave her thunderous applause. This seemed to defuse an explosive situation.

The next day the newspapers in Boston charged P.T. Barnum with fraud in selling too many tickets. Barnum was visiting friends outside Boston and he later claimed that he was not aware of what happened, but he wasted little time in leaving town on a train for Bridgeport, while having his manager refund money to all those who showed up with tickets from that disastrous evening.

Jenny Lind was married in Boston on Valentine's Day, 1852, to her accompanist. She stayed in the United States and sang on tour for most of that year. The Fitchburg Railroad extended its tracks to the west and its castle-like station was a busy place, one of four terminals on Causeway Street. The other three served the Boston & Maine, the Eastern, and the Boston & Lowell.

The Fitchburg was the northern route in Massachusetts to the Hudson River and connections to the New York Central and the traffic to and from the west. To the south of its line was the rival Boston & Albany, which had close associations with the New York Central, which in the 1890s was looking to lease a line from the Hudson to Boston. Since it would be difficult to get the Massachusetts legislature to approve leasing or outright buying both lines, the Central felt the Boston & Albany was the more desirable. The Fitchburg was in a difficult position, since it depended on the Boston & Maine for a great deal of its New England traffic and for the New York Central and the Delaware & Hudson in upstate New York for western traffic, heading eastward. The Fitchburg had little bargaining power and in 1900 was leased to the B & M. Earlier the New York Central had leased the Boston & Albany.

In Boston the system was consolidated and the B & M built its North Station to serve all those lines it had taken over, including the Eastern and the Boston & Lowell years before.

The North Station replaced the other depots on Causeway Street, including the Fitchburg's medieval castle, which by 1927 was being demolished. A Boston attorney saw the station vanishing and asked railroad officials if he could have one of the front towers to move to another location and erect it for posterity. They agreed he could have it, but whether he paid for the privilege is not known. In any case, it cost the attorney, Harry M. Aldrich, to have the top 55 feet of the tower from which the Swedish Nightingale's singing soothed the excited natives, disassembled and moved on the New Haven by flat cars to North Truro from which the stones were taken by truck and horse and wagon to a spot about 30 feet from the sandy cliff above the beach. A large slab of concrete was poured as a base for it and the numbered stones, some of which weighed three and a half tons, were reassembled and again lined with brick as the tower was when built originally in 1848 on Causeway Street, Boston. At Truro it took five men two months to reassemble.

Harry Aldrich owned the land on which he placed the tower. It was among a number of land holdings he had on that part of down Cape. Aldrich Road is named for him. So the question at the time the tower was moved can be asked again - why did Aldrich do it? That's the mystery. He had no professional connection to the railroad. He was a commuter and had seen the station many times, but so had others. Harry M. Aldrich died in 1945 at the age of 78. His son, Samuel Nelson Aldrich, inherited his father's land and the stone tower. The son said the connection between Jenny Lind and the tower in no way motivated his father to move and re-erect it on Cape Cod. Samuel Nelson Aldrich referred to the tower "as the most perfect of the four towers." Maybe that was his father's reason or one of them.

The land and the tower passed into ownership by the United States Government as part of the 26-thousand acre Cape Cod National Seashore in the early 1960s. The granite tower is still there, its woodwork and circular iron staircase is rusted and rotted away. The Fitchburg granite is as solid as ever - indestructible granite!

Walter Lenk of Orleans has been interested in the tower for years. Lenk says:

"What makes it unique is the fact that the legend and the tower do not concern any Cape Cod Railroad, as far as I know this is the only non-Cape railroad artifact on the Cape."

At 260 tons this is some artifact: a medieval castle-like tower on a moor in Truro, Cape Cod named for a soprano, Johanna Maria Lind, born in Stockholm, Sweden in 1820. The public came to adore this lovely lady with a rich and warm coloratura voice and her unique voice control. They called her the Swedish Nightingale and one October evening in Boston, Massachusetts she may have climbed the steps in this very same tower and sang to an audience in the street and on rooftops nearby. I like to think that she did, after all that pillar of stone on a windswept bluff is called the Jenny Lind Tower.

Below The Jenny Lind Tower in North Truro and the Fitchburg Depot **Right** from which the tower was moved on Causeway Street in Boston.

Structures

The railroad had certain structures necessary to its steam locomotive operation, especially at the end of track where locomotives had to be turned and where they usually had a long wait, sometimes overnight, until they were in service again. Fires had to be tended and steam kept up.

The New York, New Haven & Hartford had turntables serving its Cape Cod trains at Tremont, Fair Haven, Buzzards Bay, Woods Hole, Hyannis, Harwich, Chatham, Orleans, Wellfleet and Provincetown.

It could turn whole passenger trains on wyes at Buzzards Bay, Yarmouth, Harwich and Provincetown. The wye at Yarmouth is still there and most often used by Amtrak summer trains.

The nicest structures the railroads built, the most picturesque, were wooden water tanks to service steam locomotives, which used a great deal of water. In and around Cape Cod the New Haven had 12 tanks. There was one each at Middleboro, Tremont, Fair Haven, Buzzards Bay, Woods Hole, Yarmouth, Hyannis, Harwich, Chatham and Provincetown. In Eastham there were two tanks, each of which drew its water from a different pond. When the first tanks were built by the Cape Cod Branch Railroad and additional ones by the Cape Cod and later the Old Colony to keep up with expansion, the water was pumped by wooden windmills. All the tanks were there all over the Cape when the New Haven leased the Old Colony in 1893. After 1910 the windmills were dismantled and replaced by gasoline-powered pumps in little buildings adjacent to the water tanks.

Fuel for the locomotives was bituminous coal and it was stored at coaling stations, sometimes called docks, at the end of track. These docks were at Middleboro, Fair Haven, Hyannis, Chatham and Provincetown. The other was at Buzzards Bay which was the end of some runs and where extra locomotives were kept, primarily to service trains on the Woods Hole Branch. Of course from the time the Old Colony bought out the Cape Cod Railroad the facilities at Buzzards Bay were like a division point on most other lines.

The Roadbed on the Cape

In the earliest days of Cape Cod railroading the rails were iron and weighed 56 pounds to the yard, the standard way to measure rail weights. When the Cape Cod Central was built in 1865, the track from Yarmouth through Harwich to Orleans was 45 pound rail. In the late 1880s the Old Colony replaced all the track on the Cape with heavier steel rail weighing 68 pounds per yard. The next changes were by the New Haven between 1910 and World War I.

By 1917 the New Haven's track charts recorded that the double track from Middleboro to Buzzards Bay and the single track from the Bay to Woods Hole weighed either 78 or 79 pounds per yard. From Buzzards Bay to Yarmouth all the rail along that north shore run weighed 80 pounds per yard, heaviest on Cape Cod then. The rest of the Cape - the Hyannis Branch, the main line from Yarmouth to Provincetown, and the Chatham Branch - was all listed "as below 78 pounds per yard." With the heavier locomotives and steel cars, the New Haven in the late 1920s replaced most but not all the rail on the Cape. The next track charts available are from 1949 and they list weights from Middleboro to Woods Hole and through Yarmouth to Hyannis as 107 pound rail. From Yarmouth to Harwich was upgraded to 80 pounds and from Harwich to Provincetown is

Thirsty steam locomotives used a great deal of water. On the Cape Cod Division the New Haven had 12 water tanks. This is how it looked to Ted Rose when a fireman was filling a tender through the hatch.

listed then as under 80 pounds, which is what it was 30 years before.

The ballast on the Cape in 1917 was gravel between Middleboro and Buzzards Bay. From the Bay to Woods Hole they added some cinders to the gravel. From the Bay through Sandwich to Yarmouth the ballast was cinders and the same to Hyannis. East of Yarmouth all the track, including the Chatham Branch, was sand and earth. From Yarmouth to the eastward the roadbed was elemental earth.

By 1949 the New Haven had stone ballast with its superior drainage between Middleboro and Sandwich. From Yarmouth to Harwich the ballast was cinders and between Harwich and Provincetown to the mostly sand ballast was added some cinders. The source for the cinders was the dropping of burned out coal from steam locomotives into the long ash pit in the Hyannis yards. In that way the railroad used coal twice.

Buzzards Bay Before The Canal

From the tower all the semaphores and switches were manually operated. Station with bay window on main line track had a Western Union telegraph sign. Water tank is fairly new, replacing an older and smaller tank from 1872. A train is due on main line where several men wait, wearing Panama hats. Box Car back in the yard is one from SOO Line and may be a car produced by Keith Car at Sagamore, which built a number for that company.

This station at Buzzards Bay was built in 1872 the same year the Woods Hole Branch opened, using the track by the wooden platform. Tower was new, too. Passengers walked out doors the other side to board trains on the main line down Cape. The telegraph was a busy instrument here for train dispatching.

A New Haven passenger train is starting to leave the Buzzards Bay station for either Hyannis or Provincetown about 1908. Trains here always would divide with the rear coaches turning to the left behind the tower and would be a separate train with a locomotive for Woods Hole. Head cars would stay with the engine that brought them and go down the valley to the right on the main line. The Buzzards Bay yard had more facilities than most with an engine house at left with large water and coal capacities, passenger and freight depots, a turntable, a wye, lots of sidings and that beautiful interlocking tower in the background. To the right and past that line of buildings is Main Street where just after the turn of the century the New Bedford & Onset Street Railway planted its rails to the right and on to Monument Beach. Within a couple of years this line was torn up for the Cape Cod Canal and then all trains turned behind the tower to the left and crossed the canal for down Cape and Woods Hole.

This cold weather scene was taken from the windmill at Buzzards Bay after 1902 and before 1909. Main line down Cape curves under that overpass, which leads off right to road bridge across the Monument River. Freight house is the nearest building on the right. Main Street on left has a horse 'n buggy coming this way along the path of the New Bedford & Onset Street Railway.

The Railroad And The Canal

The winding Monument River was a pretty body of water in the valley of the isthmus before the Cape Cod Canal came through. The surveyors placed their stakes in left foreground for the line of the canal. This photo is from about 1909 and shows a road bridge in the center from Bourne station just behind those wooden buildings at the left. Rail line runs down the valley from behind buildings at left across deck truss bridge over the river until it disappears into those trees below the hill in the center.

The priority in railroad construction because of the Cape Cod Canal was at Buzzards Bay where both branches would turn and cross the new waterway on a bridge. In late October 1909 these carloads of ties and piles arrived. A crew of 60 experienced men started November 9 with that clam-shell dredge at the left, digging three pits for the piers to hold the bridge. That pile driver - in the middle of the floating equipment - drove more than 500 wooden piles in a grill work up to 19 feet into the subsoil of dense sand and gravel, deposits from the ice age. By April 1910 the work was ready for the superstructure of the bridge.

The old was still in service in the spring of 1910 with this load of bridge steel on flat cars pausing on the trestle of Woods Hole Branch. Merritt & Chapman Derrick & Wrecking Company's lighter, *Capitol*, spent months here in the Monument River unloading all the bridge steel that came by rail at the Village of Buzzards Bay. Bridge piers - the three of them clearly visible - had facings of granite to protect the concrete beneath from corrosive action of salt water.

By June 1910 the new railroad bridge to ca[rry?] New Haven tracks across the canal looked [like] this. The 300-foot long pile trestle to [the?] Woods Hole Branch is at the left with [the] movable span in the center to allow dredg[es,] tugs and lighters through. There were [no] masonry abutments, as the connection fr[om] the draw bridge to the shore on each side [of] the canal was supported by the wooden p[ile] trestles built to New Haven Railro[ad] standards.

By late August 1910 all the prefabricated bridge parts arrived from the Pennsylvania Steel Company and the bridge with its huge counterweight was complete and tested. In front of the pier in the water on this side are two posts which will help hold wooden fenders ten feet in front of the piers as protection from ships colliding with the bridge. Fenders also channeled ships through the draw. Trestle on the other side had been around since summer of 1872 as the longest bridge on the Woods Hole Branch. This steel bridge would replace it.

The railroad relocation changed just about everything at the Buzzards Bay junction of the New [Have]n. The old tower next to the station was [repla]ced by this concrete one next to the new [stati]on. This tower is still there and is still in service [for tra]in control.

The station area was expanded to include four tracks with platforms, where previously there had been two. There are two steam locomotives in this picture, and beyond the one at the left are work cars, one of which looks to be from the same time and design as those in the Lincoln funeral train.

By late fall 1911 trains were running across the bridge to Woods Hole as only a short stretch of track had to be relocated from the 1872 trestle to this new structure. Trains for down Cape continued to use the old track until relocation of south side tracks was completed in 1912. The bridge was a Strauss trunnion bascule with a single span 160 feet long that pivoted on the north foundation. The control of the bridge was interlocked with the main railroad tower controlling all signals and switches in the Buzzards Bay yard, although arranged so that the tower operator could free the bridge for independent operation.

After the canal opened in the summer of 1914, much of the marine traffic was coastal tows. The clearance between the water and the span when the bridge was closed was only 12 feet. The channel was dredged to 25 feet. The total cost of rail relocation, including the yard, switches, the bridge, 6.3 miles of main line and 1.2 miles of sidings and signals was $379,274.05.

The rail bridge enabled the New Haven to make a single crossing of the Cape Cod Canal just below the Buzzards Bay yard on the south bank of the waterway. Double tracks came into Buzzards Bay; single tracks left this way. The rail bridge was the most efficiently built part of the entire canal project. The substructure and the bridge took from November 1909 until September 1910. Subcontractors did the work and they didn't let any grass grow. A delay in relocating tracks, especially along the south side of the canal, held up the actual use of the bridge for more than a year. Lever action to move switches and signals - the old system could not be used on this draw bridge with its home and distant signals on the other side of the canal all interlocked and controlled from the tower, so the older, mechanical system had to be replaced with a new electro-pneumatic one. This is the north end of the bridge with its huge cement counterweight that balanced the single span so well that two, 65-horsepower electric motors could raise or lower it in one minute. There were three sources of power: Southeastern Massachusetts Power & Electric Company, storage batteries and the New Bedford & Onset Street Railway. The wooden fenders were attached to piles extending both sides of the bridge and ten feet in front on the piers. White gates closed automatically when the bridge opened for ship traffic. The track on the left ran to Sandwich, on the right to Woods Hole. Only railroad workers were allowed on this bridge, but everyone used to walk across as a short cut.

At Buzzards Bay this track gang is laying rail with a popular ballast on Cape Cod - sand. Train at left may be a special, since the only car is a caboose. Photo is from 1909 or '10.

It is June 24, 1912 and the relocation of the New Haven main line single track is almost complete. This safety-conscious Cape Codder has wisely chosen the now abandoned old right of way for his noontime stroll. This scene is in Bournedale. The train is headed east toward Sandwich.

The same day - June 24, 1912 - the photographer went to the west end of the relocated section of track in Bournedale where the train is headed for Buzzards Bay. Old right of way is to the left and it crossed the line of the canal three times, because when it was built - to avoid heavy cutting - it followed the easiest contours of the valley. The canal company had to pay for relocating the tracks. That expense amounted to just under $200-thousand. Wilson & English, one of the canal steam shovel contractors, did the work.

This is William Stoddard Crocker, a civil engineer, who helped survey a new route for the tracks down the valley of the isthmus of Cape Cod. He is using a hatchet to drive line stakes. His smile indicates he is camera conscious. There was no date or place accompanying this photo, so it probably was the spring of 1909. Crocker married a woman from Sandwich, Dorothy Crane, in 1911. He later was the town engineer of Bourne before moving to Boston where he joined an engineering firm.

Crews who relocated the New Haven tracks back from the Cape Cod Canal lived and ate in these older wooden box cars which were converted to bunk cars and mess cars on the south side of the valley in Bourne. Track looping to the right of picture was narrow gauge for removal of material dug by steam shovels. The 6.3 miles of single, main line track relocated was through this region both sides of the photo.

The Wilson & English Construction Company of New York did the railroad relocation work as a subcontractor for the Boston, Cape Cod and New York Canal Company. Shovel #3 removed parts of the Ellis Cemetery in Bournedale by loading these sidedumping single-truck cars behind the narrow-guage saddletank locomotive in the center. New Haven Railroad tracks are in the foreground.

Construction Railroad

The last railroad line to be built on the Cape had no name, no permanent tracks, and was submerged by water after its work was completed. It was the construction railroad that was used to dig a part of the Cape Cod Canal. It had been suggested earlier by William Barclay Parsons, the chief engineer, to the contractors that steam shovels be used in the land cut of the isthmus. Canal construction was almost two years underway when finally in May, 1911 the C. W. Reynolds Company put temporary tracks down in Sagamore and loaded flat cars with hand labor. At that rate it would have taken through two world wars and the Eisenhower presidency to finish, but work stepped up when a Marion steam shovel arrived in August. It had been preceded in July when the Wilson and English Construction Company put two steam shovels to work to the west near Bournedale Village. Four saddletank locomotives and forty side dump cars moved the material out of the trench and over to the sides on track that was laid and re-laid as the shovels progressed.

The work continued through that winter and this successful "dry" digging prompted the canal construction company to increase that effort. So the summer of 1912, the third year of canal construction, saw bigger steam shovels of the E. W. Foley Company of New York loading single-truck cars in the valley between Bournedale and Bourne. They were so successful that the contract was extended beyond the original dimensions so that almost 7,000 feet of excavation was steam shovel work. If started sooner, as Parsons suggested, the canal could have been finished two years earlier in 1912, or at least by early spring of 1913.

Parsons knew that the Panama Canal was mostly a steam shovel job, which meant temporary tracks, dump cars and locomotives. On Cape Cod from the beginning in June, 1909, shovels could have opened up the valley for most of the eight miles between Sandwich and Buzzards Bay.

No matter the weather, the construction railroad operated daily, except Christmas and July Fourth, and its success brought a new contract in February, 1913, after which Foley's shovels were to dig to a depth of twenty feet below ground water which is ten feet below sea level.

Keeping the trench dry was never a problem. A series of natural dams were left and electrically-driven pumps were used with two steam pumps as stand-by. When an area was cleaned out to the agreed depth, the tracks were removed to the next section along with the shovels and trains. More than 800-thousand cubic yards of material were removed by the narrow gauge trains. The dredges moving toward each other finished the work, cut through the dams and removed the spoil to an eventual depth of twenty-five feet in the channel.

Sub-contractor, Wilson & English, was dry digging with two shovels, four of these narrow gauge, tank locomotives and forty of these sidedumping cars. One of these locomotives could move six to nine cars quite easily when the rails were laid on fairly level ground.

Another New York contractor took over the steam shovel work in August, 1912 and its big machines seen here in Bournedale are loading cars from three cubic yard buckets. These machines were rugged and reliable and the work trains scooted around with great efficiency. With no set distance for tie centers, these tracks went down fast, lasted a month at best and were quickly moved. Spiking was directly to the ties.

Steam shovels were by far the easier way to remove the smaller boulders that were found in abundance along the path of the canal. Shovel operators had to be careful with them when loading these narrow gauge cars.

In June, 1913, August Belmont, the New York financier whose company built the canal, brought a group of investors to inspect progress of construction. At Buzzards Bay they rode on a tug through the western end and the railroad bridge. Three cars were converted to open air passenger service for the occasion by adding wooden benches. The trip over these tracks this day is the only passenger train the temporary construction railroad ran in the two and one-half years of its existence. The small engines, cars, and rail arrived by flat car on the New Haven. It left the same way in late winter, 1914. Its job well done.

Lot of construction activity here. Start way back at the dredge Herrick in the background toward left. Two steam shovels load an eight car train, while two trains wait to move this way to be loaded. Train on natural dam on the right carries a load of ties that will be used to lay more track in the next section. That long fill of sand across the trench was a disposal area and the flimsy trestle carried trains farther back. New Haven Railroad's single track main line runs under the trestle parallel to canal route. Natural dam here is later called Foley's Dyke and will be the last barrier to opening the canal. There were three steam shovel sections divided by natural dams, so that dredges approaching from either end could reach the middle gradually where the final digging would take place. This was the longest steam shovel section, 4,200 feet.

One of the worst weather jokes on Cape Cod says, "it never snows here." It does, however, snow and on occasion quite heavily. This double-headed passenger train from Provincetown stalled in heavy drifts in Orleans in the late 1880s. This crew hand shoveled the train out.

Ten years or so later the New Haven ran a plow
ahead of this engine in the cut just west of the
Chatham station. The snow had drifted in too
deeply and hand shoveling, which always works,
was needed to extricate the buried plow.

At Buzzards Bay in the early 1900s a wedge plow is pulled back to make another run in this direction down the main line toward Sandwich.

Some gigantic snow drifts in North Truro on January 10, 1910 stalled the local freight from Sandwich to Provincetown. It took more than three days to clear the railroad here, as some of these drifts were around 15 feet deep. The fireman on the locomotive, George A. McComisky, had enough coal to maintain the fire, but he had to shovel snow into the tank for water.

This scene was unusual enough to fine its way onto post cards.

In the locomotive behind this plow the engineer is maintaining enough speed to butt through the snow and avoid stalling in it. This is down Cape, maybe South Wellfleet, where the station agent had cleared some snow from the platform. Whoever took this picture must have jumped back fast.

At Pleasant Lake a wedge plow hasn't much to move on the front of this work train in the early 1930s.

PORTLAND STORM

One of the worst storms to hit New England was actually a combination of two storms that met, combined their forces, if you will, and created a nightmare for shipping. The storm is still known as the Portland Gale or Hurricane or just plain Portland Storm.

It was the worst maritime tragedy in New England during the nineteenth century. It is named for the steamship *Portland,* a beautifully graceful white sidewheel vessel that sailed out of Boston bound for Portland, Maine on Saturday evening, November 26, 1898. The *Portland* had sailed with 176 passengers and crew. She was seen or some people think they saw her the next day off the tip of Cape Cod. That was Sunday and objects from the *Portland* began to come ashore around 7 p.m. About four hours later and before midnight a mass of wreckage piled up on the beach between Race Point and Peaked Hill Bars. Bodies were washing up on the shore, too.

The *Portland* and her sister ship, *Bay State,* were owned by the Portland Steam Packet Company which ran them between Boston and Portland year round, usually sailing from each city at 7 p.m. for the overnight trip.

On that Saturday the weather bureau had warned of a severe storm moving east toward Boston from the Great Lakes. At the same time another storm was moving north up the coast. The general manager of the steamship line called his Boston agent around 5:30 p.m. to speak to the captain of the *Portland,* Hollis Blanchard, who wasn't around. Word was left for Blanchard to hold the *Portland* at the dock until 9 p.m. and if the weather was threatening then, to stay in port. It was never established whether the captain received the message, but if he did, he ignored it and the *Portland* sailed on schedule.

It started to snow in Boston, according to the weather bureau, at exactly 7:37. The wind was rising as the steamer ran north and it was snowing harder as she passed the twin lights on Thatcher's Island off Rockport, Cape Ann. She passed that spot at about 9:30, the usual time, and the lighthouse staff thought the snow and wind to be about normal for late November - but not for long. Those two storm systems came together a short time afterward and created a vicious hurricane centered around Cape Cod. The wind gauge at Highland Light in Truro registered 90 miles and hour and then it blew away.

Against this kind of northeaster the *Portland* could not make headway and she was seen several times farther and farther south of where she normally would be. Captain Blanchard may have headed out to sea to ride out the storm, but in that kind of wild night a sidewheel paddle steamer with vulnerable guards along her hull is not a safe ship. The high winds and turbulent seas were probably too much for the *Portland* and the storm relentlessly drove her across Massachusetts Bay toward the tip of Cape Cod.

A remarkable thing happened the next morning, Sunday, when apparently the eye of the storm, a calm period, moved in between 9:30 and 10 or 11 o'clock. The wind died down, the snow stopped and the sun came out briefly. During that lull several people said they spotted two coastal steamers off shore near Highland Light, North Truro. One of the ships may have been the *Portland* and the other the *Pentagoet,* a smaller propeller freighter that was en route from New York to Rockland, Maine with a cargo of Christmas merchandise for local stores. There were no other steamers in the vicinity.

Then the storm returned with its high winds and heavy, blowing snow. That was shortly before noon. Possibly the *Portland* survived until that night. No one survived of her passengers and crew. The author, Thomas Harrison Eames, investigated the tragedy for years. Of course there was no one to tell him what the end was like, so he put it this way: "It seems probable that the intense smashing she received through the night had weakened her, and finally the pounding of the sea under her guards opened her up and allowed tons of water to rush into the hull, flooding engine and boiler rooms, drowning the men working there, and depriving the ship of her power." Eames went on: "The water crashing into the helpless vessel would smash any lifeboats which may have remained, tear off doors, and burst through windows and ports, and washing helpless occupants of staterooms to death in a churning sea. Those inside were thrown into the icy water as the wooden deckhouse disintegrated, some being killed outright by falling beams, and other debris...many who had equipped themselves with lifebelts or grasped floating wreckage were benumbed by the frigid water and hammered so unmercifully by the gigantic waves that they soon died."

On the shore a surfman, walking near the beach between the Peaked Hill Bars Life Saving Station and a half way house to the west toward Race Point, saw something thrown up by the waves. By the dim light of his lantern he discovered it was a lifebelt with the words "Steamer Portland of Portland." About a half hour later he found more objects, a number of creamery cans. Another surfman at 9:30 discovered doors and other light woodwork on the beach. A great mass of wreckage came ashore shortly before midnight and them the first body was discovered. It came out of the surf at North Truro and was wearing a *Portland* lifebelt. Through the night there were more bodies and on Monday they were found near Nauset Harbor. In the days following and for more than a week bodies were picked up at Wellfleet, Orleans and Chatham. There were 35 of them recovered from the 176 who sailed that Saturday from India Wharf, Boston. When the storm struck late Saturday night there were more than 200 vessels at sea. We know that 141 of them were lost. At Vineyard Haven on Martha's Vineyard there were three sailing ships sunk and 22 others driven on shore. Four schooners at anchor there were dismasted. In Provincetown Harbor there were 30 vessels wrecked. Ships and shore property were pounded from Casco Bay, Maine to south of Cape Cod. The loss of life at sea was more than 450, including those from the *Portland* and 16 from the *Pentagoet*.

William Swan, who covered the story for the Associated Press, tried to telegraph Boston from Provincetown, but the lines were down. All over the Cape they were down, so he hired a horse and rode to Orleans and sent dispatches through the French Cable Company there. The messages first went to Paris, then London, Ireland, Newfoundland, New York City, Albany, Springfield, Worcester - and finally to Boston. It was the only way.

Another reporter tried to wire his paper and decided to carry the story himself. It was late Monday afternoon when Charles Ward, Chatham correspondent of the Boston Herald, was in Hyannis when a brief message came through from an assistant of his in Truro. "The *Portland* is lost and there appear to be no survivors." Then the line stopped transmitting. He ran to the Hyannis station and talked his way onto a work train, leaving at 6:30. The train got to East Sandwich where it stopped at a washout. He walked through the heavy drifting snow and finally arrived at 11 o'clock in Sandwich, where he managed to hire a horse, which he rode to the station in Buzzards Bay. He took an early morning train that came from Woods Hole and went to Boston, arriving before noon. That was Tuesday.

The Herald chartered a tug to carry reporters to Provincetown. Accompanying

210

them was the Boston agent of the steamship company. Once they were in Provincetown the agent visited the two undertakers to identify personnel from the *Portland*. Bodies had washed up at Orleans and Mayo's Blacksmith Shop had been converted to a temporary morgue there. The agent had a number of photographs from relatives and friends of *Portland* passengers, and he and Dr. Samuel Davis of Orleans used the photos to help in identifying storm victims washed ashore. Within a week the Orleans railroad station was piled with caskets carrying identified bodies. Those bodies that came ashore first were in better condition and easier to identify than those found later farther down the coast toward Chatham. Of the victims who carried watches, most were stopped at about 9:15.

The New Haven's tracks were cut in five locations. At Pamet River in Truro there was a washout of one-thousand feet. Along the marshes in West Barnstable about 300 feet of line was out. Around Sandwich there were three breaks: one from Dewey Avenue to Liberty Street, another from Jarvesville to Town Neck to Sagamore. These are all low-lying areas and the damage happened on Sunday morning between 10 and 11 when the tide was high and the storm surge caused by high winds inundated the track and created a softening of earth beneath. Then waves caused by continued high winds battered the tracks and moved them out of line, and in some places knocked down the telegraph poles at flood tide. The washout at Truro was the worst, so to and from Provincetown there was no rail service. Monday evening the work train from Hyannis went to repair the break at West Barnstable. On Tuesday it was back in service and trains from Hyannis could come as far as Dewey Avenue crossing and wait. Work trains on Monday and Tuesday arrived from Boston and started to repair the break around Sagamore, where trains could come and unload passengers and mail into wagons for the trip to Dewey Avenue and onto the train from there to Hyannis, Harwich and Chatham. One train came through Sandwich over repaired roadbed on Wednesday, but more work was needed.

On Thursday a long passenger train arrived from Boston carrying relatives and friends of passengers and crew from the *Portland*. The bodies of those recovered had been moved to Eastham from the other towns, and these visitors were there to look for familiar faces. All but one was given a name. He was unclaimed. Three days later on Saturday, December 3rd, the long washout at Truro was finally repaired and a freight train went through to Provincetown with food and coal. There had been no service to the tip of the Cape since the week before on the same day the *Portland* sailed from Boston into history and legend.

On the next Tuesday, December 6th, the last body was recovered from the surf at Chatham. He had been a passenger on his way back to Maine following a Thanksgiving trip to visit around Boston. Several days after that a young woman was notified by the steamship company that possibly her father's remains were in a Chatham undertakers' parlor. The following day she arrived on the late train and that evening identified him. The next day she accompanied his coffin to the Chatham station and saw it put in the baggage car. She asked if she could ride in the same car and a trainman got her a chair.

In the spring of 1989, a group of marine scientists - Historical Maritime Group of New England - found the wreck of the steamer *Portland*, 350 feet down off Gloucester some 27 miles north of Provincetown. They used side-scan sonar, video and still cameras. John Perry Fish of Cataumet looked for years for her wreckage, crossing Massachusetts Bay again and again. His book, "Unfinished Voyages," details the search and its methods.

The sidewheel steamship *Portland* sailing down Boston Harbor and heading for her namesake city. She was a popular ship with graceful lines. This photo was taken about 1890 and early in her coastal career after she was launched from the yard of the New England Company in Bath, Maine on the Kennebec River. On a Saturday night in November, 1898, the Portland sailed from Boston into one of the worst storms ever to hit the coast. On board were 176 passengers and crew. She sank the next day off Cape Ann. There were no survivors. From Martha's Vineyard north the storm was a maritime disaster. We name hurricanes today, but as a rule they did not name them then. In that case they did, and the storm is still called "The *Portland* Storm."

On the Monday morning following the Portland Storm, these four railroad men examined the damage to the line east of Liberty Street, Sandwich.

Top Here at the Liberty Street crossing in Sandwich the tidal surge, pushed by heavy northeast winds, cut the main line of the New Haven Railroad during the Portland Storm. It took four days to repair the damage in Sandwich, East Sandwich and West Barnstable. **Above** Around the depot at Truro the Portland Storm wrecked the road bed and disrupted service with more than one-thousand feet of fill washed out. Typical scenes like this were a commonplace for the week that this part of the line was cut. This photo was made after a northeast storm that stopped all trains just after Christmas in 1909. A number of places on the Cape were vulnerable to high water during storms, but none were more so than this stretch below and above the Truro depot.

Hurricane of 1938

The weather in the summer of 1938 was different, unusual. The first of June had a record low temperature at Boston of 44 degrees. The rest of the month saw rain, lots of it, which totaled about nine and a half inches. Rains continued through July with another nine and a quarter inches falling that month. For July it was the rainiest in 17 years. August had plenty of rain and temperatures up to the nineties for a week. In September the rain came back, and especially hard on the 19th and 20th. Then with all that ground saturation in New England, the weather turned ugly, no, it turned brutal! For what came then was the storm of the century.

It was a Wednesday, September 21st and warm. The sky had a pale blue color with thin clouds, wisps of clouds moving northward rapidly. Off shore, though, like a fog bank were sulphur-colored clouds down close to the horizon. The forecast predicted rain and turning cooler that night. In early afternoon the wind was noticeably higher, by three o'clock there were gusts of 60 miles an hour and rising. So was the water. This was soon to become a New England hurricane.

The day before it was off Miami and moving north at great speed. The assumption about Caribbean hurricanes was that they would reach Cape Hatteras, North Carolina and veer out into the Atlantic - away from land. Usually, but not this time.

That afternoon of the 21st the punishing winds of more than 100 miles an hour, pushing a storm surge of water (they called it a tidal wave then) first struck eastern Long Island. At Montauk, a fishing village, over 150 fishermen lost their homes. More than 80 fishing boats were badly damaged or destroyed along with nets and traps. There was no power. The Long Island Railroad was torn up for miles and in some places the roadbed had vanished before that wave of water that some witnesses described as 50 feet high. Roads were cut and trees were down. Wreckage was literally everywhere. There was no communication, except ham radio. The loss of communications would be repeated as the storm crossed Long Island Sound and slammed into Connecticut, Rhode Island and Massachusetts.

In Wareham the beach sections in the outlying areas saw nine people killed. On lower Main Street the water rose to a depth of 12 feet, causing one million dollars in damages. At the Narrows the railroad bridge and the highway bridge were washed away by the tidal surge.

A New Haven passenger train from Hyannis was approaching the bridge at Wareham. When the locomotive was within a few hundred yards of the Narrows, engineer William Reed watched a boat float over the track ahead. As he applied the brakes a wall of water engulfed the bridge and was rolling toward his train. He backed the train quickly to the station at Onset two miles away. In front of him the water had torn up the tracks and ties. The train stayed at the Onset station, for Reed couldn't go that way either, because the water rose in Buzzards Bay and up Cohasset Narrows through Buttermilk Bay Channel, washing out 5,000 feet of track to a depth of eight feet. In the other direction, toward the Village of Buzzards Bay the destruction of both tracks was also 5,000 feet long and to a depth of seven feet. A Cape Cod reporter, Donald G. Trayser, of the Boston Globe, had tried to call his paper with news and finally reached Middleboro where his search ended for a telephone in service.

After he made a lengthy call to an editor, Trayser, using back roads to Onset in order to avoid the washed out bridge at Wareham, drove past the train at Onset station.

The lights were on in the cars and the 60 passengers were making themselves as comfortable as possible in the day coaches. The fireman was keeping up steam, but the only movement was the quiet whir of the steam generator. Trayser drove up and asked William Reed where Reed was going. The engineer said, "Buddy, I can go back two miles or forward a mile, and that's all."

The following day the railroad sent buses for the passengers, the mail, the baggage and for Reed and his fireman. They went to Boston; the train stayed for three weeks.

South of the Cape Cod Canal the Woods Hole Branch was heavily damaged. From Grey Gables to Monument Beach the high water had gouged a half mile of track out 12 feet deep; at Monument Beach another half mile of the line was out to a depth of four feet; at Pocasset one mile of roadbed was washed out four feet deep; at Red Brook Harbor in Cataumet the line was gouged 10 feet deep for a length of 500 feet; at West Falmouth the track for one mile was washed out down five feet. Woods Hole was hard hit and just north of the station over 500 feet of roadbed was removed by the water and some distance north of the station there was one mile of damage down eight feet. From Wareham through Buzzards Bay to Woods Hole there were six and one-half miles of washed out railroad.

To repair all of that required 1,500 hopper cars of fill and ballast. There was bridge work needed, too. At Wareham, Onset, between Gray Gables and Monument Beach and at Pocasset construction crews spent weeks re-building bulkheads, wing walls and timber piling.

Since 1848 when the railroad came through Wareham to Sandwich there had never been anything like the destruction that Wednesday, September 21, 1938. The wall of water and the pounding of waves had altered the shore lines of Buzzards Bay and south through Rhode Island and Connecticut. The ticket office on Steamship Dock, Woods Hole, was washed out to sea. The fill at the wharf washed out and the slip filled with sand, so that vessels had to tie up at the end. Later a dredge removed the sand.

The New England Steamship Company was lucky. Two ships were tied up at New Bedford and the *Martha's Vineyard* was heading there. The steamer *Naushon* had left Nantucket for the Vineyard. The steamers suffered no damage and passengers had no injuries. But train service to Cape Cod was as far as Middleboro; from there south one went by bus.

In Woods Hole and Bourne there were 16 people killed by the hurricane. Five of them were in one house in Gray Gables that was washed off its foundation and carried up the Canal where it lodged against a pier of the Bourne Bridge. Around midnight the Bourne police and fire chiefs and some naval reservists climbed onto the roof of the house and chopped their way through to a second floor room where they found all five drowned.

Low-lying areas were hardest hit with buildings broken up and strewn about, trees and telephone and light poles broken and fallen, wires everywhere. Small craft washed inland with considerable damage to hulls and superstructure. All kinds of buildings floated away, so did automobiles with their windows closed. The coastal areas were unprepared.

On the Shore Line Route of the New Haven the worst problems were from Saybrook, Connecticut to Providence. At Stonington, east of Mystic, a passenger train was stopped by a red signal because of a train up ahead. The engineer started walking to the tower about 1,000 feet away for orders. On the way back the water had risen in a wave and was up to his waist by the time he reached his locomotive. Some of the passengers left the train and were walking forward toward higher ground. The rising water forced many of them to swim for it. Meanwhile the fill under the last three cars collapsed and they leaned

The hurricane pushed a wall of water, the storm surge, up Wareham Narrows where it took out most of the railroad and highway bridges. Tracks at the left were broken loose and upended. Not far from here on Main Street, Wareham, the water was ten feet deep at the peak of the hurricane.

No trains today! The incredible storm surge flooded the whole area of the Village of Buzzards Bay, including the depot and all the railroad facilities.

This late afternoon scene was taken near Buzzards Bay that frightening day, September 21, 1938.

From the bridge over Cohasset Narrows toward the Village of Buzzards Bay the storm surge gouged the New Haven roadbed down ten feet along this fill.

This is just part of the storm damage to the Woods Hole Branch. Here at Monument Beach the track is washed out up ahead and farther than that it is covered with sand. The waters of Buzzards Bay are off to the left.

This is most of Train #14, *The Bostonian*, which was trapped on the Shore Line's causeway west of Stonington, Connecticut. With the water rising quickly in a tidal surge, the engineer had the crew rush the passengers from these cars up to the front coaches, which were uncoupled and pulled ahead into Stonington and safety. It was a close call. The water was well above these tracks that September day in 1938.

One way New Haven work crews rebuilt the line after hurricanes was to put wooden cribbing under the tracks as shown in this Connecticut photo from 1938. Cribbing was used on the Cape at Buzzards Bay, Monument Beach and Cataumet in the hurricanes of '38 and '44.

The next day the bridge at Back River looked like this with the stream back to its normal height, but the New Haven's Woods Hole Branch was left with miles of devastation.

dangerously to one side. The train crew rushed the remaining passengers forward to the head car, which was uncoupled and pulled eastward a quarter mile to safety, but not before the locomotive pulled telegraph poles, and knocked a house and a large boat off the track in order to move forward. It had been a very close call for those passengers who left Grand Central at 11 a.m. There were two deaths, however, a woman passenger and a dining car employee drowned.

Communications were out for the New Haven with the loss of telephones, telegraph and dispatching circuits. Signal systems were dead and there were many locations where tracks were blocked by poles, trees, houses, boats and every variety of debris. For some time the railroad didn't know where its trains were. At New London a large government lighthouse tender, a steamship, the *Tulip,* was across the main line. A special channel was dug to float her off.

Rhode Island was directly in the main path of the hurricane. At 5:16 p.m. all power failed as the tide rose 13 feet and nine inches above mean high water in downtown Providence. By nightfall more than 300 men, women and children had been killed in the state.

As the storm swirled inland it lost none of its power and its heavy rains. The winds as far north as Vermont damaged buildings and uprooted maple sugar trees and lost most of the apple crop. Seven people died from the storm there. The toll of trees in all New England has been put at 250 million. More than 20-thousand buildings and 2,000 boats were destroyed. The death toll on Long Island and in New England was more than 700.

To have a sense of the power of this greatest of natural disasters to strike this area you should know that when that huge storm surge - as high as 40 feet and some say it was 80 feet - roared through eastern Long Island it struck the land and was recorded on a seismograph in Alaska. So many people on Cape Cod went out that next morning and still today, over a half century later say, "we could not believe the destruction."

The first trains between New York and Boston rolled over the Shore Line Route on October 1. It had been ten days since that fateful Wednesday. On the Cape, service was not restored for several more weeks. That was the hurricane of September, 1938.

THE NEW YORK, NEW HAVEN & HARTFORD

The New Haven added trains on the Old Colony System, which included the Cape Cod Division from Middleboro. The Old Colony had referred to trains leaving Boston as outbound and those toward Boston as inbound. The New Haven changed that to southbound toward the Cape and northbound toward Boston.

The New Haven added a passenger train on Sundays during the winter season to Hyannis and from Hyannis to Boston. Only main line stations from Yarmouth north were served under this arrangement. The train left Boston at 8:15 a.m. as an express to Middleboro. After that scheduled stops were Tremont, Wareham, Onset Junction, Buzzards Bay, Sandwich, West Barnstable, Barnstable and Yarmouth. It reached Hyannis at 11 a.m. Flag stops were Bourne, Bournedale and Sagamore.

The train left Hyannis at 5:30 p.m. for Boston again as a local express passenger with the same scheduled stops and flag stops as the morning train. The Old Colony had offered no Sunday service after the third week in September.

The winter service on the Cape on week days and Saturdays was also increased. The New Haven stayed with the old idea of two trains a day to and from Provincetown, except it ran them later. The morning local passenger left Boston at 9 a.m. and reached Provincetown at 1:23 p.m. The flag stops on this run were Parker Mills, Bournedale, East Sandwich, Pleasant Lake, East Brewster and South Wellfleet. The 4:10 from Boston in the afternoon was an express passenger that did not stop at Rock, South Middleboro, South Wareham, Parker Mills, Bournedale, and East Sandwich. This train arrived in Provincetown at 8:25. It took four hours and 15 minutes to cover the 120 miles from Kneeland Street Station to the Cape's tip.

The New Haven ran two passenger trains in the afternoon from Boston to Hyannis. The 1 p.m. reached Hyannis at 3:30 and the 5:10 reached Hyannis at 7:48.

On the Fairhaven Branch there were three passenger trains a day and one local freight each way every day except Sunday when there was no service. Passenger trains covered the 15 miles in 30 minutes. Local passenger trains either way on the Fairhaven Branch connected with through trains. There were two morning trains from Fairhaven, at 8 and 9:45. The one afternoon train left at 4:35. From Tremont the morning trains left at 8:40 and 10:30. The afternoon train departed at 5:37. The ferry from Fairhaven to New Bedford across the Acushnet River ran frequently during the day, but it always arrived just before trains left and it departed after they arrived.

The one local freight left Tremont at 2 p.m., arriving at Fairhaven an hour later. From Fairhaven the freight left at noon and was scheduled into Tremont at 1 p.m. From Fairhaven to Boston was 60.3 miles and local passenger trains covered that in two hours.

The Woods Hole Branch had three passenger trains and one freight daily except Sunday. The morning train left Kneeland Street Station at 9 o'clock and reached the Hole at 11:38. The two afternoon trains departed Boston at 1 and at 4:10. Passengers reached the Hole at 3:22 and 6:39 respectively. All three daily trains either dropped cars or had passengers change to another train that was a shuttle between Buzzards Bay and the Hole.

From May through late October the New Haven ran the *Dude Train* from Boston to the Hole. The private subscription train of parlor cars for the wealthy was carried in employee timetables, but not public timetables, as leaving Boston at 3:10 and reaching the Hole at 4:57. That was the best time any train made on the 72-mile run. There were stretches when the *Dude* clipped along at 60 miles and hour and sometimes faster. Its average over the distance was 44 miles an hour.

There were two local passenger trains from the Hole in the morning besides the *Dude*. They left at 7:15 and 10:40, reaching Buzzards Bay at 7:59 and 11:23 respectively. The average time to cover the 17.4 miles of the Woods Hole Branch was 44 minutes. The *Dude* left the Hole at 7:35 a.m., stopping at Falmouth, West Falmouth and Cataumet. It reached Buzzards Bay at 8:03. The *Dude* ran through to Boston with its parlor cars. The passengers on the public trains changed trains at the Bay, getting on mainline cars there.

Six days a week there was a local freight each way on the Woods Hole Branch. The morning freight left the Bay at 8:30 and was due at the other end at 9:45. The freight north left the Hole at 4:25 p.m. and was due at the Bay at 6:10.

Two local freights left Middleboro every day except Sunday at 3:40 a.m. for Yarmouth where it was due at 8:10. Cars would be added from Hyannis and that train would leave Yarmouth at 8:35 for the 44.6 mile run to Provincetown where it was scheduled to arrive at 12:25 p.m.

The second freight left Middleboro at 12:30 p.m. after picking up cars from Providence, Fall River and Newport. That train was due at Yarmouth at 5:12 and at Hyannis at 5:30.

The Chatham Branch had two trains a day each way between Harwich and Chatham. The trains were shuttles running on the 7.4 mile branch only and meeting trains on the main line at Harwich. From Chatham the morning train left at 6:30 and reached Harwich at 6:49 where passengers, mail and express changed to the early train out of Provincetown which came through Harwich at 6:56. That train was turned on the wye at Harwich where it waited until 12:12 p.m. to leave with passengers who came in on the train that left Boston at 9 that morning and any freight cars that arrived about 9:33 from Yarmouth. That train became a typical branch line mixed, carrying freight and passengers.

The afternoon out of Chatham at 2:45 was also a mixed train daily except Sunday and was due in Harwich at 3:19. Seven minutes later the 2:10 out of Provincetown arrived and picked up passengers, mail and express from Chatham. That train arrived in Boston at 6:38, a distance of 91.4 miles from Chatham and 84.4 miles from Harwich.

From Provincetown there was one freight a day six days a week. It left at 5:30 a.m. and was due in Yarmouth at 10:10, Buzzards Bay at 11:55 and Middleboro at 1:58.

At this time - the year was 1894, and the New Haven had been running the Old Colony for a year - the Cape had automatic electric block signals operated by batteries with the blocks either a half mile apart and never more than one mile.

This was an important safety feature, especially on single track lines and from Buzzards Bay on, all Cape track was single.

The fortunes of the New York, New Haven & Hartford Railroad were bound up with the fortunes and attitudes of America's most famous banker: John Pierpont Morgan. Morgan did not build up the New Haven, he merely presided over its destinies in the early years of the twentieth century. It wasn't that many years that he controlled the New Haven, but the damage he did contributed to the slow death of what had been a fine organization when he won control.

As a railroad the New Haven had reached its peak in 1900. Here is what had happened: the company represented the consolidation of 25 separate lines. The motive power and rolling stock were first rate and maintained as was the roadbed. Since its formation in 1872 the New Haven had paid 10 percent dividends, annually. The same year the Old Colony and its Cape Cod tracks were acquired by the New Haven, 1893, the general business depression forced the New Haven to reduce that to 8 percent.

In 1887 the best president the New Haven ever had, Charles Peter Clark, came to that position from the New York & New England. With the twelve year reign of Clark the New Haven soared. Annual revenue rose from $8-million to $38-million. Trackage increased from 450 miles to 2,047 miles. The locomotive roster was 133 in 1887, and it reached 900 by 1899 when Clark resigned. Passenger cars, the principal revenue producer, reached 1,800. There had been 400 when Clark assumed control. The New York Division from Manhattan to New Haven, with all those commuting trains, was four-tracked and became the busiest section of any American railroad. Besides the elimination of many grade crossings, the New Haven experimented with branch line electrification, some of it just south of Boston, and this lead to the main line electrification from Manhattan to Stamford and later to New Haven. It's still there. Clark also was instrumental in seeing Boston's huge South Station planned, built and finally opened January 1, 1899.

South Station in downtown Boston was badly needed. It had 28 tracks and a major concourse. The concourse was originally open but later it was enclosed, 620 feet long and 130 feet wide. Its train shed was gigantic, spanning those tracks with 570 feet of steel and glass. South Station was built as a combined terminal for the New Haven and the Boston & Albany to replace four older ones, those of the Old Colony, the Boston & Providence, the Boston & Albany and the New York & New England. Its architects, Shepley, Rutan & Coolidge, designed it as the first steam railway station to include trackage for electric trains as the New Haven was already running some on branches and was planning to convert its New York Division to electrification. There was a lower loop designed to be used by electric locomotives. It never was.

For years South Station was the largest and busiest railroad terminal in America. In the 12 months ending June 30, 1916, South Station handled 38-million passengers, which was 16-million more than Grand Central Station in New York handled.

From January 1, 1899 on that morning - it was a Sunday - the trains to and from Cape Cod left and entered South Station on tracks 27 and 28 until June 30, 1959.

The one big change came in 1930 when that mammoth train shed was torn down and those thousands of tons of glass and steel were carried off in gondola cars. The shed was replaced by individual butterfly canopies over the platforms.

The modernization program started in 1930 cost $2.5-million. The 3,750 tons of steel girders and 70-thousand square feet of glass filled 273 gondola cars. The work was completed in 1931 when 466 scheduled trains used the station daily, besides many unscheduled ones.

Cape Codders found that they didn't have to leave South Station to take a train for New York or the west on the New York Central. The frequent expresses to Manhattan left from Southie as did the trains of the Boston & Albany which connected at New York State's capital city with the luxury varnish of the Central's famous Water Level Route to Chicago. For years there was a Boston section of the *20th Century Limited* that joined at Albany with the *Century* that left Grand Central.

A separate operations unit, the Boston Terminal Company, was set up to run South

223

Station. It was a joint subsidiary of the New Haven and the Boston & Albany.

The tracks of the Boston elevated ran past the main entrance with its Ionic columns and illuminated signs up high, reading "South Station" and at the very top a stone structure, almost a triangle, with a large clock with "Waltham" above it and "Watch" on the left and "Time" on the right. Above this advertising material was a large eagle with wings at the ready.

They didn't call it "The Consolidated" without reason. That nickname was appropriate for a railroad that swallowed up every railroad nearby and some not so near. In fact the only line in Connecticut the New Haven didn't control was the Central Vermont, a Canadian Railway that ran to New London.

"The Consolidated" or New York, New Haven & Hartford, its legal name, was under the nineteenth century direction of conservative presidents who improved the property, expanded the company and ran a financially stable corporation. The New Haven would grow to be an industrial umbrella covering more than 300 separate, former companies. The men who ran it, including its greatest president, Charles Peter Clark, hated competition. They were definitely not free market people.

The change that ruined the New Haven came in the 1880s when private banker J. Pierpont Morgan of New York won a place on the board along with his friend William Rockefeller, the brother of John D. It was not until 1903 that Morgan began a decade of moves that would alter the financial framework of the New York, New Haven & Hartford Railroad.

In 1903 the capital stock of the New Haven was about $71-million with funded debt of $14.5-million. That year the man who with Morgan would change the railroad became its president. He was Charles Sanger Mellen, a New Englander who first clerked on a small New Hampshire railroad and worked himself up through the years to be second vice president of the New Haven in 1892, the year before the Old Colony was leased for 99 years. Mellen was an intelligent man who carefully chose his words, spoke well and had a rather devastating wit. Mellen knew how to gather information and when to divulge it, usually to Morgan who watched Mellen and was impressed by what he saw.

In 1897 Charles Peter Clark was still at the helm of the New Haven and doing well, but not with enough daring to suit Morgan. Still Morgan waited and in the meantime he had taken over the Northern Pacific and he wanted to put his own man in there as president. He offered it to Mellen who accepted. Mellen built up the Northern Pacific and turned it into a prosperous road.

In 1903 Morgan was ready to move and move big! He brought Charles Sanger Mellen back to the New Haven as its president. Mellen believed you could spend your way to prosperity, which he had done with the Northern Pacific. He was to do it with the New Haven all the time cheered on by J.P. Morgan.

The two of them wanted to create a monopoly of transportation in New England. Morgan bought up steamboat lines on Long Island Sound that were in competition with his Fall River Line, which he had acquired when he leased the Old Colony. Morgan wanted nothing that was afloat to challenge the water routes he controlled. Morgan succeeded, including buying up the Metropolitan Line's academic twins, the *Harvard* and *Yale*, which were running from Boston to New York around Cape Cod. He banished those ships to the West Coast through dummy corporations.

Meanwhile, Mellen was on his own buying spree with Morgan's blessings. In the 1890s when the trolley age hit America, no area was immune to the attractions of electric street railways. They seemed to be growing everywhere. As competition and often running side by side and parallel to steam railroads, they took away passenger income and even freight, which they often delivered at night to businesses along the tracks. To Morgan and Mellen trolleys were the enemy. So they bought out many street car lines, including the unsuccessful and even marginally successful ones. This was an expensive financial exercise.

Mellen began in Connecticut by buying out the trolley lines, especially the interurbans, after which he moved to do the same in Rhode Island and finally Massachusetts. Closer to Manhattan he made one of the most outrageous purchases when he paid a bit more than $36-million for a non-essential electric line, the New York, Westchester & Boston. The tracks ran for 18 miles toward New Rochelle with a branch to White Plains. That atrocity cost $2-million per mile. Its only threat to the New Haven was its parallel line!

The figures cited a little earlier on the 1903 capitalization and funded debt had grown with all these purchases in just six years to $356-million. Capital stock issued had grown by 72 percent and funded debt or corporate bonds sold by 1,500 percent. The New Haven was deeply in debt with large interest payments necessary on those bonds. The trolleys, boats, utility companies and other concerns brought into the corporate fold were purchased by over capitalizing the New Haven.

Still the growth went on as Mellen and Morgan reached out to control transportation throughout New England until at one point they did. Consider this: the New Haven managed to get a bill through the Connecticut legislature allowing it to buy stock in other railroads that in fact gave the railroad status as a holding company of other securities, of other companies.

The Boston & Maine Railroad controlled the Maine Central, a total of 3,000 miles of track. Mellen bought $16-million worth of B & M stock and that was enough for majority control of both roads. Somehow the New Haven couldn't get control of the Central Vermont, so Mellen bought enough stock to have the principal say in the Rutland Railroad that ran from Bellow Falls, Vermont across that state to Burlington and then across Lake Champlain to Canada. The New Haven shared ownership of the Boston & Albany with the New York Central. In other moves in addition to buying out the Central New England with its tracks across the Hudson on the Poughkeepsie Bridge to Maybrook, New York, the New Haven bought control of the New York, Ontario & Western whose main line ran from Weehawken northwesterly through Central and Upstate New York to Oswego, a port on Lake Ontario. The O & W also ran from Cadosia, New York down to the anthracite mining regions of Carbondale and Scranton, Pennsylvania. The New Haven wanted tracks to anthracite country. This move made the New York Central nervous. Of course J. P. Morgan made many of his competitors nervous.

Morgan and Mellen set out to enlarge the plant of the New Haven by putting in heavier bridges, greatly increasing the size of some freight yards, and ordering locomotives and rolling stock. The New Haven participated in the building of a new Grand Central Station, a Pennsylvania Station and the Hell Gate Bridge, also a joint effort with the Pennsy with the purpose of creating a link by rail between the south and New England via Penn Station at 34th Street in New York. The Hell Gate project was started in 1912 and finished five years and $28-million later.

The Hell Gate project has three bridges and many miles of track on a viaduct from the state line of Connecticut, across the Bronx to Randalls Island, to Wards Island, then the main Hell Gate Bridge to Queens County, Brooklyn where it loops toward the East River and under it through a tunnel to Pennsylvania Station. The massive twin towers rise 250 feet above the water. Through trains from New England use Hell Gate to enter New York and then exit under the Hudson tunnel to New Jersey and to Philadelphia where they can either go south to Washington and below or turn west to Harrisburg, Altoona, Pittsburgh, Chicago, Detroit or St. Louis. Also a branch was built from Hell Gate to Bay Ridge, Brooklyn on New York Bay where tugs move freight cars on car floats to Greenville, New Jersey on the upper Harbor and the interchange with the Pennsy. With the completion of the Hell Gate project a few weeks before America entered World War I, the New Haven became the only railroad that served this country's largest city through its two major terminals. Morgan and Mellen committed their railroad to its share of the Hell Gate project.

Of the $356-million in stocks and bonds issued by the railroad, the Interstate Commerce Commission said $200-million was spent on corporations not directly involved in transportation.

In 1911 business dropped off on the New Haven and the management began cutting costs. Men were laid off to reduce payrolls. Maintenance was cut back. And there was human tragedy, too.

A long series of train wrecks caused death and destruction. The worst may have been a rear-end collision in North Haven when the *White Mountain Express* plowed into the stopped *Bar Harbor Express*, killing 21 and injuring 50. There were others and the main reason for them was management trying to run too many high speed passenger trains with an old signal system. Also trains were run too close together. There was a lack of coordination and little training of employees. Management kept after train crews for speed. One bulletin said: "Engineers are requested to do everything possible to make time." What they did too often was make wrecks.

Mellen was indicted for manslaughter, but he agreed to be a cooperative witness. The railroad's directors were tried for conspiracy. No one was ever convicted. Morgan was in Paris in 1913 when he died and within a few months Mellen was gone, retiring to his home in the Berkshires.

The road back to rebuilding the New Haven which by then had a terrible reputation was led off by Howard Elliott who became president in 1913 and served until 1917 when a most able successor, E.J. Pearson, was named. The heavy debt load was crushing the road when it was saved by the entry of America into World War I. The takeover by the federal government's United States Railway Administration saw millions poured into the line which gave it at least a fighting chance when it was returned by the government to its management in 1920.

The New Haven had borrowed $44-million before we entered the war, and owed the government $60-million for improvements made during the war. The New Haven was forced to borrow another $30-million later. Money seemed to leak out everywhere.

In the 1920s the New Haven, under skilled leadership, was slowly working its way out of a fiscal mess created years before by those who were gone. The Boston & Maine had been independent of the New Haven for years, but all those steamboats and their many routes, including the line to Martha's Vineyard and Nantucket, were still operating. Even the night boat that sailed between Manhattan and up the Connecticut River to Hartford was a going concern. Many of those trolley lines had been torn up, but a few were still running. The New England Transportation Company was operating buses as replacements for steam trains. On Cape Cod this meant Yarmouth to Provincetown in the winter with

The railroad to Sandwich and beyond crossed this deck truss bridge over the Monument River a short distance east of the Bourne depot. Most of this valley was unspoiled with this river, marshes, meadows, uplands and hills. There were three small farms and nature - deer, fox, chipmunks, squirrels, woodchucks and thousands of birds. It was a pretty ride behind a New Haven steam locomotive. Russ Lovell always described the valley as a big park. It was before the canal was built through this spot and down the valley. After the canal was dug, this railroad line crossed to the south side at the Buzzards Bay rail bridge and ran along the side of those distant hills.

This is Bourne in the marsh and flatlands about one mile east of the Village of Buzzards Bay. The Monument River runs through the middle of this picture and under that road bridge. Trolley line to Monument Beach is also on the bridge. Behind the buildings at left was the railroad station, which was called Monument when this area was part of Sandwich before 1884. After that, the legislature carved out the Town of Bourne with its six villages. This picture is circa 1905. When the Cape Cod Canal was dug through here after 1910, the passenger depot and freight house were moved to the south bank along the relocated main line less than a mile from here.

Assistant section foreman Jerry Taylor worked for the New Haven Railroad and he used this velocipede to get to and from track work. On the platform that water barrel was used for firefighting. Up those steps and through the door that potbellied stove had to be cold and unused this time of year. You can tell it's warm not only by Taylor's rolled up shirt sleeves, but see that hay wagon to the left of the depot? Someone put Jerry Taylor's portrait in this oval frame. Mrs. Taylor?

South Station in Boston where trains to and from Cape Cod ran on those last tracks on the right into that huge train shed. For many years after its completion South Station was the busiest railroad terminal in America.

e interlocking tower at Middleboro
ld control the movement of as many
tches as there were levers here. This
ture is from 1900. About ten years later
these were changed to the then new
ectro-Pneumatic system that actuated
tches by electricity and moved the rails
compressed air. It was a method
veloped by Union Switch & Signal of
issvale, Pennsylvania, a Pittsburgh
urb. The system was installed at the
zzards Bay yards when the canal
nstruction brought so many changes at
at junction. The New Haven was a major
stomer of Union Switch & Signal.

This is Milton Healey, a signal maintainer who
worked out of Buzzards Bay, and this is his means
of getting to his job. There was an electric crossing
signal to warn highway traffic in North Truro at a
place called Knowles Crossing. On Sundays, Healey
would hand pump this velocipede 65 miles from
Buzzards Bay to the tip of the Cape, stopping off to
test that crossing signal. On the day this picture was
taken in North Truro, Healey's friend, the
photographer, who accompanied him, snapped the
shutter and then the two of them pumped six miles
into Provincetown where they loaded this vehicle
into the baggage car of the next train back to
Buzzards Bay. Milton Healey loved the railroad
and it hired him in 1911 at Middleboro. Two years
later he was transferred to Buzzards Bay where he
spent the rest of his working life.

A young woman and her work in East Sandwich. Anna Fish was the Postmistress of East Sandwich, and her work depended on many things, but nothing more important than the arrival and departure of passenger trains with Railway Post Office cars. Here she is hanging a mail bag for a train that is leaving the Cape. These bags made of tough canvas had a ring on the top and a brass lock on the bottom, as they appear in the photo, but actually they were suspended upside down and tied tightly in the middle so the car's hook could grab them for the Railway Post Office clerk to bring the sack easily into the car for sorting. Anna Bodfish married William Fish and they lived in East Sandwich not far from the location of this stand at what is now the Talbot's Point Railroad crossing. This picture was taken by Delia Nye Blossom in 1898, or close to it.

trains back in the summer and a similar arrangement by seasons between Hyannis and Chatham. The New Haven even had a fleet of trucks to pick up and deliver freight.

In working its way back the line finally was able to declare a one percent dividend on its common stock in 1928. These dividends continued through 1931. Meanwhile in the heavy financial maneuverings of Wall Street before the market crash major railroads were buying control of smaller ones "in order to bring about a consolidation of railway properties..into a limited number of systems." That quote is from the 1920 Transportation Act returning the rails to private operation after World War I. The Pennsylvania with its 23 percent ownership of New Haven common stock had control of the New England road. The big rails had mergers on their minds, but those ideas were soon dropped with the coming of the Great Depression. With that event, existence, even survival became uppermost in the board rooms.

All business was off during the depression, but the railroads suffered more because of their huge debt and operating expenses. From the market crash of October, 1929 until 1933 railroad revenues fell off 51 percent. Bottom line net income dropped by 97 percent!

In this grim picture the New Haven had it no better. From its 1927 income of $143-million the total had shrunk by 1934 to $68-million. The railroads, along with everybody else, were hoping for an upswing in business. The New Haven borrowed on short term from banks and from the federal government's Reconstruction Finance Corporation it got a $16-million loan to meet the interest payments on its considerable debt load, which by then was $312-million, and that was not counting debt incurred for buying new equipment.

The New Haven was a transportation company running on red ink. It was all too much and in October, 1935 the railroad petitioned the Federal Court in New Haven to allow it to reorganize under the bankruptcy laws. The court granted the petition and the great break for the railroad was being relieved of the crushing weight of paying interest on its debts.

In May, 1937 the New York, Ontario & Western went into reorganization and bankruptcy. The New Haven owned a majority of O & W stock, but was unable to help the serious fiscal and physical deterioration of that charming 544 mile country railroad that wandered around from Weehawken through the Catskills, up the Chenango Valley to Oneida and on to Oswego, New York on Lake Ontario. Twenty years later, in 1957, the O & W was abandoned after continuous bankruptcy.

In 1938 the Rutland Railroad, the New Haven's pathway to Canada, owned jointly with the New York Central, went bankrupt, but staggered on until 1964 when the scrap dealers picked up most of it. The New Haven was a little luckier with the Rutland than it had been with the O & W, for it sold off its stock in 1941 at a loss, but at least it got something for its stake in the Rutland.

One of the saddest losses of all during the 1930s was a New Haven federal court ruling to shut down the Fall River Line in July, 1937. There had been a brief strike on board the ships and the company, feeling it could not grant wage increases, petitioned the court for permission to abandon the line, which had been losing money for some years.

The through bus service of the New Haven, was sold two years later in 1939 to Greyhound. The New Haven, seeing a growing network of highways and an expansion regionally of small air lines, began planning with TWA to jointly fly four-engined stratoliners from Boeing in southern New England. The plan was dropped during World War II.

In the 1920s America was well into its love affair with the automobile, and the states and towns had embarked on an extensive road-building program that made a major impact on railroad branch lines. Cape Cod felt that impact. By 1930 long lines of cars clogged the two lane roads to the Cape. The highway bridges over the Cape Cod Canal at Sagamore and Bourne had approach roads that resembled long, thin parking lots stretching back for miles from the Village of Buzzards Bay through Onset to Wareham. The number of private sailboats and yachts had increased in the waters of both Buzzards Bay and Cape Cod Bay, especially after the federal government bought the Canal from a private company that had charged tolls for its use. That purchase was effective in March, 1928 and the following summer a stream of boats transited the waterway that was now free of charge. On most late spring and summer days that year and thereafter the cantilever bridges were in the open position for boats much of the time, creating the lines of stopped cars heading for Cape Cod. But still they came undaunted, and they would be the future means of getting there, too.

Of course the railroad bridge at Buzzards Bay was left in the open position between trains, but it could be lowered in one minute and the train could cross quickly and the span opened again. There were no lines of trains waiting to cross the Canal, just cars. And still more cars came.

The 1930s were the years of track abandonments on Cape Cod. Since 1931 the New Haven had stopped using the siding that ran from the Main Street Station in Hyannis to the wharf. It was a mile and a quarter of track. In the summer of 1937 the Interstate Commerce Commission gave its permission to the New Haven to abandon that track. It was one of many the New Haven had asked to be ripped up. There would be more.

That same summer the New Haven abandoned the Chatham Branch much against the wishes of the town and many of its businessmen. It was the last branch built on the Cape fifty years before in 1887. It became the first branch to be declared superfluous on Cape Cod in 1937. Before that in the summers there had often been private railroad cars parked for weeks on end on the siding opposite that Chatham station with its marvelous candle-snuffer, pagoda-like roof. It's still there, that station, an architectural wonder without trains.

Still the cars came and fewer people rode the train. The next year in July, 1938 passenger service ended to Provincetown. Ticket holders got off at Yarmouth and took the bus along the north shore. From Hyannis others rode a bus to Harwich and Chatham. In 1940 the New Haven reinstated local trains to Provincetown for the summer. One reason was to take parlor cars and sleepers from the *Night Cape Codder* to the tip of the Cape. There was enough business for that. In September the passenger trains vanished again from the main line east of Yarmouth. Freight service continued, however. There would be miles of abandonments in that part of the Cape, but not until the 1960s.

Under the bankruptcy laws, the New Haven started in 1935 to unload itself of fixed charges of $17.6-million a year, which included rentals of more than $5-million a year on leases, including especially the burden imposed on the New Haven by operating the Old Colony. In 1936 the Old Colony lease and those of the Boston & Providence and some others were discontinued. The reorganization allowed the railroad to default on those rentals and the money earned from traffic then was diverted to maintenance and purchase of equipment.

Office staff had been reduced in number, wages were cut and maintenance pared in order to survive. Now that would change and the New Haven would work its way back.

Quite soon after the New Haven's reorganization started in 1935, it became apparent that a generous portion of the New Haven's ulcers was from its leasing of the Old Colony. The $2.5-million rent per year was by 1936 gone, as we have seen, but its operating losses on short-haul passenger trains were losing another $2.5-million annually.

The owners of Old Colony stock insisted their road was terribly valuable and profitable too, and that anyone who said otherwise was incorrectly analyzing the figures. However, the one thing they were sure of was they didn't want the Old Colony returned to them. Through the years since J.P. Morgan had leased it in 1893, the stockholders had cashed handsome dividend checks; for them it had been profitable. The court, which had eliminated the rent for the Old Colony and those dividend checks, did insist the New Haven continue to operate the Old Colony, and that meant Cape Cod service.

Since the litigation, the investigations, the reports, expert testimony, charges and counter charges that swirled around the New Haven bankruptcy had started in 1935 and continued after the rental paid for leases was eliminated, it was obvious that major changes had to be made in the Old Colony or it should be scrapped.

The federal court created a committee to look carefully at the situation. They did and came up with a plan involving the closing of 95 stations, of which 88 were in Massachusetts and many of the 88 were on Cape Cod.

The Massachusetts Department of Public Utilities in those years would not approve major changes in train service requested by the New Haven for the Southeastern part of the state. In those days the most the railroad got was permission to make some of its stations into flag stops that were not staffed by depot masters, and many of those moves had been made prior to the bankruptcy. Some stations were physically removed as the one at Bass River was in 1937.

The New Haven wanted to simply shut down the Old Colony, cut its heavy losses and run high speed express service between Boston and New York and New York to Hartford and Springfield. Those runs were profitable. The only runs to and from the Cape that made money - and lots of it - were the summer trains from Grand Central. The New Haven said it wanted to shut down local Cape service in the fall of 1939, as they had said before. A citizens group with the support of elected officials met in Hyannis on October 16 and passed a resolution demanding that train service continue. A short time later the railroad, without state permission to abandon service, suggested that buses be run to and from Boston and trains would operate summers only. Again the state did not approve.

The New Haven made every effort wherever it ran to reduce or eliminate unprofitable lines. In Connecticut it had more luck than it was having in Massachusetts. One area of considerable success for the railroad was its major rebuilding programs for track and structures, including bridges. More than 400 new lightweight, air-conditioned cars were in use or under order and the wooden coaches were all retired as were many of the older, heavy steel cars. The money came from earnings and the elimination of fixed charges. Employee training was intensive and thorough with emphasis on courteous service to the public. Passenger cars were cleaner and time tables more attractive. Passenger trains were speeded up. The age of the automobile had arrived but in the final years of the 1930s the drive between New York and Boston was a lot slower than today with roads running through the heart of all cities and towns with traffic lights on each corner. It was a painful drive, slow and dull too. The fast trains covered the 239 miles between Boston and New York in four hours and 15 minutes and between 8 a.m. and 7 p.m. a train left each end terminal every hour on the hour. The New Haven was in good physical condition to carry the extensive burdens of World War II traffic and they were not far away.

In the summer of 1940 with Europe already at war and the first draftees in uniform the United States Government was expanding its military quickly. On Cape Cod a five mile spur from the Woods Hole Branch was under construction in North Falmouth into Camp Edwards. The plan was to have 30-thousand men in winter quarters by Thanksgiving. They would require 1,200 buildings, including barracks, headquarters, training centers, warehouses, a 1,000 bed hospital and dining halls. The spur to the camp was not finished in September when the government called the New Haven Railroad with the information that a siding to hold 80 box cars had to be built at Sagamore, along side the main line and under the Sagamore Bridge. The spur had to be 4,000 feet in length. The engineering department went to Sagamore and looked over the ground and put out a rush call for rails, ties, spikes and switches and most of all the men who could put them together. Five days after the New Haven got the phone call the siding was finished at Sagamore and the contents of box cars were being unloaded onto trucks for the drive to Camp Edwards. The crew who installed the tracks had 24 months before helped the Shore Line reopen after two frantic weeks, following that devastating 1938 New England hurricane.

Through that siding came 40-million feet of milled lumber, 120 carloads of cement, 20 more of sash, 15 of roofing material, 25 of plumbing and another 50 cars of pipe and fittings. The United States Army wanted 20 buildings a day to be completed. In order to funnel that material at a steady pace, the New Haven was moving cars over the Poughkeepsie Bridge to the north and on car floats from New Jersey across New York Harbor to Bay Ridge, Brooklyn and then over Hell Gate and up the Shore Line then through Middleboro to the Cape. A terminal building was under construction at Edwards to receive materials once the spur was finished. It also was to be used by arriving troops. Throughout the war thousands of cars entered and left Edwards.

Once America entered the war the railroad traffic picked up on the Cape with troop trains, some double-headed, using the main line to bring recruits and training enlisted men and officers to Camp Wellfleet where anti-aircraft units were in training. These trains always stopped at Yarmouth for water at the big tank there.

The Woods Hole Branch had heavy traffic to and from Edwards, the Coast Guard had men on every ship sailing in convoys through the canal to prevent sabotage, the navy had convoy headquarters at Woods Hole for the merchant ships that gathered in Buzzards Bay inside the anti-submarine nets before sailing east and up the coast for reassignment at Casco Bay, Maine or Halifax. These activities required lots of personnel and most of them got to the Cape by rail. There were many people trained in amphibious landings using Washburn's Island off Cotuit. Later those lessons would be used in North Africa, Sicily, Italy and Normandy. The Landing Craft Infantry steel vessels were all brought to the Woods Hole railroad yard on flat cars and unloaded directly into the water by a crane. Long trains of them came to the "Hole" and their crews lived in barracks on Washburn's Island along with the training officers and enlisted men.

Between 1938 and 1944 passenger traffic tripled on the New Haven while freight tonnage doubled. Gasoline and tires were severely rationed and new automobiles, what there were of them, were for the military and for doctors. If you traveled any distance at all, you went by train. In the years from 1941 to 1945 the New Haven received net earnings of $130-million. Although the various parties to litigation were still in conflict, the company remained in reorganization until 1947 when it emerged from 12 years of bankruptcy.

The reorganization that had eliminated the Old Colony rental lease had wiped out $206-million in old common and preferred stock. In its place new stocks and bonds were issued and this included new preferred, which represented part of the settlement of claims by former owners of stocks and bonds.

Some men had bought up securities of companies the New Haven had taken over a half century before. During the long period of reorganization much of this paper was thought to be worthless and so it was purchased at far below its face value. To pay off the claims in the incessant litigation during reorganization, the federal court awarded some of the new preferred and common stock to the holders of these older securities that had been bought for fire sale prices on the chance they might be valuable. They turned out to be.

The Interstate Commerce Commission approved a plan that was suggested in order to keep speculators from grabbing the New Haven "and trading on the equity." The plan was to issue preferred stock to institutions like banks and insurance companies, since they were the major bondholders before the company entered bankruptcy in 1935. The court agreed it was a good idea, believing these institutions would hold the stock as the New Haven looked as if it had a bright future. Furthermore, the holders of the preferred stock were given the privilege for five years to elect two-thirds of the directors. This again was to prevent stock speculators from grabbing the railroad. It was a good idea that didn't work out.

First off the stock had no record of dividends, of income, so the banks and insurance companies had no interest in holding it. They hadn't earned anything from the New Haven in well over a decade. They did not view the railroad as a producer of income for their institutions, so they sold the preferred when approached by buyers. And they sold it for whatever they could get. What they got on average was $22 a share which made the cost of gaining control of the company between $4- and $4.5-million. Consider this: the New Haven at that time was holding cash and government securities worth $45.3-million. Perhaps all kinds of people in different positions were naive in those days.

Two separate groups of investors gained control of the New Haven by buying shares of preferred. Frederick C. Dumaine described himself as an investor which he certainly was, and an industrialist, which was only partly true. Dumaine had run the famous Amoskeag Mills for many years. He did well as his bank account expanded and later the Mills closed. Amoskeag had been a huge textile operation. In the early 1930s it died and Dumaine thrived financially. But earlier he got himself appointed president of the Waltham Watch Company. Once there, Dumaine laid off workers, while cutting the pay of others and spending very little on new machinery, research or watch designs. During the 1930s one of its principal products was speedometers. Its watch business had all but vanished as the quality had previously. Waltham staggered into the 1940s and was saved by war business, which, of course, couldn't last, and in 1944 Dumaine sold his interest. Dumaine always came out of these enterprises doing well personally. Not so the businesses.

The second group of investors was lead by another man who had always done well for himself, although the companies with which he was associated did not always thrive. This second power was Patrick B. McGinnis, a stock broker who called himself a railroad expert. These two were the powerful men in the New Haven financial picture. They moved quickly but not before Howard Palmer, the chief trustee during the bankruptcy, had been elected president. Palmer was a good choice and he deserved the office. Within five months he was gone.

An election had been held and with a new board in place they put their own man in. That was Dumaine. He went on to cut maintenance programs, slash payroll and sell off real estate. The line started to deteriorate once again. A number of top executives were fired and some two-thousand employees were let go. Morale was at a new low. In May 1951 Dumaine died. He was replaced by his son, Frederick C. Dumaine, Jr., whose nickname was Buck.

Service had deteriorated so far and public distaste for late and uncleaned trains had risen so high that Buck Dumaine decided to move in a different direction from his father. In 1951 and 1952 he increased the budget for maintenance, and the railroad stopped - at least for awhile - talking about shutting down the Old Colony and its Cape Cod trains. The beginning of a large fleet of RDC (rail-diesel-cars) was ordered from the Budd Company. Many of these eventually ran to the Cape. But the tenure of Buck Dumaine was not to be a long lasting affair, because Patrick McGinnis did not believe that money for maintenance was the best way to spend the railroad's income. McGinnis preferred high dividends. By keeping up dividends the price of the stock would be higher and that was a great advantage to stockholders and other insiders. There was a proxy fight brewing for control, and McGinnis was figuring how to win it.

In 1954 a rugged proxy fight lasting 41 hours took place at a stockholder's meeting. McGinnis won barely, but he won and he and his supporters named eleven of the 21 directors. The New Haven belonged to Patrick McGinnis who became the new president. Buck Dumaine was out.

McGinnis had been involved in management at two southern railroads, a small company called Norfolk Southern, which is not the same line that bears that name today, and the Central of Georgia. He became involved with financial adventures that included paying himself a large salary, generous expenses, bonuses and excessive dividends at Norfolk Southern. The Department of Justice filed a criminal information against McGinnis, several of his close associates and the railroad with violations of federal law under the Clayton Act. The charges were dropped when McGinnis left the Norfolk Southern and he soon appeared at the Central of Georgia, another line recently emerging from bankruptcy. There were problems there and he left much to the relief of the other directors.

McGinnnis didn't stay long at the New Haven. He didn't have to. He was a great talker, glib. In addition to slashing maintenance as the elder Dumaine had done, McGinnis manipulated the financial records, worked hard at making sure the preferred stock always had its dividends, paid himself a fine salary and additionally about $40-thousand a year in expenses, besides several suites in New York hotels paid for by the New Haven. McGinnis made grand statements about "The Railroad of Tomorrow" and bought those three low-slung, streamlined trains that were expensive - $5-million - and didn't work very well. They were the *Daniel Webster*, the *Roger Williams*, and the *John Quincy Adams*, three names to evoke the past and the affection that New Englanders generally feel for their history.

One year and ten months after Patrick McGinnis took over he was thrown out on January 18, 1956 by stockholders who turned against him. The damage he had done to the New Haven was incalculable. He moved on to the presidency of the Boston & Maine where similar things happened except for a serious criminal indictment that charged him with illegally profiting at the expense of the B & M. For that caper he was sentenced to a year and a half in a federal penitentiary and fined. That was in 1965. His appeal failed and he went off to occupy a cell.

The next president was a Boston attorney and former New Haven director. The line's earnings at the end of 1956 was about a quarter of a million dollars; it would be the last profit the New Haven ever made. The new man at the helm, George Alpert, did

United States Government
...ted a long siding under the
...amore Bridge on the canal, so
...struction materials could be
...ght in to build Camp Edwards. In
...days the siding was completed.

...w In July, 1955 eleven gondolas
...a crushed stone for Otis Air Base
... the Cape derailed in South
...reham tearing up 1,500 feet of the
... to Cape Cod. The crane arrived
...r local spectators did.

increase the maintenance budget by more than $4-million. But there had been too many years of neglect and this amount was not nearly enough to stop the slide to near chaos. It did slow it down, however.

The autos that had won the battle of carrying people and the trucks that had taken away so much freight were soon to enter Connecticut and Rhode Island on a modern highway, the Connecticut Turnpike. Begun in 1956 and completed in 1958, this road stretches 129 miles from Westchester County, New York on the state line through Connecticut to Rhode Island. It was a high speed road that for much of the distance ran parallel to the main line. The year it was finished, railroad revenues dropped by $14.5-million. In addition the air lines were flying more people between Boston and New York and Eastern had started its shuttle. All traffic was down and the New Haven was headed for another bankruptcy.

The Old Colony Division trains in Southeastern Massachusetts including Cape Cod were by then on borrowed time. The New Haven had negotiated a state appropriation of $900-thousand that kept passenger trains running to the Cape through June 1958. Another year's appropriation saved the trains, but it would be the last. Governor Foster Furcolo refused to approve a larger appropriation the next year, so the New Haven announced that on Tuesday, June 30, 1959 all passenger trains on the Old Colony Division would stop running. And they did. The last train left Hyannis in late afternoon and then a service that had begun in the spring of 1848 was over. The New Haven had been trying since 1938 to close down Cape Cod passenger service. It succeeded 21 years later. There were no more passenger trains on Cape Cod, and even those successful trains from Grand Central: the *Cape Codder* and the *Neptune* didn't run that summer. That wasn't a smart business decision, since they showed large profits.

The following year, 1960, the tracks above North Eastham were abandoned and the weeds and bushes started reclaiming the railroad line all the way to Provincetown.

Freight traffic, such as it was, continued to the Cape, but much of it came in by truck south from Boston on the newly-opened Southeast Expressway and rolled down the spine of Cape Cod on Route 6, the Mid-Cape Highway that ran all the way to Provincetown.

The freight cars that did cross the canal carried mostly building lumber and supplies that had either come from Canada, the Pacific Northwest or cement plants in the northeast. Bottled gas came in tank cars to Sandwich and Hyannis. Maintenance had been reduced to a point where the tracks were dangerous at speeds more than 20 miles an hour. Commuters went to Boston by bus or in private automobiles.

The New Haven in 1961 did not have income sufficient to pay its debts or even survive for long. It had been living on loans that had finally dried up. Seven different managements and all sorts of personnel changes and the effects of no long-range planning had done the old lady in.

She was broke and broken and on July 7, 1961, the New Haven was in bankruptcy again. Within six months the railroad had to pay obligations - taxes, interest, rents, etc. - of $33.8-million. On hand to pay that sum was $9.3-million. Bankruptcy was the only temporary solution.

The long term solution, or so it was thought, was to include the New Haven in the coming eastern railroad merger, a move that had momentum and would come about. The trustees of the New Haven worked diligently to be sure that a Penn Central merger would include their bankrupt line, which could not exist separate from the Pennsy and the New York Central. They filed with the ICC in 1962 to be included in the merger. By March 1965 an agreement was reached to sell all New Haven property to the Penn Central for cash and securities valued at between $140- to $160-million. This agreement was negotiated on the condition that the Penn Central would be under no obligation to continue carrying passengers. In modern times almost every railroad had shown a complete disinterest in moving people. Freight was what they wanted to carry.

This proved to be a sticking point and finally the Penn Central agreed to include the passenger service. The other problems in the way of completing the merger were the litigation by railroads to also be included in the merger.

The merger was approved in February 1968 and the bondholders took their case to court to prevent the merger until they were guaranteed their money. They lost and the Penn Central, including the New Haven in its entirety, was one big railroad on January 1, 1969. It was the largest industrial merger in American history.

New Haven Railroad Passenger Cars & Traffic

The New Haven Railroad earned after World War II, 55 percent of its revenue from passengers. It was the 30th largest line in America in miles of track, but third in passenger income. From the time the New Haven Railroad was incorporated in 1872 it had been at heart a passenger railroad. Of course its predecessors on Cape Cod - Cape Cod Branch, Cape Cod Railroad and the Old Colony - also had earned more money from passengers than they ever did from freight. Commuter rail and inter-city passenger trains that carried mail under government contract and express was the most successful part of the business.

The stages of development of the passenger car on the Old Colony applied to the New Haven's equipment starting with wooden cars lit by oil lamps and heated with coal stoves. Pintsch gas lamps and steam heat replaced those devices, while Miller platforms and Westinghouse air brakes made for greater safety when trains were underway or involved in an accident. They, of course, replaced link and pin couplers and hand brakes.

A major expense in the use of wooden passenger cars was the work and time involved in taking care of the finish on the outside. Faced with the high costs of all that labor and long drying time for paint and varnish required for wooden cars, it seemed time for another approach and this change came from the master car builder of the New Haven. It was 1897 and he was William Ledyard with an idea to cover wooden passenger cars with metal. So he applied copper sheathing to the sides and ends of a day coach. The copper weighed a bit more than all that paint, but it didn't take long to apply and it could be salvaged when the car was taken out of service from old age. In the meantime the cars treated in this way spent more time earning revenue, because they weren't in the shops being painted. The copper did not deteriorate and its ultimate salvage value for re-use was an important factor. This copperizing of wooden cars was mostly associated with the New Haven and with William Ledyard.

It was a positive idea and the New Haven coppered hundreds of its wooden cars before Ledyard died in 1905. Within three years after his death the railroad was back to painting and varnishing its wooden cars, but some of Ledyard's 800 to 900 cars painted dark green and varnished rolled on into the 1930s.

From 1860 to 1930 the railroad passenger car was the chief means of getting from one place to another on land in America. Great changes took place in the size, weight and cost of day coaches from the time the Old Colony was leased by the New Haven in 1893 and even a dozen years later, let alone 20 or more years. We shall look at what happened on the New Haven.

In 1890, the typical day coach was 57 feet long and had a seating capacity of 73. The total weight of these wooden cars was 22.5 tons with most of that weight in the trucks and wheels and hardware - 15.7 tons. By 1905 the new steel coaches which were just coming in to replace wooden cars were 72 feet long, weighed 55.6 tons and could seat 86 people.

The new steel underframes were the foundation of the car's strength; the body contributed little. The New Haven got its first steel passenger cars in 1912, which was a year before Congress started to investigate requiring the railroads to replace their wooden cars with steel ones. There were long hearings on the proposed bills requiring steel cars with the railroads in opposition. They protested that it would be an economic burden on them if they had to convert quickly as some of the proposed bills required.

It was a matter of cost. Consider this: in 1913-14 wooden railroad coaches cost between $5,500 and $7,000. Steel cars went for $12,500 to $14,000. Since the railroads still had tremendous economic and political clout and the fact that money usually carries the day, it was not surprising the bills were defeated. Of course the railroads won and were not required to purchase steel cars, although new cars were almost all steel after that while huge fleets of passenger cars were wood, but gradually phased out.

An interesting side note to the arguments was the fact that in order to protect mail clerks in Railway Post Office cars the federal government in 1911 had required that those cars be steel framed. So the public could not be expected to enjoy the greater safety of steel cars, although postal employees could.

The New Haven had operated sleeping cars and parlor cars for years in some cases by agreement with other companies, especially the Wagner Company, but in 1913 the Pullman Company got exclusive rights as the New Haven sold its 252 parlor and sleeping cars to them for $3.3-million.

In the early days of railroad travel there were stops for meals at larger stations for trains that covered greater distances. Some railroads started serving meals in dining cars and the New Haven bought its first two such cars in 1884. They were used on through trains between Boston and New York with one of them dropped off at New Haven for the noon run to Worcester. That was an early development to make better use of equipment with diners working all over a system on a number of trains during typical meal times before returning to company-owned commissaries for re-stocking of food and linen for the tables. The New Haven purchased more diners and even added lunch counter cars to serve lighter meals that were fast and economical for passengers. Through the years the New Haven was one of the few railroads to show a profit on its food service.

In 1925 the New Haven owned 20 dining cars, eight of which were steel. The other 12 were wooden with steel underframes. Within five years the ice boxes on these cars had been replaced with mechanical refrigeration.

That same year, 1930, in April the New Haven began running the *Yankee Clipper* daily except Sunday between Boston and New York, one train each way. The trains left Grand Central Station and South Station at 1 p.m. and were due at their destinations at 5:45. Afternoon tea was served all passengers and the diner offered only the choicest cuts of meat. All fruits and vegetables were fresh, no canned goods. The steward was dressed in a tuxedo and all the waiters wore white suits and white shoes with black bow ties. The New Haven called the extra fare *Yankee Clipper* "The Aristocrat of Trains." Some of New England's finest maritime artists were commissioned to paint the most famous clipper ships and those original oil paintings were framed and hung, one in each of the pullman parlor

This is a wooden day coach, a smoker with seats for 77. The Osgood Bradley Company of Worcester built this and other cars for the New Haven in 1912. This car had steam heat and electric lights and was used until the end of all-wood coaches on the line in 1938.

New Haven dining cars had the usual arrangement of double-width tables on one side and single on the other. The New Haven usually had diners on the Cape Cod summer trains to and from New York. It was one of the few railroads that made money on its food service.

cars named for those ships, including the *Flying Fish* with its 12 parlor seats, one drawing room, a buffet with 14 lounge seats and an eight-seat sun room. It had a short observation platform with room enough to put a brass railing and a drumhead with the train's name on it facing the tracks. There were no coaches and no baggage carried.

At the dedication of the trains, there were wooden platforms built for guests and those ceremonies with company officials and politicians were broadcast over WEEI radio in Boston, WTIC in Hartford and WOR in New York.

The Pullman Company delivered six new diners to the New Haven in 1935-36, and the following year built five grill cars, which specialized in low-priced standardized meals, but where a passenger could get anything from a snack to a full course dinner, or from an ice cream soda to a Scotch and soda, a soda fountain and a bar being part of the equipment. Several years later the New Haven hired hostesses for its grill cars and club cars.

The New Haven's investments in passenger equipment were for main line Boston-New York express service or some of its other through trains to Washington, Philadelphia or Pittsburgh. Branch lines or commuter service did not receive the kind of attention in new cars that the Shore Line did. In fact branch lines or commuter areas, including Cape Cod, got some new inventions to cut down on the expenses of steam railroading, which included a locomotive, several regular-sized cars and a full crew.

In 1897 the answer from the Schenectady Locomotive Works was a steam car, which was a coach with one end having a boiler and cylinders to drive the contraption and perhaps pull another car or two. It was a small, economical train to carry the lighter passenger loads on some lines. The steam car weighed 57 tons and had a two-man crew. The fire could go for 12 miles and its 1,500 gallon water tanks supplied the boiler for 60 miles.

The Central New England bought the car to carry people on one of its Connecticut branches that had lost business to a parallel trolley line. Larger trains were not necessary, so the railroad put the steam car in service on that 20-mile long branch. There were too many grades and the tiny boiler couldn't handle them, so the New Haven which had leased the Central New England brought the steam car to Cape Cod with its almost flat road beds and gradual grades. Once on the Cape, the steam car did well, pulling six box cars several times and once even eleven box cars. In fact, the steam car often hauled a full-size day coach. On several straight stretches between East Sandwich and West Barnstable, Yarmouth and Hyannis, Eastham and South Wellfleet and on the Woods Hole Branch, the steam car easily did 60 miles an hour. However, that was considered too fast for the small driving wheels and the management told crews not to run faster than 45.

After six months on Cape Cod the steam car was moved to the Dedham Branch of the New Haven where it ran until October, 1904 when it was sold off line. In a number of areas away from the main line, passenger business was often light, so the New Haven in 1921 bought the first of a number of Mack rail buses for local service. They were 32 feet long and seated 35 people. They were buses on wheels and made by the Mack Truck Company of Allentown, Pennsylvania. By 1931 the New Haven had 36 of them with several assigned permanently to the Cape, where they ran until all were scrapped in 1939. The New Haven had other rail buses that ran on the Cape too. They were all gone by World War II. The only complaint from passengers was that the exhaust smelled.

In 1936 the New Haven took another chance on a steam train by having a Besler engine installed in a two car affair run regularly between Bridgeport, Waterbury and

With declining passenger traffic forcing management to look for less expensive trains the New Haven ordered three railbuses from the Mack Company at Allentown, Pennsylvania in 1921. Actually Mack built the engines and chassis and Osgood Bradley in Worcester the car bodies which were almost 28 feet in length with seats for 35 passengers in three seats on one side of the aisle and two on the other. This car, 3001, was the first to enter service, running between Tremont and Fair Haven. Later they were used on the Woods Hole Branch and on the Cape's main line. They were hard riding and the gasoline fumes could be obnoxious. The Macks were the beginning of a pioneering effort by the railroad in self-propelled transportation.

The *Comet* was an experimental diesel streamliner built by the Goodyear Company when blimps weren't selling. It regularly ran between South Station and Providence, but on weekends ran to Cape Cod and to Plymouth on so called "Daisy picking excursions."

Hartford. It was a high pressure steam engine housed in a small compartment. It ran in a similar way to the steam car that Schenectady had built. The Mack rail buses were the most economical with a per mile operating cost of eight cents compared to $.43 per mile for a full-sized steam train with a locomotive, several cars and a full crew. The Mack buses and Besler steam cars were not repeated on the New Haven. The New Haven in 1935 did have the only experimental train built by the Goodyear Zeppelin Company of Akron, Ohio. This train, the *Comet*, was a double-ender equipped for operation from either end for short haul quick turnaround service between Boston and Providence. It was a three car, articulated train of aluminum construction and streamlined. The *Comet* cost $250-thousand and was made possible through a loan for that amount from the Public Works Administration, a federal government agency.

Comet made a test with its diesel-electric power in April 1935 between New Haven and Boston in which it easily did 110 miles an hour several times. It was put on the Boston to Providence run of 44 miles and scheduled for a mile a minute, including two stops. It covered that territory in 44 minutes.

Before *Comet* started regular service on that run in June, 1935, the New Haven ran it all over its rails on exhibition and published the times it visited the various stations. On the Cape, the *Comet* was on display at Buzzards Bay, Falmouth and Woods Hole and later Sandwich, Yarmouth and Hyannis. Then it moved to Harwich, Chatham, Orleans, Wellfleet and Provincetown. *Comet* was on the Cape for two days while it visited those towns.

The *Comet* ran between Boston and Providence six round trips a day. Its patronage was fair after a beginnning that on many trips had a passenger in each of its 160 seats. *Comet* made money and ran on until 1951 when the New Haven sold it for the scrap value of aluminum.

That same year the New Haven ordered a Mack Company double-ender and another nine units two years later - all of them for Cape Cod service. They arrived in 1954, but were never used as new management put them in storage.

The Budd Company's Rail-Diesel-Cars, or RDCs, were seen on many lines, but more of them were in local New England service than any other geographic area. In fact Boston saw more Budd RDC cars than any other city with the New Haven's 46 and the Boston & Maine's 109, the largest fleet.

They ran to the Cape variously as one, two and three car trains. They had a diesel engine and a direct drive. Those Budd cars pleased everyone. They were economical to operate and the public response was most favorable.

The New Haven bought its last heavyweight steel passenger cars in 1930. By January 1, 1931 the railroad had 733 all steel, heavyweight coaches, combination cars, baggage cars and diners. The older steel coaches were moved from the Shore Line express trains to Old Colony commuting service, including Cape Cod to Boston. Some of these older steel cars were re-built in Company shops.

In a further move to increase passenger business the New Haven began an air-conditioning program in 1933 by installing it in four diners and two coaches. By the end of 1934 hundreds of main line cars were air-conditioned. That same year the Pullman Company installed·air-conditioning in 80 of the parlor cars it assigned to regular New Haven service. Both the New Haven and Pullman continued until all cars on day trains between New York and Boston had air-conditioning by 1936. Local commuter cars did not get such benefits.

In 1934 the third and last era of passenger equipment began on the New York, New Haven & Hartford. It was the era of lightweight, streamlined cars. The first 50 were built at the Pullman plant in Worcester, Massachusetts, formerly Osgood Bradley, an old and major supplier to the New Haven's passenger fleet.

These cars had arched roofs with no clerestory, had ten double windows, seated 84, were 84.5 feet long, had air-conditioning built in and were lightweight cars at 54.5 tons. For the New Haven they were the first of the future. By 1938 their numbers had grown to 200 coaches and five grill cars, featuring a continuous seat lengthwise under the windows on both sides with tables before them on either side of the aisle. The grill cars were popular with travelers because of the menu that ranged between sandwiches and full meals or wine to whiskey. The 200 coaches were an outstanding benefit to the railroad and proved their worth in the heavy traffic days of World War II. Years later in 1969 when the New Haven was absorbed into the Penn Central there were still 135 of those cars operating. The last of them was running in Boston for the Massachusetts Bay Transportation Authority in 1985!

In 1946 the New Haven was operating 545 passenger trains a day. The largest post-war car orders were for 207 cars from the Pullman plant at Worcester. They were delivered between 1947 and 1950 and were streamlined and lightweight. All were air-conditioned. This order was for a mixture of equipment, including parlor cars, coaches, baggage-lounge-parlor cars, baggage-lounge cars, diners, sleepers, grill cars and observation-lounge cars. The final 15 cars were sleepers that arrived in 1954-55. By 1957 the New Haven fleet of 1,070 passenger cars was 54 percent modern, streamlined lightweights.

The older heavyweight cars were mostly used in Boston commuting service, including Cape Cod. Between 1949 and 1954 the heavyweight parlor cars were converted to day coaches for Old Colony commuting service. After all passenger service in Southeastern Massachusetts stopped on June 30, 1959, many of the heavyweights were scrapped. The older Railway Post Office cars for that region were retired too. On the Cape and other similar branches the Railway mail section was a 30 foot compartment in a baggage car.

In 1956 two Talgo trains from American Car & Foundry came to the New Haven and named the *John Quincy Adams* and the *Daniel Webster*. They were not as successful as the regular equipment the New Haven had. In 1967-68 two more streamlined and futuristic trains came from United Aircraft in East Hartford with help from the Pullman Company of Chicago where they were built. They were turbo trains and their general failure and creation of grief condemned them to a place on the list of technological flops.

They were part of the Department of Transportation Northeast Corridor Demonstration Project. The idea was to run two turbo trains between New York and Boston. The first was tested on New Haven rails, reaching 157 miles an hour. The second train arrived in late 1968 too late for the New Haven which was vanishing into Penn Central Corporation.

Walt Gifford loved trains and music. During World War II he played in a dance band and traveled around by train and car. Whenever he was near the Cape he visited his family and the New Haven. His favorite was the Woods Hole Branch. These pictures are from June and July, 1943. Gifford liked to take pictures of morning trains, whenever he could like this shot of the 7:05 from Woods Hole as she rolls past Vineyard Sound on the left on her way north. This train carried island passengers who came into Woods Hole on the early steamer.

Some morning trains were longer as 9:55 from Woods Hole is, entering yard at Falmouth.

On another day Gifford stood among the grout along the shore of Little Harbor to catch the 9:55 as she left the Woods Hole yard behind one of the light Pacific type locomotives that were used so much on the lighter rails of the Cape Cod Division.

At Lyster Pond crossing the late afternoon 5:40 from Woods Hole reaches speed along Vineyard Sound in Falmouth on a misty June 27, 1943. America and much of the world are in a global war and on these rails the New Haven has been running trains for a half century and the Old Colony for 21 years before that. The ocean, the track and this train have an almost timeless quality.

This is the 8:45 from Woods Hole pulled by light Pacific #1306, whistling for the Locust Street crossing in Falmouth, July 16, 1943.

It's early afternoon and the *Day Cape Codder* is pulling away from Falmouth station at Locust Street on the last lap of its New York to Woods Hole run. This summer train left Grand Central at 8:20 that morning and split at Buzzards Bay at 1:45 with the head end cars going to Hyannis and these cars including two Pullman parlor cars run into Woods Hole.

On another day the Buzzards Bay to Woo[ds]
Hole section of the *Day Cape Codder* ro[lled]
past the cool waters of Vineyard Sound belo[w]
Oyster Pond crossing in Falmouth. Th[e]
roadbed was well ballasted and maintaine[d]
through here and kept company with lar[ge]
chunks of granite in that seawall to the righ[t.]
The view of the water was spectacular throug[h]
here.

This is the morning Cape Cod train from
Boston speeding past the Moors, a
summer resort in Falmouth, pulled by
Pacific #1306. One of the better known
engineers on this run was Johnny Sylvia of
Provincetown, who used to give cab rides
to rail fans, strictly against company rules.

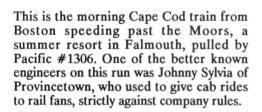

During the war there wasn't a great deal of freight
below the switch to Camp Edwards and Otis Air
Base, but this little Consolidation locomotive pulled
six gondolas of coal to Woods Hole, and on the way
had her picture taken at Oyster Pond crossing on a
bright July morning. The locomotive number is 161.

...e a look at these cancellations! All this mail ...k a ride on a train - "Boston & Wellfleet ...O.; Boston & Woods Hole R.P.O.; Boston & ...e Cod R.P.O. and even one with a New ...ford & Nantucket R.P.O." Mail came by train ...he Cape when the Cape Cod Branch opened to ...dwich in May, 1848. The first regular passenger ...ns to Hyannis carried mail, but later in the ...0s there was added a route agent who rode one ...n a day each way. He was a postal employee ...o often sat in a day coach, if there was no ...gage car or no room for him to work in the ...gage car on that train. He would drop off and ...up mail at each station that was brought there ...either the local postmaster or by the railroad's ...ion agent; he would quickly check the new mail ...ee if there was any for the next station, which ...the Cape was, in some cases, as close as a mile. ...would put the postmark on that next local mail ...I be out on the car's platform to hand off and ...eive mail. During the Civil War, in 1864, a more ...ensive system was created with post offices built ...ailroad cars, usually in one end of a baggage car ...part of an express car. They were called Railway ...t Offices or R.P.O.s. In 1869 there was a regular ...P.O. car on the Boston to Orleans run. In early ...1, the R.P.O. car was run through on trains to ...llfleet when the Cape Cod Railroad extended its ...ck there late in 1870. The postmark was changed ...reflect the terminal point, Wellfleet. That Boston ...Wellfleet designation was used for 19 years, ...en it was replaced by Boston & Cape Cod ...P.O., which meant Provincetown. In 1902 a ...ston & Woods Hole car was added. Railway ...il service to the Cape ended with the last ...ssenger trains on June 30, 1959. Trucks have ...ried mail since.

Camp Edwards in Falmouth was one of the largest army training centers in New England. Troops arrived and departed by train during World War II and afterward.

In the late 1940s, photographer Ben Harrison took this aerial of a train leaving Buzzards Bay for Boston.

New Haven Steam Locomotives

Half the steam locomotives the New Haven had on its roster were 4-4-0s, the basic American type that had brought the United States into the Railway Age. Those 500 engines were the mainstay of New Haven power in 1900. That fleet came from a variety of places, including the New Haven's own shops, the railroads that had been acquired, and outside builders, foremost of which was the Rhode Island Locomotive Works in Providence. In 1896 the New Haven turned to the Schenectady Works for twenty 4-4-0s, which was the last large order for that type, although the New Haven built a few in 1903 and 1904 in its own shops.

Some of the 4-4-0 relics built as far back as the Civil War were scrapped in the 1890s, but the younger machines ran until the late 1920s when they were taken off Boston-based commuter service. In those last years some of these teakettles ran to Cape Cod with light trains. They had graceful proportions, were reliable locomotives and had made history. On Cape Cod they were about the only engines seen from the beginning in 1848 until the turn of the century. But rolling stock was getting heavier and trains were longer.

The next order of increase in size was the Mogul type with a 2-6-0 wheel arrangement. It was designed for heavy, fast freight service. The first successful ones were built by Baldwin at Philadelphia and Rogers at Paterson, New Jersey and those engines date from 1860 and 1863 respectively. A number of Eastern anthracite coal railroads adopted the Mogul early, but they were a rare machine on the early New Haven, which used the 4-4-0 for freight and passenger service into the 1890s. But with its mergers the New Haven acquired lots of Moguls from the Old Colony and the New York and New England and it ordered some from the Rhode Island Works, so by 1900 Moguls were the favored freight engine. The oldest Moguls from the other lines were scrapped between 1906 and World War I. The New Haven bought 246 heavier Moguls and most of them were pulling trains through World War II. These engines were some of the few that could be run from Harwich to Provincetown, because of the light rail in that line, in fact, the lightest rail on the Cape.

In 1903 the New Haven brought order to its locomotive roster, which up to then was a strange mixture of types of engines and different numbering systems from those roads it absorbed. The former engines from the Old Colony were changed to #601 through #861. The numbering system lasted until the end of steam in 1954.

In a modernization program in the early 1900s, the New Haven ordered 72 larger locomotives from two builders. These engines were 4-6-0, or ten wheelers, and 20 of them were built by the Rhode Island Works at Providence, which by the time these engines were completed in 1903 and 1904 was one of the companies which joined with Schenectady and six other builders to form American Locomotive Company. These ten-wheelers were to supplement the New Haven's Moguls. The larger order for ten-wheelers was placed with Baldwin of Philadelphia for 52 engines built between 1904 and 1907. The first 20 cost the railroad $13,853 each or $277,060 for the lot. The first 50 were numbered 800 to 849, but the last two, #858, 859, were balanced compound engines with inside high pressure cylinders that drove the first set of driving wheels with inside main rods and a cranked driver axle. The steam was compounded, or used again, in outside low pressure cylinders and then exhausted up the stack. One of these compounds is pictured on the cover painting at Woods Hole. The road name and numbers were painted yellow. In 1935 the New Haven scrapped 23 of the 72 ten-wheelers and within five years another eight were cut up. But the

251

others were born again during the Hitler War when the incredible traffic crunch and a lack of new, replacement locomotives forced the New Haven, and indeed, the entire railroad industry to look at the dead lines of old engines to see what could be brought back to life. At the Readville shops near Boston there were long lines of rusting hulks at the beginning of the war, hulks that never could run again, or so it seemed. But in that time of testing of America's will miracles did happen and her railroads performed many of them.

The rebirth of old steam power on the New Haven was mostly a Readville operation and in those shops locomotives were literally rebuilt from the frames up, and in fact many of those rebuilt engines ran until the end of steam. The Australians were short of motive power during the war and a few New Haven ten-wheelers were carried there by freighter to run on the light, 80-pound rail. The rail workers down under and those living within ear shot of the tracks recall those transplanted New Englanders as "having such melodious chime whistles." The ten-wheelers made many runs to the Cape where their whistles rolled beautiful tones over towns, woods, meadows and beaches. A number of them ran past the war and into the late 1940s.

In 1907 the New Haven had Schenectady build a dozen Atlantic type locomotives, 4-4-2s, for high speed passenger service. They wound up on secondary runs, but in the 1920s they were pulling passenger trains out of Boston to Providence, Fall River and New Bedford. Five of these engines were on the dead lines at Readville for several years and were finally torched before Pearl Harbor. The other seven received class repairs - a new firebox, some boiler shell courses and the entire locomotive rebuilt from the underframe up - for wartime service in the Boston area pulling commuter trains. Some of them occasionally ran to Cape Cod. In an age where most steam locomotives had automatic stoking equipment, these Atlantics were a throwback, since they were hand-fired. In 1944 three of them were retired. Two years later another three followed and in March, 1947 the last one was scrapped. These were fast locomotives.

One of the most popular passenger locomotives was the Pacific type, with a 4-6-2 wheel arrangement. It was the next advance following the ten-wheelers, adding a set of wheels under the firebox and cab. The Pacific type is a twentieth century locomotive.

The New Haven had 138 of them and their purchase covered nine years, 1907 to 1916. Two companies split the business, but not evenly. Baldwin completed the fewest: 27. American Locomotive built all the others, including the two largest orders of 50 each at Schenectady and at the Brooks Works at Dunkirk, New York on Lake Erie west of Buffalo. Those Brooks engines, completed in 1913 and classified as I-2s, were as beautiful as any passenger locomotives in the country with their clean vertical lines, boiler and piping. They were a medium-sized Pacific designed to haul heavy passenger trains of steel cars between Boston and New Haven on the Shore Line. The railroad numbered them 1300 to 1349.

Although the I-2s were bought as fast passenger engines for Shore Line service, in three years they had been replaced by 50 heavier Pacifics, the I-4s. More on the I-4s later.

The I-2s began to show up on Cape Cod after 1916. Because of their length the turn tables had to be extended. With their heavy driving wheels, they were especially well suited for commuter service. They could start fast and move smartly, a necessary requisite on the Cape with so many station stops and close together, too. These locomotives found an additional career as fast freight engines, something not contemplated when the New Haven's mechanical department drew up the specifications. Most steam locomotives on the New Haven ran between 50- and 60-thousand miles a year. They got a boiler wash to remove scale once a month and a major overhaul in the back shop at Readville,

Massachusetts once a year.

The New Haven raised the clearances down through Braintree and that allowed these classes of Pacifics and the earlier I-1s to use that line southbound. Some of these 82 early Pacifics, showing age and great fatigue, were moved to the locomotive graveyard at Readville in the 1930s where shop foremen cannibalized them for parts to keep healthier engines running. Many locomotives on the dead tracks were rebuilt for war traffic that set new highs for tonnage and mileage. Some of the I-1s and I-2s were among them. And five years after the war in 1950 there were 23, or almost half the class, I-2s on the New Haven roster. In the following fall there were still eight of them running in commuter service from South Station to the Cape, to Plymouth and elsewhere on the Old Colony lines. By spring, 1952, only two of the I-2s were running and they represented half the steam left on the roster, which by that time was almost all diesel-electrics. That May those I-2s were retired after nearly 40 years and more than two-million miles.

The passenger engines that bumped the I-2s from the Shore Line to secondary runs and commuter service were the I-4s that came from Schenectady in 1916. Those 50 new locomotives, numbered 1359 to 1399, were the busiest engines on the New Haven, hauling the crack express trains between Boston and New Haven where electric locomotives took over for the run into Manhattan. The I-4s showed up on Cape Cod with the summer trains: *Cape Codder* and *Neptune*. They also pulled the heaviest passenger trains of 14 to 16 cars with the extra tonnage of air-conditioning added. And they did this with one locomotive, no doubleheading. Around the inlets of Long Island Sound there were some 50 speed restrictions with all those curves. There are sections along the Shore Line that looked as if they had been laid out by a snake with an engineering degree. It took a fine locomotive to maintain tight schedules with those speed restrictions that required frequent slowing of the train then speeding up again and soon after another restriction. Those miles were the toughest test with all those heavy cars strung out behind. The additon of automatic stokers and superheaters and other weighty gadgets increased their weight to 145 tons, making them the biggest engines to come through Buzzards Bay and on to Hyannis in the summer months after 1926. They never went east of Yarmouth, but on occasion they steamed to Woods Hole.

The New Haven decided it needed more help on the Shore Line and it ordered ten streamlined 4-6-4, Hudson type, steam power from the Baldwin Works at Eddystone, Pennsylvania, Baldwin's new home south of Philadelphia and just north of Chester on the Delaware River. Baldwin beat American Locomotive and Lima with a low bid of $126-thousand per engine and even lowered it to $110-thousand when the bankrupt New Haven insisted it couldn't afford the higher figure. They were classified as I-5s, numbered 1400 to 1409, and the first of them entered service early March, 1937. By that May they were all working as no other Shore Line engines ever had and they averaged covering 130-thousand miles a year, which was more than twice what the I-4s had done. These I-5s at 182 tons were simply too heavy for Cape rails.

The basic freight locomotive of greater weight from the 1890s was the Consolidation, 2-8-0, type that on many roads took over main line duties from the smaller Moguls. The New Haven had 70 of them and most had come from other lines, i.e., the Central New England and the New York and New England.

The flood of traffic during World War I that entered New England on New Haven railroad car floats across New York Harbor from New Jersey terminals of the Pennsylvania, Central of New Jersey and the Lehigh Valley over to Bay Ridge in Brooklyn and on the northern route from Maybrook, New York, west of Newburgh across the Hudson River on the Poughkeepsie Bridge and on to Cedar Hill Yards at New Haven, created an emergency requiring heavier motive power. The Consolidations couldn't handle the extra tonnage, so the New Haven had to lease bigger locomotives from the Erie, the Pennsylvania and the New York Ontario & Western. The Consolidations were never successful, but some of them survived as switchers and a few were used on local freights. They showed up on the Cape as late as 1945 during World War II. The Consolidation that had found such favor on other roads didn't perform on the New Haven and many of them were restricted to running at no more than 20 miles an hour when the speed limit between Boston and Buzzards Bay was 50 miles an hour, and between the Bay and Hyannis 45, the same as the Woods Hole Branch. Such locomotives slowed down operations, but during the war just about any old engine that could work was helpful. Motive power was that crucial to keeping all that traffic moving. In this country, America's war effort moved on the railroads; they did an incredible job.

The locomotive that was bought to help the New Haven move freight in the optimistic days of 1916 was the Mikado type, or 2-8-2. Schenectady built all 33 of them in two lots. These J-1s weighed 146 tons and were numbered 3000 to 3024. The final eight engines, classified as J-2s, were numbered 3100 to 3107. These freight locomotives ran all over the New Haven and on Cape Cod to Hyannis and Woods Hole, but only rarely east of Yarmouth because of their weight. Some of them received new boilers in 1942 and continued to run to Cape Cod from Boston for the rest of the war and from Providence to the Cape as late as 1952. The final three of them were still on the roster and used as snow melters in yard work through the winter of 1956.

When Hell Gate Bridge was opened the J-2s were used to move freight through Queens to and from the New Haven's Bay Ridge yards in Brooklyn where car floats could be used between there and across Upper New York Bay to Greenville, New Jersey and interchange traffic. It was much shorter than floating cars down the Harlem River as was done prior to opening Hell Gate Bridge.

One other steam locomotive used by the New Haven that brought freight to New England and eventually some cars to Cape Cod was the huge Santa Fe type, or 2-10-2. Fifty of these bruisers were delivered from Schenectady in 1918 to help move wartime tonnage from Maybrook, New York where thousands of freight cars arrived daily from the Erie, Central of New Jersey, Lehigh & Hudson River, New York, Ontario & Western and the Lehigh & New England. All those lines converged on Maybrook and from there the New Haven had to overcome grades through Danbury to Cedar Hill yards at New Haven where the trains were broken up and cars reassembled into freights to move east and north to factories and the docks at New England ports for ships heading to Europe in convoys. These Santa Fe types were some of the heaviest steam engines in America, weighing 180 tons. They were too much for Cape Cod rails and never came closer than Providence.

Steam lasted longer on other railroads than it did on the New Haven, but on other roads their motive power was newer. The New Haven's locomotives were mostly old and many of them had gotten World War II reprieves only because of a critical national emergency. The demands of that emergency wore out a fleet of steam engines and hastened the arrival of diesel locomotives that were seen by management as the saviors of the railroad industry in the post-war years. A salvation trumpeted by the manufacturers of diesels, but a song listened to in board rooms. So it was farewell after the war to a machine that since 1830 had a grip on the public imagination and affection that no other invention has ever had - the steam locomotive.

This photo was taken shortly after the Baldwin Locomotive Works delivered #148 to the New Haven in 1888.

Steam locomotives had more lives than a cat. Consider this shiny machine, which began life in March, 1876 at the New Haven shops at New Haven. Its first number was 33. Twenty-five years later in 1901 at the same shops it was rebuilt including some parts that dated back to 1860 and given a new number, 1511. These engines were fast starters, and so were excellent in local passenger work, but were powerful enough to haul branch line freight, too. They were in Cape Cod service until 1930.

This small, 4-4-0 was part of the last o[rder] for such locomotives by the New Ha[ven]. She was built in Providence by the Rh[ode] Island Locomotive Works in 1903. [The] Rhode Island plant had become part of [the] American Locomotive Company. T[his] class of engines was designated C-3-c. T[he] picture was taken in Buzzards Bay. M[ost] of these engines were scrapped by 1930[.]

Baldwin delivered this locomotive in 1904. With six-foot diameter driving wheels, this class of engine was ideal for passenger service. This machine is the one painted on the cover by railroad artist Ted Rose. These engines ran to Cape Cod through World War II.

An earlier ten-wheeler was #344, built by Rhode Island Locomotive Works in 1889. She pulled The *Flying Dude* to the Cape for several summers.

The American Locomotive Company of Schenectady, New York delivered 50 of these machines to the New Haven in 1916. The order was the last by the line for Pacific type engines, and they replaced as main line passenger train power those Pacifics purchased only three years before. These 133 ton locomotives were years ahead of their times and they ran up extraordinary mileage, including pulling heavy trains like the various *Cape Codders* from New Haven to Woods Hole and Hyannis. That crosswise tank in front of the stack is an Elesco feedwater heater. The two tanks back of the stack are for compressed air for the brake system. With their 79-inch diameter driving wheels these locomotives looked fast even while standing. The New Haven classified the 50 as I-4s.

New York to the Cape by Train

From the earliest days of the tracks that reached Cape Cod in 1848 most travelers came to the Cape from New York or beyond on the steamers of the Fall River Line to the city of Fall River and the rest of the way by train. Those ships became the most famous overnight boats anywhere.

Competition for the Fall River Line reached a new high when the Eastern Steamship Company brought out its two steamers, *Boston* and *New York*, to sail between those namesake cities, starting in June 1924. Eastern had begun an all-the-way-by-water service through the Cape Cod Canal in late spring of 1916 when the newly-completed waterway was dredged to charter depth of 25 feet in the channel which allowed good-sized coastal steamers to pass through, avoiding the older route around the Cape and over the shifting shoals of Nantucket Sound. The older route had its perils and passenger discomfort, but the Cape Cod Canal offered a smooth voyage through protected waters, and passengers embarked in one city and got off their ship in the other. It was a great convenience and the twins were instant successes. They drained off large numbers of passengers, especially heading north from New York. The Fall River Line, a New Haven Railroad subsidiary, was suffering. For passengers heading to Cape Cod and the Islands the railroad had an answer.

Direct rail service from Grand Central Station to the Cape with no changing trains. It was an appealing idea, since those who took Eastern's ship to Boston still had to go to South Station and take a train to reach the Cape. Thus in the summer of 1925 the *Cape Codder* was born. It was a weekend, sleeping car train between Manhattan and Hyannis that left late Friday evening and returned on Monday morning in time for work. The first *Cape Codder* ran on Friday night, June 19. The train enjoyed excellent patronage and rolled on every summer through the rest of the 20s and was marred by only one mishap.

The New Haven's worst boiler explosion caused it. Almost a year to the day from the first run of the train a freight train's locomotive boiler exploded at 2:45 a.m. near a tidal swamp in Kingston, Rhode Island. The engineer, fireman and brakeman were in the engine cab and all three of them were killed when the boiler blew completely off the frame. Within three minutes the *Cape Codder*, rolling at high speed, crashed into the wreckage of that freight locomotive. Turning over, the passenger train's locomotive left the rails as did four of the *Cape Codder's* Pullmans. One sleeper turned over. The fireman was killed. No passengers were injured because of the heavyweight steel cars. It was a foggy night with little visibility and because of the death of all three men in the freight locomotive that was running in the opposite direction, there was no one alive to flag down the *Cape Codder*. Given the speed through there of the express, there were a great many lucky passengers on that train and a lucky engineer, too.

In 1929 through sleeping cars from Washington were added to the *Cape Codder* Friday night at New Haven. There was at least one Pullman added from the *Montrealer* and another from the *Washingtonian*, sometimes two. These sleepers were on the return trip Sunday night from the Cape and were dropped off at New Haven for those trains to pick up for the run via Hell Gate Bridge and Pennsylvania Station, New York, to Philadelphia and Washington Monday morning. Of course the rest of the cars were bound for Grand Central and the *Cape Codder* proceeded there after the steam locomotive had been replaced by an electric at New Haven for the final 72 miles into Manhattan.

In June, 1930 a Pullman sleeper was added from Grand Central on the *Cape Codder* to Provincetown. It was at the end of the train and was dropped off and picked up at Yarmouth early Saturday morning and returned from Provincetown Sunday night to be coupled onto the *Cape Codder* before midnight at Yarmouth.

The *Cape Codder* used to make its last weekend run late in September, but because business fell off so dramatically to the tip of the Cape; the sleeper to Provincetown only ran through September 7. The *Cape Codder* continued for several more weeks to Hyannis and Woods Hole.

In 1937 the Fall River Line was shut down and a memorable American institution was gone in July of that year. The Fall River Line had always carried passengers to the Cape, and so the New Haven decided to carry as many of those as possible by rail.

The *Night Cape Codder* had been a three day a week train, so it was changed to a daily operation. A *Day Cape Codder* was added, leaving Grand Central in the morning and splitting its cars at Buzzards Bay with the last five for Woods Hole and a steamer connection to the Islands, and the front end cars to Hyannis and on occasion a parlor car to Provincetown. The *Day Codder* ran to the Cape daily except Sunday and to New York daily except Saturday and Sunday. It is possible that the New Haven might have added a parlor car for Chatham, but on July 6 that summer the Chatham Branch was abandoned between Harwich and Chatham. They had even stopped running freight there.

Since the Cape and Islands had always been important destinations on the New Haven, that same summer the Fall River Line died, another train was added: the *Neptune*. It was a weekend train, as the first *Cape Codder* had been, leaving Grand Central at 4:45 p.m. Friday and splitting at Buzzards Bay with the rear cars for Woods Hole and forward for Hyannis. The return trip to Grand Central left the Cape late Sunday afternoon for the six-hour run. Two *Cape Codders* and a weekend *Neptune* were moneymakers, even at the government-imposed fare in the 1930s of two cents a mile in coaches, and by that time the *Day Cape Codder* and the *Neptune* had some coaches in the consist.

In the summer of 1938, actually it was late July, passenger service to Provincetown was stopped by the New Haven. It started up again just for the summer of 1940. The New Haven had started running buses from Hyannis to Chatham in the summer of 1937 when the Chatham Branch was abandoned. The New Haven did the same thing for the north shore of the Cape when passenger trains stopped running east of Yarmouth. Buses left the Yarmouth station for Dennis, Brewster, Orleans, Eastham, Wellfleet, Truro and Provincetown.

Business was so good in those later depression years that in 1939 the New Haven added another summer train to the Cape. It was named the *Islander* and it ran Fridays to the Cape and Sundays to New York as a slightly earlier *Neptune*. The *Islander* ran through to Woods Hole with the entire train going there and meeting a steamer for the Vineyard and Nantucket. The two trains were close with the *Islander* leaving first at 2:45 p.m., followed five minutes later by *Neptune*. The *Islander* usually carried seven cars with *Neptune* longer at eleven cars. The *Neptune* still split into two trains at Buzzards Bay. After four years of running, the *Islander* was discontinued in September 1942. The *Cape Codders* ran on through the war and afterward there were three summer trains from Grand Central to the Cape from June to September and occasionally into October. They were the *Day* and *Night Cape Codder* and the *Neptune*. The new stainless steel cars were put on those trains at once, including coaches, diners, grill cars and Pullman sleepers some of which were named for Cape and Islands areas: *Race Point, Monument Beach, Long Point, Dukes County, Popponesset Beach* and *Monomoy Point*.

259

Here is the wreck of the *Night Cape Codder* in June, 1926 near Kingston, Rhode Island when she plowed into the wreckage of a freight engine whose boiler had exploded, killing the crew. No passengers died.

The *Cape Codder* paused in the summer of 1961 at Buzzards Bay on its way to New York. The diesel-electric locomotive, #2032, was one of the last 30 made by its manufacturer, Electromotive Division of General Motors in 1960. They were the second batch of Fl-9s bought by the New Haven.

After the summer season the New Haven in 1954 ran Budd RDC cars from Providence to Hyannis on Friday and back to Providence on Sunday. These trains which the New Haven called the *Junior Neptune* met trains to and from New York at Providence. In the spring of 1958 this service ended as all New Haven passenger trains in Southeastern Massachusetts were on borrowed time that soon would run out.

When the state of Massachusetts ended its passenger train appropriation in June 1959, the New Haven suspended all New York to Cape Cod summer service. Even though that appropriation was for Old Colony trains only.

It was an economic mistake for the railroad to cancel the summer trains. The *Neptune* in 1958 had 600 round-trip passengers on the weekend. The *Night Cape Codder* averaged 175 passengers and the *Day Cape Codder* had from 90 to 250 daily.

In June 1960 the New Haven promoted the restoration of *Day Cape Codder* and *Neptune* by advertising "The New Haven Goes Back to Cape Cod." The *Day Cape Codder* ran daily except Wednesdays and Fridays from June 30 to September 10. The *Neptune* was again a Friday afternoon only train, leaving Grand Central at 4:45 with coaches, parlor cars, a diner, a grill car and a tavern lounge car to Woods Hole. As before the *Neptune* returned from Hyannis and "The Hole" late Sunday afternoon with a Grand Central arrival before midnight. The *Neptune* through the years was a major contestant for the national award of the fun train of America. Just picture all these people, many of them in their early 20s, heading out of the city on a Friday for a weekend on Cape Cod or one of the Islands. The Friday night trip was what gave the *Neptune* its great reputation as a social enterprise. The railroad hired a man who played the accordion and he strolled from car to car entertaining as he went. There were always a few amateur musicians who brought their instruments along to form impromtu bands and combos. Spontaneous singalongs broke out and the grill and bar cars served drinks without end all the way to the bumper posts at Woods Hole and Hyannis. Phone numbers and addresses changed hands amid the constant revelry and some young men heading for Hyannis or Woods Hole changed destinations to pursue some lovely creature they had been holding hands with or kissing in the grill car, or any car for that matter.

Jerome Beatty, Jr. described one trip he made on the *Neptune* this way: "A man was seen carrying a large unwieldy sack aboard. He opened it to reveal a large slap bass. He was soon joined by a clarinet man, a saxophonist and a man with a trumpet. These paying passengers joined Don, the accordian man, and entertained the crowd all the way to the Cape.

"Afterwards, that combo appeared often on the *Neptune*. Once they paraded through the coaches to the dining car and right into the galley. The visit was reciprocated on a later trip when the chef, a West Indian with a ring in his ear, emerged with his bongo drums and gave his own concert that had the joint jumping."

Indeed the train was usually jumping and there were a group of more or less regulars who easily welcomed newcomers and broke the social ice for some of the shyer types who at first didn't know what to make of all these uninhibited Friday evening folks on a rolling party to Cape Cod. It never took long for newcomers to join in, usually before Stamford and always by New Haven.

Can you picture such fun on an air liner? A greyhound bus? A two-seater Nissan on Route 95? No!

The New Haven, having come to its senses in 1960 and restoring the summer Cape Cod service, kept the trains running for five straight years and ending all that joy on

September 13, 1964 with the last run of the *Neptune*. It was a Sunday evening, of course. As late as 1961 the New Haven made a minimum of $220-thousand profit on those summer Cape Cod trains from New York.

The fares were reasonable too. From New York to Hyannis one way in a coach was $13.18. Round trip was $23.75. Your own individual parlor car seat was only $3.14 one way, $6.28 round trip. To Woods Hole from Grand Central was $12.85 one way in a coach, $23.15 round trip. In a parlor car, one way was $3.03, round trip $6.06. By boat to the Vineyard was $2.10 one way and double that for a round trip. To Nantucket was $4.30 from Woods Hole and double it for round trip.

The end of the *Neptune* in 1964 was really the last of the connections that began in 1847 when the Fall River Line brought people from New York to Fall River by boat and on to the Cape by train. That service was in its 91st year when it ended. The direct trains from New York had been running 13 summers when the Fall River Line died. The New York to Cape Cod trains ran for 39 years and when they ended the New Haven was in such sorry financial shape that they couldn't muster equipment to run a profitable train up the Shore Line and through Buzzards Bay to Woods Hole and Hyannis.

In the middle 1980s Amtrak would renew weekend trains to Cape Cod on a summer to summer basis. When the first Amtrak train reached Hyannis in June, 1986 it ended a 22-year drought on that run.

This Ted Rose sketch is the Brewster depot in 1927.

Three days in the summer of 1965!
Within an eight day period in late June and early July the New Haven's locomotive #517 pulled way freight BX-20 on the Cape Cod Division's tracks to Harwich, Orleans, Eastham and North Eastham. Railfan H. Bentley Crouch spent those three days photographing the train and he shares those moments with us. On June 24 the freight went to the New Haven's sand-loading spur at Brackett Road in North Eastham to pick up gondolas of company sand. The youngster in the cab window is Ben Crouch's son, who rode in the locomotive from Orleans to North Eastham.

Later #517 pulled five gondolas of company sand south along the embankment by Depot Pond in Eastham.

When the train left Harwich, Ben Crouch walked a few feet to the other side of the road bridge and snapped it again as it crossed the switch. The sandy trail without tracks that bears off to the right in the background is the abandoned Chatham Branch that was shut down 28 years before. Not far ahead of the engine was a wye between the two lines where whole trains could be turned. That was removed with the Chatham Branch.

Opposite Five days later BX-20 pauses at Harwich with a gondola filled with stone for Roach's Ready-Mix plant at North Eastham. The passenger station at Harwich was located where those automobiles are parked on the left. Harwich Lumber was one of many Cape building supply firms that bought large quantities of Canadian wood, especially cedar shingles.

Right Just west of Route 6 in Orleans the train paused for more picture taking in the dense woods that were reclaiming the right of way. The signs of pending abandonment were never more obvious than here.

Below Two days later, July 1, Crouch again stalked the lonely branch line and caught BX-20 returning empty from Eastham and south bound at mile post 96; that's the distance by rail to Boston. A railroad had been here for 95 years. The locomotive, #517, was a 1,600 horsepower all-purpose machine built by Alco in 1950 and classified as type RS-3.

PENN CENTRAL

The new railroad handed out buttons that read "Call Us Penn Central" to its more than 100-thousand employees. It was a public relations gimmick that didn't wash well with the workers that had been with the old New York, New Haven & Hartford. From the same office of heavy thinking came the Penn Central logo, PC, and a statement of new purposes, naturally. It read this way: "This symbol is designed to give a feeling of strength and modernity. It suggests forward motion - a company on the go. It's simple, but distinctive - the symbol gives immediate identification and is easily remembered. We believe that it effectively expresses the dynamic quality of this exciting and challenging new enterprise we call the Penn Central." It reads like something created by a committee.

In front of the former general offices at 54 Meadow Street in the City of New Haven they unfurled a large, green banner with PC in the middle. The headquarters of course had moved to Pennsy offices in Philadelphia. The first day of this creation the number of trains between New York and Boston dropped from 27 to 16. Within a week the chairman of Penn Central, Stuart T. Saunders, gave a press conference in Boston, saying: "Penn Central, henceforth, will pay a great deal more attention to its trucking subsidiary, New England Transportation Company." The ex-New Haven would be a poor relation for those years of the Penn Central. Over the New Haven logos and letterboards above the windows were riveted plastic replacements with the green Penn Central on former New Haven passenger cars. Timetables were changed frequently with trains disappearing. So far as Cape Cod is concerned it was a local freight-only line and had been since June 1959. Trains were scheduled as needed and that wasn't very often. A road diesel switcher with three box cars and a caboose was about average, though many trains had no more than two box cars. Sometimes there was only one. Building supplies were the usual cargo often carried in Northern Pacific cars. Everything else came to the Cape by truck. It was often difficult to see the tracks because the weeds grew along the right-of-way as richly as in a meadow of an abandoned farm.

The merger of two industrial giants - the Pennsylvania and New York Central Railroads - at that time was the most ambitious in American corporate history. All throughout the business world people were impressed by the Penn Central, the new industrial giant. But there were incredible weaknesses, cracks in the structure that no one seemed to see. First, the company had only about $13.3-million in cash. It should have had a minimum of $40-million. It's true that there were assets of $7-billion, making it the largest transportation company in America and the largest real estate dealer, that it owned or controlled 186 companies, including trucks, hotels, pipelines, barge lines, factories, warehouses, even amusement parks, but there wasn't enough money to keep it running.

The Penn Central had enormous problems. It was "yard heavy" and it had too many terminals where the individual carloads had to be reclassified into other trains, a slow and expensive process. This was inefficient and a problem the line never solved. So many miles of their tracks were in poor condition that the average freight car covered only 37 miles per day at an average speed of 17 miles an hour and earned revenue for only three hours a day.

266

The congestion in the many yards was beyond measure and the irritation on the part of shippers was constantly at or above the boiling point.

At first losses were at least $400-thousand a day with passenger traffic accounting for $250-thousand of that. Those figures rose through the years of Penn Central. The railway mail service was being taken away from the railroads and more of it given to air lines and trucks. There was a chronic shortage of cars, and the railroad ran up new records for cars borrowed and per diem charges paid out to other lines. The percentage of cars awaiting repairs was more than twice the railroad industry's average.

A rigid rate structure worked a severe hardship on the Penn Central as it did on all railroads. Some freight rates were set at below cost because they were considered in the public interest by either the ICC or regulatory groups in the 16 states served by the line. The ICC especially was slow in responding to requests for rate increases. As the Penn Central staggered through the early months of 1970 the ICC granted an interim five percent rate increase in June for the next six months. That would have earned the line an extra $36-million, but retroactive to January 1 were new labor agreements that cost an additional $62-million. And so it went with income dropping and expenses mounting. In 1969 income rose by $138-million; expenses increased $188-million. Much of this was interest on debt as the railroad borrowed to keep going.

The New Haven was no help. The former "Aristocrat of New England Railroads" as it used to call itself lost $22-million in 1968, and besides that Penn Central in its short, unhappy life spent another $22-million to refurbish New Haven equipment. Soon it was apparent that Penn Central was losing more than $500-thousand every day and those figures never seemed to improve. The railroad had an appetite for cash like an elephant. One answer was to mortgage property. At one point the legal department was almost fully engaged in writing up mortgage agreements. In time there was little left that wasn't mortgaged. Finally, the incessant executive bickering, corporate disloyalty, powerful unions hanging on to archaic work rules, a glacial federal bureaucracy with no sympathy for severe problems, recession, tight money, top drawer bungling, a railroad in need of maintenance and new and repaired equipment, and a cash flow that always outstripped income made Penn Central a railroad wreck, the largest in American history.

The Penn Central lasted for 871 days, a bit less than 30 months. On June 21, 1970 "the dynamic quality of this exciting and challenging new enterprise" collapsed, floating in red ink. The company was broke and in bankruptcy. The ex-New Haven employees were not surprised. It was a condition they knew, having been there before - twice.

In bankruptcy the Penn Central still ran trains, although less frequently. There would come out of the bankrupt Penn Central a new super railroad. It would be called Consolidated Rail Corporation or Conrail, and it would run freight trains to Cape Cod.

The freight traffic was decidedly modest in the mid-1970s when this train of two box cars paused at Buzzards Bay to wait for the bridge span to be lowered.

The train went to Falmouth, and picked up some empties, returning several hours later and crossed the Cape Cod Canal on its way to Middleboro that Friday afternoon, November 28, 1975.

Track maintenance was close to being non-existent in the last days of the New Haven and in the short term ownership by the Penn Central. This is a renumbered New Haven diesel engine at Old Dock Road crossing, West Falmouth on April 28, 1970. Penn Central took over the year before.

This young man is Eric Choate of East Falmouth who was on a summer afternoon walk with his father, Philip Choate, who took this picture in 1970. The two would drive to a different station on the Woods Hole Branch and then walk along the track, for them a regular Sunday routine. Eric has just emerged from the shadows of a cow bridge slightly north of Curley Boulevard Bridge, North Falmouth. The cow bridge is an old New England idea that allowed cows to be moved to and from grazing fields and to the barn under the tracks and in safety. Eric was six years old.

CONRAIL AND BAY COLONY

With Penn Central in bankruptcy since 1970 and the other eastern railroads in serious trouble financially, the national government finally stepped in again if only to create a planning agency. President Richard Nixon in 1973 signed into law a bill called the Regional Rail Reorganization Act. The group created the United States Railway Association which made plans to create a company that would replace Penn Central.

That same year, 1973, the State of Massachusetts bought the railroad line from Attleboro through Taunton to Middleboro and from there through Buzzards Bay to Falmouth and to South Dennis and to Hyannis. So the state owned the tracks on Cape Cod; it still does.

But the freight service to the Cape continued to be operated by Penn Central until its replacement came about.

In 1976 it was born. The new company was the Consolidated Rail Corporation, or Conrail. It included the companies that had been combined into Penn Central: the New Haven, the Pennsylvania and the New York Central. To them it added six other railroads - the Erie Lackawanna, the Central Railroad of New Jersey, the Lehigh Valley, the Lehigh and Hudson River, the Reading and for a time, the Ann Arbor.

The new system had 34-thousand miles of track. The rails ran from Boston through much of the northeast and the midwest as far as St. Louis, Chicago and Detroit with lines to Washington, D.C. and to Montreal.

Some $4-billion in federal funds were poured in with the idea of making it a successful business and them selling it. New agreements were reached with the rail unions, the work force was reduced and some unprofitable lines were abandoned.

On Cape Cod the rails were maintained by the state and the freight moved by Conrail diesel road switchers. Aside from military traffic into Camp Edwards and Otis Air Force Base on the single track branch, most of the twice weekly trains consisted of fuel and building supplies. A company from North Eastham was trucking sand down to Yarmouth and dumping it into big hopper cars on the siding there. It was the only traffic that seemed to originate on Cape Cod. The usual train heading off Cape was one of empty cars.

Everything that moved was on slow orders, as the track was reaching the dangerous stage. A diesel was standing at Sandwich one afternoon in the late 1970s and with no warning the rail on one side fell over from the weight. It is called turning a rail, and it usually happens when a train is moving. Not this time, and on close examination the ties were so badly rotted that the spikes had nothing to grip. It was not an isolated situation, since inspections had warned of many sections of track where a train could easily derail.

In 1978 the state signed a $1.768-million contract with Hamel, a Minnesota firm, to replace old ties, realign the rails and cut back brush that was encroaching on the tracks. Hamel brought a collection of state-of-the-art track equipment and shipped ties from Georgia, 37,800 heavy oak ties, and stored them temporarily at Yarmouth and at Falmouth. By that November the work was completed and trains were running with greater speed and their crews did not view a run to Cape Cod with the apprehension they had felt earlier on the uncertain roadbed. One more - and this time major - railroad rehabilitation project would put most of the Cape rails in fine shape. That project was to cost $30-million with half of that sum coming from the state and the other from the federal government. The Perini Construction Company won the contract which reworked the 64 miles of track from Attleboro to Hyannis. It included heavy rock ballast, new ties, fish plates, spikes and new rails where necessary. Pirini's crews began work in October 1983 and finished in 1986. The track from Buzzards Bay to Falmouth and from Yarmouth to South Dennis did not receive the same attention as that from Hyannis to Attleboro.

Conrail wanted to get out of running Cape Cod freight trains and companies willing to step in and handle the service were invited to submit their plans to the state transportation secretary. Eventually seven companies did and in April 1982, the company selected was Bay Colony.

Bay Colony was conceived at Edaville in 1972, which was the second year that George Bartholomew owned that narrow gauge line that Ellis D. Atwood had bought in pieces from the remains of several Lilliput lines in Maine. Atwood had brought down most of that equipment after World War II. George Bartholomew loved trains and he used to visit Edaville after Atwood built it into an operating museum. Bartholomew worked at Edaville as a teenager when Nelson Blount, a Rhode Island seafood executive, owned and operated it from the late 1950s. Atwood died in November 1950 and his estate later sold it to Blount.

Bartholomew was a conductor and a fireman at Edaville on the narrow gauge engines. His ambition was to be at the throttle as a steam locomotive engineer. He spent much of his time as a freshman at the University of Arizona studying for his locomotive engineer's license. He enjoys a heavy laugh when he recalls that his textbook in 1958 had been written in 1906: "The Locomotive Up to Date."

He got the license at age 18, the first year of his eligibility. It was 1958. He spent his summers at Edaville and then started working with Blount at the Steamtown Locomotive Museum in Bellows Falls, Vermont where Blount was collecting rescued standard gauge steam engines before the scrap dealers cut them up.

Bartholomew was back running locomotives at Edaville during the Christmas seasons when, in 1966, he asked Nelson Blount for first refusal if Blount ever wanted to sell Edaville. Blount agreed. In September 1967 Blount was killed in a plane crash and his family ran Edaville and Steamtown for awhile after that. In 1970 they offered Bartholomew the opportunity to buy Edaville in a highly leveraged purchase. He has owned and operated it ever since.

George Bartholomew and Gordon Fay, a friend of Bartholomew's and a railroad expert, started talking about how rail service to the Cape might be saved. At that time Penn Central owned the railroad and it was on the schedule to be abandoned. The two men approached Penn Central and the giant company was receptive to the idea of selling the line. There was not enough freight business to make it pay for Penn Central who was basing their costs on full crew operations and sharing the overhead of offices and executives in Philadelphia and New York and the other aspects of financing a concern from which money was pouring out the door in a growing financial calamity.

Bartholomew's idea was a short line concept using employees who could each do a number of things rather than one. He saw a railroad to the Cape as a part time service with trains operated by two-man crews rather than five as was Penn Central practice. Before anything could be done, Penn Central went bankrupt. State law in Massachusetts regarding

271

The first major work on Cape rails in more than 20 years was in the late summer and fall of 1978 when the Loram Construction Company of Hamel, Minnesota replaced ties, realigned the track and cut back brush under a $1,768-million state contract. Ed Robinson took these pictures that September in Cataumet and West Barnstable. **Left** After the ties were sheared off, the next machine pounded them apart, **Below** then the pieces were thrown aside and new ties **Bottom** placed under the rails.

Below A Conrail diesel pulls a freight train past a 500 foot long pile of new ties from Georgia at Yarmouth Junction. At Falmouth 20 gondola cars of ties were unloaded. The Loram people put 37,800 ties down. The gondola cars in that train at Yarmouth Junction will be spotted on that siding on the right. Ed Robinson took the picture from a wooden framework where trucks brought sand from Eastham and dumped it for shipment off Cape.

Above New spikes were driven into the ties by machine and then a gauging crew **Bottom** made sure the rails were exactly 56-1/2 inches between the inside edges.

One August morning in 1979 a car inspector for Conrail checks box cars at Yarmouth before they will be pulled off Cape. This man drove in his car from Middleboro. Later that day he inspected cars at Otis Air Base and at Falmouth.

On August 11, 1979, Governor Edward J. King and United States Senator Paul E. Tsongas attended a reception in Barnstable for the beginning of a week-long demonstration of a new Budd diesel car, the SPU-2000. They were strong supporters of bringing back passenger rail service to Southeastern Massachusetts, and the King administration was on record favoring restoring Cape Cod to Boston rail service through Braintree by 1982. At the Route 6A crossing in West Barnstable, people stood in the rain to watch the Budd car on its way east. Free rides were available daily for a week from Buzzards Bay, Falmouth, Sandwich and Hyannis.

railroads is old - from the first half of the 1800s. Hearings on such a petition are necessary and then an act of the legislature is required to incorporate. Bay Colony was granted that incorporation in 1977, but then some others thought they would apply; eventually there were six others. There was, however, one big difference - all the others had asked for an on-going state subsidy.

The Bay Colony approach asked the state - since they had since purchased the railroad from Penn Central - to rehabilitate the line, using Federal Railroad Administration guidelines to Class 2, which permitted 25 miles an hour freight trains and 30 for passengers. Once the tracks were in good shape, Bay Colony would maintain them at their own expense and never allow them to fall below Class 2 standards. Furthermore Bay Colony agreed to pay the state a small percentage of their revenue that would increase as their business improved.

The state liked the Bay Colony proposal and it selected Bay Colony to run freight to Cape Cod and on several other branches in the state, including the line to Plymouth. The state had bought the tracks from Conrail, and Loram had done some track work in the fall of 1978, and there would be more work on the line in the mid-1980s. In June, 1982 Bay Colony started its Cape Cod freight service in Hyannis. It is a terminating railroad with cargo coming in and empties leaving. Packaging Industries in Hyannis used to ship machinery out, but the company closed its local operations and moved out of state.

Bay Colony has seven operational diesel-electric road switchers and two that are not operating. Parts from those two will be combined to make one running engine. The company has a small fleet of freight cars with which they ship fly ash from an oil-burning electric plant at Sandwich on the Cape Cod Canal. The fly ash is shipped to the middle west in a special car and once there vanadium and other minerals are extracted and used in steel making. The biggest shipping business has started and that is trash, solid waste, that can be burned to turn out energy at a $250-million plant at Rochester, Massachusetts, a mile north of Tremont. The plant is called Seamass and Bay Colony will haul one-thousand tons of trash a day from the Cape and south from Boston and Seamass will turn it into electricity. There are two transfer stations on Cape Cod. The first was erected at Otis Air Base and serves Falmouth, Mashpee and Sandwich. The first eleven cars run out of there with 42 tons capacity each. The cars have three bins, removable roofs and are teflon coated inside.

The other transfer station is at Yarmouth and serves the mid-Cape and any other towns that may make arrangements. At the transfer stations the trucks back into the upper level and drop off refuse and the Bay Colony freight cars are on the lower level. The refuse is sorted, so that burnable materials only get to the furnaces at Seamass. With a 27-year contract with Seamass, Bay Colony seems assured of a long future on Cape Cod railroad tracks.

A champagne christening inaugurates a new railroad at Hyannis. It is 9:55 a.m., June 11, 1989, and Mary Bartholomew, the wife of George who is watching and encouraging her, makes it on the first swing. Five minutes later service began with this locomotive pulling the first train.

CAPE COD AND HYANNIS RAILROAD

With one diesel engine and five coaches the Cape Cod & Hyannis Scenic Railroad began its first season's operation in 1981. It had two schedules with the first one in place from June 14 to 19 and September 9 to October 11. During that time three trains a day left Hyannis at 10 a.m., 12:15 p.m. and 2:30 p.m. The trip took 45 minutes to reach its destination, Sandwich station. There were a number of crossings without automatic warnings for street traffic, so a flagman had to climb down from the engine and stop automobiles, allowing the train to pass. When it did the flagman got back on at the rear car. There were three options that year: a family package cost each adult $5 and each member under 12 cost $3; the trip to Sandwich was $7 for adults and $4 for children. The most expensive was the train to Sandwich with a bus trip to Heritage Plantation Museum that included admission to all exhibits. For that package adults paid $10.50 and children $6. All prices were for a round trip on the train. The summer schedule from June 20 to September 8 and included Labor Day added one round trip and featured trains from Hyannis at 9:15 and 11:15 a.m. and 1:45 and 4 in the afternoon. Return trains from Sandwich left there one hour after their departure from Hyannis. That first year the new tourist line mentioned the possibility of acquiring a steam locomotive by late August. They never did and such talk was not part of their promotional material after that. The Cape Cod & Hyannis ran for eight warm weather seasons behind diesels.

In the second season of operations additional coaches were purchased and some leased. In rolling stock the new pride of the line was a parlor car built for the Pennsylvania Railroad in 1912. It was outfitted in one of its areas with tables where drinks were served and on some runs a meal, Sunday brunch and evening dinner. The car had heavy six-wheel trucks and rolled over the Cape Cod tracks like the *Queen Mary* in a bath tub. It offered a splendid ride and its new name was *Nobska* after the point on Vineyard Sound east of Woods Hole.

That season of 1982 saw a more ambitious itinerary with trains running across the canal bridge to Buzzards Bay and down the Woods Hole Branch to end of track at Falmouth. Mondays and Thursdays there was one round trip to Falmouth, leaving Hyannis at 9 a.m. On the other five days the trains left Hyannis for Buzzards Bay at 9 a.m., 12:30 p.m. and 3:45 p.m. Adult prices to Sandwich were $7 and the side trip to Heritage Plantation $12.50. To Buzzards Bay the cost was $8 and for $6 more a trip down the Cape Cod Canal and back by boat was an added attraction. To Falmouth and return with a two hour layover for sightseeing was $12. A seat in the *Nobska* from Hyannis was an extra $5 round trip to Sandwich, $7 to Buzzards Bay and $8 to Falmouth.

In 1983 a new package tour was offered that included a boat trip from Woods Hole to the Vineyard and from there to Hyannis. The price was $19.75. The basic trips remained Hyannis to Sandwich and on to Buzzards Bay with tickets on sale at Buzzards Bay for Sandwich and Hyannis.

The Cape Cod & Hyannis was supposed to be paying its share of maintenance to the state-owned railroad but the CC & H somehow had made a contract with someone in the

Department of Transportation that said it didn't have to pay maintenance. The earlier agreement between the state and Bay Colony said Bay Colony would be the controlling railroad, the primary lessee, and that CC & H would have to work under Bay Colony rules, Bay Colony dispatching and Bay Colony control. So Bay Colony had under state rules the right to charge the Cape Cod & Hyannis for its share of maintenance, and the CC & H was running far more trains than Bay Colony. But under the other contract the CC & H had the right not to pay maintenance costs to Bay Colony. Since the mess was a state creation, the state was asked to clear it up. They did so by paying the CC & H a subsidy that at first was in the low six figures and which was then turned over to Bay Colony as its share of maintenance.

Through the 1980s that annual subsidy grew as CC & H ran over the canal and down to Falmouth and in 1984 to Braintree and a connection with the Red Line from Boston of the Massachusetts Bay Transportation Authority. That daily connection was a state demonstration project for commuter rail. What the Cape Cod & Hyannis did during the warm season was reinstate Boston to Cape Cod railroad passenger service on the two systems. In 1988 the CC & H added a weekday run between Cape Cod and Attleboro and a connection there with Amtrak trains. That service was also included as a demonstration for the state and was part of the reason the subsidy had grown to $4.1-million.

Early in 1989 the word came from Boston that the state subsidy for the CC & H would not be available, because of the seriously deteriorating state financial picture. Such subsidies were being reviewed and many eliminated.

President Mark Snider of the CC & H decided to close the business and sell off the locomotives, the rolling stock and the other assets in the Hyannis station such as furniture, computers, dining car china and the like.

The six locomotives were all GP-9s built by the Electromotive Division of General Motors between 1955 and 1959. Two of them were originally New Haven engines, three from the Burlington Northern and one from the Southern Pacific. The company owned ten passenger cars and leased 23 from the MBTA.

All of this was announced around February 1, 1989. The brochures listing the equipment for sale had barely arrived at the office in Hyannis when one night the parlor/observation car, *Presidential*, was destroyed by an intense fire that appeared to be arson, but that was never confirmed. All the equipment was on tracks in the Hyannis yards. A dealer in used locomotives bought the engines, George Bartholomew of Bay Colony bought four coaches, the *Nobska* - a parlor, lounge, diner - and one of the tavern cars with "the longest bar in the world." The latter is used for beverages, sandwiches, soup and snacks.

Bartholomew bought the passenger equipment to run short excursions from Hyannis to Sagamore on the canal. His first season, 1989, was a financial success with some 20-thousand passengers carried from early June into October with a summer schedule of three trains a day leaving Hyannis at 10 a.m., 12:30 and 3:00 p.m. on Tuesdays, Wednesdays and Thursdays, Saturdays and Sundays. In its second season dinner trains were scheduled with all seats reserved.

George Bartholomew decided when the Cape Cod & Hyannis went out of business he would start his Cape Cod Railroad as a tourist excursion during the warm months, not as transportation since that requires a subsidy. "You can make it pay as a tourist trip," he says. "I have done it."

Bartholomew believes that in a transit, tourist market such as Cape Cod people do

277

not have a lot of time to spend on one thing, so he timed his trips to be under two hours. The run from Hyannis to Sagamore on the south shore of the canal lasts an hour and 45 minutes. The CC & H crossed the canal after its first year and if it went off schedule it had to wait for the bridge at Buzzards Bay to be lowered. If there were big ships in the canal it could be a wait of a half hour to 45 minutes. If the railroad notifies the Corps of Engineers, who operate the canal, of the railroad schedule and the train is on schedule then the train has the right of way, because the railroad was there first years ago and it has priority. If there is a big ship in the canal and the train is not on schedule, the Corps can delay the train. A big ship in the canal with a following tide is a point of no return, so the ship proceeds, the bridge remains in the up position to clear water traffic and the train just waits for the bridge.

Bartholomew has purchased four Budd Rail Cars, which are used as extra coaches on his tourist runs, but they are insurance in case the state starts running rail service to Middleboro. If that happens then he can offer a connecting passenger service to Cape Cod. If that becomes a possibility, then he wants to run it. He does not want to return to the frustrations of sharing the tracks with another railroad company as he had to with the Cape Cod & Hyannis. He has to share some with Amtrak's summer service from New York, but that is only a couple of trains on the weekend.

The first year the Cape Cod & Hyannis ran to Falmouth was 1982,
and they made a scheduled stop here at Cataumet.

RAILROAD PEOPLE

In Truro

When the Old Colony Railroad laid its tracks through Truro on the way to Provincetown the first station agent hired at Truro was George Hamilton. The construction was the final stretch for the main line on the Cape. It was started by the Cape Cod Railroad and completed by the Old Colony. The year was 1873.

The Truro station was just south of the Pamet River where the tracks crossed on a long timber trestle. The station was on the right going north with a freight house close by and a siding for freight cars on the Bay side. Depot Road wound through the sand hills between the station and the middle of the Cape where the sandy road ran one way to Provincetown and south to Wellfleet and Orleans. That road had for years seen the red and yellow stage coaches slowly rolling, sometimes stalled, and being pushed by frustrated travelers on their way in either direction. The stages were gone the day the trains ran to the tip of the Cape.

The Truro station had a ticket office, a baggage room and a waiting room. Two long settees were placed at right angles to each other in the waiting room where there also was a pendulum clock, a penny gum machine with Chiclets, a door to the agent's office, another door to a bathroom, a window where you could buy railroad tickets, a number of excursions advertised on long strips of paper, usually printed with red ink and a round-bellied stove for heat.

Along the front of the station, both sides and the rear were wooden platforms. The baggage room had sliding wooden doors facing the track and the lot on the other side. There was a car house just north of the station for track maintenance equipment: hand cars, motor section cars, velocipedes and tools for section men.

These buildings were painted with the standard scheme of tan with trim boards in a darker brown. The bright yellow passenger cars of the Old Colony stood out as pure visual excitement when they appeared along side the rather drab stations and other buildings nearby.

George Hamilton lived just up Depot Road from the station. He and his wife had one child, a daughter, Almena. When Almena returned from private school in New Hampshire, her father taught her Morse Code and telegraphy. She was the first woman telegraph operator on Cape Cod and possibly on the entire Old Colony system. He built a small office for her inside his stationmaster's office at Truro.

Almena married Isaac Freeman who in time became the stationmaster at Truro.

In addition to his passenger and freight duties, Ike Freeman was also the agent for Adams Express which provided him with a small truck to pick up and deliver items coming and going for that service. His grand daughter, Helen Freeman Olsen, remembers the big steel box like a safe that he had and the revolver he was issued, a big weapon. She can recall how busy he was with his duties, meeting all trains and working a split shift with 12-hour days. If there were any freight cars on the Truro siding, he would have to report them

279

by telegraph to Boston each night.

A photo of a horse and wagon next to the Truro depot is identified as belonging to Eben Paine who twice a week went to Provincetown for meat, which he would sell door to door. He also sold fish and vegetables from the wagon, weighing them in a scale hanging on the back. Paine delivered mail as he made his rounds.

Long before prohibition became law in 1920, Truro and Wellfleet were dry towns. However, liquor was shipped by express in barrels with the bottles packed in straw. The barrels were always stamped with another name that would not reveal the contents. This system was so successful for many years that it was continued during prohibition with bootleg whisky riding down to the Cape as express shipments on the railroad, despite the fact that Cape Cod was a major landing spot for bootleg liquor from the sea.

Helen Olsen said her grandfather, Isaac Freeman, was the only person the whole length of Depot Road who had a telephone. "People would come to his house to use the phone," she said. "There was a little coin collector on the table, but not much was ever put in it. It was a party line, and we loved to listen in on other's calls."

In the late 1920s the fare from Wellfleet to Provincetown was $.28 and about the same time a one-way coach ticket to Boston was $3.83. In the 1930s the ICC reduced the fare to $.02 a mile and so the Boston ticket was cut to $2.12.

Ticket prices were of no concern to Helen Olsen. "When we were kids we had grandpa's pass. We thought it was pretty sharp to ride the trains free. It was a family pass," she said.

There were two peddlers whom she used to see when they came to her home in Wellfleet. John Lewis lived near Old County Road in South Truro where he raised vegetables. In season he would fill several buckets and one day a week take the morning train for a three mile trip to Wellfleet. He sold his produce door to door and one of his regular customers was Mrs. Olsen's mother. When his stock was gone, he would walk back to the Wellfleet station and sit on one of the settees under the agent's window on the track platform and wait for the afternoon train and his seven minute ride to South Truro, the next station north. John Lewis followed this routine for years, starting in early June with peas and rhubarb and continuing through the summer with broccoli, beans, cucumbers and corn and into the fall when carrots, beets, turnips and potatoes completed the harvest.

Earlier John Lewis lost his wife when she was struck by a freight locomotive near her home. She was walking on the track with her back to the train and because of her deafness never heard the whistling of the locomotive by a frantic engineer who tried but could not stop his train in time. She was killed instantly. That happened in 1916. Mrs. Olsen remembered John Lewis from the 1920s.

She also remembered Ephraim Hill from Truro. Eph lived near the Truro station at the mouth of the Pamet River with its ten-foot tides and the exposed flats at low water where he would patiently dig for clams. The clams were his business and his living. He, too, came to Wellfleet once a week and sold his clams door to door. He would always arrive on the morning train and carry two buckets of clams on a regular route through town. At each house he would put the clams in a regular container for the customer.

Mrs. Olsen was a Miss then, Helen Freeman, and she had a male tiger cat with a bobbed tail. He was Tige. Now Eph Hill came to Wellfleet once a week and always on the same day. On that day, and that day only, Tige would go and sit on a knoll where he could see down the road where Eph would walk toward the Freeman's home. When Eph would be close by, then Tige, who was waiting for him, would walk over and be given a couple of clams, a wonderful treat for the cat, a special lunch. It was what Tige was waiting for. Helen said, "I don't know how Tige knew that Eph was coming, but he did and he never sat on that little knoll and watched down the street except on the day Eph came to Wellfleet. My mother always gave Eph lunch; he never talked, may have had a speech deficiency of some kind. He would do his shopping in Wellfleet where we had an A & P and he could buy groceries that he couldn't get in Truro. After he had sold all his clams and done his shopping he would carry his buckets and groceries back to the station and wait for the afternoon train, or if he were running late, it would be the evening train. He always gave me a penny, which I would take to the station where there was a Chiclets machine on the wall. It was candy-coated gum, white and two of them in a little yellow or green box. It was a treat. A week later Tige would go out in the morning and sit on that knoll, waiting for Ephraim Hill and sure enough he would come up the road and stop to give Tige a couple of clams. The only day the cat sat out there was the one day of the week that Eph came to town. This was a regular occurrence between 1922 and 1928."

Mrs. Olsen recalls the early days, the 1920s, when she would go down to the depot to watch people eating in the dining cars that came through with their spotless, white linen tablecloths.

Her brother, Raymond R. Freeman, Jr., used to shoot the green, glass insulators on the telegraph pole cross-arms with a .22 caliber rifle. They would shatter and fall off. New Haven Railroad police would come down by train and ask questions and try to find out who was doing it, but they never did. The green insulators were popular targets, as highway signs

In 1915 a cameraman took this scene from the hill to the north of the Wellfleet station. The passenger train is about to leave for Truro and Provincetown. The rear cars are out on the dyke the Cape Cod Railroad built in the fall of 1870 when Wellfleet was the end of track. Ted Rose drew this sketch in pen and ink.

'915

Almena Hamilton, the daughter of Geor[e]
Hamilton, Truro's first station agent, was one [of]
the first lady telegraphers on the Old Colo[ny]
Railroad. Her father taught her the key, sendi[ng]
and receiving, and he built a small telegrapher[s]
office for her use inside the Truro depot, the fir[st]
station there that was built in the late spring [of]
1873. Miss Hamilton later married Isaac Freema[n]
who eventually became the second station agent [at]
Truro, succeeding her father who retired. Whe[n]
this picture of her was taken in 1915, her husba[nd]
was the depot master there.

Three generations later, her great granddaughter, Cynthia Olsen, watched a freight
train steam into Wellfleet while she clutched a stuffed rabbit, or maybe it's a teddy
bear, in her left arm. It's the spring of 1952 and Cynthia Olsen is five years old.

In Wellfleet the railroad cut through this hill and under the bridge carrying Holbrook Avenue. Local people called this "The Tunnel." The Wellfleet station is behind the camera and these tracks head north to Truro. Those rods between the tracks and the granite blocks of the abutment on the right control semaphore signals behind the hill to the right as the track curves.

The evening passenger train from Boston had slowed down as it crossed the railroad dyke at Duck Creek at ten minutes before eight in late June, 1908. It always was running slowly through there as it eased into the station, but that night it never reached the station. There was a siding just west and parallel to the main line on which there were three freight cars of fresh mackerel in barrels. They were to be picked up later by a freight from Provincetown. The switch had been left open instead of closed and set for main line traffic, as it should have been. The north bound train entered the switch and lurched left with the locomotive passing through the first box car, derailing the car and itself. The engineer and fireman were not hurt, but the following day a man in the wrecking crew from Middleboro was killed when a gasoline lantern exploded. The locomotive lies on its side in front of the tender and in back of the overturned box car at the right. The wheels and trucks in the foreground snapped off the box car. The passenger cars were moved the following morning to Provincetown as the main line rails were not damaged. The early morning passenger train from Provincetown to Boston was delayed. The passengers on the train that crashed walked down the railroad dyke to take horse-drawn barges from Martin Holbrook's Livery Stable. When the locomotive lurched unexpectedly to the left in that open switch, the engineer dove out his window on the right hand side and the fireman did the same from the left. They got up as escaping steam from the locomotive cooked the mackerel that had spilled from broken barrels. A wrecking crane righted the box car and then the locomotive.

Above Wellfleet, early fall, 1966 and these men take a moment off from their work removing the rails from the line down to South Dennis. These tracks were in the same location as the original light rail that was spiked down in 1870.

Left In this photo from the early 1960s at the Orleans depot, Jack Walsh, the stationmaster, is standing at the left on the platform with a member of the train crew. There were very few years left for the railroad in Orleans when this was taken.

are today in areas where there is a lot of hunting. Raymond collected a basket full of them after the railroad was abandoned out to Provincetown. Some people use them for door stops and they are still for sale at antique shops and flea markets. When the rails were taken up in the 1960s and removed in gondola cars, the wooden ties were left along the roadbed or thrown aside. People backed up small trucks along the right-of-way and loaded the ties and took them home.

Raymond Freeman worked on the steamer *Dorothy Bradford* that for years made summer runs between Boston and Provincetown as did the *S.S. Steel Pier*. The run across Massachusetts Bay was a popular one. Many passengers took the morning boat from Boston and then the train from Provincetown back to Boston. Others went the other way with the train from South Station to Provincetown and the boat to Boston. Most, however, took the boat round trip and in the evenings there were excursions advertised as Moonlight Cruises which lasted three or four hours. These were popular voyages to nowhere, featuring live music with a dance orchestra. During prohibition, Raymond would buy bootleg liquor in Provincetown for $1 a bottle and sell it to boat passengers for $3. Another fine source of additional income on the *Dorothy Bradford* was buying up staterooms from the purser and then once out on the water keeping a lookout for heavily romantic couples in need of a bed and privacy. Negotiating the rental of a stateroom with the man was often a quick transaction. The *Dorothy Bradford* could hold 1,200 passengers and whether on a daytime cruise to Provincetown or an evening trip, there were times when all the staterooms were occupied. Human nature greatly augmented the small salaries paid to some enterprising crew members on those ships.

John Herman Walsh

John Herman Walsh spent his working life as a New Haven Railroad man, most of it in Orleans. As so many boys did during the Railway Age, Jack Walsh used to hang around the New Haven station in Braintree, his home town. The trains in those days were frequent but not constant. The one element that was seldom quiet was the sounder of the telegraph system. On warm days with the windows open the clattering sounder could be heard hundreds of feet down the platform and across the parking space around the station. It was a railroad sound as steam whistles, bells and locomotive exhaust were railroad sounds.

Jack Walsh liked everything about hanging around the Braintree station, but the telegraph held a special fascination. The station agent recognized that and offered to teach the youngster Morse Code, or "Morse" as it was called. He learned to send letters, words, sentences and ideas with the key and to understand incoming sounds that filled the office with dots and dashes.

Jack Walsh was hired in 1912 by the railroad as a tower-man at Braintree and he worked the lobster shift - midnight until 8 a.m., moving switches and signals from the interlocking tower and eventually he was sent to Orleans. Strict seniority was the rule and when another man with more years wanted a position he could always "bump" the junior employee. Jack got bumped at Orleans and went to Milton. After that he was sent to West Barnstable and when a vacancy occurred at Orleans he took that position as station agent. He stayed there until his retirement.

Jack Walsh first lived in a rooming house on Main Street in Orleans. It was Mrs. Bassett's place and it was less than a thousand feet from the station. He would run through a field between the rooming house and the ell on the back of the Wilcox Building facing Main Street and past the post office next to it and cross the parking lot on the east side of the station to unlock the building at least 15 minutes before train time. He would raise the window at his office so as to serve passengers with cardboard tickets from a big rack next to the window after first placing the ticket in his dating machine.

In season a great deal of agricultural products were shipped through Orleans and through Eastham. Cultivated asparagus, turnips and cranberries were brought to the stations in barrels and crates.

On Beach Road, Orleans, William Cummings raised chickens and sent them by rail to Boston. Seafood was shipped daily in barrels and packed in ice. Fish, clams and eels were the mainstay of local fisheries. In 1925 a New Haven train struck a truckload of eels at Skaket Road crossing in Orleans. There were eels all over the road, some on the boiler side of the locomotive, fricasseed no doubt. It was an amazing scene. The truck was demolished and its driver killed.

H.H. Snow's was a railroad customer and they had a coal trestle along side their store. One day a tank car ran part way off the track on the trestle and the New Haven had to bring a crane down to rescue the car from its position.

A potentially dangerous situation at Orleans resulted when a locomotive was switching box cars on the main line next to Snow's. The engine gave too hard a shove to a car which took off at high speed north bound. A brakeman was on top of the swaying car which raced through four grade crossings with the steam locomotive in pursuit. The car lost momentum around Eastham Flats where the locomotive coupled to it and brought it back to Orleans. There were, however, some anxious moments for the brakeman and in the engine cab as the engineer frantically blew the whistle as the racing box car approached each crossing ahead of the locomotive and by itself.

Senior class trips at the high school always began and ended at the Orleans station. The tradition was to travel on the Fall River Line to New York and then by train to Washington, D.C. This had been an annual June ritual since anyone could remember. The last time the Fall River Line was used by local seniors was in 1935. Jack Walsh sold them round trip tickets.

He was also the agent for Adams Express, which had the franchise for the New York, New Haven & Hartford until the late 1920s, and for the Railway Express Agency after that. Freight shipments required paper work, waybills and so forth and that was his responsibility, too, when there was no freight agent assigned to Orleans. Telegrams came into Orleans on the wire through his office in the station and he had to see that they were delivered by one of the trustworthy local youths with a bicycle. When school was out there were always some youngsters hanging around the station waiting to carry a telegram. The task usually paid a quarter. There were times when Jack had to close the station and deliver the wire himself. Some of those times were his most difficult. It was during World War II and three wires came from the government. Each message began with these words: "We regret to inform you..."

Jack Walsh knew some of those boys before they went into the service, knew them as youngsters from Orleans; and he knew their families. Allen Walker lived across the street from Jack on Route 28. Jack got a family friend to go with him to tell the Walker's of their son's death. He called a friend of the Atwood family whose son, Hilton, was killed on military duty. On another day a government telegram came to Jack's office for the family of Albert Nassi. It, too, was a message of death. Jack called a minister and after closing the

286

office, the two of them went to that home with news of yet another life taken. Three visits to homes where a son from Orleans had gone to war and been killed far away. Jack's daughter, Jean Deschamps, recalls how difficult each of these telegrams and then the family visits were for him. "Bringing that news to those families and sharing their overwhelming grief was as difficult a time as he had during World War II," she said. "It affected him deeply."

Beginning in early June each year the heavy steamer trunks would start arriving before the summer visitors did. Then a message would reach the station by letter or telegram that on a certain day the trunk or trunks should be delivered to a summer camp or house. Jack had to move the trunks out of a storage area reserved for express shipments and load them into a small pickup truck he used for deliveries around the area and for packages to put on trains leaving. Sending blankets, bedding and extra clothes ahead was common and practical before the war. It made Jack Walsh's summer days busy ones.

The express car was usually a section of a baggage car, but not always; sometimes the express area was partitioned off from the mail in a Railway Post Office car. Jack had mail bags to handle as well and they were piled on a grasshopper two-wheeler and he pushed the contraption over to Main Street past the three-story Wilcox Building and next door to the Post Office. He would bring sacks of out-going mail to the grasshopper and push them back to the platform for the next train from Provincetown.

In the winter the last train from South Station for Provincetown left Boston at 3:30 p.m. and reached Orleans at 6:31. During Daylight Saving Time the train ran an hour later. Every second or third night there were cans of film with features, previews, short subjects and newsreels placed next to the door of the express car for Jack Walsh to take over to the Orleans Theatre in the Wilcox Block.

This would be hard to imagine today, but in Orleans in the 1920s and 30s, Jack would receive from an express car canvas bags from the Federal Reserve in Boston, containing cash for local banks. He would pile all the money on the front seat of that pickup truck and then go into his office at the station and find a revolver issued to him by the express company and put the weapon on the seat and drive to the Cape Cod Bank & Trust branch just down Main Street on the other side from the Post Office. He would carry as much of the money as he could lift, because there were always coins in the shipment, and walk into the bank and deliver it. One of the tellers would have to sign for it, and afterward he would stop for conversation, since he was so well known in Orleans. In the meantime the other bags of cash were sitting on the front seat of the express truck along with the pistol. Nothing was ever taken. Jack's son, Donald, was a Lieutenant on the Orleans Police Force and later was chief. When he tells the story of those frequent cash deliveries by his father, he shakes his head in wonder at those trusting times.

Jack Walsh was a member of the school board and even served as its chairman. As station agent he had to be there when every passenger train came through and that meant a split shift from early morning until evening, usually a 12-hour day, so school board meetings were often held in his office in the station.

After the war the New Haven started closing stations but the Orleans depot stayed open and Jack Walsh was the agent from Harwich to Provincetown. Of course passenger service had stopped on the railroad before the war from Yarmouth east, and buses were used after that, so Jack was a freight agent for the 35-miles of track from Harwich down Cape to P'town.

In 1962 the New Haven Railroad gave him a 50-year service pin. He retired soon after that.

His last months were spent in a nursing home in Orleans where on Christmas Day, 1977 he died. John Herman Walsh was 81.

Robert Clifton Neal

On March 31, 1962, some 125 people from the New Haven Railroad and their guests went to a restaurant in Taunton to pay tribute to Robert Clifton Neal and thank him for his friendship. It was a retirement party and a goodbye for Neal who had worked for 46 years for the New York, New Haven & Hartford Railroad. Most of those years - 31 of them - Neal spent in Woods Hole. The final 15 were in Taunton as a supervisor, and he commuted from his home in Woods Hole for that job.

Robert Neal was born in Wareham in March, 1897. His father later became section foreman for the New Haven, working out of Woods Hole. Neal left school at 15 and went to work in the Standard Horseshoe Works in Wareham, a job he had for four years of almost continuous disenchantment with the position. The day his father called him with the information that there was a baggageman's position open at the Hole, Bob Neal took the first train and was hired. "That's how I started railroading, and I never regretted it," he said.

"The train crews were in unions, railroad brotherhoods, but I was station help and we didn't have a union," he said. "We worked from before the first morning train until the last one got in at night, even if she didn't get in until three nights later. Not a damn nickel's worth of overtime. You got a flat rate when I started working there. I got $14.18 a week with no minimum hours." Neal described his working condition this way: "When everything was on time you had at least a 12-hour day, seven days a week. None of that Monday to Friday stuff. No vacation unless you wanted to cut into that $14.18 a week, and you couldn't cut very deep into that or you wouldn't have enough to live on."

Neal did considerable work as a clerk at Woods Hole in addition to handling baggage and he also worked with the steamers to the Islands. That company was part of New England Steamship and the local division was the New Bedford, Woods Hole, Martha's Vineyard and Nantucket Steamship Company. That meant passengers and freight going from and coming to the Hole.

He was promoted to assistant agent and later to yard master, which had its headaches making up passenger trains and freight as well. They used to receive seven or eight freight cars a day and most of the cargo had to be unloaded and put on the steamers. Most of the freight to the Islands was coal, lumber, hay, feed, grain, groceries and cement. Although much of the grocery shipments were ordered through New Bedford and reached there by train and were on the steamers from New Bedford when they reached the Hole. Every day there were two cars with LCL, less than carload shipments, one from Middleboro transfer and the other from Boston. Carloads of ice would arrive daily to be used for storage and shipment of seafood.

Sam Cahoon had a thriving fish and lobster business at Woods Hole and he was a major shipper with at least two freight cars every night for Boston. Cahoon owned his own dock and he leased part of the railroad wharf and installed an ice crusher on it next to a track where the New Haven would spot the cars. He and his workers would separate the fish, its called culling. They packed the fish in boxes two feet by three feet and up to 18 inches deep. He shipped cod, haddock, yellow tails, bass, flounder - everything you get

around there, plus lobsters. The fishing industry was an every day business. The waters weren't fished out then, so you didn't have to go so far for a catch. Cahoon was a good shipper on the railroad. He bought ice at Barreville, Massachusetts near Norton and had it shipped to him in refrigerator cars. He later had his own ice plant at the Hole. He shipped car loads of fish to New York by rail and some by the steamers running to New Bedford and from there to Manhattan by the overnight boat, the New Bedford Line. Those boats were owned by the New Haven Railroad, too.

The summers were busy with 15 passenger trains a day, two freights and ten boat landings. There were passengers, mail, express and freight and tickets and waybills. Many of the employees were local residents. He recalls the agent, Jack Vallis and Emmy Smith who sold tickets and was a telegraph and telephone operator. Bob Neal called Emmy "a great gal." Another local person was Bob MacKenzie, the mail agent on one of the Railway Post Office cars. There were two R.P.O. cars each day each way.

There was a car knocker's shanty that was occupied in the summers for the man who was busy hooking up steam lines, air hoses and coupling the cars with those big knuckles. The railroad had several sleeping cars for the train crews that stayed over and a boarding car with a kitchen and showers. Some of them cooked their own meals. They had a locomotive repair area and mechanics to maintain the steam engines, a water tank and a turntable. The tank is to the left of Ted Rose's cover painting for this book. Behind the wall and beyond the tank was the turntable. In the early years of this century there was a small roundhouse for locomotives. It later was torn down.

They named the tracks at Woods Hole: Wall track, Kitchen track, Caboose track, track five for arrivals and departures, track six for Island freight, tracks eight, ten and 12 for

289

passenger cars and track 14 for locomotives. "The place became so busy that the railroad put a switch in on the other side of that bridge and we used to store cars in there. It was called Portagee Alley for the section crew that had a building up there with hand cars, velocipedes and a motor car with quarters for sleeping and eating. The section men were Portuguese. The Alley was expanded after the New Haven added the New York to Cape Cod trains summers. Two long tracks that could hold at least 16 passenger cars were installed," Neal said.

As yardmaster, Neal had to make up trains seven days a week. These included the regular local passenger trains to Boston plus freight. The summers were a problem with the *Day* and *Night Cape Codders* and the *Neptune*. Neal said, "We used to make them up in a certain way. Passenger coaches in the rear, parlor cars next, dining and grill cars ahead of the parlor cars. Sometimes we had what we called a bar car and that would be on the rear. Bar cars operated mostly on the *Neptune*; that's what we called the Happy Train. The *Neptune* would often run two sections a day from Grand Central with one to the Hole and the other to Hyannis. Front end business cars - baggage and R.P.O. and express cars - were right behind the locomotive."

Sunday nights in the summer were the worst for Bob Neal. He had to make up trains for New York with as many as ten Pullman sleepers in each train, plus parlor cars and a diner. Occasionally there would be added a coach for those who couldn't get a berth or a seat in one of the Pullmans. In the heart of the summer season there would be as many as 63 separate units at Woods Hole, including parlors and sleepers, grill cars, bar cars, day coaches, baggage cars, R.P.O. cars, freight cars and steam locomotives. It taxed the space and Neal's ability to sort it out and put the trains together so they could leave on time. When Frederick Dumaine was the New Haven's president, he used to come to Woods Hole in his private railroad car on Fridays. He'd lock the doors and walk over to Neal and throw him the keys and say, "take care of this, look after the car and I'll see you Sunday night." Dumaine had a place in Chappaquoit. Neal thought Dumaine was a great guy.

Railroad workers like Bob Neal had to master a number of jobs and he did. Besides baggageman he was a ticket clerk selling day coach seats, parlor car seats and Pullman space on trains and tickets on the steamers to the Islands and to New Bedford and on to New York from there and Fall River Line tickets to Manhattan. He also worked as baggage master on the trains, trainman and brakeman. When one of them called in sick, Bob Neal would get on a train for Buzzards Bay and fill in. He had to take exams to qualify as a substitute. He did everything except conductor and engineer on trains.

The winter of 1918-19 was the worst he ever saw. He said, "The boys were dying so fast from influenza at Camp Devens they couldn't get coffins fast enough. The bodies at Devens were put into boxes and shipped to wherever they lived. At one time we had four bodies in boxes at the freight house waiting to be taken to the Vineyard and Nantucket. All kinds of other freight and mail were piling up here because of the ice around the Islands. The temperature never got above zero and the boats couldn't get through. Finally the Navy sent a minesweeper and we took the sacks of mail off the boxes of bodies and loaded all of it with groceries onto the minesweeper. No boat had gotten through for two weeks, but this time it did and by going around the Atlantic Ocean side of the Islands they managed to land all that stuff over the ice."

Through the years there was steady freight with the United States Lighthouse Service which maintained the aids to navigation along this section of coast. The Marine Biological Laboratory had need of the railroad since they shipped a couple of carloads a week of specimens they had collected to Chicago. The U.S. Bureau of Fisheries and Woods Hole Oceanographic Institution also used the railroad.

In the late 1920s on Saturdays in the summer a group of the younger scientists at the Marine Biological Laboratories in Woods Hole used to buy lobsters for $.35 per pound for a picnic in the evening. With all the boats bringing in their catches including lobsters, a large supply at such a reasonable price was always available.

Cooking three dozen or so at a time was a problem. The New Haven Railroad or rather one of their employees and his equipment came to the rescue. The Marine Biological students took a galvanized ash can and installed an inlet pipe on the side down near the bottom. After putting some large stones in the bottom and the lobsters on top of them and seaweed as a cover, the can would be put on a two wheeled cart and rolled down to the rail yard and up next to a New Haven locomotive. The students had consulted with a railroad engineer earlier in the week about their needs. He agreed to help and when the cart arrived he hooked up a pipe from the engine and released steam into the can for about 15 minutes, which because the 200-pounds per square inch of the steam in a locomotive boiler contains a great deal of heat was enough to cook all those lobsters. Then the valve was turned off, the pipe disconnected and the cart and its can wheeled off to the beach and the picnic.

It is not recorded whether or not the engineer of the locomotive got a lobster for his help, but I'll bet he did.

World War II saw a huge increase in rail traffic and Bob Neal remembers it. "Camp Edwards and Otis Air Base added tremendous traffic on this branch. So much so that they had a yardmaster at Camp Edwards and we used to send a switcher in there five days a week. I remember those landing craft and the training at Washburn's Island. They had hundreds of those steel boats for infantry to hit the European beaches from North Africa to Italy to Normandy. They all came in here by rail, and they left by rail. Finally they wanted them all back at Tallahassee, Florida and we loaded them on cradles mounted on flat cars. One craft to one car. They had several shifts a day to load those boats. There must have been 400 of them. I used to work often until 2 a.m. and be back at 6:30. Sometimes the convoys heading east through the canal would hold up a train for a half hour or so and then they'd lower the bridge at the Bay during a break in the convoy."

In 1947 the New Haven offered Neal a promotion to Taunton as General Agent in charge of all passenger and freight traffic. He was there 15 years in that supervisory position. He commuted on the early morning train from Woods Hole to Middleboro where he kept a car to drive another ten miles to Taunton. At night he repeated the trip in reverse. In 1959 when they took off passenger service to Cape Cod, Bob Neal drove the 50 miles to his office and back every day. He did that for the final three years of his 46 with the railroad. Compulsory retirement at age 65 and Neal was toasted at his farewell dinner in Taunton.

He spent that first summer as a special policeman at one of the beaches "looking at young women in tiny bathing suits." When the water at the beach turned cold he approached the Falmouth National Bank and applied for a position as teller. He was a cinch for that job. Hell, everybody knew Bob Neal and besides he'd handled money and people. To keep busy in the evenings he served on the town Finance Committee for 18 years.

One of his many railroad jobs was as telephone operator at Woods Hole in 1919. One of the young telephone operators at the Bourne exchange, Bernice Angus, caught

Neal's interest and after many conversations with her he suggested a date one night. It was a foursome with one of Neal's friends and one of Bernice's girl friends. Things got mixed up a bit and Neal wound up with the other girl. That wasn't what he had in mind, but he was patient. After several more dates that way, Bob and Bernice became a twosome. That first date was his birthday, March 15, 1919; he was 22. They became engaged in September, 1920. Neal would drive several nights a week to see Bernice, picking her up at her home in Bourne and more often than not going to a movie in Onset.

They were married on June 7, 1922, at her home in Bourne by Reverent S.J. Rook, a Methodist minister. They went to Boston by train and took the Eastern Steamship boat from India Wharf through the canal to New York, then up the Hudson on the Day Line to Albany and the train to Boston and back to Woods Hole.

They had a daughter, Avis. When she married, Bob Neal, made sure his grandson was frequently dressed up in a locomotive engineer's outfit with cap and bandana.

One sunny July afternoon in 1978 Robert Clifton Neal sat in his living room that overlooks the Coast Guard Station at Woods Hole with Martha's Vineyard on the horizon across that glistening water. For several hours he talked about his life and the railroad all the time keeping his pipe filled and burning. Phil Choate was there and so was Ed Robinson with his camera. Ed took a number of pictures of Neal and I kept the reels turning while he talked his story into my tape recorder.

Bernice would show up occasionally and listen and nod her head in agreement. At one point when she was in the other room he said: "Bernice was the most important part of it all." He paused to clean the ashes from his pipe, refill it and fire it up again with a lighter.

"Every day was different...something to look forward to. I loved the railroad, loved every day of it," he said. "These days, Bernice will say to me in the morning 'did you have a nice night's sleep?' And I dream of it today and I've been through with the railroad since 1962, and you'd be surprised the many nights that I dream of doing one thing or another on the railroad. She will ask me 'what's the matter?' in the morning at breakfast. And it's always the same," he says. "I worked on the railroad all night long."

Gerald Otto Cash

Gerald Otto Cash worked 30 years for the New Haven Railroad as a clerk-baggageman. He was born in Yarmouth Port, the son of Freeman Studley Cash and Florence Cobb, his mother. He never went far from his birthplace on October 10, 1909. All his schooling was in one building on Old King's Highway, across the street from the First Congregational Church. That two-story wooden school had classes from first grade through high school. That building is gone now, replaced by a fire station.

When he was in the first grade, his parents moved from Weir Village to a small house next to Hallett's Store, which at the time was a drug store. Today that store is literally unchanged from its beginning in 1889 when the Old Colony Railroad locomotives whistled through the north side. Gerald Otto Cash as a youngster remembers steam trains and their whistles in the night.

"We used to enjoy hanging around the station. We would walk through there on the way to and from the Cummaquid Golf Course just down the tracks to the west where we would caddy for the members," he recalls. He had one early and frightening experience at the Yarmouth station.

"We were small, probably 9 or 10, possibly 12. A heavy summer storm swept in quickly. It was bad, lots of lightning and close, too. We ran like mad from the golf course down the tracks for the station. Of all places it was the worst one to go to because of the telegraph. We ran inside the station and now here's Bill Ormsby, the station agent, and in those days they didn't have any telephones. It was all telegraphy and there's Ormsby on the telegraph key and the lightning was coming through the board." Cash said, "I never forgot it, and Ormsby said to us 'any of you fellows got rubbers on?' I says I got rubber heels. He says, 'you better stand on your heels, so you don't get electrocuted!' Scared us to death; it was a very bad storm, and I never forgot that."

Cash started driving a mail truck when he was in high school, and that is how the men at the station got to know him and later made him a job offer. "I drove the truck for Pat Hannon who had the mail contract to and from the station; he ran a taxi, too. The mail truck was a trailer on the back of a car. They had those two-wheel carts called grasshoppers on the station platform and we'd carry the mail from the truck to the Railway Post Office car and from the car to the trailer on the incoming."

Gerald Cash was graduated from Yarmouth High School in June, 1928. He was one third of the senior class.

"There was Mary Thatcher and Charlotte Duchemie and the three of us went on the graduating class's trip to New York. We took the train from Yarmouth station to Boston and walked from South station to India Wharf and boarded the Eastern Steamship boat for New York. What a thrill! We sailed down Cape Cod Bay and entered the canal about 8 p.m. and half of Yarmouth was there along the banks to wave and yell to us, 'cause they knew we were making that trip. There were people all along the canal watching the steamer go through. We stayed up late and awoke in New York City. Mary Thatcher married an Urqhart fellah and Charlotte married a Johnson. Their husbands are gone now. Charlotte lives in West Yarmouth; Mary's in Chatham."

After a long career with the railroad Pat Heffernan took his pension and retired, leaving the Yarmouth station short of help. Cash took his place. It was January, 1929.

"People asked me how did you happen to get that job? You'd think I struck gold. Of course in those days it was a good job. The salary was fair, starting around $25 or $26 a week. My title was clerk, baggage," Cash says. He used to get to work at 6:30 in the morning to handle all the baggage and freight. He would be there when the early passenger train from Provincetown pulled in just before the train from Hyannis reached Yarmouth. Chatham passengers would take an early train for Harwich where they got on the train from Provincetown. That train would continue to Yarmouth where its passengers would transfer to the train from Hyannis which ran on to Boston. Cash had to help move baggage on large four-wheeled wagons with stakes on the sides. He worked until about 10:30 a.m., that is four hours "and then if there wasn't much to do they lay you off until afternoon. It was a split shift; in other words you put in 12 hours to get eight hours pay."

Cash says: "I started with Bill Ormsby as the station agent. He was in charge of the whole thing. Trains always stopped at Yarmouth. It was a central place. They had a big water tank there with a gasoline engine to run a pump to fill the tank. It would sometimes take two of you to turn the wheel to start the engine on the pump. There was a pipe that ran down into a well. A lot of locomotives took water at Yarmouth. That train from Provincetown in the morning would take on water there and then turn on the wye and stay there all day until late afternoon when a Boston train would arrive with a lot of people for Down Cape and for Chatham. That crew would sit there all day waiting for the afternoon train," he said.

While they were waiting, Cash was busy with his duties. One of which was taking care of the train signals. "One of the things was to crawl up there and put kerosene in the lamp and trim the wick. It was on the station's roof. That was part of my area."

Freight used to come in by the car load and he had to unload it all into a freight house by a siding next to the track for the Hyannis Branch. He would on many days spend all his time unloading a box car.

In the summer there would be baggage cars filled with trunks, especially after the Cape Playhouse opened. Cash remembers, "the first one I recall was when Mary Pickford and Charles Farrell came down by train to appear in a play. They got off the train at Yarmouth and were taken by station wagon to Dennis. They probably had ten or 12 trunks. Big trunks, you know. We'd unload them from both sides of a baggage car. I suppose those trunks had costumes for the Playhouse. We'd climb into those express cars and lift those steamer trunks down and put them out through the doors to those four-wheel express wagons. When they were leaving we would have to stack those trunks one on another until the cars were filled. It was heavy work and you had to move. I helped throw mail bags around, too. Unbelievable the work we'd do in those days."

Gerald Otto Cash is alone now in his home on Willow Street where he has lived since 1931. His grandfather who used to be a crossing tender just up the street invited Cash and his wife to move in with him after the older man's wife died. Cash met his wife through the railroad, as he puts it. "Olga Marie Johnson lived in West Barnstable. She used to be a nursemaid for John Hinckley. They lived right in Cummaquid and she would take the train to and from Yarmouth. I met her at the station." They had two sons. She died in 1986 after being with him for 57 years.

Cash worked at Yarmouth station for five or six years and after the railroad abolished the position there he was transferred to Hyannis in the same job. Bill Ormsby was still at Yarmouth and Cash would go back for the summers only when business was heavy with the *Day Cape Codder* always stopping at Yarmouth and the Fall River boat train as well. That was also the time when famous Hollywood personalities would walk down the steps of a parlor car to be greeted by someone from the Cape Playhouse: Bette Davis, Henry Fonda, Gregory Peck, Paulette Goddard, Basil Rathbone, Gertrude Lawrence, Humphrey Bogart, Myrna Loy, Tallulah Bankhead, Ethyl Barrymore, Anne Baxter, Claudette Colbert, Van Johnson and so many more. Cash says they always got off - and on - trains at Yarmouth.

He has special memories from World War II of driving a bus after he got finished work. The bus ran from Hyannis to Camp Edwards. "You'd drive those guys and you knew you never would see some of them again, and in some cases they didn't come back."

Travel was difficult during the war with so many people on the go and incredible movements of military personnel and war supplies, most of which went by rail.

"The trains were packed," he says. "The railroad was wicked busy, and they'd fight like cats and dogs to get on trains and get a seat, like jumping on subway cars in Boston. Of course in the summer the trains to the Cape were so crowded that people would be sitting on suitcases in the baggage cars. That was true after the war, too," said Cash.

He moved from the Main Street station in Hyannis to the new station out on Yarmouth Road in the early 1950s. The railroad had created too much congestion with its trains stopped across Main Street. He remembers John Kennedy and his brothers, Robert and Teddy. "They came into Hyannis quite frequently by train," he said.

A New Haven train crew on the platform at Hyannis with baggageman, Gerald Otto Cash, second from the right. This is about 1950.

Cash finished loading the baggage car of the last regular train from Hyannis June 30, 1959, and then he stood in the car door for the final time as a railroad man. He had joined the New Haven in January, 1929, working as a baggageman - among other duties - at the Yarmouth station.

Below A few minutes later the passenger train is heading north on the Hyannis Branch on her way to Boston. She has just passed the Camp Grounds and is about to run beneath the Mid-Cape Highway, Route 6. Regular passenger service on this line began in July, 1854.

Cash remembers a wild ride to Buzzards Bay from Hyannis. It was an emergency but he can't recall what it was for. The trip was made at high speed in a single Budd rail car. It was in the 1950s; he's sure of that. "They had to have so many men in a crew and I was at the station. They were short and I was there. We went around those curves and I thought we'd tip over. I don't remember why we had to go so fast. Bill Quirk was the engineer. He was a wild man anyway. It was excessive speed. That car was swaying and I remember saying, 'if I ever get out of this alive you'll never get me in another Budd Car again.' They didn't carry passengers. I was it. Bill was noted for speed. He was from Hyannis. He isn't alive now. He was old then. We sure did speed to Buzzards Bay. I can't remember why."

Gerald Otto Cash left the New Haven Railroad the same day regular passenger service stopped. It was June 30, 1959 and he loaded baggage into a car for the afternoon train to Boston. It was his last day of 30 years a railroad man. The next day he started work in the Yarmouth Town Hall as Town Clerk Treasurer. He retired from there in 1972 after 14 years.

He can still hear the diesel horns on the Bay Colony as they cross Willow Street up the block as he heard locomotive whistles across town when he was just a youngster and before he moved next to Hallett's store. Gerald Otto Cash never left home.

P'town Local

The trip that Samuel Dexter White of East Sandwich made was on the legendary *P'town Local*. That was the daily mixed freight that ran from Hyannis to Yarmouth where it was assembled and then off to Harwich and north to Provincetown - thus the name *P'town*, a Cape Cod localism that is still used.

The train was one of the last LCL, less than carload, freights on the New Haven. They would stop at stations along the way and using two-wheel hand trucks unload the boxes and barrels and roll them into the freight houses. When the whole train crew couldn't move a heavy object like machinery, someone would go into town nearby and bring back some more men they knew to move it out of a box car onto the freight platform. Obviously the schedule was loose on purpose with the train moving onto sidings and "going into the hole" when a passenger train was due.

Once the passenger train was gone, the *P'town Local* would steam out onto the single track main line, whistling for crossings and roll to the next stop. Loaded cars would be dropped off and usually the empties would be picked up on the way back.

It was a friendly train and completely against company rules often took visitors in the caboose and in the cab. The locomotive was usually a light Pacific type or a Mogul, but if only a J-class Mikado was available, it was used although they were the biggest to run on that light rail from Harwich north. At less than 80 pounds to the yard, that was the lightest rail on the New Haven.

Most of the railroad men picked up nicknames and on the *P'town* the engineer was Long John Silver and the conductor was Bedbug McGuire.

The freight had a lot of fans who had ridden the engine or the caboose and many more who would wave from backyards and were regulars recognized by the crew. Some days McGuire would buy a stack of Boston Globes and stand out on the rear caboose platform and toss a copy of the morning paper to anyone who waved.

The unusual part of that trip on any train was from South Truro when the track was close to the waters of Cape Cod Bay and at Truro with the station and small yard on the west end of Pamet River with its wooden trestle. The five mile stretch from North Truro where the railroad had filled in a salt water inlet to the end of the line at Provincetown was right along the beach and water. After dark when returning you could see the beacon from a lighthouse across the harbor, another one from around Plymouth across the Bay and still another from Highland Light at Truro.

Besides gondolas filled with sand, the *P'town Local* would carry barrels and boxes of fish and crates of curtains from Wellfleet where there was a factory near the tracks.

From its start in the mid-morning at Hyannis, the freight would often not return for 16 hours. The locomotive burned up at least 15 tons of coal and the tender was nearly empty. The fireman would climb up and pull a water spout over the side and drop the end into the hatch for a refill at Eastham, if he hadn't at Provincetown. They were thirsty locomotives.

One fall day in the early 1930s, Archie Cahoon took his box camera across the track from his home on Pleasant Lake Avenue. He stood on the beach at the west end of Long Pond and waited for the *P'town Local*. When it came through heading north, Archie snapped what became a slightly fuzzy portrait. One day in 1948 Samuel Dexter White rode the train from Hyannis to Provincetown in the cab of a Pacific type engine hauling the *P'town Local*. Many photographs later, White was in the caboose on the return. Their cameras caught the most legendary freight on the entire New Haven, a train that became a rolling Cape Cod social institution: the *P'town Local*.

This is the P-town Local, a mixed freight that left Hyannis around 9:30 in the morning and returned about 16 hours later, more or less. Archie Cahoon took this picture across the tracks from his home on Long Pond in the village of Pleasant Lake.

This is the old right of way at the same place. Archie's home is about a hundred feet to the left. The tracks were removed in the late 1960s. Ed Robinson took this picture the day we went to interview Archie in July, 1979. I wanted Archie to stand here on this old railroad bed, which had tracks from 1865. He didn't want his picture taken. I wish he had. He died several years later. This is now a bicycle path with black top from South Dennis.

In the spring of 1948, Samuel Dexter White of East Sandwich took a ride on the P'town Local freight to Provincetown and back. The railroad had a spur that lead into the dune area where sand was loaded into hopper cars and gondolas. That sand had the right quality to use on locomotives to help traction when driving wheels slipped on wet or oily rails. The New Haven took thousands of tons of it and shipped it off Cape for its own use. **Top left, above** The locomotive was one of 50 built by Alco in Dunkirk, New York, in 1913. As a Pacific type it was purchased for passenger service on the heavy trains that ran along the Shore Line Route between Boston and New York. They were replaced by heavier engines three years later, and by 1929 they were the mainstay of commuter service around Boston and were in constant use on Cape Cod, first in passenger service then hauling freight as well. They were fast no matter what they were pulling, and despite their age they ran on the Cape right up to the end of steam in the 1950s. Samuel Dexter White knew railroad men and he accepted their invitation to a ride and he took these pictures to remind him of a wonderful day in his life. **Top right** The sand was loaded by a mechanical dumper behind the locomotive, **Opposite top** then the train was reassembled to return. The fireman and engineer posed beside their engine, and on the way back in the caboose the conductor turned toward White's camera.

Old Colony Notes from Newspapers

August 28, 1874: President Ulysses S. Grant visited Barnstable. Grant traveled by special train from Newport to Woods Hole the previous evening, then to Martha's Vineyard for the night. His party visited Nantucket in the morning and sailed for Hyannis at noon on the steamer *River Queen*. She docked at Railroad Wharf, Hyannis, at 2 p.m. Grant then took a train from the Village Center. Large crowds cheered Mr. Grant. At Harwich station, where 2,000 awaited, banners hung on the depot said: "Harwich for Grant in 1868, 1872 and 1876." Returning that evening from Provincetown, the special train paused for a moment at Barnstable where Major Phinney delivered a brief greeting to the President.

January 24, 1880: Weather reports are regularly received by telegraph each morning, and posted in the Yarmouth depot.

March 20, 1880: Yarmouth and Yarmouth Port: The freight train from this place to Provincetown, it is rumored, will run independent of the passenger train, commencing on the first of May. The extra train to West Barnstable was well patronized by our people on Thursday evening, who attended the cantata of the "Haymakers."

April 17, 1880: Hyannis: Our people have been somewhat inconvenienced by the absence of the mail at noon. It is quite frequently left at Yarmouth, or carried down the Cape, which is certainly an annoyance.

May 29, 1880: Train to Brockton to attend the London Circus will run on Friday next. For the round trip from Yarmouth the fare will be $2.30.

June 19, 1880: The Old Colony is building a house for the handcars, east of Hyannis Road.

July 10, 1880: The Provincetown Band passed through Yarmouth on Saturday on their way to Nantucket. They gave us a touch of their quality at the depot and played very well.

September 18, 1880: The cranberry carts have commenced running to the depot, with small loads at first, but increasing every day until the season is at its height. The fruit is generally reported of good quality and the yield quite abundant.

November 13,1880: One of the greatest pleasures of railroad travel for lovers has been destroyed. Now, just before a train enters a tunnel, a brakeman goes through the cars and lights all the lamps.

February, 1881: A severe winter. Special trains ran from Hyannis to Harwich for an ice boat regatta on Long Pond.

May 28, 1881: Extra trains will be run over the Old Colony Railroad, Wednesday, June 1st to accommodate all who wish to attend the Barnstable County Sunday School Convention at the Congregational Church, Yarmouth Port on that day.

July 23, 1881: The roof on the Hyannis depot has been painted red, which sets the building off handsomely.

September 17, 1881: The mid-day express from Woods Hole for Boston on Monday the fifth, ran into a steer of Captain Joshua Handy near his residence in Pocasset.

November 5, 1881: Yarmouth: Some graceless scamp threw a stone through one of the windows of the train between Yarmouth and South Yarmouth, on Monday evening.

April 15, 1882: The old "Patriot Gun" that used to be on the hill where the old Patriot office stood in Barnstable, which was carried off about July 4, 1880, has turned up at North Sandwich; it having been tendered to E.C. Howard as old junk. Mr. Howard refused to receive it at his foundry, and it now lies besides the railroad track in that village.

June 17, 1882: Mrs. George Young, of Yarmouth, took the train and went to Boston yesterday for the first time in 30 years.

December 2, 1882: About 50 from Orleans took advantage of the free ride to Boston on stockholder's day, although not half that number owned a cent's worth of stock in the railroad, or ever did.

January 24, 1885: Large quantities of oysters in the shell are being shipped from Falmouth to Boston and New York.

March 27, 1886: The Hendersons of Cambridge are building a passenger carriage for Mr. Richard Hefler of Dennis to be run from the Yarmouth station to the new hotel, East Dennis, with a carrying capacity of 12 persons.

April 3, 1886: Charles H. Nye, assistant superintendent of the Old Colony Railroad, states that 9,210 barrels of shellfish, much the larger part of which were oysters, were shipped from this division (including Wareham, East Wareham, and the Cape) during the year ending March 25.

April 10, 1886: The Old Colony Railroad Company has extended a double track across Main Street in Hyannis for the greater convenience of freight trains.

June 19, 1886: The Old Colony Railroad will put out about 50,000 potted plants and shrubs at its depots along the line this year.

July 24, 1886: Ten thousand watermelons, cargo of the *Gate City,* were forwarded to Boston via Woods Hole Railroad (Old Colony). Forty-three thousand watermelons were thrown overboard, and a crowd of all kinds of sailing craft picked them up.

September 18, 1886: Wellfleet Shoe Factory is an assured fact. Stock in the new company has been sold and the building will be located in the lot on the northerly side of the railroad station. The sum of $23-thousand was subscribed.

May 14, 1887: Professor Dudley's Dynagraph and Inspection Car made its annual inspection of the tracks of Cape Cod Division, Old Colony Railroad this week. The Dynagraph is an ingenious device which detects low joints in the rails.

May 12, 1888: An iron bridge with stone foundation is being built across Bass River for the Old Colony Railroad, in substitution for the wooden bridge which has been announced unsafe.

August 18, 1888: Isn't it almost time to have that long talked of Harwich Centre depot? We presume that the travel at this station is equal to any on the Chatham branch.

September 15, 1888: All of the Sunday trains on the Cape Division will be discontinued after Sunday, September 23rd.

September 22, 1888: The three Wellfleet wharf companies shipped two boxcar loads of mackerel direct to the west on Monday. This is the second shipment.

June 15, 1889: Messrs. John Hinckley & Son have entered into a contract with the Old Colony Railroad Company to build a new depot in Barnstable to take the place of the one destroyed by fire. It will be somewhat larger than the old one, and in style of architecture we expect will be as pretty as any on line.

July 17, 1889: Ex-President Grover Cleveland was a guest on the Old Colony special train which carried the railroad commissioners to Provincetown on their annual tour of inspection of the railroad.

August 10, 1889: Special Old Colony trains will be run from Boston, New Bedford, Falmouth and Provincetown for the 250th anniversary of the founding of the Town of Yarmouth.

August 31, 1889: Barnstable's new Railroad station is handsomely finished in hard woods and is as pretty a room as can be found on the entire Old Colony line.

November 2, 1889: Time has worked wonders in regards mail accommodations from the Cape and from Boston. Twenty years ago Uncle Lisha used to sit on a trunk in the baggage car and sort letters and today it requires three men to work the stacks of mail matter of various classes.

New Haven Railroad Cape Cod Notes from Newspapers

November 1899: It looks as though Chatham might soon have an electric railroad if her people want it. Parties were in town last week looking over the ground. If it is built, it will come down direct from Falmouth, down the south shore to Chatham.

January 1900: Marstons Mills: Dr. J.H. Higgins has lately purchased an automobile. It arrived Thursday last and was driven by him from West Barnstable station to this place. We learn it is the first to arrive on Cape Cod. It is an object of great interest in the community. And we understand it will be hard to beat on the road.

February 20, 1904: The storm which prevailed all day Monday (the 15th) and turned into a howling blizzard at night produced one of the worst conditions which this winter of storms has yet developed. The evening train from Boston somewhat late in reaching North Truro, plowed through big drifts until about half way down Beach Point, when it stuck fast, could neither back out or go ahead, and there it remained all night and far into Tuesday.

January 14, 1905: Much interest has been taken in the plans of the New York Central Railroad to substitute electric for steam locomotives in the terminal service of the road. The electrically-driven engines will begin their work of drawing trains at a point a short distance out of New York, and one advantage...will be the abolition of dangerous smoke and steam nuisance in the tunnel by which trains reach Grand Central Station. Tests of new electric locomotives were recently made and proved successful in every respect.

January 29, 1905: The heaviest storm of the season prevailed Wednesday and Thursday ((25th & 26th). The wind reached a velocity of 70 miles. A howling blizzard from the northeast, with blinding snow, crippled the train service and blocked traffic in general for 24 hours. The snow and sleet cut like a razor, and those who were not exposed to the storm failed to realize its severity.

The mail team from Dennis for Yarmouth was overturned by the wind in Yarmouth Wednesday afternoon.

The express freight from Boston for Provincetown, with two powerful locomotives, was stalled in Barnstable from Wednesday afternoon to Thursday and arrived at Yarmouth at about 3:30. The train from Provincetown for Boston was held up at Yarmouth, the stalled freight at Barnstable blocking the main line and preventing trains from going in either direction. Passengers spent the night on board the train and came to the Old Corner Grocery for supplies in the evening and the next morning.

April 28, 1905: Captain Eleazer K. Crowell, a retired shipmaster, and one of the most prominent citizens of Dennisport, with his guest, Walter Nickerson, a Gloucester fish dealer, narrowly escaped instant death at a railroad crossing near the Pleasant Lake station of the N.Y.N.H. & H. Railroad Saturday (the 22nd). The carriage in which they were riding was struck by the north-bound Cape train and badly smashed and the occupants were thrown some distance.

April 29, 1905: Orleans: A new policy adopted by the New Haven Railroad of dismissing the telegraph operators here for more than 40 years, without a position. The milk of human kindness is often condensed.

May 6, 1905: The 6:45 train set five fires between Eastham and Orleans station Monday morning, May 1st. The prompt arrival of the fire fighters extinguished the flames.

June 3, 1905: A hearing was granted the railroad commission on the petition of the selectmen for gates at the East Sandwich crossing.

November 4, 1905: For the first time in 40 years Capt. Cyrus Smith, 74, broke away from Barnstable, where for a generation or so he has driven the depot wagon, and came by train to Boston to "look 'em over."

December 2, 1905: An attempt at suicide was made Saturday morning on the railroad train at Bournedale. Captain John Ryder of Wellfleet jumped from a moving train and received internal injuries which are very likely to prove fatal. Captain Ryder had come from Boston with the body of his wife and it was probably grief which left him to commit such a rash action. He was master of the schooner *Highland Light* until she was seized by the Canadian government for fishing inside the three-mile limit. He never fully recovered from the effects of the loss of his vessel. He was devotedly attached to his wife, and his friends say her sickness and death was more than he could stand.

December 9, 1905: The rear-end crash is the new life destroyer. It appears to be infectious on the Boston & Maine road. President Roosevelt's annual message to congress...first takes up the question of corporations and railroad rate legislation.

March 17, 1906: New York Central lines, Boston & Albany R.R. Low Rates to California from Boston $52.

April 7, 1906: Three carloads of ice arrived at the station (Yarmouth) last Saturday for the railroad company, which was placed in the company's icehouse.

April 14, 1906: Yarmouth & Yarmouth Port: Winnie Cahoon, who has been running on the freight, was at home with a bad sprain of the ankle last week.

May 5, 1906: In the severe lightning storm of Monday, the signal mast at Harwich depot was struck and slightly damaged. Mr. J.W. Raymond, station agent and telegraph operator, said things got pretty snappy and lively at the keyboard and he stepped out as a matter of personal safety. All wires were burned out.

May 12, 1906: Business at the Keith Car Manufacturing Company at Sagamore is on the increase. The company now employs 150 workmen and between five and six freight cars are turned out daily.

June 23, 1906: During a dense fog steamer *Cape Cod* with two hundred passengers aboard grounded on a sandy bottom about a mile and a half below her docking place in Provincetown. The excursionists were taken ashore in small boats and landed safely in time to take the afternoon train to Boston.

July 14, 1906: An extra engine and car which came to Buzzards Bay early Monday morning to run an extra passenger train from here to Boston owing to the heavy travel, got off the track in the yard and necessitated sending for the steam wrecker from Boston. No trains were delayed.

August 4, 1906: The Keith car factory at Sagamore closed down, having filled the last contract of 1,000 cars for the Consolidated road (New Haven). It was hoped that another good contract would be secured in the near future.

August 25, 1906: An automobile came into Provincetown, the occupants a man, a woman and a dog. The woman wore a heavy auto veil, while the man and the dog wore auto goggles.

September 1, 1906: At the baby show at the Barnstable fair there was but one contestant.

October 20, 1906: W.O. Holmes of New York, a traveling salesman, narrowly escaped death at the Sandwich station, by being struck by the engine. The engine was almost at a standstill, so he escaped with a few cuts and bruises.

October 27, 1906: Mr. E.T. Francis, station agent at North Harwich, took his first vacation in five years.

November 10, 1906: The removal of the publication office of the Patriot from Barnstable was a matter of great regret. Since 1825, when the plant of the Barnstable County Gazette was located in that village, the public has taken great pride in the fact of having a printing office located in its environs. The only newspaper now located on the northside of the Cape is that of the Register of Yarmouth Port.

January 5, 1907: An order of 1,000 more cars was received by the Keith Manufacturing Co. at Sagamore.

June 15, 1907: John M. Lewis, who was thought lost while drawing nets off of Block Island, was picked up by the schooner *Dorothy Palmer*, Capt. Harding from Philadelphia to Boston. After being adrift for 24 hours, Lewis was nearly exhausted. He proceeded to Boston on the schooner and reached Provincetown by rail.

June 29, 1907: A special town meeting was held at Dennis to see if the almshouse could be moved. A freight train blocked the South Dennis Highway and delayed the delegation from that side and when they arrived the meeting had convened, and the article postponed till the next annual meeting.

July 20, 1907: The demand for cottages in some localities on Cape Cod far exceeds the supply.

September 14, 1907: Messrs. John Hinckley and Son are building an addition to their business office in Yarmouth Port next to the station.

October 19, 1907: There were 58 tickets sold at the Yarmouth station for the excursion to the food fair in Boston. The stay was short, as owing to engine difficulties, the train did not reach Boston until 2 p.m., so instead of partaking of the "pure food" at the fair they were obliged to resort to the quick lunch.

November 23, 1907: A shortage of freight cars in New England does not explain the delay in getting coal. Barge and vessel owners hungry for cargoes cannot get the coal from the mines to the ports. It looks as if there were some cunning in hanging back on the coal roads or by the wholesalers.

August 1909: The railroad travel on the Cape this year is reported to be larger than ever before. The New Haven Railroad's extensive advertising of the Cape has undoubtedly been a paying investment. The whole Cape, individually and collectively is receiving the benefit.

January 14, 1911: There are only two autos in Eastham.

February 18, 1911: The Chatham Railroad company voted to lease its road and franchise for 81 years to the N.Y. N.H. & H. Railroad Company on a guarantee of 2 percent semi-annual dividends in addition to taxes and organization expenses. The road was built 23 years ago and the last bond was paid off in 1910.

May 27, 1911: Several of the Normal School students are planning to live at the Yarmouth Camp Ground this summer. They will rent cottages and have an outing in the grove and attend summer school in Hyannis. The train service between the Camp and Hyannis is favorable, and the fare is only five cents.

October 21, 1911: Great changes will be made in the N.Y. N.H. & H. Railroad yards at Buzzards Bay, including a signal tower and a new station and the railroad expects to be ready in time for the changed conditions.

November 25, 1911: The first passenger train to cross the new railroad bridge at Buzzards Bay was at 5 o'clock Sunday evening. Several people watched it from the new highway bridge at Bourne.

May 18, 1912: Just before the 1:08 train from Boston arrived at Buzzards Bay on Friday, Conductor Osborne arrested five men for refusing to pay their fare. Officer Maloney, who was on the train, took them in charge, but as he had but one pair of handcuffs, three of the party escaped when the train stopped to cut off cars at the bridge. The two captured were taken to Barnstable and had a hearing that evening where they were sentenced to the State Farm for three months. Late Friday the other three were arrested, but at the hearing no case was found against them.

October 5, 1912: The biggest trainload of cranberries ever shipped from Middleboro was sent last week. It comprised a solid train of 41 refrigerator cars and was bound for western points.

January 4, 1913: East Brewster: The snowstorm jolted the trains badly. The mail schedule was all upset. Christmas cards from Brewster to East Brewster reached us via Martha's Vineyard. They were of ancient vintage when they arrived but were welcome, all the same.

May 31, 1913: Mr. Elmer L. Eldridge of East Brewster took up his new duties as brakeman on the Cape train on the 21st.

August 2, 1913: A tank car of naptha was recently received in Provincetown and delivered to the submarine S-4, which is being tested in the harbor, this type of boat needing more refined fuel than gasoline.

January 17, 1914: Jack Frost marked low on Tuesday morning. The thermometer registering from 2 to 10 below. At noon Tuesday the glass stood at zero. Train service was interrupted on Tuesday and Wednesday. A huge waterspout in Cape Cod Bay frolicked about on Tuesday.

January 24, 1914: In Yarmouth, the Sandyside, Thacher and Anthony Silver ice houses have been filled with the Dennis Pond product. Much of the ice was nine and a half inches thick.

February 28, 1914: It is reported that the railroad company is to change the name of the South Yarmouth station to Bass River.

March 21, 1914: For the first time in nearly 50 years the 7:04 train from Woods Hole to Boston tomorrow morning will leave without Captain Isaiah Spindell, for the oldest commuter in the world has quit. A "forty-niner," he has come unharmed through many dangers; he has escaped shipwreck, Indians and thieves, and in 50 years of commuting on the railroad he has never seen an accident. Now, at the age of 82, he has retired from the field of business "to give the young fellows a show."

April 11, 1914: The railroad station at Pocasset was destroyed by fire on the evening of the 20th.

September 12, 1914: The czar has changed the name of St. Petersburg to Petrograd. He evidently has more "pull" than the folks who tried to change the name of the East Brewster railroad station.

October 17, 1914: According to the schedule just announced, there are four trains a day during the winter running from Sandwich and towns in between to Provincetown.

October 1929: A parlor car has been added to train 667, leaving Boston at 4:30 p.m. for Hyannis where it is due at 7 p.m.

May 24, 1930: Thirty-six hundred tons of stone have been used on the riprapping of the mouth of Bass River, first coming by rail to Bass River station, where a derrick loaded the stone on two large trucks, to be carted a distance of two miles to the banks of Bass River, transferred by another derrick to a scow, which was towed to the mouth of the river, and there unloaded and used at the end of the eastern jetty. Some of the rocks weighed two and three tons each. The work is now finished, and the tug, scow, trucks and crew have returned to headquarters.

May 31, 1930: After a good deal of discussion of the Hyannis railroad facilities, railroad officials promised that the smoke nuisance caused by the afternoon passenger train waiting for its off-Cape run would be abated. Parking of autos around the station would be restricted and freight handled more speedily.

June 28, 1930: The first run of the *Cape Codder*, the Pullman special from Washington, Philadelphia and New York to the Cape, arrived Saturday morning. In this, the third season for the *Cape Codder*, its run will be extended to Provincetown, with a section making up on its return trip from Falmouth.

July 5, 1930: The new Cape Cinema, whose opening last Tuesday night brought so many notables to the Cape from New York, Boston and even Hollywood, was instantly hailed as one of the most beautiful talking picture theatres ever built.

July 12, 1930: Hyannis: Fire in the roundhouse of the New Haven Railroad broke out at 5:20 Monday morning and gave firemen of the Hyannis fire department a two hour battle, and caused damage estimated at $6,000. The fire started in a locomotive which was to have made the 7:10 run to Boston.

July 19, 1930: The holiday weekend trip of the *Cape Codder* broke all records for the number of Pullmans and passengers carried, being undoubtedly the heaviest train ever hauled on the New Haven road, veteran trainmen say. The train of 36 pullman cars returning to New York, Philadelphia and Washington Sunday night, was run in three sections. Appreciation of this deluxe service is apparent.
  Bette Davis, charming young actress, will appear at the Cape Playhouse next week as heroine of "Broken Dishes."

August 23, 1930: Following the practice of other seasons, the New England Transportation Company proposed to operate extra service between the Hyannis railroad station and Barnstable Fair Grounds on the dates of the Fair, August 27, 28 and 29.

August 30, 1930:The *Cape Codder* will operate from Provincetown, Hyannis and Woods Hole to New York next Monday evening September 1, instead of Sunday.

September 6, 1930: Automobile traffic was exceptionally heavy on the Cape over Labor Day, with many summer residents making their departure. The *Cape Codder* left

Monday night with four extra Pullman cars for New York. All previous traffic records for Hyannis were broken Saturday when more than 25,000 vehicles were checked passing the corner of Main and Ocean Street in 13 hours up to 10 Saturday night.

October 4, 1930: The *Cape Codder* made its last summer trip Sunday night and the Fall River boat train made its last trip from Hyannis last Saturday at 5:20. The only trains out of Hyannis on the winter schedule, which is now in effect, are at 7:05, 9:55, and 4:05 to Boston, with one at 10:45 to Provincetown.

October 18, 1930: Proposed Mid-Cape Highway (reprinted from the Boston Transcript, Charles F. Marden); Where ever Cape Cod folk get together now-a-days, one of the subjects they are pretty sure to hear discussed is the Mid-Cape Highway. This ambitious project which aims to provide a third through motoring route from the canal to Orleans along the backbone of the Cape has been talked about for some time, but it is now emerging from the embryo stage and is attracting more and more attention.

It is an undertaking that probably will cost in the vicinity of a million dollars, for it comprehends a broad land taking and the building of 35 miles of wide bituminous concrete road.

By diverting the bulk of the through motor traffic from the villages it is believed that two definite advantages will result immediately. The person bound down the Cape will be able to get there more quickly and easily. The quaintness of the settlements will be preserved and their streets made safer; the load will be lifted from the existing main highways, and a large part of the Cape, now not easily accessible, will be made available for settlement.

The proposed route opens to travel a region of Cape Cod little known to the tourist. Cutting through the heart of the lake country, it offers a scenic way comparable with the best of any land. It skirts the shores of innumerable lakes and ponds. The grandeur of the forest, the peacefulness of the meadow and the flash and sparkle of the dancing water will greet the eye on every side.

October 25, 1930: Cranberry shipments moved west Wednesday, the first of the season. The shipments were exceptionally late, latest in several years, owing to the recent warm spell. The price, $11 a barrel, that held at the opening of the market still stands, although the market in cranberries has been sluggish.

January 3, 1931: Massachusetts, leader of the country in cranberry production, had a 1930 crop estimated at 380,000 barrels.

January 24, 1931: Having decided that the bus service now furnished by the New York, New Haven & Hartford Railroad between Chatham and Hyannis is "reasonably adequate" for the amount of traffic involved during the winter months, the state Dept. of Public Utilities has dismissed two petitions of officials and citizens of Cape Cod towns, requesting the department to order the road to restore train service on the Chatham branch.

February 7, 1931: The 65-year-old Harwich station of the New York, New Haven & Hartford Railroad burned to the ground at 5 a.m. last Friday in a fire that aroused the entire village and seriously menaced nearby buildings including one holding the tanks of the Standard and Texas oil companies.

It was a real touch of winter the first of the week when the thermometer registered six above with a considerable fall of snow.

June 6, 1931: The first shipment of Falmouth strawberries will be made the latter part of this week according to the present appearance of the berries.

June 13, 1931: The first run of the *Cape Codder* for the present season will be made on Friday June 19 with the return trip leaving Hyannis June 21.

August 29, 1931: Forseeing the days when highways will take the place of railway transportation on the Cape, Charles Henry Davis, Bass River, made the suggestion at the Rotary Club luncheon in Hyannis that Cape railway lines be turned over to Barnstable county to be used for roads.

September 12, 1931: A traffic count at Ocean and Main streets in Hyannis showed 22,867 automobiles passing in the fourteen hours between 8:30 a.m. and 10:30 p.m. Saturday. This was a drop of some size from the 26,363 count made a year ago on the Saturday before Labor Day.

October 3, 1931: Among Railroad Employees: Agent Slade says he has heard of "Carrying Coal to New Castle," but never heard of sand being shipped to Provincetown until this morning, when several carloads of sand were received from West Virginia.

November 14, 1931: The Buzzards Bay railroad bridge was built by the Boston, Cape Cod and New York Canal Company and has never been the property of the New York, New Haven & Hartford Railroad Company. The bridge has been operated and maintained by the railroad company and the canal company, up until March 31, 1928 and since then the U.S. Engineer Dept. has taken over and continued the existing agreement.

June 1932: A survey indicates that the asparagus and strawberry crops on the Cape will yield more than $650,000 this year.
Asparagus will bring about $50,000 through 18,000 boxes. And the outlook on strawberries, the survey shows, is even more promising, 4,000,000 quarts are expected to bring in about $600,000 to the growers. Much of this is shipped by rail.

September 3, 1932: Never in its long history has the lower Cape seen half the crowd that came by automobile, bus, train, boat and airplane to witness little more than one-minute's wonder in the skies, a solar eclipse. Local and state police had their biggest traffic problem.

Shortly after 10 in the morning, police clocked 1,000 cars an hour whirring through Orleans and gave up their stoplight system at the crossroads. By noon 2,000 cars an hour were rolling by towards Provincetown to view the eclipse of the sun.

January 26, 1935: Storm: Twelve passengers spent Wednesday night in a Yarmouth-Provincetown bus in North Truro where high gales blew sand and snow across the highway.

The motor was left running to keep the occupants warm. There were also fifteen private cars abandoned on this road.

February 7, 1936: The Barnstable Fire Department put in a busy day last Thursday. Following an automobile fire at Chester Jones' in the morning, they were called out again in the afternoon to extinguish a grass fire on Old Jail Lane, presumably set by sparks from the engine of the afternoon train for Boston. Only slight damage resulted.

July 17, 1936: The *Cape Codder* the weekend train from New York and Washington to the Cape, is carrying more cars this year than ever before. The holiday business necessiated running the train in two sections.

September 18, 1936: The last visible section of the old railroad bridge at Buzzards Bay, which serviced trains crossing the Cape Cod canal for many years until the new lift span was opened last summer, was dynamited last Thursday to clear the canal of obstructions.

October 30, 1936: Fourteen bags of mail were found near the Tupper Road railroad crossing in Sandwich last Tuesday, evidently having fallen from a carelessly closed door when the down-Cape train rounded a slight curve at that point. The bags contained parcel post material for Cotuit and Centerville.

November 27, 1936: The United States government has agreed to take 50 carloads of Cape Cod turnips at 50 cents per 100 pounds, f.o.b., it was announced by Ralph A. Chase, newly elected vice president of the Cape Cod Farm Bureau.

December 10, 1937: The Orleans-Provincetown highway as proposed would follow a scenic route on the South shore of the extreme lower Cape and would cost $1,900,000. When completed it would form the first section of the proposed mid-Cape highway which has been under discussion the last decade. The road itself would be wider than existing highways on the Cape, probably four or six lanes.

December 17, 1937: Cape trains were delayed when a locomotive of the New Haven Railroad headed down Cape, left the rails about 200 yards east of the Bourne station when it split a switch, leaving a siding. Passenger were jolted but no one was injured.

March 4, 1938: A carload of surplus oranges arrived in Hyannis last week and has been distributed all around Cape Cod.

April 15, 1938: Arrival of two carloads of oranges in Hyannis for distribution to Cape residents on relief rolls was announced last week.

July 8, 1938: Officials of the New York, New Haven & Hartford Railroad said incoming rail traffic was "very, very heavy" on the holiday weekend and outgoing traffic light. Eleven cars of the *Night Cape Codder* were filled with passengers when the train arrived in Hyannis. The *Neptune* hauled ten cars to the peninsula on Saturday. An exceedingly heavy volume of traffic also was evident on the Woods Hole branch, railroad officials said.

August 1939: The date for abandoment of Old Colony Rairoad passenger service was changed from September 24 to January 1st, 1940 by a conference in federal court at New Haven.

January 15, 1950: New Haven patrons will pay a 25 percent boost in rail fares January 15.

January 28, 1955: Mr. Gerald Cash has returned to work. He is now located at the New Haven Railroad station in Wareham, the baggage office at Hyannis where he was formerly baggage master, having been closed.

July 21, 1955: To avert possible death or injury, President Patrick McGinnis of the New Haven Railroad closed 18 private crossings on Cape Cod during a Sunday inspection tour.

September 8, 1955: We have heard that they are painting the Yarmouth station of the New Haven Railroad so this morning we got on our two little feet and toddled up to take a look. So far the ends of the building are white, the roof is black and each door is a different color. The door on the Railroad Avenue side is orange, the door on the track side is blue, and the door on the end where the office is is yellow. The door to the gents is black with white letters and the door to the ladies is yellow with black letters. The general effect is rather startling.

Bibliography

Books, Articles, and Documents

Abdill, George B. *A Locomotive Engineer's Album*. Seattle,WA: Superior Publishing Co.,1965.

Adler, Dorothy R. *British Investment in American Railways 1834-1898*. Charlottesville: The University Press of Virginia, 1970.

Albion, Robert G. and William A. Baker and Benjamin W. Labaree,. *New England & The Sea*. Middletown,CT: Wesleyan University Press, 1972.

Allen, Everett S. *A Wind to Shake the World: The Story of the 1938 Hurricane*. Boston, Toronto: Little, Brown & Company, 1976.

Alexander, Edwin P. *Down at the Depot, American Railroad Stations From 1831 to 1920*. New York: Bramhall House, 1970.

anonymous. *History of the Old Colony Railroad*. Boston: Hager & Handy, 1893.

Archer, Robert F. *The History of the Lehigh Valley Railroad: The Route of the Black Diamond*. Berkeley,CA: Howell-North Books, 1977.

Bachelder, John B. *Popular Resorts and How to Reach Them*. Boston: John B. Bachelder, 1874.

Baker, George Pierce. *The Formation of the New England Railroad Systems: A Study of Railroad Combination in the Nineteenth Century*. Cambridge,MA: Harvard University Press, 1949.

Baker, Stanley L. and Virginia Brainarad Kunz. *Collector's Book of Railroadiana*. New York: Hawthorn Books, Inc., 1976.

Barbour, Harriot Buxton. *Sandwich, The Town That Glass Built*. Boston: Houghton Mifflin Company, 1948.

Beebe, Lucius. *The Big Spenders*. Garden City,NY: Doubleday & Company, 1966.

_____. *The Central Pacific & The Southern Pacific Railroads*. Berkeley,CA: Howell-North Books, 1963.

_____. *High Iron*. New York: D. Appleton-Century Company, 1938.

_____. *20th Century*. Berkeley,CA: Howell-North Books, 1962.

_____ and Charles Clegg. *Hear the Train Blow*. New York: E.P. Dutton & Co., Inc., 1952.

_____. *The Trains We Rode*. Volume I and II. Berkeley, CA: Howell-North Books, 1965.

Benson, Lee. *Merchants, Farmers and Railroads*. Cambridge,MA: Harvard University Press, 1955.

Berchen, William and Monica Dickens. *Cape Cod*. New York: The Viking Press, 1972.

Beyle, Noel W. *Eastham Illustrated*. Eastham, MA: The First Encounter Press, 1978.

_____. *Entering Eastham*. Eastham, MA: Eastham Bicentennial Commission, 1976.

_____. *Go Eastham Young Man or Eastham or Bust!* Eastham MA: The Innermost House, 1977.

Biographical Sketch, Personal and Descriptive of Sylvanus B. Phinney of Barnstable, Massachusetts on His Eightieth Anniversay, October 27, 1888. Boston: Rand Avery Company, 1888.

Blackweel, Walter. *Tracing The Route of the Martha's Vineyard Railroad 1874-1896.* Miami,FL:1973.

Blanton, Burt C. *400,000 Miles By Rail.* Berkeley,CA: Howell-North Books, 1972.

Blum, John M. *The National Experience. Part II.* New York: Harcourt Brace Jovanovich, 1973.

Bolles, Frank. *Land of the Lingering Snow.* Boston: Houghton Mifflin and Company, 1891.

Boston Map Guide, 1920. Boston & Albany Railroad/ New York Central Lines.

Botkin, B.A. and Alvin F. Harlow. *A Treasury of Railroads Folklore.* New York: Crown Publishers, 1953.

Bracegirdle, Brian. *The Archaeology of the Industrial Revolution.* London, England: Heinemann Books, 1974.

Brewster, A Cape Cod Town Remembered. Brewster MA: Brewster Historical Society, 1976.

Brigham, Albert Perry. *Cape Cod and the Old Colony.* New York and London: G.P. Putnam's Sons, 1920.

_____*Geographic Influences in American History.* Boston: Ginn & Company, 1903.

Brown, Dee. *Hear That Lonesome Whistle Blow.* New York: Holt, Rinehard and Winston, 1977.

Cape Cod Branch Railroad Treasurer's Reply To Response of Stockholder's Committee, 1852.

Castonquay, Harold. Album of photos of Old Hyannis and Hyannis Port.

Catton, Bruce. *Waiting For The Morning Train.* New York: Doubleday & Co., Inc., 1972.

Chandler, Alfred D. *The Railroads: The Nation's First Big Business.* New York: Harcourt, Brace & World, Inc. ,1965.

Covell, William. *Short History of Fall River Line.* Newport,RI: Ward, 1947.

_____. *Steamboats on Narragansett Bay.* Newport,RI: Historical Society, 1933.

Daughen, Joseph R. and Peter Binzen. *The Wreck of the Penn Central.* Boston: Little,Brown and Company, 1971.

Decker, Leslie E. *Railroads, Lands, and Politics.* Providence,RI: Brown University Press, 1964.

Deyo, Simeon L. *History of Barnstable County, Massachusetts.* New York: H.W. Blake and Company, 1890.

Digges, Jeremiah: *Cape Cod Pilot.* Provincetown and New York: Modern Pilgrim Press and the Viking Press, 1937.

Dunbaugh, Edwin L. *Era of Joy Line.* Westport, CT: Greenwood Press, 1982.

Eavenson, Howard N. *The First Century and a Quarter of American Coal Industry.* Pittsburgh, PA: Privately printed, 1942.

Edwards, Agnes. *Cape Cod New and Old.* Boston and New York: Houghton Mifflin Company, 1918.

Edwards, Ford K. *A Financial Study and Analysis of the Transportation Costs and Revenues of the New York, New Haven and Hartford Railroad.* Washington, D.C.: Edwards and Peabody, 1962.

Edwards, William Churchill. *Historic Quincy Massachusetts.* Quincy, MA: City of Quincy, 1957.

Falmouth On The Sea. Falmouth,MA: The Board of Trade and Industry, 1896.

Farson, Robert H. *The Cape Cod Canal.* Yarmouth Port,MA: Cape Cod Historical Publications, 1987.

Faught, Millard C. *Falmouth Massachusetts Problems of a Resort Community*. New York: Columbia University Press, 1945.

Feininger, Andreas. *New York in the Forties*. New York: Dover Publications, Inc., 1978.

The First Railroad in America. A History of the Origin and Development of the Granite Railway at Quincy, Massachusetts. Boston,MA: Privately printed, 1926.

Fish, John Perry. *Unfinished Voyages*. Orleans,MA: Lower Cape Publishing Co., 1989.

Fisher, Charles E. *The Story of the Old Colony Railroad*. Taunton,MA: Privately Printed, 1919.

Fishlow, Albert. *American Railroads and the Transformation of the Ante- Bellum Economy*. Cambridge, MA: Harvard University Press, 1965.

Fleming, Howard. *Narrow Gauge Railways in America*. Oakland, CA: Grahame H. Hardy, 1949.

Fogel, Robert William. *Railroads and American Economic Growth: Essays in Economic History*. Baltimore, MD: The John Hopkins Press, 1964.

Foley, Ruth Howard."History at the Throttle." *The New England Galaxy*, Spring 1975.

Freeman, Frederick. *The History of Cape Cod: The Annals of Barnstable County Including the District of Mashpee, Volume I, 1858 and Volume II, 1862*. Boston: George C. Rand and Avery.

From Pocasset to Cataumet, The Origins and Growth of a Massachusetts Seaside Community. Bourne,MA: The Bourne Historic Commission, 1988.

Frothingham, Ted. Series of articles on Cape Cod Railroads between 1971- 1975. *The Yarmouth Register*.

_____. *With a Grain of Salt*. Yarmouth Port, MA: Privately Printed, 1972.

Goodrich, Carter. *Government Promotion of American Canals and Railroads*. New York: Columbia University Press, 1960.

_____. *The Government and the Ecomomy*. Indianapolis,IN: Bobbs-Merrill Company, Inc., 1967.

Guidebook for the Eastern Coast of New England. Concord, NH: Edson C. Eastman and Company, 1871.

Hand, Victor, and Harold Edmonson. *The Love of Trains*. London: Octobus Books, Inc., 1972.

Harlow, Alvin F. *Steelways of New England*. New York: Creative Age Press, Inc., 1946.

Heckman, Richard. *Yankees Under Sail*. Dublin, NH: Yankee Incorporated, 1968.

Herrick, Paul Fairbanks, and Larry G. Newman. *Old Hyannis Port*. New Bedford, MA: Reynolds-Dewalt, Inc., 1968.

Holbrook, Stewart. *The Story of American Railroads*. New York: Crown Publishers, 1947.

Hough, Henry Beetle. *Martha's Vineyard Summer Resort 1835-1935*. Rutland, VT: The Tuttle Publishing Company, Inc., 1936.

Husband, Joseph. *The Story of the Pullman Car*. Chicago: A.C.McClurg & Co., 1917.

Johnson, Arthur M., and Barry E. Supple. *Boston Capitalists and Western Railroads A Study in the Nineteenth-Century Railroad Investment Process*. Cambridge, MA: Harvard University Press, 1967.

Joint Transportation Committee. *Present and Future Prospects of Rail Service*. Cape Cod Planning and Economic Development Commission.

Joyce, James M. *Railroad Spikes, A Collector's Guide*. Lititz, PA: Sutter House, 1985.

Keene, Betsey D. *History of Bourne from 1622 to 1937*. Bourne, MA: Bourne Historical Society, 1937.

315

Kimball, Carol W." Victims of the Fog". *Sea Classics*, May, 1978.

Kirkland, Edward Chase. *Men Cities and Transportation*. Cambridge MA: Harvard University Press, 1948.

Kittredge, Henry C. *Cape Cod, Its People and Their History*. Boston: Houghton Mifflin Co., 1930.

_____. *Mooncussers of Cape Cod*. Boston and New York: Houghton Mifflin Company, 1937.

_____. *Shipmasters of Cape Cod*. Boston and New York: Houghton Mifflin Company, 1935.

Kyper, Frank. *The Railroad that Came Out at Night*. Brattleboro, VT: The Stephen Greene Press, 1977.

Lancaster, Clay. *The Far-Out Island Railroad*. Nantucket, MA: Pleasant Publications, 1972.

Lawson, Evelyn. *Yesterday's Cape Cod*. Miami, FL: E.A. Seemann Publishing, Inc., 1975.

Leavitt, H. Walter. *Some Interesting Phases of the Development of Transportation in Maine*. Orono,ME: University of Maine Press, 1940.

Lincoln, Joseph C. *Cape Cod Yesterdays*. Boston: Little, Brown and Company, 1937.

_____. *The Depot Master*. New York: D. Appleton & Company, 1910.

Lindahl, Martin L. "The New England Railroads". *Public Transportation for New England Reports*. New England Govenor's Committee on Public Transportation, March 1955-November 1957.

Lockland, D. Philio. *Economics of Transportation*. Homewood, IL: Richard D. Irwin, Inc., 1972.

Lombard, Asa Cobb Paine Jr. *East of Cape Cod*. Cuttyhunk Island, MA: privately printed, 1976.

Lovell, Irwing W. *Story of the Yarmouth Camp Ground and the Methodist Camp Meetings on Cape Cod*. Yarmouth, MA: Irving W. Lovell, 1985.

Lovell, Russell A. *Sandwich, A Cape Cod Town*. Sandwich, MA: Town of Sandwich Archives and Historical Center, 1984.

Loxton, Howard. *Railways*. London , England: Hamlyn Publishing Group, Limited, 1963.

Lyon, Peter. *To Hell In A Day Coach. An Exasperated Look at American Railroads*. Philadelphia: J.B. Lippincott Company, 1968.

Martin, Albro. *Enterprise Denied Origins of the Decline of American Railroads, 1897-1917*. New York: Columbia University Press, 1971.

Mayer, Lynn Rhodes, and Kenneth E. Vose. *Makin' Tracks*. New York: Praeger Publishers, 1975.

McAdam, Roger Williams. *Commonwealth*. New York: Stephen Daye Press, 1959.

_____. *Floating Palaces*. Providence, RI: Mowbray Publishers,1972.

_____. *The Old Fall River Line*. New York: Stephen Daye Press, 1937.

_____. *Priscilla of Fall River*. New York: Stephen Daye Press, 1947.

_____. *Salts of the Sound*. New York: Stephen Daye Press, 1939.

McPherson, James Alan, and Miller Williams. *Railroad Trains and Train People in American Culture*. New York: Random House, 1976.

McReady, Albert L. *Railroads in the Days of Steam*. New York: American Heritage Publishing Company, 1960.

Meeks, Carroll L.V. *The Railroad Station*. New Haven: Yale University Press, 1956.

Moore, Les. *The Book of Summer Limericks for Cape Cod and the Islands*. Hyannis, MA: The Cape Cod Times, 1978.

Morse, Frank P. *Cavalcade of the Rails*. New York: E.P. Dutton & Company, Inc., 1940.

Nelson, James C. *Railroad Transportation and Public Policy*. Washington D.C.: The Brookings Institution, 1959.

Nightingale, Lloyd Turner. *From Falmouth's Past*. Falmouth,MA: Privately Printed, 1936.

"No-Name Hurricane." *Yankee Magazine*, September, 1978.

"The Old Railroad Wharf Hyannis." New Bedford Standard Times, February 9, 1939.

Otis Task Force. *Report on Cape Cod Railroads, 1976.*

Pannell, J.P.M. *Man the Builder*. London,England: Thames & Hudson Ltd., 1964.

Parks, Pat. *The Railroad That Died at Sea*. Brattleboro, VT: The Stephen Greene Press, 1968.

Parsons, Frank. *The Heart of the Railroad Problem*. Boston: Little, Brown and Company, 1906.

Pavlucik, Andrew J. *The New Haven Railroad, a Fond Look Back*. New Haven, CT: Pershing Press, 1978.

Perkin, Harold. *The Age of the Railway*. Trowbridge, Wiltshire, England: David & Charles Publishers, 1970.

Phillips, Lance. *Yonder Comes the Train*. New York: A.S. Barnes & Co., 1965.

Reed, Robert C. *Train Wrecks*. New York: Bonanza Books, 1968.

Report of Joint New England Railroad Committee to the Governors of the New England States. Boston: 1923.

Rex, Percy Fielitz. Collection 1902-1975.

Reynard, Elizabeth. *The Narrow Land*. Boston: Houghton Mifflin Co., 1934.

Rich, Earle. *More Cape Cod Echoes*. Orleans,MA: Salt Meadow Publishers, 1978.

Rose, Albert C. *Historic American Roads*. New York: Crown Publishers, Inc., 1976.

Ruckstuhl, Irma. *Old Provincetown in Early Photographs*. New York: Dover Publications, 1987.

Sagendorph, Robb, and Judson D. Hale. *That New England*. Dublin,NH: Yankee, Incorporated, 1966.

Semple, David W. *The New York and New England Railroad*. New York: Carter & Co., 1886.

Shaughnessy, Jim. *The Rutland Road*. Berkeley, CA: Howell-North Books, 1964.

Shaw, Frederic. *Little Railways of the World*. Berkeley, CA: Howell-North Books, 1958.

Silitch, Clarissa M. *Yankees Remember*. Dublin,NH: Yankee, Incorporated, 1976.

Snow, Edward, Rowe. *Great Storms and Famous Shipwrecks of the New England Coast*. Boston: Little, Brown & Company, 1976.

Stanford, R. Patrick. *Lines of the New York, New Haven and Hartford Railroad Co.* Unknown publisher.

State of Massachusetts: Public Document no. 41.

Sterling, Dorothy. *Our Cape Cod Salt Marshes*. Orleans,MA:The Association for the Preservation of Cape Cod, 1976.

Stetson, Judy. *Wellfleet, A Pictorial History*. Wellfleet, MA: The Wellfleet Historical Society, 1963.

Stevens, Austin N. *Yankees Under Steam*. Dublin, NH: Yankee Incorporated, 1970.

Stover, John F. *American Railroads*. Chicago: The University of Chicago Press, 1961.

_____. *The Life and Decline of The American Railroad*. New York: Oxford University Press, 1970.

Strahler, Arthur N. *A Geologist's View of Cape Cod*. Garden City,NY: The Natural History

Press, 1966.

Swanberg, J.W. *New Haven Power, 1838-1968*. Medina, OH: Alvin F. Staufer, 1988.

Swift, Charles F. *History of Old Yarmouth*. Yarmouth Port, MA: The Historical Society of Old Yarmouth, 1975.

Taylor, George Rogers. *The Transportation Revolution, 1815-1860*. New York: Rinehart & Company, 1951.

Taylor, William Leonhard. *A Productive Monopoly*. Povidence, RI: Brown University Press, 1970.

Thomson, Betty Flanders. *The Changing Face of New England*. Boston: Houghton Mifflin, 1977.

Thoreau, Henry David. *Cape Cod*. New York: Bramhall House, 1951.

Three Centuries of the Cape Cod County Barnstable, Massachusetts. Barnstable, MA: Barnstable County, 1985.

Travelers Official Railway Guide of the United States and Canada. New York: National Railway Publication Company, 1868.

Trayser, Donald G. *Barnstable: Three Centuries of a Cape Cod Town*. Hyannis, MA: F.B. & F.P. Goss, 1939.

Turner, Gregg M., and Melancthon W. Jacobus. *Connecticut Railroads*. Hartford, CT: The Connecticut Historical Society, 1989.

United States Department of the Interior. *Geologic History of Cape Cod, Massachusetts*. Washington,D.C.: U.S. Government Printing Office, 1976.

Valle, James E. *The Iron Horse at War*. Berkely,CA: Howell-North Books, 1977.

Warner, Paul T. *Locomotive Development on the Central Railroad of New Jersey*. Baldwin Locomotives, July, 1926.

Webb, Robert N. *American Railroads*. New York: Grosset & Dunlap, 1957.

Welcome to Cape Cod. Cape Cod Chamber of Commerce and Cape Cod, Martha's Vineyard and Nantucket Hotel Association, 1933.

Weller, John L. *The New Haven Railroad Its Rise and Fall*. New York: Hastings House,Publishers, 1969.

Westing, Fred. *The Locomotives That Baldwin Built*. Seattle,WA: Superior Publishing Company, 1966.

White, John H. Jr. *The American Railroad Passenger Car*. Baltimore, MD: The Johns Hopkins University Press, 1978.

_____. *Early American Locomotives*. New York: Dover Publications, Inc., 1972.

Wiggin, Ruby Crosby. *Big Dreams and Little Wheels*. Clinton, ME: Privately printed, 1971.

Ziel, Ron. *The Story of Edaville and Steamtown*. Edaville, MA: Privately printed, 1965.

Newspapers and Periodicals

Along The Line
Barnstable Patriot
Boston Globe
Cape Cod Compass
Cape Cod Life
Cape Cod Magazine
Cape Cod Times

Falmouth Enterprise
Railroad and Railfan
The Register
Sandwich Observer
Trains
Yankee
Yarmouth Register

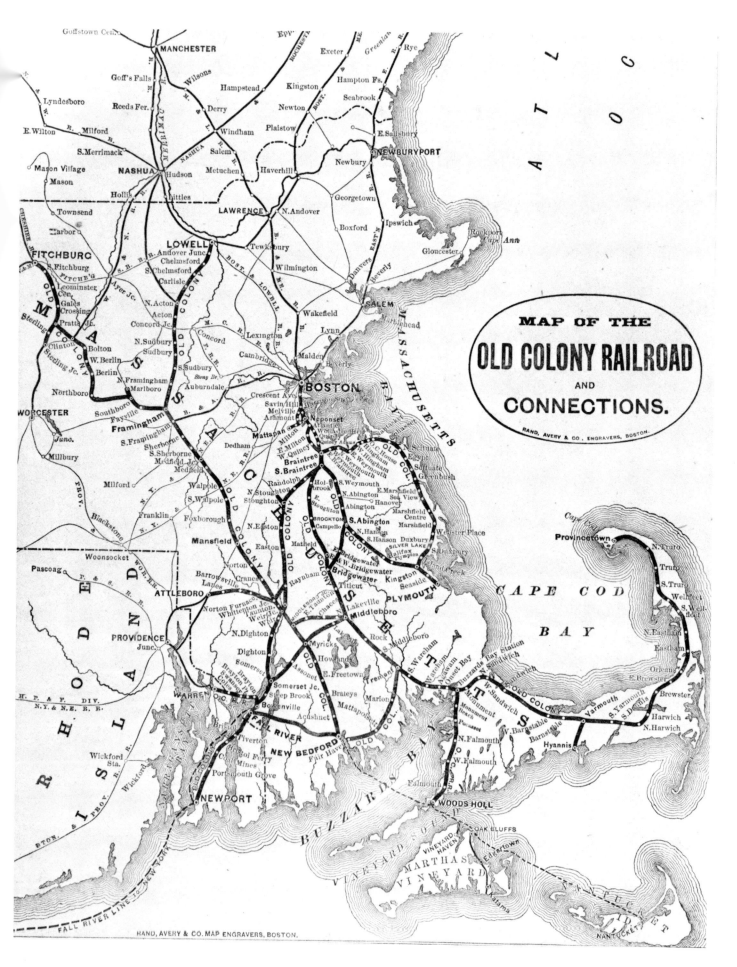

The Old Colony looked like this in 1880. The Martha's Vineyard Railroad is running, but the Nantucket Railroad and the Chatham Branch hadn't been built.

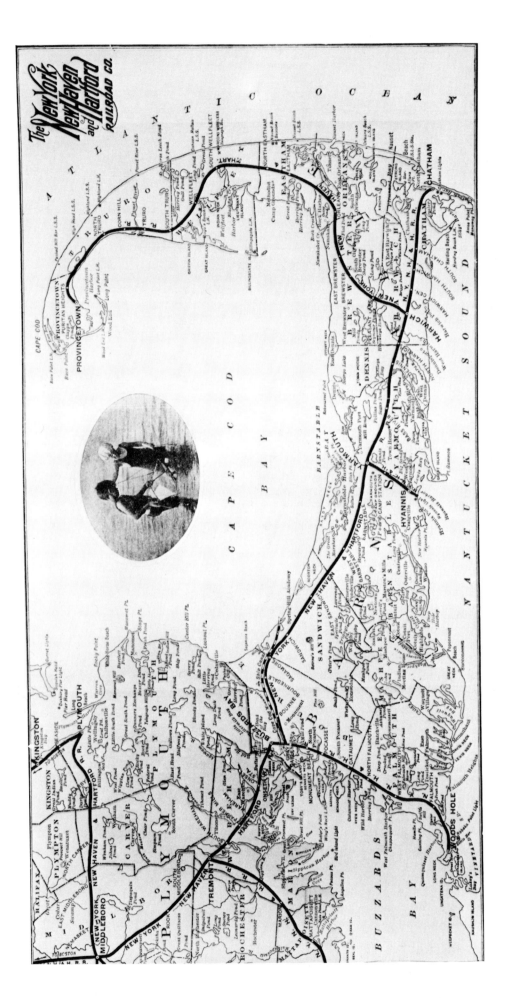

The New Haven issued this map in 1910.